This Is My Country, What's Yours?

This Is My Country, What's Yours?

A Literary Atlas of Canada

N O A H   R I C H L E R

I L L U S T R A T I O N S   B Y   M I C H A E L   W I N T E R

McCLELLAND & STEWART

LIBRARY AND ARCHIVES CANADA CATALOGUING IN PUBLICATION

Richler, Noah

  This is my country, what's yours? : a literary atlas of Canada / Noah
Richler.

ISBN 13: 978-0-7710-7533-9
ISBN 10: 0-7710-7533-2

  1. Canadian fiction (English) – 20th century – History and criticism.
2. Canada in literature. 3. Literature and society – Canada. I. Title.

PS8071.5.R52 2006   c813'.54093271'09045   c2005-907325-x

We acknowledge the financial support of the Government of Canada
through the Book Publishing Industry Development Program and
that of the Government of Ontario through the Ontario Media Development
Corporation's Ontario Book Initiative. We further acknowledge the support
of the Canada Council for the Arts and the Ontario Arts Council for our
publishing program.

Typeset in Richler by M&S, Toronto. The Richler font was commissioned by
Jack Rabinovitch and designed by Nick Shinn to celebrate the late Mordecai
Richler's memory.

Printed and bound in Canada

McClelland & Stewart Ltd.
75 Sherbourne Street
Toronto, Ontario
M5A 2P9
www.mcclelland.com

1   2   3   4   5   10   09   08   07   06

To Sarah, Nathalie, and Sophie.

A man sets out to draw the world. As the years go by, he peoples a space with images of provinces, kingdoms, mountains, bays, ships, islands, fishes, rooms, instruments, stars, horses, and individuals. A short time before he dies, he discovers that the patient labyrinth of lines traces the lineaments of his own face.

Jorge Luis Borges, Afterword to *The Maker* (1960)

CONTENTS

Author's Note

A couple of strategic decisions were made that are fundamental to *This Is My Country, What's Yours?: A Literary Atlas of Canada*. First of all, I chose to restrict its scope to contemporary writers because to have let even a few dead authors through the door would have been to give in to the juggernaut of the past and produce a book about Canada already written. History is of the essence, true, but she can also be a bully. A project like this one is by nature subjective, and the choice of authors was my own. The *Atlas* does not pretend to be a comprehensive survey. I had the privilege of spending time with about one hundred Canadian writers and storytellers in the three years it took to gather the material for this book and the preceding CBC Radio series. Still, there are many writers whom I regret not having found the time or the means to speak to – *mea culpa* – and there are plenty of others whom I did meet and who are remembered with admiration and gratitude but for a gamut of reasons are not represented in the final text. Other authors I did not include because either they had written excellent novels that simply lay outside the scope of this book or because they had written a body of work about which I felt my own views contributed little.

Secondly, the *Atlas* is not intended as a work of reference, though some may choose to use it that way. I did not want it to be necessary to have read Canadian novelists to glean anything from the book, though I would be delighted if, subsequently, it made some curious to do so. The *Atlas* is intended as a cultural portrait of the country, and at times an argument for it. It is a tribute to some of its best authors, a literary travelogue, and on occasion an inquiry into what it means to tell stories at all. My ardent belief is that novels are not whimsical texts to be consumed in literary salons or in academe, as if they stood outside of the present day and its concerns, but are incendiary things born out of a particular time, and place, a mirror to ourselves and our politics. The *Atlas* is also something of a paean to Canada – this extraordinary, fortunate country – and a pitching of views into the argument that is our developing society. The book was born out of the belief that story is often the best way to know a place, and that culture matters for this reason. Novelists and storytellers – as well as painters, musicians, playwrights, poets, and architects – give form to the times and places that we occupy. They tell us about ourselves – and we have much to learn if we listen. The arts are not an indulgence.

I

The Virtues of Being Nowhere

What was Canada – a distant place most did not know where, a pink mass on the
map beside the green of Greenland. Suddenly everyone was talking of Canada:
visas, medicals, interviews, "landeds." In Canada they needed plumbers, so those
who did not know one end of a spanner from another, schoolteachers, salesmen,
bank clerks, all joined plumbing classes and began talking of wrenches and dis-
cussing fixtures they had never seen in their lives. Toronto, Vancouver, Montreal.
You got the most recent news outside mosques after prayers, when men await
their women, and during morning and afternoon teatimes at the A-T and other
tea shops: who had left, the price of the dollar, the most recent black-market-
related arrests. They talked of Don Mills as if it were in Upanga. The buildings of
Rosecliffe Park were known, it seemed, in intimate detail.

M.G. VASSANJI, *No New Land*

January 2004. Iqaluit is the North – but the *new* North. It used
to be that outsiders came this way for adventure, to make
their fortune, or simply to get away. From debts, from the old
girlfriend, or from the person that you were but did not want to be.
The North was off the map, a place of wilderness and the unknown

I

that offered an opportunity for instant reinvention. In 1991, the first time I visited Iqaluit, you could walk the town in ten minutes, hitch a ride with a bush pilot, or pop into the bar they called the Zoo for a few beers and a night with no rules. This was *beyond* the frontier, the far side of the end of the road, though now Iqaluit is a tame government town. Since April 1, 1999, Iqaluit has been the administrative capital of Nunavut, and now my friend Jack Hicks needed a car and time as well to show me round its streets. There was even traffic holding us up – and Tuesdays, well Tuesdays for Jack and his pals are "Quebec Cheese Nights." On arrival, Jack had taken me to his Iqaluit condo and poured a glass of good French Burgundy with some chèvre noir lait cru, no less, and it turned out that the Inuit kid on the couch, the one in the dark blue parka, who was in his twenties still, *owned an airline*. And the woman who looked like she'd graduated from high school the day before was a *deputy minister*. But there was a reminder of the old and more reprobate town of Frobisher Bay that lay beneath Iqaluit's new gleam in the bloodstains on Jack's carpet.

"Someone had a nosebleed?" I asked.

"The babysitter brought over a friend," said Jack, "and they got into a bit of a fight."

"Take him home, did you?"

"Took her home, yes."

Jack's place was near the town's old Hudson's Bay Company general store, in view of the promontory where the American army base used to be. The presence of American soldiers here, from 1942 through the height of the Cold War and the active days of the Arctic's Distant Early Warning System – the DEW Line – provided the town's beginnings and a link to the outside world, if less pervasively than the World Wide Web now does. Dropping out of anywhere is just not as *easy* as it once was. The day I visited, Jack, a sociologist by trade, had been taking time out from his spirited daily routine of email vigilance (messages supporting the Inuit, the Palestinians, the environment, and against George W. Bush and the war in Iraq), and now here he was driving me to the edge of town and the foot of the plateau that was *meta incognita* – "beyond the unknown" – in Martin Frobisher's day. The maps of the Elizabethan explorer, templates provided by William Borough, commander of the Muscovy Company, have a wonderfully tentative quality. A few disparate sketches on a blank parchment criss-crossed by rhumb lines recorded Frobisher's journey, in 1576, around the bays and inlets of the Unknown Shore – only now it will be a real estate agent and not an explorer who takes you there.

We passed an architect's folly that resembled three big blue crates, precariously stacked. On a sloping road was a row of elegant townhouses that would have appeared equally *in situ* on San Francisco's hilly streets.

"I never liked this place," said Jack convincingly. "The Inuit communities I so enjoyed living in felt real. All this feels fake."

The new developments petered out, but the road continued away from town and I asked Jack its name.

"Technically, we're on 'The Road to Nowhere.' There's a small municipal gravel operation at the end of it."

Along the road were bollards connected by pipes and flagged with orange markers.

"Fire hydrants?" I asked tentatively.

"No. They're protective barriers around the sewage and fresh-water system that has been put here to support new subdivisions," Jack explained. "If they were to run subdivisions all the way till the end of the road, then I suppose the last one would have to be 'Nowhere.'"

◇　◇　◇

IF YOU ARE CANADIAN and travel at all, then you learn very quickly that the place you come from is just that – Nowhere – that Canada is not on the map.

One summer's day in London, England, in 1978, I sat on a bench in Covent Garden watching the buskers perform and the tourists pass. I was sharing the bench with an elderly Eastern European woman, who was feeding breadcrumbs to the flock of pigeons that had congregated noisily at her feet. We started to talk. I'd visited the Soho offices of the publisher Andre Deutsch that afternoon, looking for a job, and that's how we touched on to the subject of literature. The woman enthused at length about the German author Jakob Wasserman, whose books had been burned by the Nazis in the 1930s. I apologized because I had not read him.

"He always had a problem finishing his novels," she said, scattering a few more crumbs to the birds.

"What do you mean?" I asked.

"He never knew what to do with his characters. He was always tossing them overboard, or sending them to Canada."

Canada, *meta incognita*.

Nowhere, in its first incarnation, is Off the Map and *oblivion* – the place of the forgotten. Alberto Manguel – the author, with Gianni Guadalupi, of *The Dictionary of Imaginary Places* – recalls that his erstwhile employer, the Argentinean novelist Jorge Luis Borges, once described Canada as being "so far away that it hardly exists." Diego Ribeiro's world map of 1529 declared Tierra del Labrador "discovered by the English and there is nothing there worth having." The sixteenth-century cartographers were in the habit of filling in the great blank spaces on their maps of not-yet-Canada with pictures of mythical beasts and savages and complete fantasies about the geography that lay here. The Canadian Arctic is where Mary Shelley's monster, Frankenstein, like a character of Wasserman's, was finally discarded. As was the gooey stuff in the 1958 sci-fi flick *The Blob*. Our country's very name, wrote Pierre-François Xavier de Charlevoix in 1744, was derived from the distress of the first Spanish sailors who, arriving here, reiterated Ribeiro's observation and cried out, "Acá Nada!" (Here's nothing!)

When I was in England in the 1980s, a travel section of *The Independent* newspaper featured a map of the world and suggested novels to read in the instance of holidays to various countries. The considerable space of Canada's landmass gave researchers opportunity for a few, but no Canadian books were on it. Canada is the place where no one has to think about you any more, the country that issues every spy's favourite passport. For want of what to think when someone says "Canada," most default to something else.

The Booker Prize shortlist of 2002, in which three of the six nominees were Canadian, was a wonderful illustration of this rule. Rohinton Mistry was described as South Asian, which in England essentially means that he was regarded as a former *British* subject who for some unexplained reason was writing from the Indian diaspora in . . . umm, Canada. Carol Shields was a transplanted American, though she did not see it that way. And Yann Martel, who won, was far too exotic to be Canadian. He was Spanish, Portuguese, French, anything but – Canadians, in the British view, being dull whites, a few Red Indians, and some "Eskimos." (This is still how most British refer to Inuit.) Margaret Atwood, the recurring Booker nominee, and winner in 2000, was the exception that proved the rule. As a women's icon, she lay beyond the limits of national identity. Three years after Atwood's victory, Douglas Coupland published *Hey Nostradamus!*, a novel set in Vancouver with roots in the high-school massacre at Columbine, Colorado, and a British reporter who interviewed him wrote that murder of the kind he described was just not *credible* in Canada, putting Canadians in the untenable position of having to say, Hold on, man, what about Clifford Olson, Karla and Paul – or, just down the road, Robert Picton and his gruesome pig farm?

In USAmerica (this moniker the invention of the B.C. poet George Bowering), Canada is the vaguely threatening country where cold winds, power cuts, mad cow disease, terrorists, weed smokers, liberals, and homosexual marriages originate. It was also the place where black baseball and football players could go, and *be paid*, safely out of view, because a career in the professional leagues was impossible or too much trouble back home. Canada was where fugitive black slaves, American draft dodgers, but also Haitian *tonton macoutes*, Hutu war criminals, and the families of Lebanese terrorists knew they could disappear, the entire country a relocation program for those in need of it. Today, were such refugees to settle in Prince Edward Island, or the Yukon, they could rest secure

that their new home would not even *appear* on some maps published even in Canada, as happened in 2003 when Fodor's produced
the magazine *Pure Canada* for the Canadian Tourism Commission.

◇ ◇ ◇

ANY PLACE IS only a landscape until it is animated by the stories
that provide its identity – or, to use a term that is more popular
today, its "psycho-geography." The sum of stories that are told
about or in a particular landscape create an impression of a place
that is imaginary, but functions as any map would, for places are as
real as persons, but they have no voice and so they speak to us
through art. The possibility that place affects character – that
place *has* character and exerts itself on us – goes a long way to
restoring some mystery and humility to life. A group of novelists –
including Peter Ackroyd, Michael Moorcock, and Iain Sinclair in
England, and in Canada, William Gibson – are sometimes referred
to as belonging to this school of psycho-geography – attributing,
in their literature, human aspects to places as if they were persons.
In these writers' works, place becomes a character in the story,
because it is understood to wield effect just as a human character
would; not just these writers know that how we *conceive* of a place
is every bit as important as what is deemed to be its "true" nature.
They know that all places have a history, a collection of stories and
memories that is mostly *not* written. They know that how we grow
into what is said, remembered, or locally felt about places is a part
of their identity. Hence Ackroyd's
"biography" of London, Sinclair's of
a room.

The Canadian conviction that the
country is Nowhere has been a trait
of its psycho-geography since the
earliest days of its settlement. But
the conviction that Somewhere is
Nowhere depends on the belief that
better lives are being lived Elsewhere

and that the place in question is unremarkable. Both these views of Canada are not generally true, but for as long as the country was a colony each was widely upheld; part of the syndrome of having been colonized is that subjects will take no end of punishment in their efforts to be like the ruling powers, and the British never held Canadians in any meaningful regard. So, in its first stage of Nowhere, Canada was considered even by many of its own writers, still deferring to old colonial ties, as off the vital European and American maps. When the iconic literary critic Northrop Frye wrote, in 1965, of Canada's "garrison mentality," he was expressing this Eurocentric judgment and planted a stigma on the Canadian literary psyche for a good few decades afterwards. Raised in barely post-colonial Moncton and then Sherbrooke, in Quebec's United Empire Loyalist Eastern Townships, Frye was in the habit of looking elsewhere for his cues. Canada was most definitely off his map, a literary landscape he famously described as "The Bush Garden." He regarded Canada in the late 1950s as empty, hostile, and barren of good literature, although he did concede in that patronizing way of his that its canon was not without promise.

The title of The Bush Garden was borrowed from The Journals of Susanna Moodie, a collection of poems by one of Frye's students, a young woman named Margaret Atwood.

A generation later, things were looking up for "CanLit," as the burgeoning literature had come to be called. Atwood was able to deliver her own uppercut when, in 1972, she cast the country as an arena for Survival. The message of her famous guide to the incipient Canadian literature was that Nature was menacing and that it had become the habit of Canadian authors to present themselves as victims in the face of it. Atwood, who spent a good portion of her childhood in northern Quebec, has always been interested in the idea of the wilderness as strangely threatening – a place that swallows things up. In her story "Death by Landscape," Nature does just that. Nowhere is a wilderness, and nasty. "Everyone has to be somewhere," Atwood writes, but the disappearance of a teenaged fellow camper is hauntingly unexplained, even years afterwards. "Death by Landscape" is an example of what the author calls a "Bad Mommy Nature" story, the psycho-geographical result of waves of immigration that brought British settlers who had never been farmers and dumped them on a land of stubborn rock and a terrible climate.

"As soon as they got their little bit of land," said Atwood, "the first thing settlers did was to chop down every tree they possibly could, because they wanted to grow stuff and because they were afraid of forest fires. It's no coincidence that the beginnings of English-Canadian literature are in the nineteenth century, when people were reconsidering the idea of nature as benevolent. Canada was the place to do that reconsidering, because if you stepped off the path in the winter, you froze, and so a lot of our 'Bad Mommy Nature' writings come out of that time."

✧ ✧ ✧

NOWHERE IS A BUNCH OF PLACES. De Charlevoix's Acá Nada became, in the nineteenth century, the terrifying wasteland. It was Catharine Parr Traill's banishment from Eden and her sister Susanna Moodie's "prisonhouse," the rough-hewn country where the pair of pioneers struggled to cope and Moodie was afraid that she might have "toiled and suffered in vain." It was the place where Jakob Wasserman tossed unwanted characters overboard, but it was also where the unwanted *wished* to be tossed. For Nowhere was Off the Map but also *terra rasa*, and as such a Utopian Opportunity. It was Wayson Choy's Gold Mountain – a place so distant and unknown that all kinds of dreams could be situated here. And just as its unspoiled lands offered settlers the prospect of a new beginning, removed from all the judgments and strictures of the Old World, so did its territories provide Canadian novelists with fresh terrain. Susanna Moodie is the writer who got them going. A Scottish soldier's wife, she wrote an account of her travails in Southern Ontario in the first half of the nineteenth century that spoke to generations of Canadians – and, in particular, to novelists and poets, including Margaret Atwood, Merilyn Simonds, and Jane Urquhart. Moodie was a writer of appealing personality, though it is now widely accepted that she made a lot of things up. No matter. Her often exasperated observations in *Roughing It in the Bush; or, Life in Canada*, about servants and the relationships of the classes in early nineteenth-century Canada, make enlivened and enlightening reading. No sooner do servants "set foot upon the Canadian shores than they become possessed with this ultra-Republican spirit. All respect for their employers, all subordination is at end." Shock. Horror. Moodie was also a novelist and a poet, but her evocative memoir stands as her best work. Its story of the determined immigrant, the shadowy presence of natives, and the fairly miserable solace of Utopia's dark side – mostly a lot of Presbyterian hard work – became the template for a category of Canadian novel that was so successful that it flourished, from the 1960s on, for the better part of four decades. It thrived because, regardless of the veracity of its details, its story of unexpected and distressing experience rang true. "Every Canadian story begins with a shock," says Ann-Marie MacDonald. "*Shtetl*, then prairie. 'I was in this seething Victorian industrial city and now I'm on the coast and I've got windburn.' Or, 'I was hunting buffalo and now I've got smallpox – and who *are* all these people in their red coats?' Every Canadian story begins with a shock and a swift change of identity."

✧ ✧ ✧

JANE URQUHART GREW up in a part of Canada that was Off the Map and Utopian Opportunity. The daughter of a mining engineer, she spent her early childhood in Little Long Lac, then a bush camp in Northern Ontario – a vanished mining settlement quite like it appears in her novel *The Underpainter*. The protagonists in Urquhart's novels are often driven and impassioned figures wresting a new life from the land and its scant materials: the Irish O'Malley family of *Away*, emigrating during the potato famine or, in *The Stone Carvers*, Father Gstir, a Bavarian priest who arrives in Northern Ontario in the late nineteenth century with dreams of building a cathedral in the woods.

From Jane Urquhart's *The Stone Carvers*:

What lay before him was a view of his first deep Canadian valley, one with signs of settlement near a shining stream, and he fell in love at once. He had to admit, however, even in the midst of his sudden infatuation, that the place was a cluttered mess, all vegetation having been recently torn up or chopped down, leaving behind acres of mud littered with uprooted and rotting tree stumps. Any attempts at architectural construction – even the sawmill and gristmill – looked temporary, haphazard, and dangerously frail, the boards from which the structures were built pale and raw in the afternoon light, men, oxen, and horses moving sluggishly around them. The humidity of the season had settled in the valley, and everything alive appeared to be swimming in a slow trance through cloudy water. Only the little river was filled with vitality – Father Gstir could hear the sound of it – as it picked up and tossed light that came from a sun barely visible in a milky sky.

He saw all this, but he also saw how it would be later, with crops and orchards growing in the cleared areas, and with painted houses and barns, and with gardens sprouting flowers. He beheld all that was there in front of him, and all that he believed would be there in the future, and he knew he was home.

Over the years, I have had the good fortune to listen to Urquhart tell affectionate tales about her brother, a prospector, and reminisce about her mother's *New Yorker*, and how it would arrive in Little Long Lac by dogsled. There are Canadian storytellers whose skills have been honed in bunkhouses, bush camps, or on fishing boats during long nights away, and Urquhart, this deceivingly delicate figure, was capable of telling stories in their line. In Toronto, I sought her out because I believed that she was one of the Canadian novelists most sensitive to ideas about land as metaphor: Niagara

Falls in *The Whirlpool*, the forests of *Away* and *The Stone Carvers*, and cleared land in that last novel and the next one, *A Map of Glass*. Hers is the Canada that the Group of Seven has remembered in paint.

"This is the landscape my father loved."

Urquhart was showing me some family snapshots: herself as a baby, being bathed in a small tin washtub outside the family cabin in Little Long Lac. Another of her father, a handsome man dressed in a loose white shirt, standing next to a few Company men in suits holding gold bricks in their hands. A third of her mother, a pretty woman in a short pleated skirt, resembling a 1950s cheerleader as she stood next to a man on the floats of a bush plane.

"What do you think about if I refer to Canada as Nowhere?" I asked.

"Mostly what comes to mind is that the organized narrative never came from the place that I thought of as Canada," Urquhart said. "I think of illustrations in children's books that had nothing to do with the world I was looking at – of freezing blizzards, of snow on the trees. There was a great deal of narrative in Little Long Lac, only not the kind that existed on paper. And often, writing my novels, I would discover a person who was forced to come here. They were almost always forced. It was very rare that someone in the eighteenth or nineteenth century actually *wanted* to come to this place that was freezing cold. People came to Canada and they dealt with what they found once they got here, and that was an interesting journey in itself. The idea that Canada was a place that was never chosen gave it an entirely different sensibility."

"Is Canada as Nowhere an exciting place for you?"

"Yes. I love the idea of the country being undefined. In Little Long Lac, everyone had a role and was acting it out on this enormous stage on the edge of Nowhere. And if you consider how conservative Ontario was, then being on the edge of Nowhere meant an escape from the rules. For a while, I thought it was appalling that we were not being taught our history properly. Now I think it's quite wonderful that we actually don't *have* much of an official history. The lack of an official interpretation is positive. We're in a place that doesn't carry any previous interpretations or explanations along with it. We are *Somewhere*, but also Nowhere."

"As a writer, that must be tremendously inviting."

"It is. European writers cannot believe how fortunate we are. Every square inch of what they have has been examined, painted, researched, and talked about – it's almost impossible to find something that one can claim as one's own obsession. Here, nobody has explained away the country's magic yet."

✧ ✧ ✧

"ONE OF THE APPEALS of Canada as Nowhere," said Atwood, "is that you don't have to deal with the weight of history. That kind of thinking is a bit naive now, because of course there is a lot of history here and we are still discovering the effects of it. But it is like the blank sheet of paper that is every writer's wildest dream and worst nightmare because it is exactly what you choose to put on it. The space is yours to fill."

✧ ✧ ✧

WHAT IS TRUE for the country is true of its parts. Consider, by way of illustration, the country's *rive gauche* – and no, not Montreal, nor St. John's, nor Vancouver's Downtown East Side, but *Don Mills, Ontario*, the planned community built in the 1950s that overlooks the ravines north of Toronto. Barbara Gowdy, in a wonderful Freudian slip, called Don Mills, the community in which she was raised, Non Mills. The new settlement of Don Mills was *utopos*, but it was, first of all, Nowhere. It sat in the Canadian bush garden as the eighteenth- and nineteenth-century towns of Upper and Lower Canada had done before it.

The revolutionary town envisioned by Edward Plunket Taylor and his urban planner, Macklin Hancock, was a garrison in the wilderness. For the post-war families of the late 1950s and early 1960s, the suburb of Don Mills offered the chance of a better life – materially, but also politically. By the 1980s, however, it had been gradually absorbed into the Greater Toronto Area's urban sprawl and became a place that was often mocked. Don Mills was seen as dull and ordinary, though now it is home to one of the largest congregations of South Asians in the country.

The ravines at its edge were an instance of the Canadian wilderness as the first settlers saw it, alluring to children and writers in the same way that the great blank spaces of early Canadian maps had been to cartographers. Its ravines have been used by the novelists Barbara Gowdy, Catherine Bush, Anne Michaels, and Margaret Atwood to convey the disturbing and sinister. They are a place to get lost in – land that cannot be domesticated and cleared. They are filled with natural hazards, bogeymen, and Indians of the James Fenimore Cooper kind such as Gowdy's young Louise Kirk imagines in *The Romantic*:

In the ravine, I enter a daydream that has me as an orphaned Indian princess called Little Feather and Mrs. Richter as a captured German settler whom the chief has renamed Nightingale and taken for his bride. Because Mrs. Richter is too old to bear children and I am like a daughter to her anyway, she and the chief have adopted me. I teach Mrs. Richter Indian songs, the ones I learned last year at Camp Wanawingo – "Indians are High-minded," "We Are the Red Men," "Pow-Wow, the Indian Boy." She teaches me the German language and customs. Everything is fine until Maureen Hellier waltzes by. Maureen is a sleazy half-breed named White Pig. When she starts throwing her weight around, the chief orders her to be tied to a tree and gagged. Sometimes she's not in the daydream at all, she has been banished to the wilderness. Sometimes I imagine everyone, including Mrs. Richter, gone. I am alone in my tee-pee. I am the sole survivor of a massacre by white men.

"The system of ravines," Urquhart said, "has entered the unconscious of many writers because there is the sense that some kind of magic could be going on in them, and if you put together magic and menace, then you have a place that is freighted with possibility."

Ravines such as are found near Don Mills are perfectly suited to the wild but also frightening idea of Nowhere in its first stage. Ravines are worn crevasses cut by running water over millennia that suggest a previous time. They are the proof, in a society that is only humanly recent, of ancient roots. In Anne Michaels's *Fugitive Pieces*, the ravines and the debris that Hurricane Hazel swept into them in 1954 become archaeological layers of time that allow Michaels to insinuate her characters into the weave of Holocaust history and make it her own. And ravines are *negative* spaces. They cannot be seen as you approach them. They are a means of escape, and of detention. They are places into which things and people quite literally disappear from view. In Atwood's novels, stuff is always falling into them – Elaine, in *Cat's Eye*, retrieves the hat Cordelia has menacingly thrown into the ravine, and in *The Blind Assassin*, Laura Chase's car falls in, with its soon-to-be-dead driver still in it. Really what the ravines are doing is offering the writer a path out and away from the world as it appears at first glance. In Atwood's *The Edible Woman*, Marian and Duncan walk to the Don Valley Brick Works, located in the south end of the ravines, and have "a vision of nothingness." Atwood took me there.

"We can go right down into the ravine now," Atwood said. "There's a beautifully gravelled pathway instead of the little muddy tracks we used to follow."

Below the mansions of Rosedale, and the smaller but still comfortable houses of Leaside on one flank and the imposing apartment blocks of Thorncliffe Park on the other, the ravines have the air of country paths. Mysterious and otherworldly from street level, they offer a strange feeling of security while you are in them. The slopes fall steeply away from the houses, built to their very rim. In the vicinity of Cabbagetown, alongside train tracks and the Don Valley Parkway, the ravines bottom out and spread into marshes. By the banks of the river, and elsewhere beneath grand bridges that ford the ravines and serve the world overtop, are camps of homeless people. A congregation of tents, accumulations of trash and discarded clothing.

"The ravines are the city's only *vertical* dimension," said Atwood. "Toronto was built on seven shores of ancient seas that you don't see easily because they are quite sloping. They are old beaches. The ravines were cut by the flow of water and they are the only places you can go up and down quite steeply."

I asked if this physical aspect, of dropping away, promoted a culture of secrets.

"All cultures promote secrets," said Atwood. "But the secrets are of different kinds. There are all sorts of places, in literature, where you go to be by yourself, places where you go to make strange discoveries of the soul. There's the frozen north, the desert, the desert island, the sea, the jungle."

Atwood laughed. "We've got ravines, that's about it."

✧   ✧   ✧

NOWHERE IN ITS SECOND STAGE is Nowhere in Particular. It is the Utopian Opportunity realized – the tamed countryside, a town, a suburban basement. Don Mills, Erindale, Glengarry, Steinbach. Bland subdivisions and malls civilize all those terrifying blank spaces filled with lions and tigers and bears, the homeless, or other beasts too scary to mention and make indistinct places of them. Nowhere in Particular is the plethora of towns in Canada that were once industrious but whose economy has failed and whose sole reason for being has become to maintain their existence because the towns are there. It is the abstract landscape of a whole generation of "urban" writers who have not yet found the ways to express their cities' differences and so speak of them in unnamed, generic terms. It is the sum of places remarkable for being without remarkable qualities – beyond their citizens being satisfied, of course. In Colin McAdam's wonderful novel of bureaucrats and developers, *Some Great Thing*, Jerry McGuinty is a builder with standards, someone who favours plaster over gyproc. He fights a variety of battles – with rival developers, blithe Ottawa civil servants, his alcoholic wife, his runaway son. But the developments and malls so easy to deride are, in his novel, also realms of possibility. They are the *point* of living in the New World, whole communities created in places that were previously Off the Map. They are Utopian Opportunities seized, though there is the shadow of the wilderness, still. When McGuinty espies his runaway son, also named Jerry, in the mall he has built, he is halted in wonder tinged with fright.

From Colin McAdam's *Some Great Thing*:

> I couldn't believe all the people in that mall. It was lunch hour, and there were men in suits walking around, women in suits, old ladies shopping, people jabbing fries into their mouths. It was still new, but it was *full*. I felt like I had planted a few seeds, forgotten about them, and now here was a forest with wildlife, flowers and nuts.
>
> Can I admit to something, just between us? I forgot about Jerry. I completely forgot about why I was in that mall. You will understand that I felt pride for having had a hand in the making of the building, but there was some other feeling that made me forget about Jerry for a minute.
>
> Look at the man looking for an electric knife, the granny looking for a bluer rinse, the woman here looking for the right speckled frame for her glasses. They depress me, my friend. They're all looking for something, and their sad little faces are telling me there's a reason for their looking and it's not roast beef or a weak shade of blue. There's something outside, I tell you, and it's making them all come in here, something scary, something waiting for all of them.

✧   ✧   ✧

THE NOWHERE OF Don Mills, the country in miniature, has touched the lives of a disproportionate number of Canadian novelists. M.G.

Vassanji knew it because he used to visit relatives in Thorncliffe Park. He used Don Mills as the setting for *No New Land*, his early novel of immigrant experience. Richard Wright worked as a salesman for the Oxford University Press out of Don Mills. Barbara Gowdy grew up there in the 1950s, as did a pair of contemporaries and childhood friends, the novelists Paul Quarrington and Lawrence Hill, a decade later. Each used the experience of living Nowhere to advantage. I gathered Gowdy, Hill, and Quarrington in the Hill family's Don Mills kitchen with a view to learning from Canada writ small. What the trio yearned for above all in Non Mills was *difference*. In Canada's Nowhere in Particular, it had to be sought out.

"Don Mills wasn't just racially homogeneous," said Gowdy. "It was religiously so. It was very white and very Protestant. I remember being intrigued by a woman named Dr. Shinobu. She was the only Japanese person I'd ever heard of or seen. You didn't even see Japanese people on TV. We treasured her because she provided some contrast in the place."

"I'm just trying to remember how I identified myself," mused Quarrington. "Mostly through the silly clothes we used to wear – clam diggers, Madras shirts, and shirts with fruit loops – did you ever wear any of that stuff?"

"No," said Gowdy, dead-pan. "We dressed as girls."

The hell of Nowhere in Particular is not Nature but a tedium that Canadians themselves often invite. The contract of the fresh start, of Nowhere as Utopian Opportunity, is that immigrants who have landed here, as nearly all Canadians have done, strive 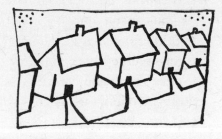 to put the often unsavoury experiences that drove them here – whether war, poverty, or a class system that dealt a bad hand – at a distance. We agree not to inquire – or to do so only in a self-serving way. Our national lack of curiosity can be a part of the refugee's nightmare, a whole life rendered obsolete. The new

Canadian is a traveller, like Odysseus carrying his oar, landing in a country that doesn't have a clue.

When Lawrence Hill's parents moved to Don Mills, wanting to put the racism of the United States behind them, their mixed-raced son virtually had to *insist* to other people that he was black. Hill's own Nowhere in Particular spawned a memoir, *Black Berry, Sweet Juice: On Being Black and White in Canada*, as well as novels of black experience that grasp at the significance of being black in USAmerica over the relatively anodyne adventure of being the other in Canada.

In *Any Known Blood*, the narrator, Langston Cane V is, like Hill, mixed blood. (The character's name is a play on the work of two iconic African-American authors: the poet Langston Hughes and Jean Toomer, the author of *Cane*.) Langston Cane V is born in 1957, in Oakville, once a stop on the Underground Railroad. His great-great-grandfather, Langston Cane I, had been a slave in Virginia, in the first part of the nineteenth century. Early on, Cane V makes a private but acerbically felt prank out of the indistinct colour of his skin.

From Lawrence Hill's *Any Known Blood*:

> I have the rare distinction – a distinction that weighs like a wet life jacket, but that I sometimes float to great advantage – of not appearing to belong to any particular race, but of seeming like a contender for many.
>
> In Spain, people have wondered if I was French. In France, hotel managers asked if I was Moroccan. In Canada, I've been asked – always tentatively – if I was perhaps Peruvian, American, or Jamaican. But I have rarely given a truthful rendering of my origins.
>
> Once, someone asked, "Are you from Madagascar? I know a man from Madagascar who looks like you."
>
> I said: "As a matter of fact, I am. I was born in the capital, Antananarivo. We moved to Canada when I was a teenager."

Another time, when a man sitting next to me in a donut shop complained about Sikh refugees arriving by boat in Gander, Newfoundland, I said: "I was born in Canada and I don't wear a turban, but I'm a Sikh. My mother is white, but my father is a Sikh, and that makes me one, too." The man's mouth fell open. I paid the waitress to bring him twelve chocolate donuts. "I've gotta go," I told him. "But next time you want to run down Sikhs, just remember that one of them bought you a box of donuts!"

"If I'd grown up in Brooklyn or South Carolina, as many of my cousins did," said Hill, "I would have been attending segregated schools, and regardless of the colour of my skin, whether it was lighter or darker, I would have been harshly and viscerally identified as black every step of the way. But in Don Mills I had to fight even to develop a sense of blackness, and so the field was thrown wide open. Sometimes I was black, sometimes I wasn't. Don Mills was a grey zone, a place where racial identity was up for grabs. It wasn't handed to you in a clear and un-negotiable way – the way it had been handed to my parents or would have been to a person of my generation growing up in Capetown, say. That was the unique thing about Don Mills."

"But perhaps growing up Nowhere in Particular offers advantage to the writer," I suggested, "because its anodyne quality makes it easier to consider and then write about Elsewhere."

"And to *accept* Elsewhere and embrace it," said Gowdy, "to be glad that not everyone is like you, thank God. When everything appears very much the same, you become more innately attuned to subtlety, just as a mother who has twins sees great differences in her children that nobody else does."

"I have certain tendencies that arise because I don't identify with anything much," said Quarrington, "and I suppose that's a virtue when you're writing a novel. I know that it has always been pretty easy for me to enter other people's consciousness and perhaps that ability comes out of being from a kind of Nowhere."

"I always feel like I'm somewhere else," said Gowdy. "And if I sneak around corners in my writing, if I sometimes don't identify things or places by name, it's because I'm far more interested in people's minds and motivations – in what it actually feels like to be a daughter, a sister, or a lover in really intimate relationships – in what it feels like to be a human being, and perhaps that is a way of *avoiding* place. I mean, I wrote a book called *White Bone*, set in Africa and told from the point of view of elephants, for God's sake. What does that have to do with a girl from Don Mills? What it has to do with Don Mills is that I felt the freedom to enter that story more easily. When you come from Nowhere, then you're not really expected to describe it. You can float out into other places. That was an appetite that the landscape gave us."

◇　◇　◇

EVENTUALLY THE WRITER floating out to other places scrutinizes his or her own backyard and sees worth in it; one of the artist's first mandates is to find *difference* in places, and the novelist does so through language. But if those places look the same, were designed to be the same, then how does naming help? Nowhere in Particular generates a yearning to be Elsewhere and an aptitude for describing other places, but also a certain literature of disaffection.

Atwood said, "I would call that the literature of the shopping mall. It deals with a sinister underworld, with mazes and disorientation. These places are not happy places."

In Vancouver, I found a master of this kind of literature, the young writer Lee Henderson. He had grown up in Erindale, outside Saskatoon – one of those seemingly generic suburbs that have come to symbolize Canada in its second stage of Nowhere. The stories of his collection, *The Broken Record Technique*, portray a rootless world of hot tubs, strip malls, and suburban basements that might have been located in just about any city in Canada – or America, for that matter. In Henderson's "sinister underworld," as in Gowdy's, salubrious streets and malls such as Colin McAdam's Jerry McGuinty built are the settings of a kind of dysfunction that had its roots in the false promise and impossible optimism of the 1950s and early 1960s. What is really being explored – what is being relied upon – is the impossibility of a happy, normal life such as it had been envisioned in the scientific and planned surroundings of communities such as Don Mills or Erindale. Utopian schemes, no matter how modest, have the certainty of failure built into them, as it is humankind that is doing the dreaming and men and women – and boys and girls, of course – are by nature flawed. In Henderson's story "W," life in the subdivision is so uniform that even people resemble one another, and a man who looks exactly like Ben, eleven-year-old Eliot's father, abducts the child. The mother, Molly, wondering –

> where the boy is, where and how he could ever have been taken out of this world, all-inclusive as it is, a shelter cruelly planted with grocery stores and discount clothing outlets and everything a person could want, supposedly, so that you never have to venture outside the walls meant to keep the noise of traffic from bothering those living next door to it. The safety of a place like this, smothered in sameness and in snow. (Molly has tried to draw the neighbourhood so many times, from so many angles, but she's never seen it from above, has always wanted to, but she doesn't have the energy to lift a pencil any more, so what's the point.) Look at how the wind comes unexpectedly and steals away the lovely things, the leaves off trees and the fluttering torn pages of catalogues from department stores –; the children who play with wood and long knotted-together shoelaces have their hats blown down the street and they run after them as their parents scream for them to come home this very instant, this very instant, this very instant.

"I grew up scarred by the experience and pretty well needing to write about it," said Henderson before I asked him if writing from Nowhere in Particular offered benefits.

"It's a good vantage point, that's for sure," said Henderson. "A lot of the details in my head were Western Canadian, but I didn't want any place names in as a way of stating that this story could be in Saskatoon, Calgary, Vancouver, wherever. You keep objects and ephemera at a distance, to ensure that should someone pick up your book in London, England, they would not be completely lost."

Canada, in its subset of "urban" novels, can seem a place ready to write itself out of existence, as if to be local would undo the idea that the city life these writers know has no borders. The one realm in which authors such as Henderson, or another writer living in Vancouver, Douglas Coupland, rely on the identifiable is that of products: shampoos, food, clothing brands, pop songs, CNN. These ubiquitous items are specific to Nowhere, the nondescript place.

"You do that to create *totems* out of things," said Henderson. "If you start to talk about a 'Toyota' rather than just a car, and if you then say 'Toyota' enough times, then 'Toyota' becomes a talisman, and you begin to associate the word *Toyota* with so much more that is in the culture. Canada is really good at taking other cultures' ciphers. These things like Toyotas, or Twinkies, they come from different countries, and we engage with them all quite happily because we don't produce very many of them ourselves."

"Is this part of Canadians' aptitude for writing from Nowhere, do you think?"

"Yes. We don't have a car manufacturer, so we latch on to these things. We incorporate them into our lives – and with *gusto*. We really like that stuff, and I do too. I like these things for their ability to become abstract items."

"Are these the props of a globalized world that is *ostensibly* Nowhere – but actually American? I'm thinking, for instance, of Douglas Coupland's two volumes, *Souvenir of Canada* and *Souvenir of Canada* 2, in which he takes products that he's picked out of larders and living rooms and sees in these objects a character that is uniquely Canadian."

"Sure, but what's problematic about Coupland's two books," said Henderson, "is that those objects have *never been*, until he said it, decisively Canadian things. The stubby bottle is not really a decisively Canadian item, though he's decided that it is. And good for him; it's cool, but fiction is so much more plastic than that. If I am writing a book in which you recognize items as the objects of a globalized community, you could say, 'Oh, this feels American,' but the weather might feel too Canadian. The situation immediately becomes more vague. And in a sense, I hope that you would be allowed to feel such geographical confusion without ever having a proper answer."

"For how long can any Nowhere really be Nowhere in Particular?"

"Well, this is where you are going, right? We might be in a transition from being Nowhere to being Somewhere Quite Distinct."

"Another way to put it would be to ask you where you think you are from."

"I'm from Western Canada. I'm definitely from Western Canada."

✧ ✧ ✧

"THE QUESTION IS a pragmatic one about audience," said Wayne Johnston, whose early novels were set in and around St. John's or, in *Human Amusements*, amid the Newfoundland community in Toronto.

"One of the reasons Canadians are reluctant to name," said Johnston, "is they don't have the confidence if they write about political issues – about Quebec, let's say, or Newfoundland joining Confederation – that people will understand the underlying stories. They're worried that they will seem to be navel-gazing. If you write about Iraq, if you write about 9/11 – those numbers are as instantly recognizable in Canada as they are in the United States. Try to think of something that is quintessentially Canadian that is as easily understood in the United States, some little phrase that instantly means Canadian, except something like 'How's it goin', eh?' Try to think of some Canadian historical event that around the world everybody says, 'Oh yeah, I know exactly what that is. I know exactly what ideology is resting on that, who is fighting who and what the issues are.' You always have that concern, so that when Canadians write political novels, they tend to be satirical, because that's a way of making issues more universal. The comedy is something that anyone can relate to. Or they are dystopian novels such as Margaret Atwood has written, set in a generic future. Think of *The Handmaid's Tale*, set in upstate New York, or *Oryx and Crake*. They're not really set in Canada. They're set in a post-apocalyptic world that is not Canada."

Yet I wondered what had been common knowledge about Wayne Johnston's Newfoundland before *The Colony of Unrequited Dreams* drew such a brilliant portrait of his reluctant province? Canadians were not about to write as Johnston had done until they started to believe that their Nowhere was *Somewhere* – and that was easier, perhaps, as a Newfoundlander. The persistent psycho-geographical idea that, at some level, Canada is Nowhere explains why a frequent motif in Canadian novels has been of the photograph or the movie house. In Nowhere in Particular, the effect of believing ourselves to be living on the wrong side of Elsewhere is that we have become accustomed to watching life as if it were happening at one remove.

◇ ◇ ◇

PAST THE WAREHOUSES and the railway tracks, past an array of chicken diners, the slaughterhouses have taken over and then even those disappear as the outlying industrial areas of Winnipeg give way to the flats that preceded the Manitoban capital. A few days away from June, nature was still not convincingly in bloom.

"Pretty, eh?" said Miriam Toews. We were driving towards her Mennonite hometown of Steinbach, sixty kilometres southeast of Winnipeg. We passed a pro-life billboard, posted next to a larger billboard for a Dodge dealership. JESUS IS THE SAVIOUR AND THE LIGHT.

"Absolutely," I said.

"I have a real love-hate relationship with this place," said Toews. She pointed at a farm to one side of the highway and said chirpily,

"I had an old boyfriend who lived there. I don't want you to think I was some kind of a slut, but there wasn't a whole lot to do growing up in Steinbach."

I was aware that my mood was not quite right. Toews was a cheery, even ebullient presence at the steering wheel of her van filled with the detritus of family, but that morning I had finished *Swing Low: A Life*, her bold faux memoir of her father – a loving man who, after the job of family was done, committed suicide by calmly getting dressed, walking to the perimeter of town, and putting himself in the path of an oncoming train. Finishing the book had brought me to tears.

"No shortage of car dealerships," I said.

"The Mennonites ruled that the railway should not pass through Steinbach because they didn't want nasty outside influences coming in."

In Toews's novel *A Complicated Kindness*, Nomi Nickel is born to a Mennonite family living in the fictional Manitoban town of East Village. Her mother has left, leaving no clue as to her whereabouts, and so has her sister, Tash. East Village is Nowhere to Nomi. She is desperate to get out and dreams of flight to that other East Village, the Bohemian one in New York City. Work in the Happy Family Farms, a chicken slaughterhouse, beckons.

The long passing trains, of which there are many on the prairie, offer the tease of a way out of Nomi's Mennonite No Exit. She says,

> I like to ride my bike to the border and stare at America. I like
> to ride my bike to train crossings in empty fields and watch
> graffiti fly past me at a hundred miles an hour. It really is the
> perfect way to view art. I silently thank the disenfranchised
> kids from Detroit or St. Louis for providing some colour in my
> life. I've often wanted to send a message back to them.
> Nomi from Nowhere says hello.

"Nomi can smell the odour of death when she's lying in her bed at night," said Toews. "When the wind is blowing in a certain direction, everybody in town can smell these chickens being killed. It's really unpleasant."

"The Happy Family Farms were an emblem of what?"

"Of a dead end, of a stupid, mindless task – now, apologies to all of those who do slaughter chickens, because I do eat chickens and I know they have to be slaughtered in order for me to do that – but in Nomi's mind it was just an abysmal, horrible job and she would compare it to the whole flock of young Mennonites being led almost to slaughter. It was a type of life that was so predestined. Death was the ultimate goal, and the belief was that in the end we'll have eternal life, we'll have happiness, we'll be free of pain, we'll be free of sorrow – this was preached in the Church and so Nomi would compare the idea of all these chickens living together, await-ing their death, to her Mennonite situation."

"She's a rebel. She wants to get out."

"But at the same time she's afraid of what that entails. East Village is all that she knows, there are parts of it that she loves – obviously her father, and some of her friends, so it's a difficult thing for her. She knows that she wants to be free and to experience the world that she fantasizes about, constantly. But at the same time, she's nervous about it. She's afraid."

We approached the model Pioneer Village just outside of Steinbach, and Toews parked the van. A crop-dusting plane was practising takeoffs and landings on the airstrip beyond the metal fence at the bottom of the mock Mennonite settlement. A wooden sidewalk ran the length of Main Street, on the side of the wide dirt road that was lined with shops and old-fashioned storefronts. The "East Village" of Toews's novel, modelled on Steinbach, is one that people come to "from all over the world for a first-hand look at simple living." In this, its ersatz inspiration was a grocery store, a printer's, a livery and restaurant. A windmill was visible in the open space behind the shops, and tall elms towered over the gardens of the houses on the other side, their borders marked by low white-picket fences. Among them were a couple of one-storey log cabins and a large farmhouse with a red-painted barn attached. The

Mennonites came to Canada in several waves, this one from Russia and Prussia in the 1870s. Canada was the Utopian Opportunity, a place where Christian Anabaptist followers of the sixteenth-century preacher Menno Simons would no longer have to live in fear of rival churches or answer to European monarchs' rules. The Mennonites of Steinbach developed plenty of their own. In *A Complicated Kindness*, the mother's rift with her brother, Nomi's uncle – "The Mouth" – leads to her shunning, a family split that was similar to one that occurred in Toews's own family and contributed to her father's suicide.

"After *Swing Low*, people were saying things like 'Miriam Toews, why is she writing?'" said Toews. "'What is she trying to prove?' 'Why doesn't she just grow up and accept her father's death and move on?' But really it was more of a head-shaking, lip-pursing thing and a lack of understanding of what I was trying to say. Besides, I'm not a part of the Church, so I can't be shunned by a Mennonite congregation."

"But people leave in other ways," I said. "Nomi's boyfriend leaves her for Montreal, and her mother and sister have walked away. You left your family, and your father did when he left Steinbach and committed suicide."

"Yeah," said Toews. "Leaving is a big thing in my work. I had a set of encyclopedias, and I would look up Manhattan, or I would look up Los Angeles. I would look up all these hotspots that you know about when you're a kid. Most of them were American, though sometimes I would imagine that my town was somewhere in Italy or in France. I mean, if it couldn't be a city, then at least it could be a little *village* somewhere that was not on the prairie!"

✧　✧　✧

AND THEN A STRANGE thing happens. Time passes, history accumulates. The work a writer does wrests Nowhere *onto* the Map. Nowhere as Off the Map and Utopian Opportunity becomes Nowhere in Particular and, finally, Somewhere – Nowhere as an Address with Virtues.

"When I was growing up," the Tanzanian-born novelist M.G. Vassanji said, "the centre of the world was London, England. London was where I wanted to go for my education. London was where my friends were wealthier, and living in London was what earned you prestige. Canada was not really on the map at all. In my consciousness, it was there as much as Greenland or Argentina was. But then people started looking around for other places where they might emigrate. Canada was a possibility, and suddenly it was *the* place. It was easy to get into, and people had heard about Canada. They had heard about Don Mills."

✧   ✧   ✧

IN THE DAR-ES-SALAAM of M.G. Vassanji's *No New Land*, the citizens of "Dar" are eager to leave Tanzania and dream not of Toronto but Don Mills when they contemplate the better life. "They talked of Don Mills as if it were in Upanga," the upmarket district of the Tanzanian capital. The dull suburbs of Canada's Nowhere in Particular – Surrey, B.C.; Glengarry outside Edmonton; Erindale, Saskatchewan; Saint Laurent, south of Montreal; and Don Mills, of course – lure new immigrants with the promise of work and a respectable address. Vassanji, a student of engineering, was born in 1950. He left Tanzania to study in America and then immigrated to Canada in 1980. The Thorncliffe Park housing estate in Don Mills becomes Rosecliffe Park in *No New Land*. Its broad, ungainly apartment blocks, on the eastern ridge of the Don Valley, overlook the original suburb that was home to Gowdy, Hill, and Quarrington, as well as the busy Don Valley Parkway that is a symptom of the community's changed status. Don Mills is the first thing many new immigrants know of Canada – but the last that many members of older, European-Canadian settler communities learn about their rapidly changing country. Thorncliffe Park has a Valu-Mart, a couple of mosques, and, a few streets behind it, the Iqbal Foods store. Trucks unload amid the cars parked at its front. The low, one-storey building could be an Asian store anywhere in Africa but it is here, in Canada. Within it, a cafeteria-style restaurant serves a variety of curries and desserts, and a lineup of workers and families push their plastic trays along to the waiting cash register. Vassanji and I ordered lunch there, grabbed some plastic cutlery, and poured ourselves some water into Styrofoam cups.

"You were going out into an English-speaking white world," said Vassanji, "but a wealthy, civilized world of order where you could be *safe*, or at least not be persecuted. What was known was that in six months, or a few years, people had established themselves and were living in apartment buildings, and that there were places of worship, and supermarkets, and friends who also lived there. In Dar, they would say, 'Oh, I saw Mr. So-and-So who used to live across the street.' *Now he is in Don Mills.* That is how Don Mills became known. It was a neighbourhood that you had never been to but your old neighbour from Dar lives there now, and maybe your son is there too. There was a sense of possibility, but also the feeling that you were not going to an *alien* place."

"And yet you describe Canada as having been a blank space –"

"It was a blank space because it was underpopulated, not because it was a place of nothingness. We knew about Canada. And we knew about Trudeau, of course. Trudeau was a big deal."

"Do you think that the nature of immigration has changed?"

"People who came earlier on escaped war, they came in boats, they left their countries, and knew they would not see their home again. There was no looking back. Now we live in a different world. We come by plane. We hold dual passports, we have email, we have telephones, we have families that are split all over the world."

"And today there are few currency controls –"

"Yes. Now economies are interlinked so that when people come to Canada they speak the old language and even *refresh* it, so that it doesn't happen that Gujarati disappears, just as English or German won't disappear. But for me, the redeeming feature is that every year immigrants are not coming to an insecure country, they are coming to a country that is sure of itself."

✧ ✧ ✧

IN ROHINTON MISTRY'S novel *Family Matters*, there is a scene that bristles – and it was written *before* the author was detained by American customs officials following the events of 9/11. The novel is set in Bombay in the 1990s, a time in which the Bharatiya Janata Party, the Hindu nationalist party, was beginning to gather strength and stir religious intolerance in the city. At one point, Yezad Chenoy, a struggling employee at a sports store, recalls inquiring into the possibility of emigration to Canada. The immigration officer at the Canadian High Commission is one Mr. Mazobashi, a Japanese Canadian, and Yezad is "thrilled. This was the beauty of Canada, I felt, that Mazobashi could be as Canadian as any other name." But Mazobashi's manner is patronizing, even racist. He insults Yezad and stonewalls the Chenoy family's application with mocking taunts that stun the Indian disproportionately, as he would not have expected the Japanese Canadian to repeat an experience of prejudice that Mazobashi's community remembers to this very day. Boldly, Yezad rebukes him.

From Rohinton Mistry's *Family Matters*:

> "You, sir, are a rude and ignorant man, a disgrace to your office and country. You have sat here abusing us, abusing Indians and India, one of the many countries your government drains of its brainpower, the brainpower that is responsible for your growth and prosperity. Instead of having the grace to thank us, you spew your prejudices and your bigoted ideas. You, whose people suffered racism and xenophobia in Canada, where they were Canadian citizens, put in camps like prisoners of war – you, sir, might be expected, more than anyone else, to understand and embody the more enlightened Canadian ideals of multiculturalism. But if you are anything to go by, then Canada is a gigantic hoax."

"Yezad knows more than most about Canada because of his interest in literature," said Mistry when I spoke to him in Toronto.

"He has a friend who lends him books and among these, I imagine, was Joy Kogawa's *Obasan* and Ken Adachi's history of the Japanese in Canada, *The Enemy That Never Was*. And he must have read some of Pierre Berton's books, I'm not quite sure."

"What do you think the great blank spaces of Canada's map would have meant to Yezad?"

"I'm not sure if Canada appeared blank, or as a basket of goodies."

Mistry, who was born in Bombay in 1952, immigrated to Canada in 1975. For a long time, he kept his home in Brampton, a small and prosperous town in Southern Ontario that has become, over the last couple of decades, another Don Mills, another point of settlement in Canada's Nowhere. Fed by the 407 Highway, Brampton was one of those places burgeoning with new houses and developments, with monster homes and even palaces, built on the whim of immigrant families that could not have imagined living in such space or splendour in the countries they had left behind.

"People often don't understand this move to monster homes," said Mistry.

"When I drive through Mississauga," I said, "I find myself thinking what a marvellous alternative those homes must be to the poverty of New Delhi or London's Brick Lane, and I'm frustrated with myself for knowing so little of what goes on there – which is why we read, I suppose. Do you ever want to know yourself?"

"Oh," said Mistry, smiling again, "one has a pretty good idea, really. Enough so that one day one may write about it."

✧ ✧ ✧

"When you come to a different country," said Atwood, "you have a couple of choices. One of them is to write about the place you came from, so that you have novels about India or novels about Africa that are being written in Canada, by people who now live in Canada. But their subject is not Canada. Their subject is the place from which that writer came. The other kind would be the immigrant novel – the kind of story in which you arrive with your preconceptions and your luggage and you find that things are quite different from what you imagined in this place that you have come to. And usually you have a number of unpleasant adventures that can end either with acceptance or with a sort of 'get me out of here' ending."

"I suppose that even in the act of writing about the old country," I said, "you are filling this Nowhere with things that are familiar."

"Writers write about what they know," said Atwood. "And it is a paradox that a number of people have to get out of the place that they have been in because it is too dangerous for them, but that is really where their imagination lies – in the old place. If you have grown up in a place, then that place supplies your material, to a certain extent, and often you have to work your way through that material before you hit another bunch of material that comes from what you've seen and experienced after setting foot in the new place."

◇ ◇ ◇

YEZAD KNEW THE country he was choosing. Canada, in its third stage, is the destination of first choice – Nowhere as the place to remain, finally – even more so after 9/11, said the Vancouver writer and visual artist Douglas Coupland. He bounded to fame with his first novel, *Generation X: Tales for an Accelerated Culture*, an expanded essay about anxious youth that was also a brilliant exercise in labelling – an activity that all Americans adore. Because *Generation X* was set in the arid North American Nowhere of the Californian desert, Coupland is still included in anthologies of USAmerican fiction, as if his country of origin was immaterial, and yet being Canadian informs all of his work, which is why the turn his novels have presented on an old theme is so interesting. The mood of the West Coast author's books is often dire, even apocalyptic. His novel *Hey Nostradamus!* was prompted by the 1999 high-school shootings at Columbine, Colorado – a natural subject for Coupland and his grim prognoses, as the shock of Nowhere in its third stage is of Utopia being taken away. The story is told from several points of view including that of Cheryl, one of the students who is slain, and who speaks from wherever it is that the soul of an innocent – this one pregnant – is transported after death. In the class she was attending shortly before the massacre, Cheryl had been contemplating that very Canadian idea of Nowhere.

From Douglas Coupland's *Hey Nostradamus!*:

> In homeroom I sat at my desk and wrote over and over on my pale blue binder the words GOD IS NOWHERE/ GOD IS NOW HERE/ GOD IS NOWHERE/ GOD IS NOW HERE. When this binder with these words was found, caked in my evaporating blood, people made a big fuss about it, and when my body is shortly lowered down into the planet, these same words will be felt-penned all over the surface of my white coffin. But all I was doing was trying to clear out my head and think of nothing, to generate enough silence to make time stand still.

* * *

> Stillness is what I have here now – wherever *here* is. I'm no longer a part of the world, and I'm not yet a part of what follows. I think there are others from the shooting here with me, but I can't tell where. And for whatever it's worth, I'm no longer pregnant, and I have no idea what that means. Where's my baby? What happened to it? How can it just go away like that?

"Part of the Canadian dream," said Coupland, "as much as it exists, is to generate neighbourhoods like this one in West Vancouver, where there is safety and freedom from the dark things in this world. The very broad theme of what I do is to take these environments and then have something happen in them. There's a shooting or a terrible accident and you are forced to reconsider your environment. I mean, in the genetic and geographical lottery that is life on earth, being Canadian and middle class in the late twentieth century is probably the biggest grand prize of all. I mean, what can be better? *Nothing.*"

Every Nowhere becomes Somewhere, true, but the corollary of its evolution is that all those once empty spaces on maps or in ravines get filled. The cost of not being alone in Utopia is that it does not seem so much like heaven any more. The dream is farther out of reach. The Don Mills that M.G. Vassanji's Tanzanians imagined was a version of Canada that Jane Urquhart's Irish ancestors and the families of Scots, Belgians, Germans, Dutch, Chinese, Japanese, Serbians and Croatians, and now peoples from whole other continents and regions – Africa, South Asia, the Middle East, and Afghanistan – envisioned. Only now the gate is closing, just a little, and if you do get through it, then you're right up against the next guy and you may not want to be that close. Nowhere becomes Somewhere and then all of a sudden it feels like Anywhere.

"I feel sorry for the Japanese translator," Coupland said, "because none of this Nowhere, Now, Here, There stuff translates into any other language."

"But in English it's a word that can be played with a fair amount. Northrop Frye did. You did."

"So how do you look at here?" Coupland asked.

"I think that Canada was Nowhere as Off the Map, then Nowhere in Particular, but that we have a stronger sense of self now," I said. "We're still off the map, but we're not *meta incognita* any more. We are a place with our own attributes. Virtues, even. That's my theory of Canada as 'Nowhere,' what's yours?"

"I suppose what used to be called Nowhere still might be Nowhere, but now it's an interesting place and it's able to generate difference," said Coupland. "It has yet to be pasteurized, it has yet to be homogenized."

"That would make it Somewhere, wouldn't it?"

"To me, the most Nowhere place on earth is Chicago's O'Hare Airport. I'll do anything to avoid going through that place because it's like going through zombie purgatory. It's like being Everywhere *and* Nowhere. It's just awful."

"And Canada?"

"Hmm. If you fly over the North, you'll see nothing happening there, and nothing probably *will* happen there unless we have the big climate change. And yet it's part of Canada. What does it mean that the land is Canadian? That was just an abstract thought until the Danes started trying to claim some of it, and now the Canadians are sending troops up there to march, and that's all they're doing. They're just walking across this land. That makes it Canadian or something?"

"It still feels like a blow to the stomach," I said. "The North was meant to be limitless territory, and I suppose that what the dispute with the Danes over Hans Island does is to define limits."

"And I think that you can still, only just *barely*, go to these Nowhere places and reinvent your life. In the old days, meaning the 1950s, if you wanted to reinvent yourself, you came to Vancouver. In the 1990s, a lot of people I knew – from Ontario, in particular – would sell everything and move to Whistler and start life over again, only when they got there all they found was a lot of other people from Ontario doing exactly the same thing. Now I suppose you would go to Labrador or to some small place up North if you wanted to go to these Nowhere places and rewrite or reinvent your life completely."

"Well, you can't go to Iqaluit any more," I said, "because the Road to Nowhere is being developed –"

"Oh. Iqaluit is the new Seattle. Haven't you heard? All the new bands are coming out of there, and the new fashion look, like mukluks. You wait and read the magazines in a year."

And then they moved to a vast space next to Greenland

Coupland laughed. "Just tell me there wasn't a Starbucks."

"But you anticipate all this development in *Souvenir of Canada*. You have a page on Baffin Island and you wonder when we'll see a Baskin-Robbins ice-cream outlet there."

"Okay," said Coupland matter-of-factly. "I guess what we're talking about is the difference between romantic Nowhere and a generic Nowhere. I think that ours is the most romantic Nowhere on Earth, and that's a good thing, whereas a place like Antarctica is still a generic Nowhere – I mean, let's face it. You can't go down to Antarctica and reinvent yourself."

Coupland put a finger to his mouth and thought about it.

"Or could you?"

Part One

THE AGE OF INVENTION

*T*here is a parallel to be made between the ways a territory is mapped and how stories are told. A human sees perhaps an animal, a tree, or a rock and identifies it with the drawing he makes. As soon as he paints a second object, or puts himself in the painting, then distance is implied and a map has been made. When the map is complete, then further maps contribute other kinds of information or contest the points the first map has made.

During Canada's period of First Contact, European explorers reached into this continent, meta incognita then. They drew tentative sketches of what they found, and fabricated what they did not. As their forays increased, so did their knowledge, and the lines they made of mountain and shore, rivers, roads, and settlements were connected until it was fair to say the whole territory had been charted. But maps are not objective things, and so we argue the truths they claim to represent. Consider, by way of illustration, how habit makes some places "close." Perhaps the cartographer has a lover in Ghana whom he sees frequently, family he visits in Digby, meetings he flies to in London, England, but hardly ever goes to Mississauga, though it's technically next door, and never, ever visits Canmore or Yellowknife. The map that is real for him is at odds with the version of the country that official maps represent.

Stories behave this way too. In the beginning, we name a thing. As soon as we name a second, then we have made a list, and a narrative is implied in the gaps between the names just as distance is between objects. Then we add to the list of things that we have named, and create stories that guide us through the world as maps do. Eventually, we believe that we've charted our world in its entirety. And, as these stories proliferate, we argue the truths they purport to tell.

As the world does to a child, the stories of any society unfold in three Ages. During the second, the Age of Mapping, novelists and storytellers chart the history, geography, and imagination of a country. Then, the mapping done, the country enters the third, its Age of Argument. But in the beginning is the Age of Invention, in which stories grapple with the very idea of a place and wish it into existence.

2

Stories and What They Do

In 1991, a BBC radio producer at the time, I travelled with the Jamaican-British writer Ferdinand Dennis to West Africa. In Ghana, we interviewed the novelist B. Kojo Laing – the author of *Search Sweet Country* and *Woman of the Aeroplanes*. His second novel had fabulist tones appropriate to the region that had spawned *anansi*, the spider Trickster figure, who is to West Africa as Raven is to the Northwest Coast. In Laing's manic story, the inhabitants of the imaginary town of Tukwan have been banished for "refusing to listen to all the songs of all the ancestors." They fend off an invading Asante force with a maze that has been built at the town's ramparts, in which a stupidity machine crushes tongues and prevents people from speaking.

The power of story is not to be underestimated.

During the brief optimistic period that followed the granting of statehood to several British and French colonies in the late 1950s and early 1960s, the novel flourished in Africa. The first, most celebrated generation of African novelists was one that included Chinua Achebe, Ngũgĩ Wa Thiong'o, Wole Soyinka, and Sembène Ousmane – writers with a future to debate. The continent was theirs to invent, map, and argue. Corruption was not yet endemic, and *coups d'états*, civil wars, and the collapse into kleptocracy had not yet become a continental habit.

The steam train was an occasional motif in the fiction of that first generation. It was a rude black iron thing that snaked its way into the dense interior of the African landscape and consciousness as ominously and inexplicably as the tall masts of the first English ships did during the same centuries of colonization in the treeless Canadian North. To disparate ends of the earth, the European imperialists carried their armaments and industry and new ways of telling stories too. The steam trains and tall ships were symbols of European technological achievement but also of settlers importing religious as well as secular ways of understanding the world into places that had previously been the domain of animist spirits, oral stories, Trickster tales, and creation myths. Eventually, Africans used the novel to fight back. Chinua Achebe did so explicitly when, in 1959, he published perhaps the continent's most celebrated novel, *Things Fall Apart*, as a response to the racism and trivialization of African life he sensed in Joseph Conrad's *Heart of Darkness*. Literature offered the possibility of argument in what was sometimes referred to as the period of the Nigerian Renaissance. But by the time Kojo Laing was writing, the pan-African dream was a blighted project and Africa's mythic past was a morass. The colonial powers were at fault, to be sure, but neither did indigenous cultures elude blame. Perhaps this was why, after Dennis sought Laing's opinion of Amos Tutuola, the great Nigerian oral storyteller, the Ghanaian thumped his fist on the table and said, "I hate this romance about oral stories! When a flood wipes out a village, we invent some *anansi* story to explain it. If we had known how to write novels – *if we had known how to tell lies* – then we would have defeated the colonial invader!"

Laing was not suggesting that creation myths have no value, and he did not mean that lies are not told in *anansi* tales, as all Trickster stories depend on ruses or on mischief that usually backfires. Rather, I believe he was saying that when, on ramparts such as he imagined in *Woman of the Aeroplanes*, the European colonist and native met, the two societies' ways of telling stories were also in negotiation, and that the novel was a wilier, more calculating form of narrative than the oral story was. The maze, in fact, belonged to the colonists.

✧ ✧ ✧

WHAT IS IT that stories do? We accept that stories reflect the way we see the world back to ourselves, but what if they do more than that? What if stories are not innocent but sometimes aggressive rivals locked in an evolutionary struggle?

In the current age, we have come to terms with the power of story over the more random, often discredited items we call "facts." Indeed, we are now so comfortable with the notion of *narrative*, once a fusty old word, that the idea of story is in danger of becoming a fad. Advertising and PR companies sell increasingly elaborate stories as ways for public and private institutions to brand themselves, and governments – mostly, though not always totalitarian ones – have been using stories to sell themselves since time immemorial. When Canadian prime minister Stephen Harper decided to control, in 2006, access to the funerals of soldiers killed in the war in Afghanistan, he was paying tribute to the power of a novel-like story to undo the bellicose message his government was promoting. In Montreal, Toronto, and Vancouver, "murmur" projects call out *hear you are* and tell stories associated with certain buildings and street corners to pedestrians who notice the street-posted signs and phone in to the initiative's digital archive. And in Toronto, in 2004, posters mounted at bus stops asked, "How do we tell our story, Toronto?", beseeching passersby to visit www.whoarewetoronto.ca.

The claims this book makes for the power of story are made without apology, for narrative is not just influential but *essential* to life. When, on the field of war, one side kills the soldiers of another, what they are doing is destroying the physical bodies that are the agents of competing stories. Western economies are eminently successful because they have recognized the power of story and that people will spend billions on stories conveyed in films, television, music videos, and books, and then tell their own with weblogs, digital cameras, and Internet-posted films and slideshows. We are all storytellers now, well accustomed to ideas that used to be the province of professors. We have learned, for instance, that the vocabulary we use is a cultural vehicle and frequently offensive. So few talk about "the nigger in the woodpile" any more, or say, "Don't Jew me" when they mean "don't rip me off." And we have come to recognize that the *content* of stories reflects the values of the age, usually those of the establishment, so that numerous Canadian novelists of the last few decades have made it their business to challenge popular accounts of who we are with stories that recognize overlooked or subjugated communities and their disregarded histories. But, hold on, what if the supremacy of one society's worldview depends not just on the vocabulary or the information of the stories that it tells, but on the actual *form* of narrative used? What if the *way* we tell a story is the thing that is in contention?

In Canada, the young country, all sorts of story forms vie for our attention. Creation myths and cautionary tales compete with novels and epic stories, and somewhere in this imbroglio the idea of a nation is taking shape. (I use "epic" to describe poetry or prose that sings the virtues of a particular hero or society – more than compositions, such as the Haida cycles poet Robert Bringhurst translated that are "epic" in length.) Ours is a pragmatic, scientific age, in which what is respected tends to be that which can be measured, though novelists do not work this way – which is why we listen to them. Their art demands an opening up to the subtle communications our world emits. The stories that ensue give form to the messages that places speak and provide clues and even information about where we're headed. The novelist acts as conduit and occasionally as seer, a storyteller standing on the cusp of human experience – much as, in the First Nations cultures, the shaman did. The writer occupies a middle space between the world as it is and as it ends up being represented by the work. It is in this space that stories are born, exist, and even do battle.

$$\diamond \quad \diamond \quad \diamond$$

THE SAME STORY, told in different ways, achieves a variety of ends. Let's think back on a nursery rhyme most of us know to make the point.

If you tell the story of Humpty Dumpty as a creation myth, you will have an explanation for the mess on the pavement. Tell it as an *anansi* tale and the story offers the tonic of a laugh and a warning to those who climb beyond their station. Give it an epic rendering and noble Humpty is elevated to heroic status. His fall was "great," and so who is surprised that mere men could not put Humpty together again? (He guarded the kingdom as Beowulf did. Fear the worse times to come.) Tell the story as a romance and the reader will yearn for the good old days when all the King's men *could* put Humpty together again. The *novel* of Humpty, however, is the form that leads to the greatest moral outrage and to *action*. Not on God's or society's behalf but for the Humpty Dumpty in all of us. For even as we are dumbfounded by Humpty's stupidity, or aghast at the failure of the King's men to have anticipated an accident bound to happen (was it ineptitude, or corruption?), *Dumpty* the novel is the narrative that elicits most sympathy. It does so because even as an expression of unrelenting despair, the act of writing a novel implies a belief that someone, somewhere, in some other time or place will identify with its hero or anti-hero and be moved by its depiction of the human condition. If only by recognizing the faults of this world, it implies that an alternate, *better*, outcome might reasonably have been contemplated for Humpty, for the King's men – and, by extension, for all *humankind*.

Told as a novel, the Humpty Dumpty story does not settle for the palliative explanation of the creation myth (this is the way things are, get on with your day) or the dubious succour of the *anansi* tale's vengeful witty medicine. (Beware the selfish act, though be encouraged too. There is a chance that fate will be subverted.) Neither is the belligerence of the epic – chauvinist, if not outright racist in its support of a narrower idea of community – nor the wan nostalgia of the romance its limited purpose. No, what *Dumpty* the novel demands is more than peace for a while, and more than peace for a select group or the restoration of a bygone order. The writing of a novel is a hopeful gesture, an almost spiritual one that does not defer to immutable natural laws that are seen to be greater than us. No matter the pessimism of its author, the novel relies on a fundamental belief in the possibility of human progress. It knows that the job of society is one of improvement.

The fact that a novel is written, often long, usually in prose form, and explores the interior life – these classifying aspects matter, but none of them is a trait of story form that is unique to the novel. What sets the novel apart is the "imaginative leap" that its author makes in order to create and then inhabit a character, and that its readers make in turn. This simple dynamic is what gives the novel its identity. *Dumpty* the novel asks that we identify with Humpty's terrible situation, as tomorrow it could be ours. And in this assumption that readers make – that we are all, at some base level, alike – lies the magnanimity, but also the aggressive and even colonizing impulse of the novel. For the novel is a hegemonic thing, righteous on behalf of a certain conception of humankind's place in the world. It is the literary vehicle of the values of the Enlightenment – which is why we tend to describe the novel as a humanist enterprise. It adheres to the idea that we are all human beings born "free and equal in dignity and human rights," as wrote Canadian John Humphrey in the 1948 Universal Declaration of Human Rights. And it is convinced that the rational sciences and *progress*, that trouble-some word, are necessary to the pursuit of these ideas. The novel's inalienable ties to these liberal democratic principles explain why *all* novels are inherently political, and reading them is a political act. It does not matter if we are speaking of Albert Camus's *The Plague*, the diary of a New York shopaholic, the last testament of a separatist in Quebec, or three generations of a Carol Shields prairie family, the fundamental, driving principle behind the novel is the assumption, in the poet John Donne's words, that "no man is an island." Think of the vocabulary we use to describe a good novel. We praise its compassionate or its *humanizing* aspects. We speak of its *timeless* qualities. If it is "regional," or set in some distant historical period, we say that it transcends these limitations and speak of its "common humanity" and its "universal values." This is the same language that is used to diffuse the basic human rights defended by Western liberal democracies and their troubled invention, the UN. And there has been resistance, note.

On the tail of the novel's imaginative leap – one that is made even when the novel's protagonist is a murderer, a miser, a sexual deviant, or horse – a common, humanitarian purpose is achieved. Even the distress that some novels deliberately engender prompts the sense that something ought to be done. The novel makes it our business – makes it humanity's business – to strive towards the best of all possible worlds. And the world it has in mind is a fair, tolerant, secular, and progressive one.

The novel is a proselytizing instrument.

✧ ✧ ✧

OF COURSE, the novel is not story's final form, or even its most widespread. Every day, each of us consumes a panoply of different kinds of stories. We may teach a child a nursery rhyme, share a tale of mischief, and advise loved ones and friends with admonitory stories. We might read the Bible – the Book of Genesis is as much a creation myth as any aboriginal story is – or in Canada, the queru-lous nation, participate in the quest for a nationally binding story that has been a habit of the times. A person might read Erich Maria Remarque's *All Quiet on the Western Front* in the morning – a wonderful novel that displays the "common humanity" German soldiers of the Great War shared with Wilfred Owen, John McRae, or you and me. Then, in the afternoon we might watch the movie of J.R.R. Tolkein's *The Lord of the Rings* with popcorn on our laps and look on indifferently, or even with amusement, as tens of thousands of Orcs are slaughtered. When we do so, we are enjoying the story as an epic, as a cartoon. For what citizens in the narrative age of the novel know is that characterizing evil in this simple fashion contravenes the novel's politics – of our common humanity, and of evil being not absolute but a matter of degree. The novelist asks, "What does it mean to say that this person is my enemy?" or "What does it mean to decide that this person is guilty?" He or she asks, "How was it possible for a human being such as I am to do this terrible thing?" They begin their work by putting themselves in their protagonists' shoes and making that imaginative leap, no matter their creations' extremities of character. The novel says, "For me to know you and portray you in good faith, I must remember that you and I are fundamentally alike. Perhaps only circumstance is what has made us different."

But the truth is that we do not like to think of the novel as political, especially within a country as stable as Canada. We prefer to think that the novel reaches across cultural divides in a *peaceful* way – as authors often do, visiting wartorn countries in times of strife. And yet it is this very tendency that renders the novel obnoxious to many societies. The novel believes in essential common causes, and in conflicts it has the incontrovertible habit – though not always the *advantage* – of putting an empathetic, rights-based view of our common humanity at the centre of its story. This quality puts the novel close to being an "end of narrative," if you like – a form of story that is as versatile and enduring as the belief in human rights that it reflects. But its reliance on the *individual* character of these human rights is the thing that puts it into conflict with other narrative cultures around the globe. Most notably, the novel is locked in contest with the epic, and elsewhere with the more eternal verities of creation myths and admonitory stories that we associate with "oral" societies.

Critically, these two other, more venerable narrative cultures differ in their conceptions of community interest and in the ways that good and evil are envisaged. Where the novel upholds the culture and primacy of the individual, epics *and* creation myths defend the rights of the group. In the creation myths and admonitory stories told by oral societies at the level of subsistence – ones such as the first English explorers encountered in the nineteenth-century Canadian Arctic – the rights of the community and not the individual take precedence because the living is precarious and the allegiance of *everyone* is necessary to the task of survival. "Evil" is thought to be an external quality, one more presence in a contingent universe, that can inhabit or leave a person at any time. In the epic, such as exists in Islamist states, but also in developed nations in a condition of war, the living is still precarious though the enemy is not nature but some other, rival society. In both those narrative cultures, the community is being protected *at the expense* of the individual. A more defensive idea of community prevails, and good and evil are construed as absolute qualities for survival's sake. A handy, if not vital belief in wartime, a person can be identified as monstrously bad, or saintly and irreprehensibly good in a way that would not be acceptable in decent novels or the frame of mind of those who read them.

In the battle of stories that is going on, the novel's assumption of our common humanity may also constitute a failing. The novel can address the existence of evil, but unlike the epic, the novel is unable to assume absolute evil in its principal characters because to do so goes against the grain of its humanizing principles. This is why, for instance, it has only recently been possible to consider writing the novel of Hitler or of Saddam Hussein. For as long as Hitler and Saddam are regarded as monsters, it is impossible for the novelist to begin. Hitler can be introduced as a peripheral character – or, as a small number of novelists and filmmakers have done, the issue of his evil nature can be tried by taking him on as a youth, as a failed artist, or in his last days. The novel can even take on the *phenomenon* of evil as it was incurred by the Führer and his Nazi regime, but to tell *his* story is impossible within the novel's essentially sympathetic light. Hitler the monster for the time being lies outside the boundary of our common humanity.

This was also the case with Saddam – though it is no longer. Saddam lay beyond the scope of the novel for as long as we considered him to be a monster. The point at which we ceased to do so is instructive. For as long as he was a caricature, for as long as he was the autocratic perpetrator of lethal gas attacks upon the Kurds and warden to the tortured, for as long as he was the enemy, the novel of Saddam could not be contemplated. But when Saddam was captured in December 2003, and television images of USAmerican doctors picking at his teeth and lice-infested scalp were beamed around the world – from this moment of his humiliation (quite against most liberal democratic principles), the novel of Saddam became possible. The novelist was allowed a way in. Not an easy entry by any means, but a crack in the door. On that fateful day Saddam was reduced from being a monster to something human – and as such he was nudged within the novel's reach.

✧   ✧   ✧

IF WE HAD *known how to write novels – if we had known how to tell lies – then we would have defeated the colonial invader.*

The possibility that the novel is a proselytizing instrument irks those who would prefer to see reading as a pleasant pastime. A conflict of narrative cultures is unpalatable because it implies a hierarchy of stories, and in Canada we tend to believe that a diversity of storytelling is as important to human society as biodiversity is in nature, and that all narrative societies have equivalent virtues. The first idea in that last sentence I have always considered to be true. The second idea I do not, which is to say that I believe that different story forms have different merits. The attempt to understand what is the worldview, in particular, of indigenous Canadian stories led me to want to learn about their difference. And so, on a clear blue day in June 2004, I found myself in the company of Robert Bringhurst, the classicist, poet, and translator of the Haida canon, following him on a trail through woods that he knew better than I. We were on the east side of Quadra Island, in British Columbia, not far from Heriot Bay. I had crossed the country to be here, on the first of this book's many pilgrimages.

I had interviewed Bringhurst for CBC Radio a couple of months before, "down the line" from Toronto, but our conversation had not proceeded well. Of course it had not. Bringhurst lives in the forest, he *breathes* the forest. It is where his spirits soar. To have asked him to share his views in the bare closet of a disembodied studio was only ever going to have been a mistake, and as hard as Bringhurst had tried to respond to my inquiries about the ways in which stories conflict, it was clear to me after only a few minutes that I needed to come find him in this, his proper milieu, for there to have been a meaningful exchange.

Bringhurst, I believe, is one of the country's literary treasures, quite possibly a genius. He is a brilliant linguist whose passions are ignited with temper. His 1992 manual, *The Elements of Typographic Style*, is considered exemplary in its field. As a classicist, he is self-taught, though Taoist and Japanese ideas figure as much as Greek ones do in his early poetry. Bringhurst's great endeavour, the one for which he stands to be remembered, is *A Story as Sharp as a Knife*, his verse translation of a substantial portion of the extant canon of the Haida, the Northwest Coastal First Nation. After his trilogy was published, Bringhurst was excoriated by angry Haida. The rallying call was that Bringhurst, a white man, had *stolen* the native stories, even if what he had really done was breathe new life into the work of Ghandl, Skaay, Kilxhawgins, and several other Haida myth-tellers, whose work had been transcribed by the ethnologist John Reed Swanton in 1900–1. (Unfortunately, as Swanton was not allowed to listen to the women, only the men's work has survived.) The Haida opus enraged a number of aboriginals and academics defending their territory against trespass, but Bringhurst was undeterred. His trilogy thrust the forgotten Haida masters into a previously segregated canon of European greats. The comparisons he made were with Aristotle, Tolstoy, and Flaubert. With bold authority, Bringhurst wrote, "In my attempts to set the best Haida poets in a global context, I have found Bach and Titian and Velásquez more immediately helpful than Racine."

Bringhurst rehabilitated old furrows that the Haida oral stories had travelled before the Europeans criss-crossed the continent and controlled it with stories of their own. His translations animated the forest with spirits and stories that had been largely forgotten and – spoken by a minority of Haida and otherwise withering in the dusty files of various library archives – had only the possibility of a diminishing circulation. His translations gave Haida poets identity, proving that Haida oral poetry was not some loose, folksy set of stories passed on by anyone in the community, but a rigorous canon of brilliantly honed poems of frequently considerable length performed by a small number of highly skilled orators. This did not mean that Bringhurst believed that this small number of Haida storytellers *invented* the stories they told. He believed, as I did, that stories exist outside of us, and those who write or speak them, Haida or not, are in the *service* of stories and articulate them as a means of a society finding its way. Maps, I suggested to Bringhurst, were the first stories.

"No," he said, correcting me. "Stories are the first maps."

I watched as Bringhurst deftly picked his way along the trail ahead of me. Periodically he would push the lower tree branches to the side with his arms, but his gaze was fixed on the wondrous details of the lichens and berries underfoot. In the world as Bringhurst sees it, the big exists alongside the small, and the forest that appeared merely dense to me was, in his view, positively *teeming* with life forms that were busily interdependent. An ecosystem in which humans, too, played their part.

"Entertain for a moment the idea that stories are the genuine inhabitants of the world and that human beings are not really in charge," Bringhurst posited. "Stories are at the top of the food chain, and our function is to nourish and tend to them in the same way that a dog's function is to guard our flocks or wake us if there's a burglar. If you think of stories as the dominant life form, then we must be necessary to that species, the *genus narrativus*, in the same way that these alders are necessary to the red-cedar and the hemlocks that succeed them. If we stop telling stories, the forest will shrivel up and die. We won't find our way, not only because we don't have the maps that stories are for us, but because without the wisdom of these stories there won't be a world for us to live in any more. Stories are the real king of the mountain here. They're like those eagles up there. They're on top of the heap."

Bringhurst spoke in a low, steady baritone, his voice rumbling and full of untried strength.

"It's a marvellous forest," said Bringhurst, "rich and young, recuperating nicely from that fire. But it has its troubles too. Too many hemlocks dying before their time, too few red-cedar seedlings thriving, sunburnt clumps of dead salal translating into bunchgrass. That's a change in climate. In a hundred years – a blink of the forest's eye – this forest that is now Douglas-fir, western hemlock, and incipient red-cedar will be Douglas-fir and shore pine. The animals will change. And the stories – those species you can't see, but who tell you how to live here – will change too."

"But if stories exist as you describe them," I said, "is it not possible that they might also be contending and even grappling with each other as other animal species do?"

"Stories feed on each other just as we feed on each other," said Bringhurst. "They swallow each other like bacteria. They fight with each other, yes they do."

"And during the period of First Contact, do you think there was a battle of stories taking place?"

"There were several battles going on. The novel is usually a book written by a human about other humans. It is organized around the life of a single species that is in charge of all the other species. People who carried that notion of story came into this New World, where the dominant literary form was the myth. But what is distinctive about the myth is that human beings are *not* the principal characters. On the Northwest Coast, there were very highly developed storytelling cultures, in which it was taken for granted that humans had walk-on parts in the great stories to be told. And of course all these novel-writing folk were members of a society that put humans first. They had Bibles in their back pockets, and the Bible is a story that confuses itself with history, and then history with singularity, to the point of supposing that there is one true story to which all other stories are subservient. It says that you must join this story because otherwise you are damned – and that makes no sense whatsoever in terms of the literary cultures that were already here in the New World. Even Time itself is not a story with a beginning, a middle, and an end. Time is just not like that in the forest."

The trees were pillars reaching towards the sky. The sunlight penetrated through them towards the ground in discernible rays that illuminated barks covered in green and brown mosses. We stopped at a log that had fallen across the path we had been taking through a shallow gully. The log was a bench. It looked to me like the kind of naturally occurring object that the English sculptor Andy Goldsworthy might have exhibited, and that the art world, in its urban astonishment, would have assumed was his creation. And then it struck me that the relationship of the storyteller to the stories that they tell is very similar. The story, like the branch that becomes a log, exists as it is and is unnoticed, until it is put into relief by the artist who sees its full shape.

"Colonial culture was certainly materialistic in its bias," said Bringhurst. "The Europeans didn't come here to commune with the forest and then go back to Bristol or Le Havre and share their spiritual experiences with their close, good friends. The Europeans came here wanting the resources of this world – the furs, the timber, the minerals, and then the land as an agricultural base. They came here to *get stuff*, and if you have a bias for putting things into material form that you can then clutch – if you favour making things like big ships, or laying things like railroads and highways, and building big structures like churches, houses, barns – then you'll want material embodiments for your stories as well. You'll want *the book*.

"And," I offered, "I suppose that the act of writing something down anticipates the need for the thing that is written to be defended at some later point. Perhaps this anticipation – this *readiness* – served the settler culture better than oral stories did the native ones that were here."

"In the myth-telling culture, the material embodiment of the stories is the landscape – the forest, the oceans; it's the clouds, the mountains, the rivers and the lakes. They're the script, the literature of reality, so that learning to write is not on the agenda. Learning *to read* is the important thing. *The text is already here.* When we pass through the forest and make up stories about it, we're deciphering the stories that are already in it. Articulating those stories is as much a part of the process of living as deer passing through here and munching leaves."

"But I wonder if, alongside the power of writing and the divine purpose that the Bible provided, the moral vindication that the novel offered the individual helped further the colonial cause?"

"In its origins, the novel is an urban art form," said Bringhurst. "Novels come out of cities, where humans are crammed closely together. As a consequence, there's more heroizing in the European novel because that's what happens when you narrow your focus to the single species to which you belong. Humans are not unique in their concern for other members of their own species. But in nature, just getting breakfast requires dealing with a world much larger than one's own, and once you have farms and cities, this may appear to no longer be the case. It still *is*, of course, but the novel may not illuminate that aspect of real life.

"The myths, on the other hand, are constantly shining their light on such things. There are protagonists in the Myth World too, but they're not *heroes*, they're just elements that get used up. *Underneath* them is where the real story is going on. The ecology of stories is always poking up through the surface of myths the way these rocks are poking up through this patch of rain forest here. They're constantly showing up the weaknesses of humans, and the dependency of humans on the larger tissue of things. There's always a lesson there – about what diminutive creatures we humans are and how we get by in the world not by confronting it squarely in the manner of a conquistador or a great industrialist but by collaborating with the ecology that we depend on. There's landscape in plenty of European novels, and there may be some twentieth-century novels, some Canadian novels too, in which landscape is the principal character, but that's a recent development."

An eagle swooped low and Bringhurst looked up.

"There's a sense in which the novel contains the cure for its own disease," said Bringhurst, "but the culture in which it operates tends to be an avidly materialistic and possessive one. The novel is trying to find its way in a world that has it outflanked."

◇ ◇ ◇

WE CAN SEE a battle of stories being played out in the current strife in the Middle East, where the narrative culture of the novel is embroiled with that of the epic. It is a conflict that has been re-iterated at home and is being used to challenge the Canadian multi-culturalist exercise. The reigning forms of story of the Islamist cultures with which the novel-reading countries of the West must contend are votive religious texts advocating tales of unadulter-ated heroism (martyrs) and outright villainy (the United States of America as the "Mother of All Evil," the "Great Satan," etc.). Osama bin Laden, should he be killed, will become al-Qaeda's Roland. The "insurgents" and rebel fighters in Iraq, the suicide bombers of Amman, Kabul, London, and Tel Aviv, and the alleged Islamist truck bombers of Toronto, are Beowulf's warriors. But the West is often duped in its negotiations because we understand these conflicts practically, and less as contests in the *narrative* world. Still, we come close to understanding the conflict of narrative cultures as such when we ask, "How do we negotiate with someone who wants to kill us?" For we have learned that in the narrative culture of the epic, it is possible to think of men and women as nonentities unworthy of sympathetic consideration. Jews, Americans, etc.

In the narrative frame of mind inculcated by such a story, it is possible to think of the world in terms of absolutes and an attack on "innocents" is permissible because there is no necessity to have to treat the other as human. The individual does not register. The hijackers of 9/11 made no imaginative leap. Doubt did not come into it. It is not necessary, even *counterproductive*, to ask – as the novelist does – "Why?" And so a slaughter on jet planes, in schools, on tube trains, and on buses is unimpeded, even encouraged, by the moral code of a form of storytelling in which the survival of the host society is what's at stake.

Perhaps it was inevitable that some Western nations should meet their Middle Eastern nemeses with epic thinking of their own – the "Axis of Evil," the existence of weapons of mass destruction, and so on. The battle of narrative cultures begins to be played out at home as individuals within one society waver between narrative views. Concerning terrorism, the debate about "root causes" is essentially one between the novel's liberal democratic view (if we are fundamentally alike, then what is it that made you the way *you* are?) and an epic view that allows for the existence of an enemy, pure and simple. The rhetoric and storytelling that President George Bush Jr.'s government has used, as well as the Christian fundamentalists and neo-conservative extremists and now the Canadian government that supports him, is an instance of epic thinking being rallied against epic thinking.

Muslim extremists list the novel alongside dance, nudity, and movies as a corrupting Western influence – not without reason, as the novel has always had repercussive social effects that our allegiance to the form prompts us to forget. In the seventeenth and eighteenth (and even the nineteenth and twentieth) centuries, the English gentry was anxious about the liberalizing influence of the novel in the hands of the working classes and women – just two of a series of communities rocked by its political messages. They were right to be worried. Eventually, as the novel's moral universe expands, it becomes a tool in the hands of those it once failed to recognize – women, Joseph Conrad's Africans, North American aboriginals, and soon, quite possibly, "terrorists." Look far enough into the future and it is even conceivable that animals should one day be full participants in the empathetic embrace of the novel – not just the cautionary tales and generally anodyne fables of juvenile fiction. Adult stories that do not pay sufficient consideration to animal species might become problematic in the way that previously admired works conveying prejudices towards Jews, blacks, homosexuals, or Muslims are – beasts shooed in from the cold as the novel tries to "find its way in a world that has it outflanked." There would be a certain irony in this. Were it to happen, then the narrative culture of the novel would have come full circle, arriving at a philosophical and political position in which it had much in common with the Myth World it once subsumed.

This was emphatically not the case in Igloolik in 1822. At the time, the Inuit belonged to an oral society that told mostly admonitory stories and creation myths. The Europeans were proponents of the written narrative culture of the novel. The stories of the Inuit upheld the interests of the community and the survival of the group at all costs. The European canon vindicated individual purpose and property as a private right.

The English were welcomed by the Inuit. No shots were fired, and nobody was killed or enslaved. Ostensibly, the two societies passed the winter in peace, but their storytelling was in conflict. In that moment of First Contact, the narrative culture of the novel began its negotiation with the narrative culture of the Myth World, and the oral stories of the Inuit served the aboriginal culture less well.

3

Igloolik, 1822

Hervé Paniaq, an Inuit Elder, said:

The Sun and the Moon were siblings and had no parents. Siqiniq, the sister, was in the habit of staying alone in her igloo. But during the time when the camp would hold festivities in the qaggiq, the large ceremonial snow house, someone would rush in to her igloo, blow the flames out, and then pin her down and molest her. She had been unable to determine who this person was, but her cooking pot always hung over the flames of her qulliq, the soapstone lamp, and when once more someone rushed in and blew the flames out she reached up and managed to touch the cooking pot and wipe her sooty hands on the face of her attacker. After she had been molested, her aggressor left the igloo and she followed behind to see where he went. She saw him go into the qaggiq where the festivities were being held. As she approached the snow house she could hear people laughing. Someone was saying:

"*Taqqiq inutuarsiurasumun asit naatavinaaluk!*" – "Taqqiq is marked with soot because he has been looking for someone who is alone again!"

Siqiniq entered the qaggiq and discovered that it was her own brother's face that was covered with soot. She was embarrassed and angry so she took her breast and cut it off and offered it to her brother saying that as he liked the rest of her so much why did he not eat her breast as well? Then they both ran out of the qaggiq with lit torches. With her breast in her hand she followed her brother and as she chased him around the qaggiq, he tripped and fell so that his torch went out, leaving only smouldering embers while the flames from his sister's torch continued to burn brightly. She chased him up to the sky where she became Siqiniq, the Sun, and her brother became Taqqiq, the Moon.

◇　◇　◇

A WINTER'S DAY as Igloolik knows it. Outside, it is -40°, a temperature at which it does not matter if the scale reads Celsius or Fahrenheit. This small Inuit community in Nunavut sits at the northeastern end of the Melville Peninsula and south across the water from Baffin Island, just inside 69° latitude. It is the middle of January in the calendar of the *Qallunaat* – the white man – and the beginning of *Siqinnaarut* in the Inuit one. The cold is crisp, the sky dark and clear. The Arctic, in winter, can feel like a landscape set inside some godly polished sapphire. The snow-encrusted land stretches out flatly in all directions, bluish and untrammelled. It looks like an upside-down shallow plate. The horizon, its distant surrounding rim, is an incandescent silvery-white. Above it looms the moon, dauntingly large. The sun has not been seen since the end of November.

Siqinnaarut is not a month that can be called "lunar" in the way that southerners understand the word, because *Siqiniq*, the returning sun that gives the month its name, and her brother, *Taqqiq*, the moon, linger and then disappear for protracted periods at the top of the world. At the peak of winter, the moon pursues a steady circumpolar course and can loom over Igloolik for a full four days. If the snow is not blowing, then the clarity of the atmosphere is magical. Noon is indicated only by a glow of increasing intensity in the area of the southern horizon, where, if the taboos are respected, Siqiniq will make her appearance again. For the four thousand years of habitation before this region of the Canadian Arctic was absorbed into the dominion of the southern clock, other measures of time were necessary. The months of the Inuit calendar were tied to events occurring in the natural world: the nesting of birds; the birth of seal pups; the shedding of velvet from caribou antlers, the time when caribou skin was at its best for clothing; and so on. The constant moon of *Tauvikjuaq*, the "great darkness" that immediately precedes Siqinnaarut, is the hibernal equivalent of the Midnight Sun. Deep winter is Siqiniq's turn to sink below the horizon – chased, in the local mythology, by her incestuous brother, the moon.

How odd it is that scenes of not much happening can be so compelling. The flame of an open fire. A steady ocean. Or this, the northern vista I was looking at. Stillness anticipates change and, in Igloolik, the event that provided it was Siqinnaarut – the time when, in their winter camps, Inuit anxiously watched for the sun to make its long-awaited return. During Tauvikjuaq, the Inuit were more likely to be assembled in camps together, and Elders would amuse themselves and the children with stories and a variety of games, hours passed in the handing down from one generation to the next of a community's traditional knowledge. Inuit shamans explained the world and its mysteries – why there was such a thing as death, the strange comings and goings of the sun and the moon. The sun's fiery inching above the distant edge of the world was cause for rejoicing, but never a moment that Inuit took for granted. When, finally, Siqiniq did appear – and stay – the moment was marked in the traditional Inuit calendar by a Qaggiq, a communal celebratory event held in an oversized igloo.

The sun's reappearance meant that the year was starting afresh. Children would rush from igloo to igloo and extinguish the flames of the *qullit*, the traditional soapstone lamps that used the oil of seal and the narwhal for fuel, before lighting them again with fresh wicks. But Siqiniq, pursued for so long, had the habit of rising and then suddenly disappearing again. In today's Qallunaat world, stories of "refraction" have solved the puzzle of the sun's coming and going, but in the Iglulingmiut cosmology it was explained by legends and taboos. In this critical time at the end of Tauvikjuaq, the string games that children played were put away, and sometimes even cut up, as parents worried that the rising sun would get caught in their mesh. When Siqiniq finally did rise again, Iglulingmiut learned to smile with just half their mouths. The upturned left side welcomed the sun, while the other unsmiling half acknowledged the hardships of Tauvikjuaq and the certainty that the severe temperatures were not yet done.

During the discombobulating events of the last century – prompted by the intrusion into the North of explorers, whalers, missionaries, and the RCMP – the festival of renewal lapsed. But since 1990, the *Iglulingmiut*, the Inuit of Igloolik, have celebrated the return of the sun again.

✧   ✧   ✧

IT WAS JOHN MACDONALD who first told me about Igloolik's Festival of the Return of the Sun. The author of *The Arctic Sky: Inuit Astronomy, Star Lore, and Legend*, MacDonald had recently retired when I met him in 2003 aboard the *Akademik Ioffe*, a Soviet research vessel leased by a Canadian company for summer travel through the High Arctic. As if to remind us of the circumstances that nineteenth-century explorers faced, an August blizzard bore down upon the ship in Lancaster Sound and obliterated our view of nearby Baffin Island completely. Large pieces of multi-year pack ice gestated in the frigid salt water and drummed against the *Ioffe*'s steel hull with such a resounding echo that it was not hard to imagine what damage an iceberg might have done to wooden ships. For centuries, the appearance of new ice melding these floating frozen chunks was an indication to the explorers passing through that it was time to seek the safe harbour of some reasonably protected inlet and prepare to overwinter there, as the English explorers William Parry and George Francis Lyon did, in the region of Igloolik, during the winter of 1821–22.

MacDonald arrived in Canada in 1959. He was nineteen, and his first job in the Arctic was as a Hudson's Bay clerk in Gubridge Bay, in what were then the Northwest Territories. He served in many HBC posts throughout the Northwest Territories in northern Quebec and was working with the Department of Northern and Indian Affairs in Ottawa when, in 1985, he moved to Igloolik. There he managed the Nunavut Research Centre for eighteen years, before his retirement. Aboard the snowbound *Akademik Ioffe*, MacDonald explained that stories were an integral part of a festival that he described as "a time of celebration and looking forward to the future." He told me of the excitement of travelling the land and collecting stories with the Inuit Elders and of logging the lore of a sky that had not yet been obscured by artificial light. In 1986, after his friend George Qulaut visited the National Archives in Ottawa, the pair discussed the possibility of creating an oral archive, and arranged a meeting with several Elders distressed by the loss of Inuit culture, values, skills – and above all, language. With Leah Otak and Louis Tapardjuk on board, the group set about the recording and conservation of Inuit *Qaujimajatuqangit*, or "traditional knowledge." The interviews with the Elders, including all of those quoted in this chapter, were conducted in Inuktitut. Igloolik's Oral History Project (IOHP) was underway.

The following winter I flew from Ottawa to Iqaluit, and then on to Hall Beach and past the defunct Distant Early Warning Line. This is Canada's extraordinary hinterland, if you are a southerner; its centre, if you are Iglulingmiut. (Igloolik lies close to the actual centre of Canada. Baker Lake, 832 kilometres southwest of the

Melville Peninsula, is the country's middle point.) MacDonald met my First Air flight, and driving in from the terminal, I could see the distant bright klieg lights of the power plant that kept Igloolik lit and its furnaces running. I could not help thinking that if there were a fire, the town would be uninhabitable in a matter of hours – a Northern Pompeii of ice and frozen pipes. In the opposite direction hung the enormous full moon – but which direction was it? North? South? East? West? I had arrived in the early hours of the afternoon, but day was indistinguishable from night, my watch a souvenir of the Canada I had left behind.

MacDonald took me to his house, where we sat in the kitchen and he helped me orient myself. He pointed to a few stars through the window, and gave me a primer on these old indicators of the day and seasons. "Soon," he said, smiling almost mischievously, "you won't be looking at clocks at all." And then he told me that in his first season in the Arctic, he had listened to a Canadian government officer lecture Inuit on the efficiency and rewards of hard work. "Time is money," the officer told the Inuit, a phrase his interpreter translated as "a watch costs a lot." The Beatles' "Here Comes the Sun" was playing on the kitchen radio, and the announcer followed the song with festival announcements in Inuktitut. There was to be an igloo-building competition on the Saturday morning, and festivities that night in the high-school gym – today's qaggiq. The evening would include performances of drum dancing, throat singing, *ayaya* songs, and informal dog-mushing and animal-call contests. The highlight of the night would be the ceremonial re-enactment of the extinguishing and relighting of the qullit, the soapstone lamps that provided igloos with meagre light and warmth. The festival would be the apogee of a "long cold lonely winter," the likes of which Lennon and McCartney had surely not imagined when they composed their springtime ballad. The Beatles song ended. How wonderfully apt its cheerful notes sounded in their strange Northern context.

"Time for a walk," said MacDonald.

Socks, more socks, thermal long johns, and winter pants. A turtleneck sweater, a heavy parka, a scarf, two pairs of mitts, a toque, and a fur-lined hat.

"The moon is at its highest round about now," said MacDonald, closing the frosted side door of the house. "It used to be that when there was a full moon like this, people took advantage of it to hunt and children would go sliding or play tag."

Out in the winter air, our layers of clothing, stiffened by the cold, made comfortable cocoons of each of us. We walked along the empty road, its surface of pressed snow, and past the white mushroom-shaped building of the Nunavut Research Centre. This was where the archives of the IOHP were held until they were transferred, in 2004, to the community's new Nunavut government offices. A few snowmobiles and a pickup truck were gathered at the stem of the building. A floor of laboratories and meeting rooms constituted its broad cap, suspended like a spaceship some thirty feet above the ground. An Inuit researcher was visible through one of its podlike windows – dissecting a polar bear, MacDonald said, collecting tissue samples for later analysis and study. The building blended surprisingly well with the landscape. Its whiteness and its circularity invoked the features of an igloo, while its spaceship aspects intoned the *sotto voce* declaration that all the Qallunaat had really done was land here.

Scrouch, scrouch, scrouch, skeerouch. We continued walking, past the limits of the town. A truck was noisily draining septic from the distant townhouses. After only a few minutes we had left Igloolik and its approximately fourteen hundred residents behind.

MacDonald showed me how an Inuit hunter used to measure the stages of the sun's return. He extended his arm out towards the moon much as a painter might have calculated a scene's proportions with his thumb.

"Pretend that the moon is the sun for a moment," MacDonald said. "If you could fit the shaft of a harpoon, held horizontally and at arm's length, in the space between the sun and the horizon, then the sun was said to be *harpooned*. The second stage occurred when you could fit your thumb in between, but it wasn't until *Pualutanitatuq* – such time as the sun, at its zenith, was a full mitt's thickness above the horizon – that Inuit were convinced that the sun had actually returned and preparations for the Qaggiq were made. It didn't mean the end of cold temperatures, mind you, but with more light the Inuit could think about longer journeys and often, in traditional times, this was when they would plan trading expeditions – to distant Hudson's Bay Company trading posts, for example."

Taqqiq, the moon, appeared close enough to imagine that a leap up to the Myth World was possible. The legend of the sun and the moon is part of a substantial Inuit story cycle that recalls the Greek myth of Persephone and her time in Hades, the daughter's abduction leading to a comparable stealing of the light. But there was a further, practical aspect to the story of the two siblings that had to do with preserving the social contract. *Beware*, was the lesson – incest in a society of small numbers is a grave temptation, but in the end it will lead to darkness. When, in the Inuit North, there was an eclipse of the sun, it was believed that Taqqiq had pinned his sister Siqiniq down again.

"Today, there are fewer stories attached to the land and more to the community," said MacDonald. "There are more distractions to life – a different tempo and different obligations. It's not just that Igloolik is growing, but that the very nature of the community is changing. There's television, there's radio, there's hockey, and there's *light*. Many of the Igloolik Elders we spoke to had not even thought about the stars for years, but we would drive them to various points outside Igloolik where there were no street lights and look up at them, and then the stories associated with them would flow."

Bruce Chatwin, the late British travel writer, novelist, and romantic, believed that stories were born so that humans might stay awake and vigilant by the night fires they tended in places where sabre-toothed tigers threatened to attack. In his notebooks, he wrote, "Man is a talking animal, a storytelling animal," that "talked his way out of extinction, and that is what talk is for."

In the Arctic, the tiger was the cold and winter's long dark night. During the worst of it, Inuit families listened to stories that explained the contingency of the world and their place in it, and in this way they made a home of *Nunarjuaq* (the Inuit Earth) and kept the Northern Tiger at bay.

"Do you see that faintish white line?" asked John. "It's getting stronger now. Those are the aurora borealis, the northern lights."

"They're playful things," I said. "Sometimes it even feels as if I can move them around by thinking."

My voice sounded muffled through the scarf wrapped around my mouth. The moisture of my breathing had formed into ice crystals and turned my eyebrows and lashes white. When I blinked, the crystals pulled away from one another with a slight tearing sound.

"The Inuit call them *aqsarniit*. They believe that by whistling you can draw them closer."

My eyeballs felt cold, an odd sensation.

The aurora borealis did one of its scurrying dances across the Northern sky, and the impression was of looking up at the folds of an enormous theatre curtain from a supine position on a stage floor.

"Inuit believed the spirits up there are playing a game of soccer with a walrus skull," said MacDonald. "Sometimes you'll see the northern lights with red in them. This is blood. The Elders say that the spirits of people who end up there are those who have died through loss of blood – those who are murdered, perhaps, killed in a hunting accident, or women who die in childbirth. The

Iglulingmiut told their children not to tempt the lights because they would kill you – decapitate you, in fact."

"So, according to the Inuit cosmology, where you go to in the afterlife has nothing to do with the *moral* circumstances of your death but everything to do with *how* you die."

"That's right," said MacDonald. "If you drowned, for instance, then you went to the bottom of the sea. The Danish explorer Knud Rasmussen recounted the story of a boy who missed his mother so much that he deliberately died in the same way that she did – by drowning – in order to be with her again."

The northern lights had become faint. No reds or greens or yellows in this display.

To *anijaaq* is to read the night sky in this way, as generations of Inuit have done. In the early morning, Inuit would leave their igloos and prepare for the hunt in a world submerged in darkness and then at best half light. The far limits of the winter landscape were beginning to delicately shimmer, and as I lay down on the snow, the sensation was of being on top of the world and a supporting bed of light. Wherever you are is technically the centre of the world, but in the Arctic your position really feels that way. The stars are numerous but do not crowd the dark sky as densely as constellations between the Tropics. This, and the elemental simplicity of the Arctic – during the winter months especially – provides an illusion of infinite space in a landscape that is open, yet curiously intimate. The way the light rises up from beneath the rim of the encircling horizon, it seemed quite rational to believe that Nunarjuaq was flat, a feeling that was augmented by the absence of any trees or dramatic hills, for the Arctic landscape is one that does no vertical reaching. In winter, the white landscape appears to spread out in concentric circles towards the horizon, and the limited number of distinct objects in view has the effect of presenting the world as a place that can be known in its entirety – and what can be *known* is by nature less threatening.

Inuit called the ecosystem of earth, sea, and air *Sila*, and the several atmospheres that made up the sky *Qilak*. The one world appeared to reflect the other, and between the two we were comfortably enclosed.

"According to Inuit Qaujimajatuqangit," said John, "the sky is analogous to the earth. It has a similar, snow-clad environment, and is populated by the same animals. There was regular traffic between the two realms and some legends tell of the sun and the moon living in adjoining igloos. Shamans would visit the moon on their spirit flights, and the moon-man would often come to earth to enforce taboos. Above all, the sky and its contents were comfortably knowable and intimate. This is quite unlike the modern enterprise of astronomy, that I find renders space increasingly unfathomable and remote."

The steam of furnaces was rising from the town, entrenched against the cold. Light shone through the small windows of the houses that, with their frosted surfaces, looked like chocolates left too long in the fridge. The blue of televisions glowed here and there. The stories that Inuit once relied on were close by but a whole narrative world away.

We started the walk back.

"Do you hear the sound our boots are making?" asked John. "They're completely frozen. It's quite extraordinary that Inuit survived here for millennia simply on the strength of the materials that they found here, don't you think?"

✧ ✧ ✧

THE MOMENT OF European or First Contact – the initial meetings of settlers and aboriginals that occurred in the Americas over the course of several centuries – took place in the region of present-day Igloolik, in the Siqinnaarut of 1822. The British explorers William Edward Parry and George Francis Lyon left Deptford on April 29 of the preceding year and entered the Arctic through the Davis and then Hudson Straits. In September, the men encountered a couple of Inuit with prior knowledge of the Qallunaat, as they had done repeatedly farther south. In October, the Admiralty pair moored

His Majesty's ships, the *Hecla* and the *Fury*, at Winter Island, 130 kilometres east of Repulse Bay and 300 kilometres south of Igloolik. Three months afterwards, Parry's men encountered the Iglulingmiut and their families. Scarce Iglulingmiut stories pertain to the moment of First Contact with the Qallunaat, and none describe the very day, but Parry recorded it in his journal, later published as his *Narrative of a Second Voyage to the Polar Sea*:

On the morning of the 1st of February it was reported to me that a number of strange people were seen to the westward, coming towards the ships over ice. On directing a glass towards them we found them to be Esquimaux, and also discovered some appearance of huts on shore, at the distance of two miles from the ships, in the same direction. I immediately set out, accompanied by Captain Lyon, an officer from each ship, and two of the men, to meet the natives, who, to the number of five-and-twenty, were drawn up in a line abreast, and still advanced slowly towards us. As we approached nearer they stood still, remaining, as before, in a compact line, from which they did not move for some time after we reached them. Nothing could exceed their quiet and orderly behaviour on this occasion, which presented a very striking contrast with the noisy demeanour of the natives of Hudson's Strait. They appeared at a distance to have arms in their hands; but what we had taken for bows or spears proved to be a few blades of whalebone, which they had brought either as a peace-offering or for barter, and which we immediately purchased for a few small nails and beads. However quietly the Esquimaux had awaited our approach, and still continued to conduct themselves, there was as little apprehension or distrust visible in their countenances or manner as it was possible for one strange set of persons to evince on meeting another. As soon as we had bought all they had to sell, and made them a number of valuable presents, we expressed by signs our wish to accompany them to their huts, with which they willingly complied, and we immediately set out together. On our way the Esquimaux were much amused by our dogs, especially by a large one of the Newfoundland breed, that had been taught to fetch and carry; a qualification which seemed to excite unbounded astonishment; and the children could scarce contain themselves for joy when Captain Lyon gave them a stick to throw for the dog to bring back to them.

Stories anticipating the Qallunaat would have preceded their arrival. Inuit travelled considerable distances to hunt and trade, and social exchanges with other Inuit, and even hostile Indians farther to the south, would have provided some intimation of the Qallunaat coming. Inuit believed the Qallunaat to be the offspring of a dog and a woman – this was not a derogatory idea, as the Inuit depended on dogs for their survival – so that the cavorting pets that Parry assumed were such a novelty to the Inuit children would not have been, though the stick Lyon brought from the ship must have appeared strange. The Elder Noah Pingaatuk told the IOHP of a song that anticipated the arrival of the white man's ship. The composer imagines that he can hear "the sound of wood" made by the vessel as it battles its way through the ice floes. And as the Arctic landscape, one that the British anthropologist Hugh Brody brilliantly described as occurring "at knee height," had no tall things in it, the sight of the high wooden masts of the *Hecla* and the *Fury* could have meant only one thing.

✧　✧　✧

"You could probably not miss it," said the man at the window, "two ships wintering with their masts up in the air."

The day after my walk with John MacDonald, I visited Zacharias Kunuk, the director of *Atanarjuat* (*The Fast Runner*) and, in 2006, *The Journals of Knud Rasmussen*. We met at the Igloolik office of his movie production company, Isuma. The office was bare: a few taped boxes, a couple of courier packages. The building could as easily have been a warehouse. I sat at a table as Kunuk stood, looking out over the frozen water that separated Igloolik from Baffin. The strait had taken longer than usual to freeze over. "Global warming," muttered Kunuk. He said something about the diminished herd and took a long draw of his cigarette.

Radio, in the North, is a bulletin board, and that morning I had listened to the day's announcements on the local station. Inutai, Kunuk's father, was preparing to leave for Baffin to hunt caribou and was looking for a companion. The elder Kunuk's departure was only the second of the year, the season was that late, and his son – "Zack," as he is known – gave the impression of wanting to be the one joining him. How many times had he accompanied his father on the journey the Elder was about to make? I asked him if he had much to do in the office and he said yes, but he would rather be hunting. When I congratulated him on the success of *Atanarjuat*, he scoffed. He didn't want to be famous, he said, he wanted to make movies.

Zack was born on the land and raised in the sod house that was the family's winter camp at Kapuiviit. He lived there with his family until, at the age of nine, he was sent to the federal day school in Igloolik. Zack hated the school, though he did learn to love John Wayne films. After he dropped out of grade eight, he carved sculptures to earn the money to see more of them. Eventually he made his own movies for the CBC, for aboriginal television – and then the big success, *Atanarjuat*. It was the first feature-length aboriginal film ever made, and won Zack the Camera d'Or Award at Cannes in 2001. Zack describes it as "a classic love and revenge story set in the mythic, apolitical past." Its story, scripted by the late Paul Apak Angilirq, also of Igloolik, was based on the Inuit legend of the same name, of which several versions exist in the IOHP, though such a story would also have been told to Zack directly. Zack's mother, he told Clifford Krauss of the *New York Times*, had been raised by a woman who gave birth only to stillborn children because of the curse of a jealous shaman.

"The Inuit who were trading at Repulse Bay," said Zack, "probably they were coming back to Igloolik, and probably they saw Parry's ships for miles. So they approached, and a mile off they made camp – and all this time, Parry's men are keeping their telescopes on them."

Zack spoke his words as if in a trance – as if the story was happening right there, again, in front of him. In a way it was. At the time he was still developing the idea for his second film about the travels of the Danish explorer and ethnographer Knud Rasmussen through this part of the Arctic in the 1920s. Zack's accent was thick and guttural. When he spoke, he did so in short, breathy outbursts, as if to the rhythm of a slow-moving metronome. The effect of his repeating certain words and phrases – "probably," "ready," "just imagine" – was mesmerizing. They were the refrains of a story that would have been related orally in the era before print, television, and film, though few indigenous mentions of it are made. Zack's sources were the journals of Lyon and Parry, the imagining was his own.

"Probably they had cannons pointing in their direction," Zack said, still looking out the window and not at me. "They are naval ships, so probably they're on red alert, probably there is someone always watching. Just imagine how Parry had his men ready, cannons pointing, muskets all loaded and ready to fire, probably. And in the morning, the Inuit, they start to come. Probably they could see the Inuit and there's only five of them coming. They look like they're carrying bows and arrows, so the English, they're ready to fire – ready, ready, ready to fire. But as the Inuit get closer they

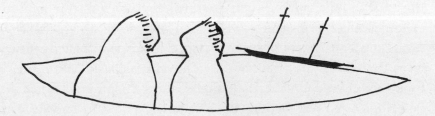

can see that it is just whalebones they are carrying. They're just trying to trade something. Just imagine how much firepower the other side had – and the Inuit, they had *nothing*.

"And that was the first encounter."

The European vessels spent that first winter of Parry's second voyage at Winter Island. The following winter, after culling Inuit knowledge for their maps, they moored hard by Igloolik. The Qallunaat came laden with guns, telescopes, and Bibles – and stories too. Parry was keen on English instruction, and his men performed a number of plays on board. His journals suggest a familiarity with Miguel de Cervantes's novel *Don Quixote*, one of the earliest volumes to be found in the Hudson's Bay Company collection from the Fur Trade Libraries. These comprised mostly histories, geographies, scientific tracts, as well as narratives of Arctic expeditions and the journals of explorers from other parts of Empire, but, over the next fifty years, also works by Charles Dickens, George Eliot, William Makepeace Thackeray, and Sir Walter Scott, as well as Blackwood's magazine, *Punch*, and the *Literary Gazette*. The libraries of the *Terror* and the *Erebus*, John Franklin's ships, sailing in just the next decade contained 2,900 volumes and among them was Oliver Goldsmith's *The Vicar of Wakefield*. Of course, to belong to the narrative culture of the novel does not require that every sailor or foot soldier arriving in Mexico or the Mackenzie Delta was up on his Thomas Hardy, or even that he knew how to read – just as you or I do not need to be computer software savvy to be the ambassadors of a society that is today on the brink of an entirely different mode of digitally enabled storytelling. We are the practitioners of a new age, just as the first imperial sailors and foot soldiers were, because a certain habit of telling stories is in the air. So, into the Arctic, Parry's ships brought narratives about faith, justice, and property. Half a century later, the stories they took out of it, and other parts of the British Empire coloured pink on the famous maps, inspired what can be described as Empire Fiction – novels of high adventure and heroism from the likes of Robert Louis Stevenson, Rudyard Kipling, and H. Rider Haggard.

The same moment of First Contact prompted the Iglulingmiut to tell stories of a wholly different quality. Inuit told mostly cautionary tales, the purpose of which was to warn against improper behaviour and the abuse of scarce resources, and creation myths that conjured and explained things into the world – including the arrival of the Qallunaat. There was no going back.

Zack emitted a long sigh that finished with the tense clicking of his tongue against his teeth, and I asked him what had been the effect of growing up in these two narrative worlds.

"I ask that question myself," said Zack, the breath still leaving him. "I notice that when I am walking on my own out on the land, I am thinking in English. *My head is going in English.*"

Zack fell into silence, and it seemed appropriate to let the moment endure. He took a seat at the table with me and started playing with his pack of cigarettes as if it were a deck of cards, shuffling it from one hand to the other. He had yet to look my way. As a settler from the South, I considered how we do not expect the Inuit, a congenial race, to hate intruders, but that perhaps he did.

"Do you see the land as a place of stories?" I asked.

"The stories tell you where there are more caribou," said Zack. "The stories will tell you where you are. Wherever you go, there are Inukshuk and tent rings. You are seeing men who used to camp here and that knowledge goes through your mind."

"Are you speaking to yourself something in Inuktitut now?" I asked.

"No," said Zack. Another toss of the pack.

"Do you believe that during the period of First Contact, when the Qallunaat were exploring and making their deals and treaties, that the Inuit understood what was going on?"

Zack let out a breath like a hiss. "I don't think so. Land is for everybody in our culture. Everybody can walk on it, everybody can hunt on it. Nobody can *own* it."

He laughed the last line out in his tense, arrested fashion. With bitterness, it seemed.

✧ ✧ ✧

BACK AT THE HOUSE, John MacDonald had prepared some gravlax from a couple of plump fillets of Arctic char and cilantro I had brought in from "outside." MacDonald had fished the char from the waters in front of Igloolik as a part of his resident's annual allocation. We followed it with a roasted shoulder of caribou. The flesh of each was delicate, mild, and lean. Arctic caribou are raised on a diet of what had been, prior to the proliferation of PCBs, the planet's cleanest water, mosses, and lichens. The char have somehow managed to avoid the slaughterhouse destiny of becoming a staple of sushi menu cards and are still fairly abundant. We ate chocolate and drank the wine I'd brought into the controlled community illegally, as all shipments of liquor should be pre-stamped and authorized. We were, nearly a couple of centuries later, as the first explorers were, living in a bubble of imported mores and goods. It is hard, if not impossible, in the Arctic, not to do so.

That night, as I warned John would happen, I experienced what I have come to call "the Revenge of the Recently Dead," the violent nightmares I have each time I eat the fresh meat of wild animals. Knud Rasmussen, MacDonald said, described the Inuit as living "on a diet of souls," which is why the indigenous made a point of honouring the animals that they hunted and depended on, as the Inuit believed they would not pass the community's way again were they offended. The dreams I had that night, animals talking back, made the concept of a diet of souls palpable and real.

"When I was a child I went to church," Zack had said, "and all our minister did was try to scare us. *Repent, repent, repent*, the minister said. They try to scare you, they try to scare you, try to scare you, so that we would go to heaven. But the only time Inuit repent is when they do something wrong and can't touch *animals*, and then everybody must repent to the shaman."

For allowing themselves to be hunted, the animals were explicitly thanked, as I make a point of doing now each time I fillet a salmon or thrust a lobster into boiling water. What I am expressing is my gratitude, but also my fear of the spirits that will come to me that night should I forget to do so.

What bad dreams have taught me, the Inuit knew by force of circumstance. Parry witnessed this scene on April 5, 1822.

> Toolooak having been concerned in killing one of the seals just brought in, it fell to his mother's lot to dissect it, the *neitiek* being the only animal which the women are permitted to cut up. We had therefore an opportunity of seeing this filthy operation once more performed, and entirely by the old lady herself, who was soon up to her elbows in blood and oil. Before a knife is put into the animal, as it lies on its back, they pour a little water into its mouth, and touch each flipper and the middle of the belly with a little lamp-black and oil taken from the under part of the lamp. What benefit was expected from this ceremony we could not learn, but it was done with a degree of superstitious care that bespoke its indispensable importance.

And then Parry himself explained the benefit just a few sentences later. The Iglulingmiut, he observed, "depended on catching seals alone for their subsistence, there being no walruses in this neighbourhood."

"The life of the community was based entirely on the co-operation and the suppression of individual needs," said MacDonald. "Life was very precarious, so that any action that upset the delicate relationship between people and the land was considered to put the whole community in danger. The demands of an elevated ego were simply not on."

"Did the stories support this moral code?" I asked.

"Yes. There were two categories. There is a set of stories that have to do with the sun and moon –"

"Creation myths."

"Yes, but they are more than that," said MacDonald. "The sun-moon cycle is one of the most widespread and complex of all Inuit legends. At its fullest, it is a statement of quite epic proportions that addresses universal concerns about creation, the social and cosmic order, as well as issues of nourishment, retribution, and renewal. Another category of stories warns people of the dangers of the land, and how to behave socially."

"Can you give me an example?"

"Earlier you referred to the Inuit 'diet of souls,'" said MacDonald. "Traditionally, Inuit relied entirely on animals. If they couldn't find animals, they would cease to exist, so you'll find many stories that warn against their abuse. The shamans who told these stories were negotiating between the human and animal spheres, and urging the observance of taboos and rooting out those who breached them. Confession usually restored harmony, but there were consequences for those who kept their transgressions secret or who wantonly abused animals. The interesting thing is that although there is retribution in these stories, it occurs not in the afterlife but in the present one. There's a story about a man who, very cruelly, took all the feathers off the body of a small bird. He left the feathers on the wings and allowed it to fly away – to a certain death. Later, the man dies of a skin disease. Or there is the story of a man who boasted that he'd killed a polar bear without making any wound. He'd strangled it. The man develops respiratory problems and dies. If the taboos were broken, the aim of punishment was always the restoration of co-operation and good relations within the community. These were the primary goals of the shamans' justice, whereas our legal system depends on punishment as retribution and for its own sake."

Inuit Qaujimajatuqangit (or "I.Q." as it is referred to in short form today) was the body of local science and commandments. It was the job of the Iglulingmiut creation myths and admonitory stories not just to explain the contingencies and cruelties of the world, but to do so in a manner that would not exasperate Iglulingmiut by suggesting that their situation might have been otherwise. The

Iglulingmiut story explaining the origin and presence of Death in the world shows the allaying purpose such creation myths have, and how this purpose is essential to the narrative culture of a society struggling merely to maintain its numbers. The outrage, despair, or want of alternatives that would have been provoked by a comparable situation of scarcity in the narrative culture of the novel was never the intention of stories such as the Elder George Kappianaq, who died in 2004, told:

> In Igloolik the first people were known as Aakulukjuusi and Uumarniittuq. There were no other people and they had no name and they were made so that they were able to bear children.
>
> The land never experienced winter. Food was readily available because the winter never set in. They knew nothing of the cold, and had no knowledge of anything that felt cold. Aakulukjuusi and Uumarniittuq were bearing children who never died and so the population became great here in Igloolik.
>
> This is the story that I have heard. None of it is of my own making.
>
> There were now many people who were born to Aakulukjuusi and Uumarniittuq and the population kept growing until the entire island became overpopulated. It was so full that it was getting harder and harder to find space because there were so many people.
>
> As Igloolik was now very crowded, one who found himself without a place cried out, though I suppose when some of the people were awake he would have been able to go to sleep on the ground. They started to push one other to the limits of the beach because it was so overcrowded. I am telling the story the way I have heard it.
>
> The one who found himself without a place said:
> *TUQU! TUQU! TUQU! UNATA! UNATA! UNATA!*
> Death! Death! Death! Fight! Fight! Fight!

He was saying that the people should kill each other. He wanted death because there was no more space. The land was too overcrowded. I imagine some of them might have gone to the mainland.

Right after he said the words, someone overheard him, and this man said:

TUQUJUUNATIGILU, UNATAJUUNATIGLLU.

No death must occur, no fighting must occur.

He was saying that the people should not kill each other nor should they fight, but because he spoke the words after the first who wanted death, he lost out. The one who wanted death and for people to fight each other was the one that won.

It was from that time that the people started to die, and winter came about. It was from that time on that the island of Igloolik was no longer overcrowded.

Who protested starvation, disease, or the arrival of rifle-toting Qallunaat into the Inuit universe, when the untoward was explained this way?

The majority of Elders who contributed to the Oral History Project were born in the first half of the twentieth century, so that Inuit Qaujimajatuqangit and then the changes that white traders brought were the stuff of living memory. Rachel Ayarsuk, approaching one hundred when I visited Igloolik, was twenty when Knud Rasmussen passed through. Her age makes her the exception, as life expectancy is short in the Arctic – more so now that depression figures. Several of the crosses at the cemetery MacDonald and I visited on the northeast edge of town marked the graves of teenage suicides, and in the brief time that I was in Igloolik, trucks, snowmobiles, and the nurse's van gathered outside one house indicated yet another Elder's death and more irretrievable knowledge lost. A plume of smoke rose from the chimney of the late woman's house and wended its way through the telephone wires and television antennae strung from its siding. The wires were connecting the building to the rest of the world, but disconnecting it from the community. String games of the kind Qallunaat call "cat's cradle" had been taboo during Siqinnaarut, as the Iglulingmiut worried that the returning sun might get tangled in their mesh and fail to rise, only now the "cat's cradle" is the lattice of satellite dishes and telephone and computer lines, and it is Inuit Qaujimajatuqangit that is caught in their web.

✧ ✧ ✧

IN LONDON, a few months previously, I had visited Hugh Brody, the British author, ethnologist, and traveller who spent several years working with indigenous peoples in the Canadian Arctic and sub-Arctic regions. Like Robert Bringhurst, he was someone whom I had known intermittently, but whose work not just I profoundly admired. Both native and settler Canadians held Brody's book about the homeland of Canada's Northern peoples in the twentieth century, *Living Arctic: Hunters of the Canadian North*, in high regard. In a subsequent book, *The Other Side of Eden: Hunters, Farmers and the Shaping of the World*, Brody revisited the territory and proposed that the conflict being played out in the Canadian Arctic mirrored those in other parts of the world where indigenous tribes still exist – and that the struggle could be characterized as one between hunter-gatherers and "aggressive, restless agriculture." In Brody's schema, the urban civilizations of the South are the nomadic societies. They are Isaac's progeny, belligerent and acquisitive, constantly roaming the world in their quest to find new lands and resources to satisfy their cities' insatiable appetites. The oil of whales. The oil of Iraq that Saddam Hussein needed to empower his cities from the Marsh Arabs, another hunter-gatherer tribe, before the Americans, in turn, wanted it from him.

A boyishly handsome Englishman, even in his late forties, the silver-haired Brody is cut in the Bruce Chatwin mould of the restless and inquisitive travellers of the Victorian era – men who held story and adventure in high regard.

"There is something about the individualism in the European tradition," said Brody, "that is starkly at odds with the individualism in the hunter-gatherer tradition – and that has been expressed in the literature. The individualism of the European tradition is that of the person who seeks to achieve the greatest possible result for him- or herself against the rest of the world, exploiting what opportunities he or she can, and defying the demons that are going to do you in. It's about maximizing advantage and achieving a winning hand, getting the girl, getting the land, becoming king, marrying the princess, overcoming your internal crises to move to more sophisticated forms of literature – from the fairy tale to the existentialist novel, the individual is seeking to triumph against an adversity in order to win something. In the hunter-gatherer world, the equivalent stories would have to be about individuals fulfilling the purpose of the society. Achieving and winning the girl could be part of the story, but it would be a winning of the girl by finding a place as an equal among equals. No one can be a hero or heroine in that society if they are securing more of the land, or more of the resources, for themselves and in defiance of others."

"But it was a culture less equipped to negotiate."

"It's not equipped to negotiate *well*, partly because it's not organized at a state level," said Brody. "There isn't a chief. There isn't a negotiating party. A critical part of Enlightenment consciousness is the idea that there is a truth out there that we can discover either empirically, by deduction, or by some mixture of the two. Built into this intellectual tradition is a dialectic of intellectual progress that is completely absent from the indigenous, hunter-gatherer world. It is not a world where discourse is seeking to defend itself against rival versions of the truth."

"Do you think that the act of *explaining* as a creation myth does, of making almost anything *okay*, impedes a kind of questioning that might have led to a more rebellious outcome?"

"Yes," said Brody, "I think it might, although the idea that there was a failure of rebellion is questionable. There are all kinds of ways in which a people can rebel. You can rebel by just moving away from the enemy, and avoiding them, which is a normal response of hunter-gatherers. They have a territory they can move into. You can rebel by not co-operating, or by pretending to co-operate. But you can't rebel with rebellion of the ordinary European kind because you don't have the numbers, and you don't have the armaments. You're outgunned from the start."

✧ ✧ ✧

AT ISUMA, Zack stepped up to the window again. Waiting.

"Why do you think stories were invented?" I asked.

"Stories were told to us so that we can choose which character we want to be. Do you want to go for the good or for the bad? Which life do you want to lead?"

"So stories are there to instruct you?"

"Totally."

"And when you tell your stories," I said, "are you instructing in matters of right or wrong?"

"No."

"You're putting your culture on show?"

"Exactly. The Inuit had many stories before the white man came."

"Do you read much?" I asked.

"Oh yes."

"Only Inuktitut stories, or do you read Qallunaat stories as well?"

Zack took another of his long, sibilant breaths.

"I hardly ever read novels," he said. "I tried that. I tried to read Westerns, with cowboys and Indians and everything, but I gave up on that. I do a lot of reading of explorers' journals –"

"Like Lyon and Parry. Rasmussen."

"Yeah."

"Why?"

"I try to think like them. I try to think what misunderstandings they were having."

Here was a man on the cusp.

"What didn't you like about the Qallunaat novels that you were reading?"

"I liked them, but I couldn't keep reading them because I learned that every novel is the same. They're like a movie. Whether you're in

Paris, or Greece, or Japan, or the Wil' Wil' West, *you're stuck with the character.*"

✧ ✧ ✧

I FOUND ZACK'S objection to the novel fascinating. The novel is not an indigenous Inuit storytelling form, as oral storytellers neither compose for the page, nor expect much of a settler audience disinclined to such stories. Nevertheless, claims are made from time to time for the "first" Inuit novel. Robert Bringhurst had pointed me to Markoosie, a Quebec-born pilot who worked out of Resolute for many years, who was the author of *Umajusiuti unatuinamu*, published in three instalments in an Ottawa-funded Inuktitut magazine in 1969–70. The novel was translated as *Harpoon of the Hunter*, in 1970. Mitiarjuk Nappaaluk, born in 1932, wrote *Sanaaq* in the syllabic alphabet, with the help first of a Jesuit oblate and then the aid of the proactive French ethnologist Bernard Saladin d'Anglure. Neither of these books are novels in any sophisticated sense. They are generally expository stories explaining a heritage through picaresque scenes.

"Were a novel of an incontrovertibly sophisticated kind to have been written, it may well have been done by Paul Apak Angilirq, the screenwriter of *Atanarjuat* who died in 1998. And it would have needed translation for its proper dissemination – often a disadvantage," argued Robert Bringhurst in a letter following our discussions in the forest.

"Almost all North American native literature," wrote Bringhurst, "is oral. There's a body of low-grade journalism and other practical writing in Inuktitut, Cherokee, Cree, and it has as a rule the same literary wattage you'd find in any rural community newspaper. The indigenous written works that have grabbed me were all written by people who still lived their mental lives in an aboriginal culture – one to which writing and much else had been introduced, but which had not yet been entirely eviscerated by alcohol, technology, and schools. All of them were also written in places where there was a counterforce to the church – a surviving sense of pagan identity, a sense of real belonging to the land, or some kind of new hybrid (the Peyote Cult, for instance). Could have happened in lots of places, but usually it didn't. Where it did, there was almost always an outside trigger.

"Apak's screenplay doesn't quite fit that model. The outside trigger was pulled from inside. The initial money came from the Canada Council, which meant that he and Kunuk had to ask for it. Like any anthropologically funded native writer, he was forced to supply an English translation, but the medium, film, is one that had been passively adopted by and accepted into his community – so there *was* a native audience in view. Would Apak, if he had lived, have turned his filmscript into a novel? If he had, the book would have been published, with a federal subsidy, in Inuktitut, and some Inuit would have read it – but its only hope of revenue or celebrity would rest, once again, on translations.

"Settler culture is spectator culture. Making a living from literature, like making a living from hockey or football, depends upon that fact."

Novels of the kind that I was looking for, and that Zack had in mind, ones that demanded a reader's allegiance to one, perhaps a few, characters and that we see the world through their or the author's eyes, were not yet a staple, although some schools were encouraging this kind of fiction. To be "stuck with the character" was, in Zack's view, a limitation, for the Myth World is generally one in which there is no single hero. That opportunity awaits with the epic, in stories such as those contained in the cycle of Kiviuq, an Odysseus-like figure, whose many lives and peregrinations are related in a body of stories that reflect the wide-ranging contact of Inuit peoples across the circumpolar North. But in Zack's understanding of the world, there were, in a sense, no celebrities, only presences. His point of view made me recall my first visit to Resolute in 1991, when satellite broadcasting was in its early stages and a quirk of atmospherics meant that residents were as likely to receive the local news from Detroit as they were *The National* on the CBC. In the house in which I was staying, Minnie's place, the family

watched TV reports of Michigan race riots, these alien stories with
their cast of black characters and inner-city settings of blistering
summer heat, as nonchalantly as they might have done news of a
Calgary snowstorm, *Hockey Night in Canada*, or the news from nearby
Iqaluit. It was an odd sight, but it fitted in with an understanding of
the world as a panoply of presences such as animism provides.
There was violence, calamity, and occasionally good things in the
news. Did it really matter if that news was from Detroit? The television was a box of spirits. In the Inuit universe, being one thing does
not mean that you cannot also be another. Men and women, animals
and spirits, move in and out of states of being – good, bad, young,
old, alive, dead. The Myth World acts itself out on and in people,
and the world is a morality play with the health of the community,
not the individual, at its heart. Elements of a recurring story, not
the fortunes of a single character, are the things that matter.

In the Iglulingmiut world of 1822, survival was paramount and
dependence on the interests of the individual and not the community was anathema. All the land was necessary to the people, and
all the people were necessary to the task of living off it. As George
Kappianaq's story of Death illustrated, there was no spare land to
accumulate, or share, and a paucity of contact with other peoples
meant there was not yet the necessity of epics or jingoistic histories to rally the Iglulingmiut to the defence of borders and society
as it was, with a view to the acquisition of more. The purpose of
Inuit stories and I.Q. was to conserve a society in which all lives – of
humans, of animals, of plants – were considered valuable. There
was no surplus in *any* of these categories.

Morality, in this way, follows on from our relationship to the
land. A century of negotiation with settlers has taught First Nations
how to tell stories for advantage, and many of the aboriginal creation myths, as they are now told, are not so much about explaining the world as emphasizing the singularity of native cultures.
Often, they do this at the expense of what could be considered Inuit
orthodoxy. In the "traditional" versions of the legend of Atanarjuat
in the IOHP, if not in Zack's film, the story ends in mayhem and

bloody revenge. A happy ending, the modern narrative requirement to put humankind on top and offer *some* possibility of redemption, is not just a Hollywood habit. Quietly, the Inuit canon is being altered into a means of rebelling that had hitherto not been available. Creation myths are being used as epics – as stories that legitimize differences in the battle between nations and their narrative cultures. Except that they are vaulting over the epic's belligerent stage and employing the values of the *novel*, insisting on the individual human rights our narrative age trumpets and that First Nations have only recently been accorded.

Listening to Zack I was aware that the narrative culture of the myth was far from dead, but that the only way for the myths to be told as myths again would be for native and settler societies to accept the instructional merits of their value system and see the world again as the first societies did. Survival would need to become the priority once more, although this time of a larger collective, a global one that was sufficiently enlightened to recognize itself as a community sharing a common territory in which all the land is necessary to the people, and all the people are necessary to the task of living off it. This new community would have to believe that a sharing of resources and respect for them is what is required. Fishers – but multilaterally, whether from Canada, Denmark, West Africa, or Spain – would need to conceive of themselves as one, and become the stewards of resources they are now rapidly depleting. They would need to learn and tell stories that warned against overfishing, and to understand these stories' point – to thank the halibut for coming their way, and not fish the last one out, just as Inuit do not shoot the last caribou in a herd so that there *is* another that will pass their way again.

It's unlikely.

✧   ✧   ✧

THE FESTIVAL OF the Return of the Sun took place, as planned, on the Saturday night a few days before modern astronomy predicted the molested sister's rise, as the Inuit calendar is now governed by electric light and requires a Saturday, a Sunday, and a working week.

Outside the perimeter of the Arctic settlement, the igloo-building contest was being held on the northwest edge of town, on the clear land above the new Nunavut government offices. The air was crisp, the snow compact and hard – good snow, this. I watched the steady progress of the only woman taking part in the competition and listened to the tearing sound of her cutting blocks of snow with a large serrated bread knife. A group of younger Iglulingmiut were building igloos beyond the dozen or so adult participants, and MacDonald pointed out how much speedier and more dexterous the woman and the other Elders were.

Inuit construct igloos by carving blocks out from the snow around where they stand, so that the dome of their traditional winter dwelling rises as the floor beneath the builder drops. The finished igloo sits slightly beneath surface level and is protected in this way from the worst ravages of the wind. The method is simple and effective well beyond the scale of the family-sized igloos that were being built this Saturday. In one of the earliest years of the revived Festival of the Return of the Sun, a truly enormous igloo was built – a qaggiq, some thirty-five feet in diameter, able to accommodate approximately eighty people.

I suggested to MacDonald and a couple of his Inuit friends that I might spend that night in one of the completed igloos, and the response was one of (full) smiles and suppressed chuckles of laughter. The igloo I had pointed to was small, perhaps seven feet in diameter. What I had not calculated was that properly it would have slept five or six – no, properly, it would have *required* five or six to sleep in it, as on my own I'd have been freezing, even in the

beautiful outfit of brown and white caribou fur that whole families were proudly wearing as they watched the igloo-building. Bundled up to several other bodies, as dogs in a litter are, then there would have been sufficient warmth, and the pastime of telling stories would have arisen naturally and the Northern Tiger would have stayed outside.

Another age.

Now snowmobiles take Inuit to where the caribou are and make winter camps less necessary. They are not yet *unnecessary*, as the Iglulingmiut need to travel farther and farther to find the caribou learning to travel in a wide arc around the humans' fixed settlements. Yet, more often than not, the hunters return by evening to their insulated homes, where the creation myths and cautionary tales that once kept order in the community have been subverted by the new Qallunaat canon and its technology. No need to visit when you can use the telephone. No need to weave into the knit of a story the things to be remembered – the valley where a catch is effortlessly made, a couple of tricks to snare your intended prey – when the new technology means your message and your bearings can be conveyed immediately.

"All the hunters take these radios with them when they go hunting," said Louis Tapardjuk, one of the IOHP's founders, "so everybody is constantly informed as to what's happening and there's no good stories coming back from the land any more." He sighed. "Memory is so different now."

A few of the contestants and their families had started the walk back to their vehicles, idling all the while so that their engines would stay warm. Some piled onto the backs of trucks, others onto snowmobiles. Leah Otak, another of the IOHP founders, gathered with her family, all of them resplendent in their furs, beautiful against the snow. Otak, I knew, had a winter cabin out on Ham Bay, on the west side of the island. It was popular with many parents who sent their children to be with her there and hear the old stories.

"When you are there, you feel as if you are alone on Earth," said Otak, after some coaxing. She picked her words carefully, one at a time and as if out of a box. So much, in the North, is about haste *not* being made, about critical energy *not* being wasted.

"Are there any legends that you have heard that explain the Qallunaat?" I asked.

She smiled carefully and showed what the French call *méfiance*, a proud woman not particularly wanting to share. "There's the story of the woman who wouldn't take a husband and married a dog and gave birth to non-Inuit," she said.

"Don't worry," I joked. "I won't take it personally."

A half smile of the conventional kind indicated that she wanted to go, and I watched as snowmobilers buzzed a noisy path around the igloos of the few remaining contestants. Others revved their engines while they chatted to friends, lifting their vehicles' hoods like piston heads anywhere. Quiet would have to wait until evening. The finished igloos looked like bubbles on the snow. Melding into the blue-white plain as if they had always been there, their domes belonged to the landscape and were organic in a way that the landed humming buildings of the Qallunaat – the A-frames and bunkhouses that can be found all over the Canadian Arctic, the churches and the huge sports centre, complete with hockey rink and curling facilities – were not. In the afternoon, I returned to the site on my own and crept inside the opening of one. The light of the moon illuminated spots in the igloo's canopy of snow and the joins between its component blocks so that the dome was an analogy of the heavens, complete with constellations and northern lights. Cold after a few minutes, I moved off the raised platform that would have been layered with furs in an earlier time, and around which Inuit would have told stories until their eyes started to droop. I shuffled out the tunnel exit on my belly and tried to imagine what set of fears, excitements, anxieties, and aspirations an Inuit hunter would have had as he did so and made aniyaq. Evening was approaching and the field of igloos appeared like the pieces of some ephemeral art installation. Within days the snow houses would crumble and be gone. Within years, the skill of building them would be esoteric.

✧   ✧   ✧

SCROUCH, SCROUCH, SKEEROUCH. This time in jolly concert. A stream of people was headed towards the school and the performances of the festival. There was laughter at the front doors and, as is the custom, the doffing of winter boots. The sea of discarded footwear included sneakers and cowboy and Harley-Davidson gear. I added my own felt-lined Arctic moon boots to the fray. In the gymnasium, several rows of chairs had been arranged on three sides of an open area at the foot of the school's elevated stage. Four women I recognized from a rehearsal earlier in the week were sitting in separate quadrants on the highly polished floor with its basketball court markings, each before a lit qulliq. Louis Tapardjuk, the night's emcee, thanked the Elders, extolled Inuit Qaujimajatuqangit, and announced the Festival of the Return of the Sun. The lights were dimmed and for a moment the only light was from the soapstone lamps. Once again, I was astonished at how we unconsciously imitate nature in the things we build. In Egypt, pyramids mimic the natural rubble outcrops in the desert around the Nile. In the Arctic, the shallow flame of the qullit, which risked being extinguished during Tauvikjuaq because of the winter's dwindling supplies, resembles the sun's low spread. The qullit offered the orange, glimmering light that would illuminate the distant horizon, and that everyone was waiting for, in miniature.

The women put out the lamps and moved to one side of the performance area, and for a couple of hours, the community was entertained with the ayaya songs, drum dances, and throat singing I'd seen at rehearsals, only this time members of the audience tried dog-mushing calls and the imitating of ptarmigans, loons, snow geese, and other Northern wildlife. Children ran in and out of the crowd, their playful screams ricocheted about the room and were ignored. There was laughter as a Qalluna tried a few animal calls of his own. Pakkak Innushuk, a man of about thirty-five and one of the cast of *Atanarjuat*, stepped into the open area and started to dance while beating a circular drum made of stretched hide. A few feet in diameter, it looked like an oversized ping-pong paddle. He turned it with a twist of the wrist while striking each side with a small mallet held in the other hand and letting out occasional whooping cries to the accompaniment of the elderly women singing ayaya songs from a bench at the foot of the stage. He quit and then the Elder Hervé Paniaq, his large broad face creased from the wind, did a drum dance that received a round of applause. A young boy stripped down to his caribou bottoms and had a go, and then two pre-teen girls performed some throat singing. The gathering had an amoebic quality. The audience and performers constantly morphed but remained loosely the same. The theatre in the round reinforced the sense that Inuit stories promote of a complete universe in which all things are contained and nothing is lost. Even the authority of the Elders appeared to be less a quality of their actual persons than an attribute of the group itself. Being an "Elder" was but another property of the circle in its entirety, the middle-aged, young ones, and the infants as necessary to the circle's balance of ages. In time, the children would become old – have their turn – and others would take the youngsters' place. In the Myth World, Bringhurst had said, time has no beginning, middle, or end. The balance of the circle would be unchanged. This is what the exported life of cities has done, I thought. It has upset this balance and rent this picture. It has allowed us to convene with our peers and forget the seat that we occupy at the round table of the ages.

Louis Tapardjuk thanked everyone for coming, the Elders especially. He held up a snowmobile part that had been found at the door and asked if the owner would reclaim it. Stories had not featured on the agenda, and nobody had played any string games, but the night had been a happy one. As the crowd began to dissipate, I caught up with Tapardjuk, a big bear of a man exuding a little melancholy.

"It's a problem," Tapardjuk said. "In our schools we teach our language but not the culture."

"And if you had a story to tell, Louis, would you tell it to your grandchild sitting on your knee, or would you write the story down – as a novel, perhaps?"

"I would write it down," Tapardjuk replied.

✧ ✧ ✧

THE NEXT MORNING, MacDonald and I took another of our walks together, this time to the top of the gentle slope above Igloolik where three large Inukshuk stand – the stone cairns often in human figures that the Inuit use as trail markers. It was impossible not to marvel at the mere fact of our being warm in the Arctic air, or of the way sound carried with piercing clarity – the loud ripping noises of snow crunching underfoot and the howling of a couple of dogsled teams staked to the warmer sea-ice offshore. We descended through the town and walked out onto the frozen water, and the insulation of our many layers made even thoughts linger close. I shut my eyes and located the position of the howling dogs easily. I opened them again and the elemental sparseness of the landscape struck me as strangely Greek. The snow-covered land extends out as the bleached Helladic hills do, and meets the sky in the far distance in a changing wash of colour, as the Peloponnesus does the sea.

We stopped to look back at the town, and MacDonald said, "The interesting thing about mythology is that it's always local. The story that Indians and white men were the progeny of Uinigumasuittuq – the Woman Who Married a Dog – occurred right here in Igloolik. The name of the place where she lived suggests it was an island, and even now people will point to various rocks and will insist to you that this is where it happened. Versions of the story are told all over the Arctic, but people here will point to a particular piece of land when they tell the story of the arrival of the British. It is local to home."

The rocks that Iglulingmiut point to belong to the isthmus of Qikiqtaarjuk. It was an island before the land in the area rebounded after the last Ice Age, connecting it by a narrow strip of shore to present-day Igloolik. In the narrative imagination of the time, the high masts of the British ships were the stems of sedge plants grown to mythic proportions.

The Elder George Kappianaq said:

The legend of Uinigumasuittuq is a story that appears to have been the beginning of the White people and the Indians. This was here in Igloolik. Uinigumasuittuq had a father, this might not be true, but then again, it might be true, who became the foundation of all shamans in years to come. The parents and the rest of the people were living here in Igloolik. That is how the legend goes, I heard it from my father's grandmother. This is Arnattiaq.

During the night, a man would enter their dwelling. This man had dog fangs on the top of his shoulders for an amulet. As it turned out it was a dog, their own dog. I suppose he was a white dog because his upper garment was clean. He would enter their dwelling in the middle of the night and when they had all fallen asleep, the man would get into bed with their daughter. This is Uinigumasuittuq.

When he discovered that the dog was wiving his daughter, the father of Uinigumasuittuq took her and the dog across to Qikiqtaarjuk. Uinigumasuittuq got pregnant, and she gave birth to a litter of twelve. One half was part human, while others resembled more of dogs, and she cast them off from the island of Qikiqtaarjuk to the strait of Ikiq in the sole of a sealskin boot. The half who were more human, she sent to the mainland to find implements for their survival, and they would become Indians. On the other sole, it might have been the right sole, she placed the rest, the ones who had more of a resemblance to dogs, and she sent them on the water to the sea. That is the way I have heard it.

I would not think that the story had any truth to it, except that she stood two stems of a sedge plant in the sole. Once she had pushed them off from the beach, it was blown out to sea by the wind. This was the time when there was open water between Qikiqtaarjuk and the rest of the island. When they had gone well away from the shore, the sole started to get bigger and bigger until it got really huge and the stems of the sedge plants became masts and guy ropes anchored the masts. She thought to herself if only she had gotten onto the small sole of footwear as well.

✧ ✧ ✧

THERE IS, in the Oral History Project, another, quite extraordinary story that the Inuit shamans told concerning Parry and his band of Qallunaat. It suggests that the Qallunaat, the offspring of the Woman Who Married a Dog, had come north to search for relics of Uinigumasuittuq. As a creation myth, the story did its job perfectly. It satisfied Iglulingmiut who might have been baffled by this strange and irrevocable moment and welcomed the Qallunaat home as family. The story answered the question "Why Qallunaat?" without encouraging any of the skepticism or sense of danger that would have been automatic to those raised in the narrative culture of the novel. Rosie Iqallijuq's story is the quintessential example of a tale that served the aboriginals less well:

> Parry had been in this area and lived among Inuit and made lots of friends. But out of jealousy shamans sent the ships away and made it impossible for them to return and that is why the ships did not come to this area for a long time. Then one time, without our knowledge, they came back and took the skull of Uinigumasuittuq because she was their mother. The skull was at Qikiqtaarjuk, which is now the northwest peninsula of Igloolik Island.
>
> Also, at the time that Arnaannuk was a baby, we had to avoid stepping on the tent stones of Uinigumasuittuq but these too had been taken away. I have heard all these stories from Ittuksaarjuat but I never seem to have heard it from anyone else. Ittuksaarjuat believed that Parry had come to this area to collect his mother's skull because that was the fact. And it was believed that Uinigumasuittuq was the maker of Qallunaat because before that Inuit never bore many babies at one time.

"THE SHAMANS in a society," Brody had said, "have the job of explaining everything that surprises us. The crucial role of shaman figures is to find, in dreams or in visions or in some of extraordinary intuition, an account for what appears to threaten or disturb, whether it's an illness or the animals not allowing themselves to be hunted or a strange boat appearing over the horizon. The shamans *have got to find a way* of describing the appearance of Parry and Lyon and their ships in terms that their people can understand."

"If you read Parry's journals," MacDonald said, "you will find that the English were shocked by the Inuit treatment of corpses that were left out in the open and prey to dogs or wolves. Sometimes they collected these remains, giving what they thought was a more dignified disposal, such as wrapping them up in canvas and putting them through a hole in the sea-ice. You can imagine how the sight of these operations or of the white men collecting samples of the flora and fauna would have fitted in very well with the story that Lyon and Parry and their crews had come here to find relics of their mother. But the Inuit needed some explanation for the arrival of the Qallunaat, and if you had said that Parry and Lyon were here because they were looking for a Northwest Passage, it just wouldn't have made any sense."

✧ ✧ ✧

AT THE BEGINNING of his journey, Parry had looked upon the Inuit as savages. By the end of it, he admired their resilience. Still, he wore his imperial mantle with *hauteur*. Although his primary purpose was to find a Northwest Passage, he undertook his civilizing mission seriously, propelled as he was by stories about the white man's place in the New World that the literature of the day had provided him.

Soon after First Contact, Parry punished a shaman he thought had transgressed during his time "on the parish." (A play on his name, this is what the boats and the ice around it was called.) Parry wrote:

Several of them visited the ships as usual on the 9th, and among the rest Ka-oong-ut and his son Toolooak. The old gentleman was not a favourite with us, being the only one who had yet begun to tease us by constant begging. We had often expressed displeasure at this habit, which, after a day or two's acquaintance, began to be extremely troublesome; but I had to-day taken cognizance of his stealing a nail, of which I determined to take a rather serious notice, as it might otherwise lead to more extensive theft. I therefore collected all the other Esquimaux who were on board, and having in their presence expressed great indignation at this conduct, turned the offender away in disgrace.

The shaman saw things differently. His stories had the purpose of explaining things into the world – and out of it.

"I've interviewed a couple of Elders," said Louis Tapardjuk, "and there is a story of a shaman blowing away the ships so that they wouldn't come back for a long time."

MacDonald provided further details: "There is actually surprisingly little testimony about the Qallunaat, and one of the few stories that we do have concerning Parry is about this administration of corporate punishment. Hervé Paniaq told of a shaman named Quliigaujaq, who'd stolen a shovel from one of Parry's ships. The shaman was caught and taken on deck, where, as punishment for his crime, the white men attempted to cut off his arms with an axe, but no matter how hard they tried, they could not sever either of his arms. The axe would not go right through him and got wedged in the deck, and Quliigaujaq would remain unscathed, so the punishment failed and he was let go. Later, with the assistance of his helping spirit, Quliigaujaq caused a great wind to come up and blow Parry's ships away. He also ensured weather conditions would be such that Parry would never come back – and he didn't. It was nearly a hundred years before Qallunaat returned. In 1913, Alfred Tremblay, a French-Canadian prospector with Joseph Bernier's private Arctic 'gold-rush' expedition to Northern Baffin Island, came here overland with Inuit from Pond Inlet. He is called Taamali in the few stories that refer to him in the archive, and he is remembered, not least, for his bizarre behaviour. Then, in 1921, Knud Rasmussen's Fifth Thule Expedition reached Igloolik, and in 1927, Newfoundland's Bob Bartlett arrived here by sea."

"And when you hear stories about these events," I asked, "do they strike you as myths, or do they have the ring of history?"

"A bit of both," said MacDonald.

✧ ✧ ✧

ZACK BRISTLED, AN intelligent caged animal patiently biding his time, waiting for this Qalluna to be gone and for the opportunity to strike out on the land again.

I was interested in the modifications Zack had made to the Atanarjuat legend – changes that had prompted one Elder to complain that the director was "not telling the truth." In so doing, Zack had effected a major break with the ardently conservative nature of Inuit stories. He had altered the legend but also given it new vigour. In the battle of stories, Zack had taken an Iglulingmiut legend and was now wielding it as a weapon. He was behaving heroically.

"What motivated *Atanarjuat*, Zack?"

"Being born on the land, living in a sod house. People visiting and coming through the door. Getting up at the crack of dawn –"

"To make anijaaq."

"Yes."

"Will the stories disappear?"

"I ask that question myself," he said. "What ground are we going to hold? Is our story lost? Why is it lost? I look around and it's still the same world, still the same animals, still winter every year, but now there's all this talk of global warming, and PCBs, there's mercury in our fish – *why, why, why?*"

Zack let out another of his hissing breaths.

"You will need stories when you are an Elder. How will you tell them?"

"On television," said Zack. "That's where the children will be looking."

"Do you think your message will be more militant?" I asked.

Zack looked away.

"Our Elders are scared of it. I think our turn will come. For now there are people that are older than us and we respect them, but when it comes our turn to speak –"

His sentence trailed off unfinished and we ended the interview, me to prepare for the journey home and he to set about more work on *The Journals of Knud Rasmussen*. It was a bit past noon. *Scrouch, scrouch, skeerouch.* I walked up the road from the Isuma offices, and through the gap between the Nunavut Research Centre and John MacDonald's house, a strip of brilliant fiery orange suddenly appeared at the horizon, like molten lava about to spill over onto the rim of the world. I knew what it was immediately and felt a pounding of adrenalin in my chest. Auspiciously, MacDonald walked into view and I called out to him.

"John!" I said. "John! Look, the sun has risen!"

"It's beautiful, isn't it?" said MacDonald, unflappable as usual. Obviously, he had known.

"I feel so lucky. I'm leaving today."

MacDonald smiled and said, "The bad news is that it's not the sun rising. It's actually a refraction."

"Come on." I laughed. "It's like the debate about whether 2000 or 2001 was the millennium year. Five hundred years ago, I doubt that Inuit parents were saying to their children, 'Don't get excited, it's only a refraction.'"

"Five hundred years ago? *Fifty* years ago."

We stopped to admire the light that truly appeared to rise and then fall again. It did so two times.

"You can see how the Inuit got the idea of the sun coming and going," said MacDonald. "I am sure that's why there was such uncertainty at this time of year."

"There it goes," I said. "No – it's back again."

"And gone."

"My God," I said, "that was less than a minute."

"I'll take your picture," MacDonald said.

"Smile?"

"That's right – but with only half your face. *Quickly!*"

✧ ✧ ✧

The Elder Rosie Iqallijuq said:

> A white man by the name of Taamali was brought over by dog team from Pond Inlet. This is the story that I have heard from Ittuksaarjjuat. He arrived here from Pond Inlet by dog team in a time before Ittuksaarjjuat was born.
>
> It is said that Taamali had a pistol. With it he shot the island of Igloolik as he walked around the shoreline. After he had shot the island he said that Igloolik was dead and that a ship will now be able to get to the island.

4

The Circle in the Square

Louis Bird, an Omushkigo Cree from northern Manitoba, took to the riser at the front of the Talking Room in Toronto's First Nations House. Bird was part of the city's annual story-telling festival, and was beginning the second of three nights recounting the myths of Jakapaish the Shaman. The house, close to the city's downtown core, is on Spadina Avenue north of Bloor Street and is inconspicuous from the street but for a sign posted on the lawn and a few smokers that congregate outside its front doors. It was hot inside the upstairs room, so the windows were ajar and the sound of traffic spilled in from outside. The Talking Room was in a house that belonged to Canada's largely ignored native ghetto and the room was almost empty.

After a time, some fifteen or so people trickled in to hear Bird (the translation of his Cree name, "Pennishish"). They were a ragtag bunch. A lesbian couple had laid out a sweater so that their child could listen as he lay upon the floor. A woman at the back of the room was carrying her baby in a paisley-patterned sling and rocking the infant gently. She was in conversation with a man beside her who had tied his grey hair into a wispy ponytail dying on his shoulders. Several members of the audience wore articles of tribal clothing – Ghanaian kente caps, Nepalese vests. The young man who took the seat in front of me had a collapsed mohawk and held his girlfriend's hand in the gap between the school chairs. She had studs in her lips and in her ears, and sewn on the back of her boyfriend's leather jacket was a patch with a red line through a swastika in the manner of a No Smoking sign. They were socially responsible punks and here on their anarchists' night off. No aboriginals were present. But for a South Asian man, whose arms were crossed over the top of his belly in a defiant manner, the listeners were white. This was troubling but also poignant. Bird's stories appealed beyond the franchise to an evident yearning for diversity in the world – for an alternative, any alternative, to the dominant Western thinking. In this room, the environment and native culture were "good." Multinational corporations, logging companies, and Republicans were "bad." It was a view of the world that did not want more defining than that because, in a universe of quantities, the specifics of complicated arguments obfuscate. So all wars are equivalent, and native cultures – well, the ideal is the thing that matters. Better to think of native cultures as one, and the First Nations' own history of bloody wars and cruel torture as an incidental, sometimes spiritual thing. Honouring the warrior and all that.

Bird started to speak. His face was broad and his expression kind. Many creases had been etched into it by the northern elements and a habit of smiling. An elderly woman with a matronly air fiddled with the PA, the art of telling stories having given way, long ago, to the archival mission of recording them. Bird's manner was gentle and soothing, and from time to time he would interrupt his storytelling to quiz one of the children in the audience.

"Do you remember there were two young people who wanted to come down to this earth, and that somebody lowered them down and was helping them?" asked Bird. "Who do you think he – he, or she, or whatever it was – was?"

"Umm," said the young boy on the floor, "was it that midget person?"

"No," Bird laughed. "That was just to see if you were listening."

This prompted a gentle volley of chuckles, but it was clear that tonight the Bird was a fish out of water. He was speaking in English, and that was a lot of the reason, but the truth is that his audience was not listening to him at the end of a long day, dozy from the feast and taking refuge from the night or bad weather. The audience was not listening so that they might better understand the miracle of a birth, or to forget the pain of a mysterious death and see whether it was okay to laugh at such an outcome. The audience was just a bunch of city people sitting inside. Beyond, the night was damp and grey, but the weather was nothing to be scared of and there were plenty of other people securely on their way to dinner, the theatre, bars, or the movies.

Downstairs there was a rehearsal of some sort, and the whoops and cries of aboriginal dancers could be heard above the beating of drums.

"What is a shaman?" the South Asian man asked.

"A shaman is someone who develops himself spiritually so that he can overcome his physical weakness," Bird said. "If you are a shaman, you can walk on water, you can travel on the air without touching the ground, you can heal a person, and you can kill a person with your mind. Before the Europeans came, before Christianity came, the shaman was powerful."

"Maybe *Christ* was a shaman," the South Asian man said.

"We have no reason to involve Christ in the story," said Bird, laughing again, but anxiously. "If you involve *Him*, then you will not enjoy the story. You will be killing the story if you do that."

The South Asian man was not satisfied. There was a certain onus upon Bird to explain himself, and the exchange reminded me of how during *pesach*, the Jewish festival of Passover, the rabbi or father presiding over the table must answer questions about the meaning of the evening until, the instruction goes, the children are satisfied or their eyes are heavy with sleep.

"If you are a shaman, you cannot live close to another shaman," Bird said. "A shaman has to have *space*. Did you ever hear that saying in the old cowboy shows? *There's not enough room in this town for the two of us!*"

Bird delivered the last line mimicking the growl of a tough guy in a Hollywood Western. Perhaps, like Zacharias Kunuk, he had seen many of those.

"Shamans cannot live together," Bird said. "So just put Him aside and enjoy the old story."

The South Asian man shrugged. His point seemed to have been proven, Christ the shaman having shunted the Moosonee ones aside. The audience was beginning to fidget. Bird suggested that we all take a break. Dispirited, I decided to quit the evening.

Outside, the aboriginal version of Canada seemed a world away, its atlas hidden somewhere in the shadows. At Bloor, the cars hurtled past, and it was hard to believe that any of the pedestrians and drivers who passed by First Nations House knew what was there or spared a second thought for life as it had been lived by the Mississauga or the New Credit prior to the existence of the modern city. It was cold and so I hailed a taxi. In a matter of minutes, the kindly figure of Louis Bird had receded into the nether regions of my thinking and I needed to concentrate to keep the spirit of him present. The odds were against managing this for long. The driver of the taxi, a turbaned Sikh, careened through the traffic just as he would have done in his distant homeland at half the speed in a white Indian Ambassador taxicab. Already, his India seemed closer. Toronto, in all its ethnic complexity, bellowed.

If the oral stories are lost, so is the world they navigate, Bringhurst said.

✧   ✧   ✧

AT HOME, I logged into my email and found a press release from the Canada Council. It announced that seven young aboriginal writers had successfully applied to a Banff Centre writing internship and congratulated them on their success. The candidates were to learn from three published Canadian aboriginal writers about "writing techniques, methodologies, genres, cultural and storytelling protocols."

What were the "protocols" these aboriginal writers were apparently compelled to live by, what were the *rules* their tutors imagined they should respect? I whipped off an indignant email to the Newfoundland writer Lisa Moore, and she replied, "You have to know the rules before you can break them." True enough. And yet there was an orthodoxy in the Canada Council announcement – one that I had encountered in many aboriginal novels – that upheld this view at the expense of the opportunity of vigour that the novel offers stories of the Myth World. The novel, it seemed to me, was a lot like the English language itself. It absorbs the tricks of its rivals. Unlike the myth, it is *not* conservative. And unlike the epic, it does not exclude. Because its idea of community is of the family of man, nothing less, it is constantly expanding its horizons. It exhorts its authors and readers to experiment – with new cultures, new subjects, new ideas, new ways to write itself. It has voracious appetites, and because of these it thrives in confronting the shadows in the corner of the room.

Eventually, this is how the novel, having served the dominant culture, goes on to champion the subjugated one. Its proselytizing purpose fulfilled, it abandons the colonizing society that used it to further its own humanitarian ends and says, on behalf of its new devotees, "Look at who we are. See what you have done to us when we are just like you." In the hands of native writers, immigrant writers too, the novel had accomplished as much as laws have done to sway minds and heighten Canadians' awareness of what it means to be the other. Good stories win us to their side; good novels do so by *reacting*. What, I wondered, were the traits of oral storytelling that had persisted in the work of native writers who had chosen to write novels instead?

In Saskatchewan, a few months before, I had visited the Cree poet Louise Halfe, her aboriginal name Sky Dancer. We had talked at the foot of what had been a buffalo jump at the Wanuskewin

Heritage Park, on the plains outside Saskatoon, where this striking and elegant woman had described the dream that had convinced her to *write* her poems down.

"When I was twenty-one or twenty-two, I had a dream about the log cabin I grew up in. It's dilapidated, and I'm filling the cracks in the logs with papers and books, fixing it with paper leaves. It's prophetic, don't you see?"

"The paper is our new buffalo," Halfe said.

Below the Canada Council missive was an email from Robert Arthur Alexie, the Gwich'in author of *Porcupines and China Dolls*. Alexie's first novel told the story of an aboriginal community in the Northwest Territories devastated by the experience of the mission schools and lost in a boozy torpor of self-inflicted ruin. It had been virtually unnoticed because Stoddart, its publisher, had gone into receivership at the time of its release. Some copies had circulated, but the bankruptcy had been distracting. I had been a literary columnist at the time and was one of those who paid the book no immediate attention. Later, when I read it, I was struck by the novel's tone and message. I made contact with Alexie, and he started to include me on his email circulars. This one had a photograph of a snow-covered building partially fallen in on itself.

From: Robert Alexie
Subject: School
Date: 5/4/2004 4:13:00 PM
To: Noah Richler

The foyer in the high school collapsed due to heavy snows on the roof and the fact that no one wanted to shovel it. They are still arguing about who had shoveling rights.

In the meantime, school, which was supposed to begin this morning had to be postponed, again. See pics.

What's next, earthquake, wind?

Fire!

Earth, Wind, Fire and Water (snow) are the ancient elements.
ra

Alexie, once a band leader and treaty negotiator, had become an alcoholic in the early 1990s, but confronted his condition and put himself through rehab in Scarborough, Ontario. That was where a counsellor read his manuscript and sent it on to Michael Levine, a Toronto entertainment lawyer, who arranged to have it published. Now Alexie was working in Inuvik again, an executive at the Gwich'in Tribal Council Land and Water Board, taking time out to snap digital photographs and keep his address list of southern buddies in the know. A subsequent email showed more pictures of the fire-damaged school, one with a couple of fire trucks and a cherry-picker attending to the gaping hole in its sidewall.

From: Robert Alexie
Subject: School
Date: 5/17/2004 3:21:09 PM
To: Noah Richler

today
samuel hearne secondary school – inuvik nt canada
more on the fire
see pics
one big hole in the west wall of the gymnasium
common opinion is they should have just let it burn – it can't
be fixed now, or if it can, it will cost as much to build a new
one – it'll save on demolition costs . . .
ra

It was hard not to be curious about this wry man or the affecting mix of dry humour and anger in his novel. The climactic moment in *Porcupines and China Dolls* is one in which thirtysomething Jake

Noland, who had been sent to a mission school as a boy, chooses to "disclose" the revelation of his abuse to the community to which he has returned. His drive towards catharsis is courageous and, as a read, heady and invigorating. I liked Alexie's honesty, what felt like rage, and that knee-jerk blame was not being launched lazily in the settler's direction. I wanted to know about these dark moods of his, and to learn what was distinctive about the techniques of the novel in the hands of native writers. Certain aspects of native stories – the use of Trickster, the repeating of certain phrases, or even the idea that oral stories tended to vary with each performance according to the teller's reading of his audience – did not strike me as exclusive properties of oral stories, or particular to aboriginal culture. Trickster, to my mind, had become a cliché of native stories, a truncated way of claiming aboriginal pedigree. And although not composed to be spoken, the reading of a novel is, in my experience, as much of a performance as the oral story is – the time of year in which we read a novel and the mood that we are in determines how many of us embraces a written story too. Alexie, I thought, could help me in this quest – and so, on June 21, the summer equinox and a national aboriginal holiday in Canada, I sat in a plane descending to Inuvik, close to the Arctic Ocean and to the Mackenzie Delta.

Within the plane's truncated compartment – the front of the jet was reserved for freight – a bevy of tidily dressed whites bantered loudly. Their luggage tags indicated that they worked for government. Other men's bags – there were few women on board – carried the identification tags of surveying companies and a variety of oil and gas outfits, but no longer was there any of the renegade excitement that used to be the hallmark of these flights. The atmosphere was one of business to be done and no surprises. The North has been settled, emphatically, and today a geologist or construction worker doing time in the Northwest Territories can call home on his cell, commute on scheduled flights, and is in possession of a truck or an SUV, an ATV, even a sailboat if he wishes.

The effect of the aboriginal world having been turned on its head has been bewilderment, misery, and anger directed inwards. Some aboriginals have made their way in the new Canada, to be sure, but the venerable cultures that existed in this country have been eroded, and the sad truth is that most of what is indigenous and still prospers has been encouraged against the tide. The modern way of life has made colonists of the Northern peoples themselves. It has retired them to administrative jobs in offices, so that the land is a kind of Arcadia now, necessary to the native soul more than it is to economic well-being.

The new *modi vivendi* have institutionalized widespread feelings of helplessness and depression. Nothing is manufactured here. Nothing is farmed. The companies that exist in the North are engaged in the extraction of resources just as the whalers and fur trappers were. It is not a good memory, this standing by and witnessing the territory's depletion, because if all the aboriginal has is the land, then as it is bartered he sells off a bit of himself piece by piece. Aboriginals who once hunted and fished and prospected the land for the sake of the community have seen these ties pass into the realm of privileges to be defended – against timber companies, diamond-mining operations, pipelines, and the courts. For the native, the truth about the land is that it is no longer about survival, but about topping up. Hunting and fishing means "country food" – free and better meat than that which dollars will buy at the Northern Store, though you'll still need bucks for gas, a gun, refrigeration, etc. In the North, there is no possibility of comfortable living that is not blatantly dependent on some distant Southern power – whether it is Ottawa or an international conglomerate such as Exxon or De Beers. Not even the best shared principles of natives and the people who had been their vanquishers can impede the deleterious advance of Southern mores and the confusion they had wreaked upon aboriginals seduced by the Ford Expedition, the fridge, and the computer.

In Inuvik, the aboriginal community has suffered a wasting of its communal memory and an obliteration of purpose. Assuaged by phony jobs and a trumped-up rhetoric of belonging, boredom is the general condition so that for years, the open sores of hearts and minds were soothed with sex, drink, and drugs.

When that didn't work, there was always suicide.

✧ ✧ ✧

ALEXIE, A HANDSOME man with dark hair, evidently not prone to smiling, met me at the airport wearing black shades, black jeans, and a black leather vest over a khaki hunting shirt. He nodded in my direction and took one of my bags and then acknowledged a Gwich'in Elder whom we passed on the way to Alexie's SUV. Alexie said that we would drive to Fort McPherson tomorrow, explaining that he had been born near there in 1955 – raised first on the land and then in a one-room log cabin that his grandfather built within the settlement. His father, said Alexie, had brought the family into Fort McPherson so that when it came time for their education, Robert and his sister might continue to live at home rather than be sent to some distant residential mission school. Aged fourteen, Alexie attended Stringer Hall, the Anglican mission school in Inuvik. Grollier Hall, the Catholic school, was right next to it – the two schools gathering their pupils from a region that stretched all the way from Fort McPherson to Aklavik, west across the Mackenzie.

"The Gwich'in you saw at the airport," I asked Alexie. "Who was he?"

"He was the first one who disclosed. He stood up before a Gwich'in gathering and he told them all the bad things that had happened to him."

"How did people respond?"

"It was like nothing had been said," Alexie said. "Sometimes that would drive me nuts. Once I almost got up and gave one woman a piece of my mind, but what's the point? People have to find out for themselves."

Inuvik – the name means "Place of Man" in Inuvialuktun – is a 1950s Canadian government invention. It was built on "Site Three," one of several possible sites recommended by federal surveyors for the location of a new town, as the old Inuvialuit settlement at Aklavik was frequently flooded. It was opened, in July 1958, by then prime minister John Diefenbaker – the first settlement north of the Arctic Circle to offer the amenities of a Southern Canadian community of equivalent size. Its spanking new buildings sat either on piles or on three-foot gravel pads, and its "utilidors" (utility corridors) solved the problem of constructing over Arctic permafrost by transporting sewage and water in a network of heavily insulated pipes suspended in uninterrupted boxy casing a few feet above ground. In 1967, a rush of patriotic endeavour meant that a small Centennial Library was added, but it was the oil and gas boom of the mid-1970s that really bolstered Inuvik's fortunes – and its reputation as a rough town – as a flurry of seismic exploration and then drilling took place in the Beaufort Sea and the land around the Delta.

Around town, a certain memory exists of those oil exploration boom years. There's the Mad Trapper's Inn for a start, but the main business of this Arctic Nowhere, true of so many Northern communities, quickly became that of sustaining itself. Following the Justice Berger Report of 1977, a moratorium on oil and gas exploitation brought a halt to the venture of a pipeline from the Beaufort Sea through to the South – and an economic slough from which the region has still not recovered. The number of permanent residents in Inuvik settled at a little more than three thousand, and the atmosphere in the town was transformed from one of bustle to one of waiting. Although some prospecting was going on, and the surveyors and front men of the oil and gas companies impatiently wanting to put the Mackenzie Valley Pipeline through have also been working the area, the activity is now of a lesser, more regulated kind. Inuvik had become a place to make a living, but not a fortune. The big companies are no longer prepared to pay massive amounts of overtime. They are more shrewd. There is plenty of labour locally, though a perusal of the job postings in Inuvik showed them to be uninteresting and few. Today, the revived project of the pipeline has become a last chance at redemption for the downtrodden characters of a Northern story of no boom, all bust, that has been going on for decades now. It is the story that Alexie himself lived in the years before he wrote *Porcupines and China Dolls*. The Mad Trapper was what you'd call an "Indian bar" then, a rowdy, hard-drinking tavern like any number that existed across the North or in the no-go areas of cities like Winnipeg and Vancouver. The Mad Trapper became the generically named "saloon" in *Porcupines and China Dolls*, in which are set scenes of afternoon destitution, and of James Nathan's efforts to avoid it, that are quite unforgettable – funny too.

James stood by the bar and looked around for the ten millionth time. *Same shit – same shitters.* He spotted Jake sitting with Alfred, Kevin and Greg, then took a deep breath and swam across the sea of misery holding his beer aloft in case one of the sharks took a bite out of it.

"Hey, James, len' me loonie!"

"Hey, James, gimme smoke!"

"Hey, James, buy me beer!"

Hey, James, eat me!

That was Angie and she was doing pretty good, considering. She'd woken up that morning, had a shower, then squeezed into her tightest-fitting jeans only to find she needed a coat hanger to pull up the zipper. She thought about getting a patent on her new invention, but realized there was already one in the ladies' room. *Prob'ly seen more crotches 'an James 'n Jake combined.* She looked at Jake. *Wonder if I should fuck him to make James jealous.* She shook that thought off. *He's jus' a kid.*

Jake smiled at James. "Hey, bro, what's up?" he asked.

"Clap rate," James answered, then sat up and took a shot of vodka.

"Hey, James, what's up?" Kevin asked rhetorically.

"Diddly."

"Hey, James," Greg said. He looked stoned and drunk. "Tell us a good one."

"What am I? A fuckin' Elder?"

"Well, you are older 'n you're always fuckin' somethin'."

Alexie and I shared a smoke on the steps of the Eskimo Inn and observed a group of Gwich'in teens gathered on the landing of the Mad Trapper opposite, waiting for its doors to open. An increase in passing traffic, at lunch hour and then at four, indicates the time of day in Inuvik. In the vicinity of the Trapper, and the ATM handily nearby, there was a parking problem.

I asked, "Is Inuvik as lively as you remember it?"

"Oh no," said Alexie. "Back in the late 1970s and early 1980s, I was a flight service specialist, down in South Mackenzie, and I remember coming home for holidays and meeting people who were working in the oil industry, and these people had *money*. Everyone had a brand-new snowmobile. I'd go into the bar at eleven o'clock in the morning and it would be packed. Standing room only. Or you can go to a bootlegger and buy a bottle for what, sixty bucks? I can't tell you what the going price is right now because I haven't bought one for a long time."

"Since when?"

"I haven't bought a drink since May 23, 1993, at four o'clock."

Alexie chuckled. Had a pull of his cigarette.

"But I'm not counting," he said.

✧   ✧   ✧

HAD I NOT been somewhere like this before? The truth about most Northern towns is that they look infinitely better under the blanket of snow that keeps the dust down and covers the refuse and old machinery left in people's yards. The utilidors appear like the town's exposed intestines, and only add to the impression of the place being gravely wounded in some way. It was hard not to be astonished that people actually *lived* in Inuvik, its population a mix of visiting workers hating their days here and an indigenous population wanting better.

Summer means bugs and endless light and the kind of stifling heat that leaves you watching the fan in your room and reminds you that Inuvik is a colony – *a colony of Ottawa*. The heat is sweltering, the constant light confusing, and the mugginess contributes to the feeling that Inuvik has something in common with some remote outpost in West Africa. The colours were less vivid than the places in Ghana or Sierra Leone that Inuvik reminded me of, but the place was familiar, depressingly so. Perhaps it was the pair of Palestinian taxi drivers, emailing digital snaps of their unlikely new home back to Gaza. (Why do people live in Inuvik? Because life can be a whole lot worse.) Or was it the slightly sour comedy of the Mackenzie Inn's Briar Dining Room, the air-conditioned restaurant where Southern executives and their local company contacts were gathered like British ex-pats in Kenya before Mau-Mau. That's what they are – these geologists and engineers and Ottawa bureaucrats with their papers, their studies, and their fat per diems – *expats*, congregating in the dining room of the one place in town where they've been told it's safe to eat. With its tables of mostly white Canadians, this was Inuvik's Hill Club such as Graham Greene might have written it – an establishment that has known better times but must now let the natives in. Sometimes you'll see a few in the diner next door, grabbing a Salisbury steak or a plate of deep-fried chicken fingers, but even the short-order restaurant is the domain of mostly blue-collar workers, some of them still cursing Indians, as a table did when I was there, for their baffling, lazy ways. "Fuckin' Indians." Why can't they handle their drink? *Why can't they be more like white men?*

If you read Alexie's work, quickly you come to understand what has been the curse of aboriginals pushed to be more like white men. The "porcupines and china dolls" of his novel's title refer to the appearance and brusque transformation that the native children underwent upon their entry at mission school, brush cuts and delousing powder, reducing them to uniformed look-alikes. James Nathan and Jake Noland belong to a community not considered, sent to alien schools, and returned home unrecognizable to their families and to themselves. Some are driven to contemplate suicide, as James Nathan does in the opening pages of the novel – and as Alexie's best friend did at the age of fifteen.

"That was the first suicide I was aware of, and it took place in 1973, when I was in grade nine," Alexie said. "My friend was fourteen days older than I was. We grew up together. That's why, in the book, I put James's and Jake's birthdays only fourteen days apart."

"The two brothers."

"That's right," said Alexie. "We've had about twenty or twenty-five suicides since then in a population of about nine hundred. It was like an epidemic. All of the suicides but two were young men and most, if not all of them, had been through the residential school system."

Across the street, an older aboriginal woman put a hand out against the wall of the Mad Trapper, steadying herself. Alexie said he knew her, and watched.

"Are you an angry writer?" I asked.

"Probably. When I write about things like the mission schools, the government, or about the things that have happened to our people that shouldn't have happened – yes, I am."

"Does anger make the writing of a novel more difficult?"

"The anger that I felt in my first book was helpful because it allowed me almost to *scream* what I wanted to say. Writing it down was a very positive experience. I remember writing the part where the Chief gets up and discloses and the story almost goes into a kind of magical realism. It was a period in the community where everybody was going about their business as if it was *normal* –

normal to drink, normal to buy bootlegs, normal to be sexually abused, normal to be the abuser or to be neglected. Everything is normal. It's so dysfunctional, it's *normal*."

Alexie and I got back into the truck for the short ride over to the Gwich'in Land and Water Board. The desk in his office was large and extremely tidy, and he sat down to upload the digital pictures he had taken that day and add them to his website. Reports, mostly relating to the Mackenzie Valley Pipeline project, sat beside faxes from the Department of Indian Affairs and Northern Development. A neatly stacked pile of about fifteen hundred pages that I had assumed to be Gwich'in business was in fact the manuscript of his second novel. Above a small, round meeting table was a map of Gwich'in territory. Next to it, a chart showed the migrations of the three major caribou herds in the region, around the routes of proposed and existing pipelines in the Northwest Territories and Alaska. In the corridor, above the office kitchen, was a calendar. The date of June 25 was encircled on it, and *1876* written in its box. The anniversary of the American Lt.-Col. George Custer's Last Stand.

"After work a bunch of us are going to get together and beat up a few white people," said Alexie, grinning. "Wanna join us?"

Alexie brought the truck around, and we started on the trip to Fort McPherson, where he had been chief before he became vice-president of the Gwich'in Tribal Council. The truck careened along a gravel highway that, in his words, "cut across the land like a rip in a painting." Outside it was hot and dry, but he was wearing his cowboy boots, black jeans, and dark vest, as usual. Fall, he told me, was his favourite time of the year. The temperature is cooler, the mosquitoes are mostly gone, and the boreal forest is so colourful that, as he wrote in his second novel, *The Pale Indian*, it is "as if the Old People had set fire to the hills in anger. *Or was it sorrow?*"

Elation, today. At the Peel River, we waited to take a ferry that made summer crossings in a triangle between the three banks of Tsiigektchie Junction. The horseflies were large and vicious, but children were playing in the tide, and somebody else was water skiing on a makeshift rig of jettisoned plywood behind a boat with a small outboard motor. The children's laughter carried across the water. On the bluff behind where the children were playing, two churches glowed in the late-afternoon light, and from a distance the grass on the bank descending to the beach looked soft and inviting. Live in any place long enough and you learn to call it home.

Out on the land, in Alexie's novel, is where the spirit can soar. When James cocks his gun and considers shooting himself, he does so on a landscape similar to this that Alexie calls the "Blue Hills."

"It's like Jake is making an effort to get back to the old ways and join the old people," he said. "He's trying to get back home, wherever home is. It's a crazy way of thinking, but better to kill yourself out on the land than on some dirty back street somewhere. Out on the land it would almost be like a ritual, but it would be a tragedy in the community."

Alexie was silent for a moment.

"There have been a lot of times when I've taken that walk up into the hills and thought about life, or the lack thereof, and contemplated suicide," he said.

In the passages of the novel that take place outside the saloon, beyond the unmade beds of who knows whose front room – outside the whole desultory town – Alexie communes with the ancestors and launches himself into a wonderful, mythic exaggeration. A *million* voices cry in the dark, James Nathan grows *one hundred and twenty-five fuckin' feet tall*. It's not magic realism. Alexie's style is colder and more brutal than its florid South American cousin, as you would expect of a landscape where dwarf trees take decades to grow just a few centimetres off the ground. The images are more sinewy, glimpses of a native Myth World that belongs to Canada's intractable Arctic and not the Amazon's anarchic jungles. Authors write to a personal music and when, in the community hall, James Nathan makes his disclosure, the poetic exaggeration Alexie employs takes the beat of a Gwich'in drum-dance. Before you know it, you are in it, *believing* it. After crouching in shame for so long – after finally expunging his festering shame – well, of course, James Nathan will be standing one hundred and twenty-five fuckin' feet tall.

Alexie drove on and as he spoke, dropped his chin so that he could peer at you over the top of the shades clipped to his glasses. "I did have one experience of the schools before I went myself," he said. It made him appear wise, this habit of singling you out in such a concentrated fashion.

"It was August, I was about twelve, and I was playing with a friend on the sewage pond behind McPherson. We were in a canoe and we tipped, and we went to the hostel to get washed up. The administrator, he was a nice man. We told him what happened and he said we could wash up. The shower area was full of baths, all separated by partitions, and we were taking a bath and all of a sudden this guy comes in and says he's the new supervisor. We've never seen him before, and he keeps coming in and out and he's talking to us and asking our names –"

Alexie stopped, chewed his gum for a while.

"And then, one moment there, he basically touched me," he continued. "I didn't realize until later that he was a homosexual, and it wasn't until later that I wondered if anyone else knew, or if he had gone further than touching with other boys. And I thought to myself, well, if that happened *in one day*, then what happened to all the kids who were away from their families and in the schools for all of the year? And then I wondered about my father, and why he had gone to such trouble for us *not* to be at the residential school as he had been. His was the first generation, you see."

"Did your father ever talk about his experiences at mission school?"

"My father never talked about it. He would say that he had been to mission school in grade six and leave it at that."

Alexie and I hardly knew each other. I thought about it for a moment and then asked, "Was your father abused, do you think?"

Alexie turned and peered at me over his glasses again. "That is a story that for the time being will remain untold," he said.

✧ ✧ ✧

WE ARRIVED AT the aboriginal days feast at Fort McPherson, where most of Alexie's extended family was present, as they were still living in or near the settlement. Alexie hovered around the edges of the gathering, bantering quietly with those he knew in the shade of the one-room cabin in which he had lived as a child. It stood, once amid tents, now off to one side of the main street that ran through the village. Behind it was a pretty white church, its small cemetery bordered by a low picket fence. Some fifty metres away from the common where the games were taking place was a Northern Store.

The cabin, about four metres by seven, was due to be knocked down in the ensuing months. It appeared a totemic shadow behind the gaiety, this coming together of neighbours and friends and generations, enjoying the feast and games in a manner that was not different from the rehearsals and performances that I had witnessed in Igloolik, an instance of the aboriginal circle again. A group of women sat at one of a few picnic tables and watched as Elders cooked whitefish and caribou, but also hot dogs, hamburgers, and corn. The caribou was charred nearly black – the meat is so lean that it burns easily – and was tender and delicious. Another woman was ladling out bowls of soup and tea. There were about sixty people milling about, the few tourists – American mostly – as well as a number of whites who were resident in the area. One of them had been married to a Gwich'in woman for nearly thirty years, and he and a Gwich'in pal were playing Elvis, Roy Orbison, and Dwight Yoakam tunes.

"Gwich'in still have the drums and the dancers," Alexie said, "but in Alaska, not here. We used to have the drums and songs and burial practices, but the old people took the old ways with them and whatever religion we had is also gone. Tradition to us, now, is the fiddle and dances that were brought by the early fur traders. I don't know how it is that the Inuvialuit, the Dene, and the Dogribs have kept their traditions going."

"And what of Trickster?" I asked.

Alexie shook his head. "No stories that I know of," he said, another of the old ties broken – but then, in almost the same breath, he told me about a short story of his in which Charlie, a Gwich'in, is picked up by the RCMP for being drunk off the reserve but really to prepare the compound's wood for winter. The Indian chops a couple of cords. After the RCMP let the old man go, they discover that he has cut each piece of wood exactly three inches too long for their stoves. I laughed. It was a good story – one of mischief, certainly. Of Trickster, I was not so sure. If I'd wanted it to be, I supposed.

I asked Alexie about his use of poetic exaggeration, and the way he repeated phrases like "the future unfolds as it should," "this is what really happened," or spoke of stories that "needed to be told." I reminded him that he started both of his novels with a recitation of history, in the North, that took the form of an incantatory list that described the shocks of Gwich'in history since First Contact – the arrival of the fur traders, the missionaries, the RCMP, the 1921 Treaty. I pointed out how he enjoyed the vernacular – talking about the Gwich'in having their "ass kicked worse than General Custer got his" – and asked if these aspects of his fiction had an oral aspect.

"Those prefaces are almost a history lesson," said Alexie. "People can object to what has happened here all they want, but it's not going to win them anything – to me, that's a pattern that we've been put into as native people. We object, and pretty soon we're nothing but whining, drunken Indians."

"And so you tell yourself that the future has unfolded as it should?"

"Or that there is too much apathy," Alexie said.

"Do you think there's something about the written form of the novel that makes it a sturdier vehicle for the anger that comes out of such wrongs?"

"The first time you disclose, or the first time you tell a story about what happened to our people, you get very angry," said Alexie. "That anger brings forth all the emotion, but after the tenth time you tell it, you don't feel any of that anger any more. In a written story, all the anger and the hate and the shame that one feels is put down as it was. If I told the story orally, it wouldn't be the same."

"The anger is forgotten, you mean. The story becomes something else."

"You've also got to remember that back in 1921," Alexie continued, "very few of us could read and write, so there were a lot of X's on the treaty, and a lot of promises being made by the commissioner to the Gwich'in and other native people up and down the valley – and a lot of these promises that were made were *oral*. Years later, the commissioner seemed to have lost his memory. So writing is important now, and I find it very ironic that now it ain't worth *nothing* unless it's in writing."

"Is that true of stories as well? Is writing a novel a defence of the culture in the same way that negotiating a treaty in the courts – as you did personally – is a defence of the land?"

"I'd like to believe that. My story is mine. It has my name on it. It tells a story that maybe a hundred years from now, maybe two hundred years from now, I'd like people to remember."

"So maybe the novel is a way to fight back."

"Well, I'm not going to get five thousand Gwich'in to listen to me tell a story, so I give them my book. Maybe they won't read it now, but they might in five or ten years. At least they'll have the *chance* to read it, and that chance will be given to others as well."

Paper, the new buffalo.

Alexie and I took turns at the wheel as we drove back to Inuvik, the light bright and white. Once in town, we stopped at ground above a ramp that boaters use to access the Mackenzie. The river figures large in Alexie's novels. It is a symbol of time passing on, and of a way out into the domain of ancestral spirits. Alexie wiped the dash of his SUV with a paper towel from the roll he kept beneath the back seat and stepped out of the car to have a cigarette, and I joined him. It was pleasing, this view across the water.

From: Robert Alexie
Subject: Inuvik
Date: 7/26/2004 4:55:04 PM
To: Noah Richler

sometimes i wonder if the gwich'in are all there
i mean, why would we live in an environment that's 25C in the
summer (that's hot for us folk), and 40 below in the winter
when it's dark 24/7?
not to mention the bugs and other blood sucking critters out
there and the high cost of living, if you can call it that
and the dust

then one day you take a drive into the hills with your wife and
pick yellow berries on a hill in the midst of gwich'in country
and there's
not another soul for as far as you can see
you can look at the mountains, drink clear cold mountain
water, pick,
look at your wife
and then you know why we stay

✧   ✧   ✧

MOST CANADIANS' ENCOUNTERS with aboriginals are still few. Too
many of them occur in cities, where the sight of a native with his
arm outstretched, or news of another young aboriginal woman
murdered, have become the emblems of a situation that approaches
ipso facto apartheid. Consecutive governments pour more and
more money into reservations hoping that the social problems of
aboriginals will just go away, or at least stay where the money
pays Indians to be, even as the aboriginals who are congratulated,
mostly artists, are ones who have participated in the broader
society – as, to name a few, Tomson Highway, Thomas King, Lee
Maracle, Norval Morrisseau, Bill Reid, and Eden Robinson have
done. But there is, in Canada, despite a troublesome history of

engagement that equates the notion of participation with *assimilation*, such a dirty word, a remarkable urge of immigrant and settler Canadians to be reconciled. Participation works both ways. At First Nations House, the evidence had been that Canadians *wanted* the stories. They wanted to learn more about the cultures and values that their own narrative world had obscured. They were eager to graft themselves onto the bark of the aboriginal tree and thereby acquire a history in a land where there is not much. Native writers such as Alexie, Joseph Boyden, Tomson Highway, Thomas King, Lee Maracle, and Eden Robinson were speaking to this pervasive need as they addressed the thorny issue of the invisibility of natives.

From Eden Robinson's *Monkey Beach*:

We drove along the highway between Terrace and Kitimat and stopped when Mick thought we'd reached a good spot. As we drove, Mick played Elvis and homemade tapes that his friends had sent him, with songs like "FBI Lies," "Fuck the Oppressors" and, my favourite, "I Shot Custer." Despite my pleading that they really were socially conscious, Abba was absolutely forbidden in Mick's cassette deck.

"She's got to know about these things," Mick would say to Dad, who was disturbed by a note from one of my teachers. She had forced us to read a book that said that the Indians on the northwest coast of British Columbia had killed and eaten people as religious sacrifices. My teacher had made us each read a paragraph out loud. When my turn came, I sat there shaking, absolutely furious.

"Lisa?" she'd said. "Did you hear me? Please read the next paragraph."

"But it's all lies," I'd said.

The teacher stared at me as if I were mutating into a hideous thing from outer space. The class, sensing tension, began to titter and whisper. She slowly turned red, and said I didn't know what I was talking about.

"Ma-ma-oo told me it was just pretend, the eating people, like drinking Christ's blood at Communion."

In a clipped, tight voice, she told me to sit down.

Since I was going to get into trouble anyway, I started singing "Fuck the Oppressors." The class cheered, more because of the swearing than anything else, and I was promptly dragged, still singing, to the principal's office.

Mick went out and had the teacher's note laminated and framed. He hammered a nail into his wall and hung the note in the centre of the living room. He put his arm around me, swallowed hard a few times, and looked misty. "My little warrior."

◇ ◇ ◇

"IT REALLY ANNOYS me when Canadians talk about 'wide open spaces,'" said Robinson, "and I really *hate* being called a 'pioneer.'"

Robinson is a Haisla writer from Kitamaat, the village on the B.C. coast that preceded the town of Kitimat that Alcan built for workers at its smelting operation upriver, in the 1950s. She is a candid woman who established a formidable literary reputation right away with the collection *Traplines*. She knows how to tell a good story, and has an attentive and often amusing eye for the contradictions and challenges of native living. As it had been for Alexie, anger was an inextricable part of the mix. The classroom scene, and another where Lisamarie gets into a slanging match with a gang of whites driving by in a truck, displayed Robinson's fury about native standing in Canadian society, and the storytelling power she possessed that put these feelings to good use.

"But anger is so easy to overdo," said Robinson as we sat together in a busy Toronto pub. "Anger is like a really strong spice that can completely ruin a dish. I find that I can't write until I have a certain distance and the emotion has been simmering for a long time. If I'm angry, then I'm inarticulate – I have no head for pressure."

Early in her career, Robinson complained that Canadian readers were in the habit of consuming the works of native writers as they would any another material good and then moving on. Later, she was at pains to describe herself as a *writer* first of all, rejecting the "native" label for the freedom that the novel offered.

"If I didn't follow protocol, there were all sorts of lectures that I would get," said Robinson.

"Have Haisla protocols impeded your writing in any way?"

"No," said Robinson. "You can be overly cautious if you're too aware of them, but they make for a good first step. Other native writers had to struggle on their own with issues of how much to tell and when to do so, but I actually *liked* the clarity of being told what I could or could not do because in terms of Haisla intelligence I'm actually quite dim."

Robinson took a sip of her cola.

"I *like* things to be written down. It was actually a huge relief for me to go to school because I love novels and book learning meant there were people who thought I was smart."

She smiled. Looked out the window at the busy terrace bar.

"Do you know who Terry McMillan is?" she asked.

"The bestselling African-American author of *How Stella Got Her Groove Back*."

"That's right."

Robinson gazed across the bar. "Native literature is still waiting for its Terry McMillan," said Robinson. "When I went to hear her speak, I was sitting there just wishing I could be her."

The tension Robinson appeared to have put behind her is felt by the writer of any community, previously closed, who suddenly finds herself the novel's ambassador and standing astride the great divide of a culture wanting to protect its integrity and the wider, bigger world of which the novel has made her a member. The lesser community finds itself exposed, mystified, and often hurt by the novelist's capacity to cut close to the bone. For writing a novel has always demanded a certain readiness to betray – family and friends, usually. The ability to do so prompted the English novelist Graham Greene to declare that "a sliver of ice lives in the heart of every important artist." These acts of betrayal occur at the level of the community too, and explain why, for Robinson or any native novelist, the very act of *writing* a story down is political. The challenge that confronts the native storyteller proud of her origins is how to respect the traditions of the aboriginal circle in the modern era of the book.

✧　✧　✧

AT THE CORNER of Carlton and Parliament, in Toronto's Cabbagetown district, the Coffee Cup, now closed, is where drug dealers used to gather and the derelict went for a smoke. FRESH DONUTS, read the marquee above the hazy windows of its smoking room. The store even sold doughnuts occasionally. Outside, sitting on her arse on the sidewalk, was a black woman repeatedly wailing, "*Two dollars, please! Do you have two dollars, please?*" Farther up the street, the man locals knew as James, shirt loose and hand out, paced frenetically. He looked my way and thought about asking but changed his mind for some private reason and moved on. It was evening and from the shadows an aboriginal man waved me over towards the dry cleaners. He was familiar, this thoughtful-looking man with the glasses, the pock-marked face, and the distant dark eyes. His hair, thinner now, fell to his shoulders. He wore a black coat and a long white scarf draped from his neck.

Yes, I knew the man.

"*Noah,*" he said. "Noah, quickly, *come here.*"

He was peering into the window of the laundromat.

"Want to see Bruce Cockburn's laundry?" he asked. "It's spinning right now."

This is how I would run into Tomson Highway on occasion – now and again and unpredictably, but always with pleasure. A Cree from northern Manitoba, the celebrated playwright and author of *Kiss of the Fur Queen* is enviably footloose and divides his time between Ontario, Manitoba, and leaves the country for France for half the year, the better to write and not be pinned down. When I set out to find Highway for this project, I needed to travel to Banyuls-sur-Mer, a French coastal village that overlooks the Mediterranean from the Pyrenees, hard by the border with Spain. I wanted to talk to Highway because Trickster was integral to the spirit of his novel.

Highway's Weesageechak was neither as menacing as the part-Ojibway writer Joseph Boyden's, nor as priapic as the Greek-American, part-Cherokee writer Thomas King's. There was an authenticity to Highway's miscreant – its sexuality, in particular – that made his Weesageechak amusing but also unsettling. It was not hard to imagine Highway himself having lived the part.

Highway's brother Rene, a ballet dancer, died of AIDS on October 18, 1990, aged thirty-six. (The obituary in the *Toronto Star*, an indicator of more censorious times, says that he died of meningitis.) It is a date the author remembers as Robert Alexie does his last drink. Like Alexie's novel, Tomson's *Kiss of the Fur Queen* is set against the panorama of Canada's residential schools and invokes the aboriginal Myth World – Cree, in this case – but the mood of Highway's story is quite different. Where Alexie's characters seethe with a slow-burning and tragic capacity to destroy themselves, one that begins its job from within, Highway's lot spend their manic energy outwards. Champion Okimasis is a classically trained pianist, as Highway himself was. Champion's younger brother, Gabriel, is a dancer, as Rene was. The two are educated in the residential schools and later tour the cities of the Canadian South, Gabriel wreaking his sexual mischief just about everywhere the pair go. When, at residential school, Gabriel senses the dangling cross of Father Lafleur over his cot, he embraces the fate that, quite literally, is about to come his way. The novel is an allegory, the exquisitely beautiful Gabriel "eating" people as Weetigo, the man-eating spirit of Cree legend, does. *Kiss of the Fur Queen* is a novel of appetites learned in the "semen-airy" and wielded in the tempting playgrounds of Southern cities and the malls, replete with food courts and more carnal temptations, that the brothers frequent.

From Tomson Highway's *Kiss of the Fur Queen*:

> "Why did Weesageechak kill the Weetigo?" asked Gabriel, as he washed down a gob of bleeding beef with a torrent of Orange Crush.

"All I remember is that the Weetigo had to be killed because he ate people," replied Jeremiah through a triangle of pizza. "Weesageechak chewed the Weetigo's entrails to smithereens from the inside out."

"Yuck!" feigned Gabriel, chomping into a wedge of Black Forest cake thick with cream.

They ate so much their bellies came near to bursting. They drank so much their bladders grew pendulous. Surely this place had a washroom hidden away somewhere. Gabriel went hunting.

There – glaring light, ice-white porcelain, the haunting sound of water dripping in distant corners – standing nearby was a man. Six feet, thin, large of bone, of joint, brown of hair, of eye, pale of skin. Standing there, transported by Gabriel Okimasis's cool beauty, holding in his hand a stalk of firewood so pink, so mauve that Gabriel could not help but look and, seeing, desire. For Ulysses' sirens had begun to sing "Love Me Tender," and the Cree Adonis could taste, upon the buds that lined his tongue, warm honey.

Highway took me to his apartment in Banyuls-sur-Mer, overlooking the sea. He sat at an electric piano and prodded at a couple of sticking keys exhibiting the first signs of wear and tear.

"Without residential school, I would have had none of this." Highway said. "There were no grand pianos in northern Manitoba."

He put an unlabelled bottle of wine on the table and started to play some evocative, rolling cascades. "The Sage, the Dancer and the Fool" was a piece that he had written for his brother.

"Rene was a gorgeous dancer," said Highway. "I started writing music for him when he was beginning to experiment with choreography. Now I play this piece each morning as part of my prayer for him.

"My brother dances with seagulls," Highway said.

To an extent, *Kiss of the Fur Queen* is a dated novel. It belongs to what could be termed the *Cage Aux Folles* period of gay expression of the 1970s, when homosexuals, in the face not only of the devastation of AIDS but of discrimination too, were essentially stating that the best possible response to an inexplicably unjust world was to live outrageously, flamboyantly, and well. In Highway's scenario, the situation was exacerbated further, as his homosexual characters were living in a country that still had a long way to go before acknowledging, let alone coming to terms with, its brutalization of natives and disregard for their social condition. They could have used Weesageechak then.

"On the reserves of northern Manitoba, where I come from – it wasn't an endless parade, but there was certainly a *procession*, shall we say, of coffins. There would be these beautiful young women going down to places like The Pas, Thompson, and Winnipeg – and next you'd see them come back in coffins. They had all been raped. Clara Dantusyu. Marie Benoni. Rose Morasty. Helen Betty Osborne – the sickest rape of them all. These were girls I went to school with, and the great majority of these cases were never reported. Nobody was ever apprehended or arrested or fined or jailed. Nothing. So I became obsessed with it, and to my mind, in religion it is the same story of God coming in and raping the lot of us. That's how it was, and I am particularly angry about the situation because, in the hierarchical Christian system, not only is God only male, he's a *heterosexual* male. You're either a man or a woman, and there is nothing in between, whereas in the aboriginal circle, there is room for all kinds of life. There is allowance in there, for man or woman to be male, or female, or both at the same time. This male God, we've just had enough of him."

Kiss of the Fur Queen is a sad novel, a story with more than its fair share of mortifying anguish. Jeremiah dies of AIDS, and the brutal gang rape and murder of an aboriginal woman in a back alley on Winnipeg's North Main deliberately invokes the death of Helen Betty Osborne, raped, murdered, and stabbed more than fifty times with a screwdriver by four white youths in The Pas, Manitoba, in

November 1971. It is also a very beautiful book. That would be an odd thing to say of a novel that is mired in loss and abuse, except that Highway's pair of brothers spoils the conventional aboriginal story because they do not behave as victims. They are residential schoolboys who, like the author, are at ease with experience and occasionally feel better off because of it. Advantage, Trickster.

"You didn't find the mission school traumatic in any way?"

"Every nation goes through trauma of some kind," said Highway. "Look at what the Jews have been through. Look at what women have been through. Think about the Spanish Inquisition or the American Civil War. The most privileged kid in Rosedale is probably traumatized. I'm a child of privilege. I come from a good family, from the kind of marriage that in Hollywood they can only dream about. So who's traumatized – me or the kid of Hollywood parents?"

Highway let his hands make graceful runs up and down the keyboard. He swore at the piano, from time to time, as the keys knocked. Then he changed tempo abruptly and mimicked the brisk, coarse chords of a squeezebox tune.

"My father played the accordion. When I hear something like this, then I think of him," Highway said. "I look back at my life, and it's an endless sequence of moving down aisles to pick up trophies – like Jeremiah in the novel. I had *carte blanche* to travel. I went to performance festivals everywhere. Sure it was traumatic, but there was plenty of good that came out of it as well."

Highway played a few overlapping phrases of another tune he had composed, and it was easy to envision the open water of some brooding Northern lake, terns or perhaps an eagle flying overhead.

Suddenly he dropped his hands to his side.

"Oh my God, this piano sounds so terrible," said Highway.

Abruptly he stood up.

"Come," he said, "I'll take you to my library."

We drove along the precipitous coastal road towards Spain and parked at the end of a farmer's track that veered steeply through cultivated terraces and then down scrub-covered cliffs towards the water. A footpath led towards an outcrop a few feet above the shore. The waves crashed against the rocks below us and were wetting us with their spray.

"This reminds me of Windy Lake and Meriah Lake and of all the lakes I grew up on," Highway said jubilantly. "I am the son of a fisherman, I grew up on those waves!"

"And they were as high as this?"

Highway nodded. "The lakes of northern Manitoba are like inland seas. On stormy days they could be even higher. The sound of these waves is a constant rhythm in my life – I was born in the middle of a Garden of Eden."

"Otherwise known as a snowbank."

In the Cree cosmology, children choose their parents, and young Champion, a.k.a. Jeremiah, is born in the novel as Highway was – dropped from the stars while his father is working the winter traplines. "'Poof!' he went on his bum, smack into the most exquisite mound of snow in the entire forest, making crystals of silver spray shoot up to join the stars."

"In the winter we worked the traplines by dogsled," said Highway, "and in December 1951 my parents were coming back to Brochet and my mother went into labour, so that's where I was born – in a snowbank, one hundred and fifty miles north of the village of Brochet. That's where I want to die too."

"And did your mother carry you in an *amauti*?" I asked, referring to the beautiful Inuit garment, a winter cloak, in which a child can be carried in an oversized hood that flips over the head and protects mother and baby from the snow, wind, or rain.

"No," said Highway. "The Cree used a piece of spruce wood – like a plank – and nailed and sewn into that plank was a thick cloth, attached in such a way that the baby could be laced into it –"

"So that it was snug and comforting –"

"Yes. We were always travelling, following the caribou, and the wonderful thing was that it kept the back straight. Like my back," said Highway laughing. "My back is very straight, which I'm afraid you can't have noticed because you haven't looked at my back once since you've been here."

"It's a nice straight back," I said.

That evening, Highway and his lover took me for a walk along the road by the quay.

"You must enjoy the languages here," I said.

"I love them," said Highway, "the French and the Spanish. The corner of Manitoba where I'm from is on the border with Saskatchewan and Nunavut, and it's just like this. It's Cree land that overlaps with Dene and Inuit. There was always Cree and English spoken in the house."

"So what language do you think and write in?"

"English, but I would like to write in French eventually, and I like to think that I'm changing my English to suit the rhythm of what I want to say. The Cree language has a comical rhythm to it. *Degegegedegegegededegegege* – it's Trickster-ish. English is so much more cumbersome by comparison."

"Does English not have that same mimicking capacity?"

"Every language has a special genius," said Highway, "but, for me, English is a language of the intellect."

"And Cree is what, a more carnal language?"

"Very much so. The way I like to put it is that English comes from here –"

Highway pointed to his head.

"French comes from here –"

"*L'estomac.*"

"– and here."

"The heart."

"And guess where Cree comes from?"

"The groin is what's left," I said.

"That's right. The *funniest* part. The most *hysterical* part. The most *sensual* part. In mythological terms it comes right smack down to the Garden from which the other two languages were evicted a long time ago. It's the garden of *pleasure*, the garden of *joy*, where the tree of knowledge is to be celebrated – and to be *sucked on*. Five times a day if possible."

Flirtation was the point of it. Anything to subvert – anything to make the rest of us reconsider the world and the ways in which we thought we had it figured.

We walked past the boardwalk and the boats, up the road and then a stone path to the house of a couple of Parisian friends that was discreetly lodged behind a small rock garden. There we drank, told stories, and Highway took his place at the piano again and encouraged everyone to sing – songs we knew, songs we were commanded to improvise, songs in round robin.

Okay, said Highway – *en français* – you'll know this one. Then he threw his head back with an impish grin, the white scarf falling towards the floor, and cajoled his French hosts into singing along to a rendition of *La Marseillaise* that he was playing to a samba beat. And it was then – seeing his alarmed French hosts sing their usually martial anthem so stiff and uncomfortably, unsure what to make of their friend's tropical, hip-swinging version of their national anthem – just when I thought I'd lost hope, that I realized I'd found Weesageechak. *Yes, I knew the man.* That was him at the piano, such a long way from The Pas. I watched keenly, the French nervously singing as Highway did his best to suppress his own laughter. He played on. We were all in his thrall.

"What is Weesageechak for you?" I asked as we left.

"Oh, man. Where do I start?" said Highway. "Ultimately, I'm on a lifelong quest. My work is fundamentally a comparative study of the three mythologies that I believe have come closest to informing Canadian society: Christian mythology, Classical mythology, and aboriginal mythology. In order to understand the Trickster fully, you must keep in mind the fundamentals of all these three mythologies, and the first thing that must be remembered is that the Christian mythology is a monotheistic system, the Classical mythology is a polytheistic one, and the aboriginal one a pantheistic system – which means that God is in everything."

"Do you believe Christians to have a Trickster figure of any kind?"

"Trickster is a mediator between divinity and man," said Highway. "He's half-man and half-God, or half-animal in many cases – so, yes, Jesus Christ, I would say."

"He is subversive in the way that Trickster is?"

"He upset the Jews, didn't he? And the Pharisees were certainly upset with him."

If you involve Him, then you will not enjoy the story, Bird said. *You will be killing the story if you do that.*

"You have to admit that he left a bit of a mess behind," said Highway, grinning widely.

Perhaps there is room for two shamans if they are both the same one, I thought.

"In Christian mythology, everything works according to the structure of that one-God system. The God is male, and male only. The collective subconscious of the society that subscribes to it is basically male, and the hero figure that stands between the society and its God is male – his name is Jesus Christ – is half-*man* and half-god and that's it. He's male too. The idea of having a woman for a female superhero figure is unthinkable.

"In polytheism, there are many gods and goddesses, as well as any number of heroes who are half-God and half-human. They are the products of sexual unions between Gods and of both genders. Zeus, the Father Sky, was forever coming down to Earth to ravish young women, or young boys for that matter, and out of these unions came the heroic figures. They were not all men, but in the collective imagination of these two societies, God was given the form of a human. But in the *pantheistic* mythology, God was never made flesh. Insofar as I know, no aboriginal language in North America has gender to begin with. There is no 'he' or 'she,' no 'her' or 'him,' no *le*, no *la*, no *der*, no *die*. God is neither male nor female, or is both simultaneously. There's no man or woman high up in the sky or deep in the Earth. There's just an *energy* that informs the movement of the spheres and all the rest of it, and there is no superhero who stands at the centre of the Dream World and its collective subconscious. There's only this clownish figure who is like a bolt of electricity – like a poke in the bum – that is basically, first and foremost, hysterically funny. And that's Trickster, who is one-third God, one-third human, and one-third animal, and at any given point in time can be male or female, because he's this endlessly shape-shifting form of energy that is a part of the Dream World, humanity, and Nature."

"And is he represented in art this way?"

"Norval Morrisseau was really the first artist to try to give Trickster physical form. He was the first to anthropomorphize these energies. That was a huge revolutionary step, back in 1962. The same thing happened about twenty years later in literature, with the birth of native theatre in the early 1980s, when, for the first time, you could see the Trickster on stage, and then in novels, as a woman or as a man.

"The second way in which these three systems are different is that in only one of them is eviction from the Garden essential to the story. Only in the Christian mythology does the one God, the male God, give the planet to mankind to celebrate, and to appreciate – and then take it away. God exiles humanity from the Garden because a woman chose to talk to a snake. In the other two mythologies, there is no such narrative. The Greeks were never banished from Arcadia, and there is no such story in aboriginal mythology either. *This is it.* We are still in the Garden, and we are still free to worship trees, water – or talk to snakes, for that matter. So when the Christians arrived up in northern Manitoba at the end of the nineteenth century – in my great-grandparents' generation – monotheism met pantheism, and basically what happened is that God as man met God as woman."

"So, in Greek terms, Gabriel, who is at times the Trickster figure in your novel *Kiss of the Fur Queen*, is there to reintroduce *eros* into the guilty Christian Garden?"

"Yes," said Highway. "Even in the Greek polytheistic system, it was perfectly okay for a male god to make love to a young man, because it was thought of as an act of pleasure –"

"But Champion struggles with the idea – more than Gabriel does, anyway. Why is that?"

"Because at the time, I struggled with it, and I'm still coming to terms with it now, but I refuse to believe that what I went through at residential school, the sexual exploitation that we all went through, was necessarily abuse. I was eleven years old, or thereabouts, and at the age of eleven, a person's sexuality is coming to life, and it's a wonderful thing. That feeling of pure physical pleasure is just so fantastic – and what on earth is wrong with that? It's just so *natural*. I had a great time. If it's anybody's problem, it was the problem of the Church, because it refused to recognize the act of homosexual love. At the risk of sounding just a tiny bit bitter and angry, in one system, our existence on planet Earth is a curse from an angry male God. In the other two systems, our existence here on planet Earth is a *gift*."

There is a moment, in the novel, when young Gabriel becomes enraged on behalf of a group of young aboriginal children he tutors, at least one of whom has been abused. Learning as much, Gabriel stumbles into "a vortex screaming with monsters." Mere homosexuality, I knew, was to be distinguished from paedophilia, but I suspected that Highway knew this and so I forewent any objection and chose instead to accept the Trickster-ish lesson that he was giving me. Eroticism need not always be equated with the Oblates' dour shame.

"To this day," he continued, "I've always wondered about the Christian God, who is also the Judaic God, and who is also the Islamic God. The God of the 'three great monotheisms,' as they're called. I mean, where is this guy's wife? How come he doesn't have a girlfriend? Greek mythology is just rife with marital unions and sexual unions. There were all these gods and goddesses of pleasure whose purpose was to engage in physical pleasure – in sex – the very soil itself was an act of pleasure. It was a garden to be celebrated. Pantheism has a similar idea, but when the monotheistic God comes into the picture, he rapes the living daylight out of the goddess, so to speak. That's the story I've been trying to tell."

Highway stopped at a small park on the far side of the quay, with a bench that overlooked the night water.

"In my play *Rose*, the conflict between the concept of male divinity and female divinity comes to a climax, and God – the male God

– begins to die and the female Goddess comes back to life. And that's what my whole life work is about. To put it in the native terms, I am a two-spirited person. I am a man with the soul of a woman, and in the Circle such people were magic people. We were the artists. We were the visionaries. We were the shamans, and ours was a sacred place in that Circle – whereas here, there is no place for us. We're *sick*. According to the vertical lines of this hierarchical, monotheistic system, the men who raped my friends were *normal*, and healthy – whereas somebody like myself, somebody who loves men and women, is a sick pervert who should be destroyed. And I just don't see that. It's so wrong."

"Do you miss your brother at all?" I asked.

"No," said Highway. "The philosophy we have about death means that in the Myth World you don't ever really go away. Where I come from, the living was also tough. Illness came upon us, people died, and the infant mortality rate was extremely high – but in the Garden even *death* was a natural occurrence."

"As it is in monotheism –"

"Except that in the Christian mythology there is a heaven and there is a hell. Heaven is up there and hell down there, just as there is a male up there, a female down below, and the rest of Nature is around us here. It's a vertically linear system. But in the pantheistic mythology, there is no God up there and Nature down here. It's not a *line*, it's a *Circle*, and we all exist within that Circle. I think of it as a bargaining table where we all have a voice at the meeting – men, women, God, trees, rocks, birds, sunlight, sound, water, the earth – even Death has a place at that table. Everything is equal, and when you die, your soul does not go to heaven or to hell. It stays in the Circle. It's a natural rhythm, and death is a part of our lives. Death is not a tragedy at all."

Highway tossed his white scarf over his shoulder.

"Oh, how do I explain it? I look in the mirror sometimes and I see my mother. I see this hysterically funny and wonderful woman who died four years ago. And I see her eyes staring back at me. And my brother, he's still here with me too. He's a part of my flesh and blood. I have his eyes, apparently, and I have his lips. I have his hands." Highway lifted his hands up in the air in front of him and gazed at them.

"Rene had hands like this, and my life is twice as exciting because I live not just for me but for him."

"So," I said, "in your Cree view, we're still living in the Garden."

"*Yes*. Look at Canada. Is it not a garden? It's the most spectacularly beautiful garden on the face of the Earth, for heaven's sakes, but at that point in time when monotheism met pantheism, we were evicted from it. Nature died, trees ceased to have a soul, water ceased to have a soul, the rocks and sunlight ceased to have a soul. When we lived up north in that Garden of Eden, I would see my mom walk through that forest and her feet hardly touched the ground. When she cooked over that open fire, with all the elements of nature that she had gathered around her – the fish from the lake, the ptarmigans from the forest, the ducks, the geese, the endless roots and berries, and all these gorgeous, gorgeous foods that we got from the land – she looked so graceful and *beautiful*. But as soon as you removed my mother from that environment and put her into a city like Winnipeg, or Thompson or The Pas, there was a pathetic aspect to her existence that I hated looking at. It was like watching a muskrat or a beaver let loose on Yonge Street."

✧ ✧ ✧

THE CITIES OF the south, in the fiction of a host of native writers, are crucibles of calamity for aboriginals. The existence that Tomson Highway envisioned as pathetic for his mother and fatal for his roll call of raped and murdered women, is the same nightmare of etiolation that drove Alexie to declare that it was "better to kill yourself out on the land than on some dirty back street somewhere." In *Porcupines and China Dolls*, Alexie's Gwich'in consume themselves as ulcers do the stomach by a situation in which their families, too, were actors. Highway's cast lashes out against the world in ironic celebration but still their rage has no direction. What Joseph Boyden, the author of *Three Day Road*, a novel of two Cree snipers and their experiences in the First World War, does is pin these native demons to the points of a compass. In his first book, the collection of stories *Born With a Tooth*, the East is "Labour," the West "Running," the North "Home," and the South "Ruin," and the stories are segregated accordingly. There is, in Boyden's work, always this double vision – the world as it is, twice over. The Sikh's Bloor Street *and* the invisible native map are the two that he lives by.

Boyden has Ojibway and Nipmic ties, though he is careful not to describe himself as native. He is a proud member of the Métis Nation, and as a younger man he worked in Northern Ontario on reservations in Moose Factory, Fort Albany, Attawapiskat, and Kashechewan. In these places, and at home, he became privy to the stories of a culture that have absorbed him ever since. I met Boyden in Toronto, on his way to Moosonee, where he is fond of hunting with his son. I was still concerned with identifying the traits of native storytelling that have persisted in the novel, though I was becoming uncomfortable with this pursuit. Stories, after all, belong to no one. They are the attributes, not the property of a place, to my mind belonging to the full panoply of peoples that live in or are merely concerned about a culture. When, for his second film, the Iglulingmiut director Zacharias Kunuk decided to tell the story of Knud Rasmussen, it was a good thing. He was recognizing the story of the Dane as a part of his own heritage, just as Bringhurst was doing with the Haida stories. Neither trespassed. Stories exist outside of us and we serve them, was one of the points that Bringhurst made. This is not a mystical idea, or even a scientific one.

Rupert Sheldrake is an English philosopher and scientist. He was busy, the day I sat with him in his North London study, contemplating the weight of the human gaze for his book *The Sense of Being Stared At*. (We think we know someone is watching us because we can *feel* the stare, was his idea.) He is best known for his theory of "morphic resonance," in which he proposes a "living, developing universe with its own inherent memory." It was his way of suggesting that information exists outside of our bodies, so that it made sense, for instance, that the discovery of oxygen was made at roughly the same time at various points across the globe. An idea, once thought, is more easily thought again. In a crass way, we recognize this. The screenwriter or inventor who comes up with an idea is often afraid that someone else will get to it first. Not without reason. Ideas – stories – are in the air. What these cautious inventors and artists are acknowledging is that ideas are *out there*, waiting to be "discovered" – like the log that became a bench in the forest I paused in with Bringhurst. A part of the "psycho-geography" of a place is that stories, once told, are more easily repeated, and that we step into these stories when we move into a place.

Stories, on top of the heap.

An incident that Boyden uses in the section of *Born With a Tooth* called "South" shows the surprising life that stories can have before a novelist gives them written form.

In Boyden's story "Painted Tongue," an aboriginal wanders about the city of Toronto and reads the landscape as a native would. He happens across a gay bashing in the story, and eyes the unfolding events like a crouching hunter. The beaten man's assailants flee, and Painted Tongue takes him in his arms and comforts him while he dies.

Boyden himself had lived through something similar, witnessing a murder on the streets of New Orleans and rushing to the dying man's aid. As expected, the experience was profound, enough so that he wrote about it in *Born With a Tooth* and later in *Three Day Road*.

Or, at least, that's what I'd assumed was the sequence of events. Here, for the record, is how the scene appeared in "Painted Tongue":

Motherfuckers! the wounded man screamed.

He's running. Grab the bitch!

A naked man came dashing from the trees towards Painted Tongue with three men close behind him. He was streaked red in the moonlight and ran hard, but with a limp. Painted Tongue dropped quickly into the shadow of a bush without the man's seeing him and held himself rigid as the other men swooped by.

They quickly caught up to the wounded one and tackled him. They took turns kicking his head and groin and stomach with their boots. Two had shaved heads and the other wore his hair long like Painted Tongue. They chanted, Dirty faggot, cocksucking faggot, through their clenched teeth. Painted Tongue tried again, but his warrior song would not come. The long-haired one pulled out a knife.

Don't. Please don't, the man on the ground said, curled up and holding himself. He was close enough to Painted Tongue that Painted Tongue could taste the copper tang of fear in his own mouth. The long-haired one dropped down on his knees with both hands held above his head.

Do it, one of the standing men hissed.

Stick him. Fuck him, the other man said.

Die, bitch, the long-hair said after a few seconds, then swung down hard. The bleeding man howled. Painted Tongue shivered as the three men ran into the darkness.

Painted Tongue stood up after a long while. He slowly walked up to the body on the ground, bent over him and peered down. The man blinked at Painted Tongue and Painted Tongue jumped back quickly. The man's chest was gurgling and his lips opened just a little. Then his chest stopped moving. Painted Tongue's legs told him to run away as fast as he could, but instead he hummed a death chant for the man slowly and quietly. Your last moments were spent in fear, he hummed, but now you are peaceful and sink into the waters of sleep. Your last moments were spent in fear and I could not help you, but now all is peaceful as you slip into sleep.

Painted Tongue thought he could see his own face for a second, reflected in the man's open eyes, but knew that wasn't possible. He realized as he ran back towards downtown that the man's last sight had been of an Indian standing over him and humming, looking down like a death angel, an Indian with a hook nose and black hair almost long enough that it tickled the man's face.

Boyden, I assumed, had lived the scene and then written it. Not so. It turned out he had *written* the story and *then* had the experience – unless you consider that stories exist outside of us, have their own morphic resonance not just in memory, and that Boyden had lived the moment long before he put pen to paper and wrote his story "Painted Tongue."

Boyden concurred. He had witnessed a street killing after a great night in New Orleans, Louisiana, where he had a job teaching, he said.

"I was driving home with my wife," said Boyden. "It had been this lovely day at Jazz Fest, with lots of music and friends. It was about nine-thirty at night and we were driving down a dark four-lane street. In front of us we saw a man in our lane and so we slowed down and pulled right up to him. It was dark outside and so we didn't see much. He was standing over another man and we thought that he was helping him get up, but I quickly saw that the man below him was covered in blood. The guy that's on top looks up at my wife and me, and he drags the man out of our lane and into the next one. We pulled up beside him and rolled our windows down – it was a warm, nice night – and then I see that this young guy has a gun in his hand and so I shout to my wife, '*Drive! Drive! Drive!*' not wanting to be shot. And the young guy on top looks up at me when I say that, and then –"

Boyden faltered. It doesn't actually happen very often, so it's obvious when a story is being told for the first time. The emotional candour that Alexie had to work hard to capture was in high relief. It is a special experience to listen at moments such as this.

"And then," said Boyden, "very quickly, as we pulled away, I watched him shoot the other guy in the head and then run away. So I told my wife to pull over because I wanted to help this guy. I've since been told that it was a very foolish thing to do, but I jumped out of the car and I ran to this man lying on the street. He was still very much alive, and moaning. I kneeled down and talked to the man and told him it was going to be okay, to try to breathe, and that help was coming, and I watched, over the next few minutes, as he died in my hands."

I asked, "Did you actually believe that everything was going to be okay?"

"I knew when I saw him lying there that he wasn't going to make it," Boyden said. "There was a lot of blood coming out of him. He had been shot in the chest and then the guy shot him in the cheek. I think that he was aiming for his temple but that in the panic of the moment, as I was shouting, he missed. I knew that he was going to die but I tried to comfort him. I held his head, and rubbed his arm, and he responded. He was moaning and I think fearful that I was the killer come to finish him off. I talked to him and told him, 'You're going to be okay,' knowing that he wasn't, and as I leaned down to him I saw the light fading from his eyes and said to him, 'You're going to a better place,' and that he didn't have to die alone. I think that – I *hope*, anyways, that the one small good thing that came out of that moment is that I did comfort him for a little bit."

"It was a shock to learn that the incident had occurred *after* you wrote the story."

"It did, yes."

"Do you think, at some level, that it was easier to act because, effectively, you had already written the scene?"

"Unconsciously," said Boyden, "I must have realized that Painted Tongue did the exact same thing in the story that I had written many years prior. But, you know, thinking about it at this moment, one of the places where that story came from was this internalized part of me. My father was a doctor in World War Two, on the front lines in Italy. He was the British Empire's most highly decorated medical officer. King George told him that, as he pinned the medal of the Distinguished Service Order to his breast, and so I've always grown up with these different myths swirling around my head, one of them belonging to my native uncle, and the other to my father – the medic – who was very Irish Catholic. It's what he did on a constant basis in World War Two on the front lines of Italy and now I'm thinking that what I was doing was something very, very Freudian – that I was wanting to be my father for a moment. When I acted, when I ran out of the car instead of driving away very quickly, I was acting on what I thought at the time was instinct. But maybe it was a little bit more than that. Maybe I was trying to relive the legends, myths, and oral stories that had been told to me all my life."

"Can you tell me about the idea of the Circle in native culture?" I asked.

"I'm one of eleven children," said Boyden. "My dad was very traditional, so that growing up we all sat around the dinner table and talked about our day. But this sitting in the Circle was as much Irish to me as it was Ojibway. We came together, face to face, and laughed and told stories and fought every day. And when my dad passed away, I was eight, his seat was suddenly empty and there was no one who could fill that chair – and so it stayed empty. But my father was still there among us. And to me, this is the strange hybrid of Irish and Ojibway, the Catholic and the traditional –"

"Or really of any culture where family and story are important," I said.

"Well, I'll tell you another story of the Circle," said Boyden. "When I wrote the first draft of *Three Day Road*, I told the story in a linear, chronological way. It began with two young Cree canoeing, going through a fire, joining the army, and eventually going overseas – and it was clear to me that it wasn't working. Something was missing. Basically, I was telling a native story in a Western way. I was applying the form of one worldview onto the content of another.

And so I bent the story like a hoop. I began it near the end, and made my way back, *full circle*. And it works far better now, in my opinion."

The novel, making new friends, puts them to decent use. In the hands of aboriginals it once helped oppress, it has offered the values of the Myth World new life.

◇　◇　◇

"FOR ME," said Lee Maracle, the Stó:lo novelist, short-story writer, and polemicist who was writer-in-residence at First Nations House when we spoke, "the novel is anything and everything that you want to make it."

Maracle's novel *Ravensong* has at its core the memory of the flu epidemic that ravaged the Sailish communities of the Pacific Northwest Coast during the 1950s.

"We believe," said Maracle, "that stories – the *sacred* stories, for want of a better word – are born in the space where the river meets the bank. There's a little silver eddy there, where the sun hits, and that's where the story creators live. The stories that begin everything are the salmon stories and the salmon rest in that eddy."

"And do you think it matters *how* aboriginal writers tell their stories?" I asked.

"I believe," said Maracle, "that we have come closer to understanding the Ojibway and the Cree saying that there are an infinite number of pathways to the centre of the Circle. What we are taught is that there is a Circle at the top of a kind of hourglass. Through discussion, the Circle becomes a human Circle, and we are fed everything. The threads that we've swallowed go in towards the centre, and so we are taken on a spiralling journey through all the layers of our existence until we come to a moment of peace, and recognition, and then we spiral back out to meet the world. A number of these threads enter our lives, but we don't know what's at the centre of the Circle – which is the direction that we want to be travelling in – until we try to spin that tornado and 'story up' whatever it is that we must come to terms with. And we believe not just that we *need* to 'story life up,' but that we cannot *not* do this. If we fail to 'story up,' then we'll become sick. So we take the story-lines that we inherit, and create myths from them."

I described to Maracle the solitary figure of Louis Bird sitting before his sparse audience at First Nations House, the microphone pointed at him like a gun. I found it heartbreaking, I said, to step out of one almost expunged world into another that has pretty well obliterated it from view.

"Novels – or at least a really *good* novel – will address that invisibility and give you a window into what is absent in your neigh-

WHERE I LIVE

bourhood, and I would hope that by taking the novel's storytelling structures and braiding them with our own, that the door would open to new writers to pursue either way of telling a story." And then Maracle spoke tenderly, as a mother might have done. "You see, we've always been on that Circle – all of us – and the 'unknown' at the centre of it is the question, 'How are we all going to live together?'"

5

House and Garden

Alas, alas, that great city wherein were made rich all that had ships in the sea, by reason of her costliness! For in one hour is she made desolate.

REVELATION 18.19

The Carnegie Community Centre occupies the corner of Hastings and Main on the Downtown East Side, a handsome turn-of-the-century stone edifice resembling a bank. It began its existence, in 1903, as Vancouver's first public library. Today the centre offers a safe, alcohol- and drug-free environment to Vancouver's down and out. On the day I went there to meet Nancy Lee, the author of *Dead Girls*, it was pleasantly sunny and some homeless people and addicts had gathered outside for a smoke and a bit of talk. Nearby, a Chinese man was selling a small envelope of something illegal before riding off on his bicycle, coriander and broccoli wrapped in newspaper and tied to the rack behind his seat. A man whistled as he pushed his grocery cart of salvage up the street. In a nearby alley, a stumbling couple passed a joint between them, in full view of police in a cruiser waiting for some more enticing misdemeanour to be committed. These were the invisible people of a forgotten black hole of a district, marginalized men and women who would eventually move on to some other part of town and be marginalized another time, once gentrification and the city's avaricious real estate market decided that value could be found in dilapidated tenements that had once been handsome streets, warehouses, shops, and hotels. The Balmoral, The Patricia, The Empress. In Vancouver, the wheel of prosperity turns relentlessly. Ten *million* dollars for a condo penthouse with leather-padded ceilings and thermal windows separating tenants from nature, still menacing, though now reduced to being the investor and realtor's commodity.

"Because Vancouver is a port city and a final destination for so many people who come here and then find it hard to settle," said Lee, "there is a transience to this city. People believe they can start something new here. The city is constantly growing, and there is a manic energy spun out of the constant activity of moving to a better place. Those who are successful are continually moving into newer, bigger, and nicer houses, and those who spiral in the opposite direction are constantly being shunted from rooming house to rooming house and then trying to get off the street."

Today, the Carnegie Centre's small library boasts a large number of Chinese paperbacks for those who left China to come to the Gold Mountain. Its collection is a testament to the culturally specific nature of immigration here, and to the fact of a mountain being broad at its base, and accommodating few on its pinnacle. The cafeteria was full on the day I visited with Lee. At the simple wooden table next to ours, a woman was playing cards with a Chinese man with a tired face and letting out long, ululating yelps at regular intervals. It seemed a suitable place for us to talk as I was interested in the way real life finds its way into novelists' work, and the centre was full of what writers call material. The woman was obviously disturbed but garnered no special attention as she was the normal one and I, the oddity. I was from the world of the accountable. Friends or family would know if I went missing and what to do about it if I did. But in Vancouver, and on these streets in particular, men and women can disappear quite easily. Many more than society cares to notice still do. This, even after Robert "Willy" Pickton was charged in May 2004 with the first seven of twenty-six counts of murder, dismemberment, and burial, on his pig farm, of more than sixty women who had disappeared from Vancouver's East Side over a period of two decades. Reports of the missing appeared regularly, and Pickton was known to police from at least 1997, but no charges were laid until DNA evidence was found on the farm in 2002. The suspicion was that the police – and Vancouver's wealthier constituents – simply had not cared enough, a situation that led to a national feeling of revulsion and embarrassment.

From Nancy Lee's "Dead Girls":

> The body count is at twenty-three. A female broadcaster, whose hair has turned from dark auburn to medium blond in the days you've been watching, announces that skeletons have been found in sets of twos, threes, and fours, an elaborate corpse orgy orchestrated by the accused. Hip against hip, skull upon skull, fingers entwined, a morbid collage. She warns that the following scenes may be difficult to watch, that parents should ask their children to leave the room. A live camera pans through a backyard with cedar fencing, past a white plastic patio set and a painted picnic table to a huge rectangular dirt pit, its muddy sides reinforced with wood planks; small orange flags dot its surface. To you it looks like the beginnings of an in-ground swimming pool. The camera moves in closer. Protruding here and there beside the orange flags, pale slivers and rounds, the bones of the unexhumed. Drowning hands. Then there are the victim photos – police record mug shots, thin, angry girls. The parents of a recently identified victim weep openly on the screen. The mother is dark-skinned, maybe Malaysian or Filipino; the father wears a baseball cap. They bow their heads, hold up a photo of their

daughter at her high school graduation and repeat over and over that she wasn't a prostitute, that the police have confused the facts, that she was a good girl. Her face is homely beneath the tasselled cap, a smatter of acne across her brown forehead; she's a little on the plump side; her lipstick is pink, not scarlet. This is how they want their daughter remembered, they say, as they push the photograph towards the camera. You wonder if you would do it differently.

"The stories in *Dead Girls* are very tied to the city," said Lee, an articulate woman with a languorous manner and a snappy intelligence. Her parents, of Chinese and Indian descent, moved to Vancouver from Cardiff, in Wales, when she was a child. Lee was in command – smart in that brash, West Coast way. At writers' festivals, I'd seen her control her audience with the confidence and aplomb of an afternoon talk-show host. "The woman's daughter is a prostitute and a drug addict. Although I did include many details of Vancouver, I didn't want to be in the situation of readers thinking, 'I know that place.'"

They would.

With its disturbing array of social problems played out brazenly on the streets, Vancouver's Downtown East Side is one of the most squalid and degenerate city districts in the country, but the peculiarity of the city's civic "at-large" system is that no single politician needs to stand up and take the rap for it.

Some days, you'd swear the good citizens of Vancouver like their bit of Bosch, because the squalor of the East Side feels oddly necessary to this hedonistic West Coast city, just as a vision of hell was to the Dutch painter's famous allegory, the *Garden of Earthly Delights*. Here, the possibility of lascivious consumption is enough to put puritanical warnings in the near regions of the most agnostic minds. Paradise requires the possibility of its opposite, and in Vancouver both are on permanent display. In *Dead Girls*, the title story of Nancy Lee's collection, a well-to-do mother is obsessed with following a news story about a serial killer who has been arrested in Vancouver, as she fears her own daughter may be one of his victims. Desperately, she searches for her runaway daughter. In so doing, she discovers the hidden hell of Vancouver's more sordid spaces.

"When I set out to write that story," Lee said, "there had been a series of garage robberies in one of the city's most affluent neighbourhoods. Within a week of the crimes, a ten-thousand-dollar reward was posted for the capture of the perpetrators. At the same time, there had been reports of missing women, but the mainstream media weren't investigating them. I knew from my research that this was likely the work of a serial killer, but all these women had gone missing and no one was acknowledging it."

The stories that inhabit the middle space between the world as it is and as it ends up being portrayed by the writer provide territories with their psycho-geography and render cities, which might have been thought of as generic places, specific. This is the gift of the space Lee Maracle described as "the silver eddy where the sun hits" between the river and the bank. The stories that dwell in it construct a city that is as true and important to the imagination of the people who live in it as its grid of streets is to the physical space. The ways in which writers are able to channel these stories explain why, from time to time, a writer appears to have not just caught the *Zeitgeist* but actually to have *anticipated* the news.

"The climactic moment in *Dead Girls* occurs when the mother comes to the Downtown East Side because of a phone call she traces back to a phone booth there," said Lee. "She stumbles into an alley and catches a girl who resembles her daughter giving a john a blowjob. The question of whether or not it *is* her daughter remains unanswered, but nevertheless it's the moment at which the mother feels some peace. If it *is* her daughter, even though she's engaged in this lifestyle, at least she is still alive. If it is not her daughter, the mother is still able to feel empathy and a connection for all girls who find themselves in that situation. For me, that was the turning point that allowed me into the story."

"What with Vancouver's long history of runaways and the missing," I asked, "do you ever wonder if you are conveying ideas that are already in the air?"

"I don't know if ideas so much as questions hang about," said Lee. "For me, everything starts with a question and the answers are never simple. When girls who are on the fringes of society go missing, it's very easy to dismiss them as being prostitutes and drug addicts. But if the city is one living, breathing unit, then we cannot separate ourselves from events that play out in it the way we do when we watch the news by thinking, 'Oh, this is happening to *those* people.' If you do, it creates this bizarre logic that says should you engage in a certain kind of behaviour then you are disposable and should something happen to you, it's your own fault. This is a symptom of something that is terribly wrong in the city as a whole – and not just in one *part* of society. What the news made me wonder was that if these girls *were* missing – because there was

no one saying for sure that they were – then who was missing *them*? That question provided the beginning of the story, and then it grew into the larger question, which was, 'If this is happening in our city, then what do these events say about the rest of us?'"

✧   ✦   ✧

THE PSYCHO-GEOGRAPHY of Vancouver as a terrain of the missing is the suggestion of a lush landscape in which a valley on the far side of a mountain might as well lie at ten times the distance and the consequence of a pace of development that is rapid and ruthless. In Vancouver, nature is beguiling; the land seems habitable in a way that it explicitly is *not* in so many parts of the country. In Vancouver, you can sleep in the forest overnight and not be killed by the cold or bitten to the point of insanity by mosquitoes and black flies. You will probably get very wet – and you may well be assaulted, abducted, or even murdered – but you will not, as the Nova Scotian poet Alden Nowlan wrote of generally inhospitable Canada, "die simply from being outside." Nature, in Canada, is no longer the intimidating wilderness that prompted Margaret Atwood to deduce in *Survival*, her 1970s guide to Canadian literature, that Canadians saw themselves as victims.

Atwood's celebrated text epitomized Canada's Age of Invention. The task of envisioning the country and wishing it into existence, in the 1970s, had not yet been completed, so that the psychological contest of the time was, to a certain extent, with the ogre to the South, though with the land most of all. But in the twenty-first century, Canadians have spread out from the towns Northrop Frye saw as the fount of a "garrison mentality" and are in the uneasy position of being occupiers. Canadians have shot the land and killed it, as Taamali, the prospector Alfred Tremblay, did, according to Inuit oral history, in Igloolik in 1913.

We have done so not with bullets but with thermal windows, Gore-Tex, and air conditioning, etc. And yet the grandeur of the land remains mythic and if in the face of it we do not regard ourselves as victims any more, we still feel something akin to *aidos* – the mix of humility and awe, often translated as "shame," that Ancient Greeks felt in the face of something great. Even as we behave like Robert Bringhurst's conquistadors, even as we pretend that the power and the resources are all ours, there is the nagging and deep-seated suspicion that title to the *moral* ground evades us. Nature is still daunting, but the anxiety that we feel is of a different character. As custodians, we suspect that ours has been a failing grade, and so we feel guilty – and what is a guilty conscience but the fear of being found out at heaven's gate? The puritanical discomfort that Vancouver induces is the trick of this fear at its most extreme – the dread that God exists in Nature and has a temper, will remember our slights. Someday, out on an enjoyable stroll, Nature will come at us like Todd Bertuzzi with a sucker punch – and it will be *our fault*, because we have been living too well.

Vancouver, this country's gleaming and most brazenly artificial metropolis, is where this anxiety about the land is at its strongest. It is the reason that so much of our unsettling literature comes from there. Vancouver is Douglas Coupland's "City of Glass," a city where Paradise has been paved over not just for a parking lot, but also for a tower of condominiums topped by that penthouse with the ten-million-dollar view that will be yours only for the short time it takes for someone else to erect a taller high rise between your new condo and the sea. Vancouver is the Canadian city that, more than any other, suspects (but does not admit) that it has bullied Nature rather than be pushed around by her, rudely irrupting its way into the Garden so that houses slide off hills as a consequence. The ungodly pursuit of pleasure means that here, "survival" *is* still the issue. In the skewed consciousness that comes from living where you were not invited, a Golden Spruce tree becomes an icon and is sacrificed by one who should protect it, and the woman who dares to chop down a city tree that blocks her remunerative vista is repudiated as quickly and with as much wrath as serial killers, Hells Angels, or blithe cops appear to be.

At the root of a plethora of Vancouver stories is the sense of having recently arrived in houses or apartment buildings that exude the feeling of having been previously occupied, or of the discovery of objects that needed to be lost before they could be found. The sense of culpability is enormous. The fear is that we are undeserving and often incapable tenants. Nature, no matter how inviting, does not feel quite like home here – or at least not like a home without liens.

✧ ✧ ✧

What thou seest, write in a book. – Revelation 1.11

IN THE VANCOUVER writer Timothy Taylor's first novel, *Stanley Park*, the tension between the new city and the natural environment is extreme, one that finds its nexus in the beautiful wooded reserve of the book's title. Stanley Park is a place of dichotomous character.

Its tall firs elegantly reach skyward and provide shelter for those walking or, today more likely, running in their shade. Their straight trunks offer a counterpoint to the slopes and jagged steps of the Rocky Mountains, and the pan of the ocean around Kitsilano and English Bay. The Park is Eden-like, the novel's original sin the murder that was committed, in 1947, of two children locally remembered as "the Babes in the Wood." The murders were never solved, and in the novel, some fifty years afterwards, Taylor's maverick academic, "The Professor," is enticed by the case. He enlists the help of Caruso, one of a number of homeless who have found room available in the arbour of Stanley Park. But the curiosity is not theirs alone. The journalists of *Stanley Park* also cannot let it rest. The murder is a story that will not go away because it has provided a narrative shape to the city's fears.

From Timothy Taylor's *Stanley Park*:

An accepted theme had developed in the small body of Babes in the Wood literature. The articles were inevitably printed in October, the anniversary month, and most of these cast the murder as an at-once tragic and inaugural event in the city's history. For Vancouver, the first of the self-inflicted wounds North Americans would come to associate with late-twentieth-century urban life. Murder, burglary, arson, car-jacking, child abduction, rape, stalking, the drive-by and the home invasion . . . all these would follow. But the murder of those two children ushered this unsettling aspect of modernity onto the stage of Canada's third city, quiet at that time in its West Coast rain forest. Gently dozing in the mists that rolled in off the as-yet toxin-free and salmon-filled ocean. And thinking of it each year, or more accurately every ten years or so, the press in Vancouver would disinter the tale. The journalists would open their articles sounding as perplexed as they had been the first time. They would run over the tragic facts, grafting on the pale analysis of sociologists or psychologists or members of the still-stymied Vancouver City Police Unsolved Crime Unit. And they would finish as perplexed as they began, as perplexed as they would be for Octobers stretching into the future. Flipping from article to article, Jeremy was forced to consider a calendar of civic passage, guilt and confusion, tracing itself up through the decades.

"The Babes in the Wood were a couple of kids believed to be six or seven years old when they were killed. The bodies were found in 1953 by Public Works staff who were removing leaves in the forest not far from here," said Taylor, a smart, neat man in his early forties who earned his MBA, worked in a bank, and trained with the Navy before he turned to writing. The man had a vestigial tidiness, would look good in a suit. That, and the office in the old Dominion Building, constructed in 1910 and for one year the tallest in the British Empire, idiosyncratic rooms today, give Taylor a certain Raymond Chandler air.

Taylor and I were sitting on the bough of one of Stanley Park's fallen trees, in a glade off the beaten path that I would have been hard put to find a second time. We'd met the previous day at the Hastings Park Track, where Taylor coached me in his pastime of betting on horses in the company of a few of his West Coast writing pals – Steven Galloway and Lee Henderson among them. This was Taylor's third place, away from his home and office, and one that had become the setting of one of his tidiest pieces of fiction, the title story of his collection *Silent Cruise*. That story recounts the death of a horse put down after an accident on the track, shot behind a raised blanket so that spectators cannot witness the scene, though Taylor's real subject is the numbers game that handicappers, bettors, and racketeers play, and the instinctual factors exemplified by the track that are not so easily explained. Writers of detective fiction have always had an extremely practical, forensic attitude to place, and although Taylor is not wholly one of these, his prose has a streak of the craft and a further, sometimes foreboding quality. His characters are often at the behest of forces they cannot identify or therefore understand. A lot of his fiction is imbued with the feeling that machinations beyond our immediate control affect us – and that these can be sensed on occasion. These intimations are detections of the stories occupying that middle space. Though we may not always know its origin, we can some-times point in a story's direction – just as, sitting with Taylor in Stanley Park, the sound of passing traffic was audible though its source was not exact. In the forest, noises disguise themselves and become a part of its fabric. We know the thing happened, but *where*?

"Is the spot where the Babes were found marked in any way?" I asked.

"No," said Taylor, "and that fact was important to me. I had always imagined there was some kind of event, tragic in nature, that was rooted here, perhaps the killing or the witness of a killing – it was inarticulate at that point. I imagined that the story of the Babes in the Wood existed, but also that I had made it up. It was only later that I realized that here was a true story and that it hovered under the surface of the lore of Stanley Park. It was tragic, unsolved, and not well known, though it was widely disseminated in a faint, distant way. It had wormed its way into the consciousness of one of my characters, and it was only upon doing further research that I real-ized I was dealing with a genuine event, at which point it felt impos-sible to extricate the book from that storyline. So I left it in and the burden fell on me to be factual about it."

"It's as if there's a sort of Braille that lifts itself out of the world once the kernel of an idea has made itself known to a writer," I said, "and once that happens almost everything that is seen or heard is interpreted in terms of that idea."

"But things grow around those kernels in different ways," said Taylor. "If the kernel is a piece of fact like the one I described, then you begin setting your constellation of characters in a manner that they become posited in terms of that fact. With most writers, an extraordinary collision of fact and fantasy occurs on the page, and though I felt an obligation to Stanley Park in terms of its topography, there was obviously some flexibility there. Where there is little flexibility is in the fact that Stanley Park has a daytime and a nighttime personality. Just as at night, the park is a place of hiding and no small amount of danger, and in the daytime, it is a place of relaxation, recreation, and of feeling safely close to the wilderness – so too is Stanley Park the flipside of the city itself. Vancouver is all shining towers and polish and postmodern gleam, and Stanley Park is this little piece of wilderness that we use as an alibi to prove to ourselves that we haven't killed it all."

◇ ◇ ◇

IN SOUTH ASIAN novels, whether written at home or in the continent's wide Diaspora, a prevalent literary metaphor is of the busy street. In the spirit of the Mahabharata, the great book of India, it is

on the street that all things happen all the time. In the Middle East, the block of apartments does the job, an appropriate setting in stories by Arabs and Jews of tenants who cannot choose their neighbours. In Canada, a fundamental literary metaphor is of the house. It appears in stories emanating the length and breadth of the country. In its West Coast permutation, the House sits in the Garden, and the fear is not only that it was previously occupied, but that it has been brusquely vacated and we are trashing it.

Taylor's second novel, *Story House*, puts this house metaphor front and centre. Architecture provides the skeleton of a novel in which a mysterious and neglected architectural gem in downtown Vancouver stores two half-brothers' history, memories, interests, and feuds. Built by their father, Packer Gordon, it is a psychoanalytic symbol and quintessentially the house that has been previously occupied. Nor is it the novel's only one. There is the eerily named Orwell Hotel, "descended to derelict, the walls alive at all hours with the sounds of the sex trade," whose tenants have been evicted by a thug who subsequently leases its rooms to an organization housing mental patients, collecting handsome rents from that most sound of creditors, the government. More intriguing is the Haida longhouse that gives the book its title. Graham, one of the brothers, is led by his Haida guide to the remains of the village of Kiusta at the north end of Graham Island, where Chief Albert Edward Edenshaw built the great Story House in 1850. In astonishment and wonder – in *aidos*, really – Graham contemplates the carved barks of trees, the ruins as well as the importuning absences and depressions in the shore where fire pits once served a row of houses on the beach, at the edge of the forest now reclaiming the site. Graham makes sketches, fascinated by the tree carvings that operated as text and how the village, writes Taylor, "worked as a symbol on other levels too. The shoreline was a boundary between the forests on the one side and the ocean on the other. These houses, standing in their long line, stood between. A physical reminder of man's position between what lies above and below. The village lay along a seam where two other worlds meet."

"I'm trying to understand what the house was built to tell us," Graham says to himself. *Maybe Story House is asking you a question*, he concludes.

"The seminal idea for *Story House* was of the house as a project on which two people might or might not succeed in co-operating," said Taylor. "I was exploring the notion of conflict in a permanently flawed relationship, but the house quickly assumed a critical importance to the whole creative undertaking, as I found it tapping into other ideas I wanted to explore – architecture, obviously, but also notions of inheritance and authenticity. In addition, I did come to think of the house as an icon derived from the Vancouver landscape. It is a city very much obsessed by real estate in all its sociological guises. Real estate as the financial behemoth that might make you rich, but might just crush you too; real estate as a force of social disruption. Real estate as an emblem of globalization. The list goes on. A preoccupation with booming real estate values is a phenomenon that can be found in many cities, but Vancouver's version of it is unique to the region. Every day, staring across the Burrard Inlet, downtown Vancouverites look up to the mountains through view corridors carefully preserved between the city's towers and up to the slopes of the Garibaldi Highlands, where North Shore development pushes back the wild a little each year. New swathes of development carve back the trees above last year's construction, each new cull inspiring the same thought: they can't go any farther up that hill, can they? They *won't*, will they? But of course they do. The house in Vancouver is like any other in the overpriced cities of the globalized world, except that here it sits perilously on a piece of reclaimed wilderness and provokes a lot of unarticulated anxiety."

"But there's also an idea of transience here," I said. "Any building is as much an empty vessel as a school, railway station, or hotel is. When you describe the Orwell, you're suggesting an idea of transience, though in the crueller Vancouver setting."

"I feel that transience every day," said Taylor. "The Dominion Building that I work in will have experienced a perfectly emblematic and sweeping change in the one-hundred-odd years it has been standing. Over that time, the epicentre of Vancouver has washed like a tide from the harbourfront at the very northern tip of Main Street westward towards the higher ground of Vancouver's corporate 'downtown' and the city's west end. The Dominion Building sits right in the middle. It used to be on the western edge of the old Vancouver. Now it's on the eastern edge of the *new* Vancouver. Over the same time, the meaning and function of the building has changed entirely.

"The now-staid Dominion Building began its life as a gleaming, high-tech example of what was possible in architecture. Just like the Sun Life Building in Montreal, it was a very proud colonial reference to the distant seat of Empire. Then it would have housed whatever businesses were at the top of their game, whatever companies needed peak profile and status. Now it represents what rental brokers call C or even D Property – desired, primarily, by people like myself, or by outfits that either don't need or can't afford shinier digs. Entire populations have washed in and out of the Dominion Building in those one hundred years. In each of them, the change in tenant profile would have shifted minutely, invisibly. But if you stand back and look at the century in *total*, then you see the change to have been an enormous, city-scale social phenomenon. The history of the Orwell would have been acted out in parallel. I only needed to use my imagination to guess how its former status might have manifested itself."

"And yet I wonder if it is just too banal to believe that there is, in Vancouver, land of the condo sliding into the sea, any real guilt or lingering anxiety about the treatment of Nature?"

"No," said Taylor. "We have plenty, though it is a perfectly recip-rocal feeling to that which you encounter among working-class residents of B.C.'s rural regions. I flew with a bush pilot up to Kitsault recently, and he dipped the wing of the plane to point out a glacier lake that was an exquisite, unnatural blue – the colour of Windex, in fact. We circled and admired it for a moment, and then swept down the face of the mountain towards the fjord. I made some very 'citylike' comments and said something about how beautiful it all was and how it must bother him to see evidence of logging just down the hill from that amazing glacier lake. The pilot shrugged and said, 'Nah, don't bother me at all 'cuz you know, the trees are like big weeds up here.'"

Shelley Ambrose, the force in the shadows of Peter Gzowski and the CBC Radio show *Morningside* for so many years, likes to tell the story of the pair travelling to the Yukon and being shown a moun-tainside cleared for the sake of a golf course.

"You had permission for that?" Gzowski asked.

"Up here," the pilot said, "we seek forgiveness, not permission."

✧   ✧   ✧

IN TORONTO, I had been discussing with Eden Robinson the macabre violence of her novels, suspecting aboriginal anger there. How much, I wondered, did the settlers' guilty schema apply to the native relationship with the land. Was the anger a barometer of anything?

"My mother liked to read *True Crime* stories," Robinson said. "In our house, they were always right beside the Harlequin romances.

The stories she liked to tell stuck in the back of my mind and they were always slightly gruesome. Really, *Blood Sports* was meant to be a more erotic book, but the sex I wrote came out silly and those scenes weren't going anywhere, so I stuck with the blood and gore. That's what I'm good at."

Robinson smiled and looked out at the pub as if from the back of the class and watching kids' antics play out before her. In Canada, we can put such an onus on writers to be significant, and here I was doing just that.

"I love blood," Robinson said, "but I could never be a nurse."

"The arc of your two novels," I said, "travels from the Myth World of the Haisla in *Monkey Beach* to the violent world of East Vancouver in *Blood Sports*. Does that progression say something about the larger aboriginal journey?"

She shrugged.

"I wanted a place that I knew and the geography was home territory. My mother's family was from Bella Bella and migrated to Vancouver, but that was before Expo 86 and the city was very different. They had laws to keep johns off the street."

"But that idea, in Vancouver, of living on the edge – of B.C. as the continent's last stop – does that reflect the Haisla sensibility of your hometown of Kitamaat in any way?"

"No," she said. Casually, but emphatically.

"Is there no fear of an apocalypse, then?"

"Well," said Robinson, "it is true that Vancouver is precarious. I mean, one tsunami and the city is toast."

◇ ◇ ◇

THE DYSFUNCTION in Robinson's most recent novel, *Blood Sports*, reaches its nadir in the sealed basement of an abandoned house in the woods where a couple is deliberately left to die. But the violence is urban more than it is "native," less the expression of the aboriginal community's plight than it is evidence of Vancouver's singular combination of beauty and its opposites – the rootedness wealth buys and deracinated poverty; the pleasures of Garibaldi

Heights versus the squalor of East Hastings or, in Lynn Crosbie's novel, *Dorothy L'Amour*, the concatenation of the gorgeous play-mate Dorothy Stratten, killed in 1980, and Paul Snider, the sordid husband who became her murderer. "I was young and impression-able: he had a certain charm. I lived in Vancouver after all," says Lynn Crosbie's Dorothy when she is not listening to Hugh Hefner's vain recitations of Shakespeare or the spouting of his own Bosch-like worldview. "We fear for you, Dorothy," says Hefner. "Beneath your dulcet voice we hear the howling of dogs."

Dorothy speaks as Douglas Coupland's assassinated schoolgirl Cheryl does, from beyond the grave, and recalls her first kiss. Ten years old, the boy she befriends on the Kingsway, at the back of the Regal cinema, is a salty-lipped poet called Michael. Young Dorothy, dead at twenty, says, "I never forgot him – watched him writing late into the night about Kingsway, pushing a pin in the map where the Regal was. His poems were impassive elegies and still, I saw myself: '*hard her face/ pressed hard*' against his, long before I fell."

A poem about a blowjob by Michael Turner is titled "(viii)" – *Hard her face/ pressed hard against/ the steering wheel/ him fat in her mouth*. It is one of the pieces in the Vancouver poet's collection *Kingsway*, a tribute to the long and historic street that has the rhythms and the course of the busy road in the explorations that it makes. Crosbie's subtle reference is a nod to a colleague, a pal who is something of a Renaissance man cut in Vancouver's new mould. Turner, a lean, smooth character, was once a musician (experiences that led to his novel of a band on the road, *Hard Core Logo*). He handles conversations with deft syncopation, keeping you on edge as he lures you in on the beckoning off beat. Vancouver, as Turner knows it, is an Eden with the problem, particular to any heaven, of just where to put those who would besmirch the place – the addicted, the perverted, the elderly, the infirm, and the poor. The missing flourish in Vancouver, it seemed to me, because sink-holes occur not just in nature but in the negligent city that Nancy Lee described. The disenfranchised can drop out of sight here, because those who can see would rather not, adding to the surfeit of physical places for runaways and the marginalized to hide. In this city that finds the immediate sexy, in this *country* where the urge to renovate is a *sine qua non* of our being in the *New* World, even close yesterdays are out of view. Turner, I suspected, would lead me to them, a writer who has made a professional point of finding contrary ways to understand our urban spaces. He situated his novel *The Pornographer's Poem* in the middle-class neighbourhood of Kerrisdale – a "wonderful combination of Norman Rockwell nostalgia and cosmopolitan city-chic," says the Vancouver neighbourhood's Internet website – though home to teenage purveyors of porn in Turner's story. What is any Garden, without the possibility of an indecent fall from grace?

The past is not impossible to find and perseveres where it has not been noticed yet. The Kingsway is one such place. It was, during colonial times, a route that the British military widened either to defeat invading Fenians or to facilitate flight from what was then the capital settlement of New Westminster, down to the Navy and the sea. Now the long street is scar tissue on urban flesh. Its diagonal line cuts through Vancouver's rectilinear grid and declares to those who, like Turner, are able to read its script, that its banks of car dealerships, low-end stores, boarded-up motels, and vacant lots offer more history than most of the newer city that its route traverses.

Turner drove me along the Kingsway, narrating the street as others would have a mountain trail.

"I like to think that I'm in a dialogue with the space around me," said Turner. "For me, the city is a novel – but one with many authors. It's an anthology. Some people get more pages than others, but everybody's contributing. The idea of *Kingsway* was that reading is like driving, and writing is like thinking. I feel like I'm reading a book right now."

Away from the centre of the city, the view of the surrounding hills was not so dramatic, but also less cluttered and more panoramic than it was downtown, where the skyscrapers jostled on the thin ocean ledge like commuters on a rush-hour subway platform. The long street was untidy along stretches but, away from the developers, free to be what it was. Where a supermarket had been intended but never built, a family sat at the edge of a great tarmacked expanse with second-hand wares and an assortment of found objects and detritus spread on blankets and up for sale. The day was coming to an end in a gentle, misty haze, and the buildings that lined the street were hoarding the dying light. The steady stream of traffic that rolled along the Kingsway seemed to have been shushed quiet. Vancouver looked as it might have been portrayed in an El Greco painting, a settlement spread over the top of hills, as the cities of Ronda or Toledo were in Spain – and not, as skyscrapers' foundations have made it, a city burrowed deep into the beaten coastal ground.

"You're missing the view," said Turner. "Look at the mountains and all their variegations."

"Actually, I was contemplating it," I said. "I was thinking about what you do to readers who make their way through your porn or erotica, and if there is anything to query in that particular literary exercise coming out of this beautiful landscape – these mountains peeling away towards this luminous pale sky and the mist in the valleys. Should I draw any conclusions?"

Turner chuckled. "Get rid of the Midas Muffler, get rid of the New and Used Auto Repair, get rid of the hydroponic simple-grow garden supply, the Vietnamese cafés, the Midland Liquidators, get rid of the construction, get rid of all the places we drive to, stop by, pick stuff up at, and drive away from – get rid of the nasty foreground, and you'll find many lithographs of that very view."

In the 1960s and 1970s, this had been a city of draft dodgers, slow traffic halting at Stop signs, and such folksy vistas painted on rocks. Not any more. The American poet Gary Snyder, I reminded Turner, had said of urban spaces such as we were looking at that their residue of litter, upended grocery carts, syringes, and polystyrene coffee cups was as "natural" an environment as any forest is, with its upended boughs and bed of fallen leaves.

"We have it in our head that the organic has to be something that comes from seed and earth," said Turner, "but the organic can also be the result of human behaviour. Witness any massive metropolis. Through its detritus, it leaves a formation that others inhabit. Junkyards become shelters, with people living in refrigerator casings or what have you. That is 'natural.' That is organic adaptation."

"And I suppose this contrariness is also intriguing to the writer," I said. "Often, you present a sort of poison in places that we think of as unremarkable. In *The Pornographer's Poem*, it's the poison of pornography –"

"I prefer to call it *sexual representation*," said Turner, grinning. "By calling it 'pornography,' aren't you the one putting the poison in the well?"

"But it would have been different had you chosen to set your story in the Downtown East Side, or in any of the more decrepit parts of Vancouver. Coming out of Kerrisdale, the story has a particular effect. We're not expecting such activity there."

"Much like Kingsway," said Turner, "Kerrisdale is a neighbourhood that has been denigrated, and once a place has been made abject then it's likely that something nasty or transgressive will happen there. There's the attraction of decay for you. Kerrisdale is a Utopia, it's supposed to be *perfect*. It's supposed to be the ideal place to grow up and you're not supposed to be curious. If you are, then you're just wrecking it for everyone else, because curiosity leads to questions and questions lead to people feeling uncomfortable.

"If you want to read me, then you've got to pay the price," said Turner.

From Michael Turner's *The Pornographer's Poem*:

Robin had a huge collection of skin magazines. Mostly gay stuff. And he was forever leaving them lying around. They were impossible to avoid. I think he did this on purpose. He was always creating situations where he could catch me looking. His favourite set-up was when he'd go into his kitchen to make coffee. He'd tell me to relax, smoke some hash, whatever. Then he'd disappear. It didn't take long before I clued in that the mirror he'd hung in his hallway provided him with an indirect view of the living room. So soon as I picked up a magazine, he'd come back real fast like he'd forgotten something, then quickly try and get me talking about whatever it is I was looking at. This used to bother me because it felt so obvious. But I got over it. After a while I didn't mind talking about what was going on in these magazines. Plus I was curious about what it was like to be with another guy.

One time I let him catch me. "Oh! *Garçons de Maroc?*" he said, running back into the room, rummaging around for something. "I just got that last week – you seen my rollies? – check out the centerfold." I held up the magazine, letting the color-spread fall onto my lap. An elderly German held his semi-hard against the cheek of a young Arab boy. The boy had his hand cupped under the German's testicles. The look on the boy's face was supposed to be awe. But I wasn't that impressed.

I refolded the centrefold, then put the magazine back on the table. Robin picked it up, reopened it, and began: "A friend of mine – Henke – Do you know him? He's a curator – yeah, doesn't matter – anyway, yeah, Henke says he can't get turned on by this photo because it's too colonial. Does that make any sense to you? That it's *too colonial?*" I shrugged. I had a vague sense of what Henke meant. Robin continued: "I mean, sure – colonialism. It's bad right? But whatever. I just happen to think that it's a really sexy photo. I mean, I would love to be this little boy, wouldn't you? I'd give anything to suck on a dick like that."

✧   ✧   ✧

"You VISITED THAT suburb I lived in, outside of Saskatoon, didn't you?" Lee Henderson asked.

"Erindale, yes."

"It's the most insane suburb. Saskatoon is only a city of two hundred thousand people. It doesn't *deserve* to have a suburb."

I was having coffee with thirty-year-old Lee Henderson, previously of Saskatchewan, at Helen's Grill, the diner at Main and King Edward that a number of Vancouver writers frequent. He was the lean young man at the counter in a railway engineer's cap and prescription glasses in heavy black frames, wearing a loose white shirt over green army pants. He had a restless, agitated air, this writer who did not put his trust merely in what flowed. Henderson, raised in Saskatoon and Edmonton, fled the prairie as soon as he could. Vancouver became the place in which he was able to dwell on the downside of the places he knew.

"Erindale was the end of the world," said Henderson. "It was really like this was the perfect place to kill yourself, though I suppose if you're a teenager, then the suburbs are one of the more interesting places to live because they're so horrible. I knew kids who went from being hardcore Nazis – freakish kids shaving their heads and wearing high boots with laces – who would then make enormous reversals of character and be, like, against drugs, against racism, against *everything*. Just taking the exact opposite route."

Or merely a route out. Henderson had the fraught sense of a man with a mission, as if there was no time to waste and always some new thought to be sorted. Vancouver was not quite Nowhere any more, its possibility of a fresh start perverted by oversubscription, the unfinished business of its ongoing construction evidence of a city struggling to keep pace with its new arrivals.

"We used to walk around downtown Vancouver and do tours of what we called the 'big pits,'" said Henderson, "'cause in Saskatoon you have nothing like that. Nothing gets constructed, it's just people doing minor refurbishments of old buildings, and you never get those deep five-storey pits that you see here. Which is great. I love those big pits. I love those empty lots. I find them remarkable."

"And what is the effect of living in a place in which people are constantly arriving – and moving once they're here? That's why all those holes in the ground are being dug."

"I'm not a city planner," said Henderson, "but I see what you're getting at. You can look at the architecture and the structure of the roadways with the sense of this place as some kind of a terminus. Kingsway is very much a street that arose from the fact that the CPR train line ended downtown, so that the road was hugely important when Vancouver was a port city. But now all it does is funnel traffic and alienate neighbourhoods from one another. A lot of people in Shaughnessy and Point Gray don't even know the layout of the Downtown East Side. They don't know the area, not only because it may not be safe but because they live so far away from it that there's no reason to communicate with those neighbourhoods.

"But one of the more positive things," Henderson continued, "is the influx of people, and yet there really isn't a sense of many cultures coming together in this city. When I first moved to Vancouver, there were a lot of people coming here from Hong Kong, buying property, dropping their kids here – so you have these satellite teenagers whose parents buy them a house, set them up, and then go back to Hong Kong while they attend high school. These kids just basically spend all their money on really nice cars and driving madly, so the city changes in terms of the cultures that come to it, but the new arrivals don't embed themselves in quite the same long-term way that you get in a city like Toronto, where you have a Little Italy or a Spanish or Chinese neighbourhood of working people. We have a Little India, we have Chinatowns, but besides those two older communities it still feels very disparate here."

"It also strikes one as a city in which the memory of arrival is recent. The place is still being invented. Maybe for that reason, it's easier to feel that humankind has spoiled things here."

"In the early days," Henderson said, "people cut down trees, the size of which you wouldn't believe. The novel I'm writing takes place in Vancouver at a time when they cut down a tree with a circumference big enough to fit a band – a whole *band* – for a New Year's dance. Then they cut down another

This one is new on the market

whole tree and its stump was big enough to use as a dance floor. These were damn big trees. And they didn't give a fuck. For them it was like, oh, perfect, this tree will be a great dance floor, let's ravage this forest and put in something Utopian."

"The new novel is set when, exactly?"

"It begins in 1886, the year that Vancouver was incorporated as a city and then immediately burned to the ground. It was a beautiful, almost improvisatory lifestyle that people were living here, where the town drunk was constantly being put in the jail cell for the night, and they were just so sick of having to put him there that they made him warden. There was definitely a feeling of plasticity to Vancouver. Nothing was set in stone. It was a mellifluous kind of lifestyle, and that can be a good or a bad thing. Sometimes I think that had our culture grown in stages – at a slower speed like Europe's did – then we wouldn't have this mentality of exploiting this place as much as possible. Do you know what I mean?"

◇ ◇ ◇

"IF STANLEY PARK had a motto, it ought to be 'More Bodies Than Dirt' – I've always maintained that there are at least a thousand people buried in that place."

Douglas Coupland was sitting in the kitchen of his north Vancouver home, a modernist Ron Thom bungalow obscured by high trees and a mix of indigenous and non-native plants that is a trait of West Coast gardens now. From within, there was a certain sense of being under siege. Raccoons had trashed garbage on the roof. A great leafy plant, straight out of Dr. Seuss, had grown higher than the eaves, almost blocking the path to the studio where Coupland creates his sculptures. The windows of the living room looked out onto forest that was inches away.

Coupland's work both as a novelist and as a sculptor is rooted in a very Canadian sense of place. The day we met, Coupland was masticating pages from the first editions of his novels in order to make papier-mâché wasp's nests out of them. Effectively, he was returning his books as sculptures to Nature. After making one called

"Royalties" from a pile of American dollar bills – they were washed, he insisted – Coupland had temporarily disabled his saliva glands.

"I want to put these books into biological, evolutionary time," Coupland said, "so that you can no longer look at them as a part of the culture, but as objects that go on beyond whenever you live or die. The ultimate – and I'm trying to figure out a way of doing it – would be if I could mix them in with sugar syrup and then put them near a hive and get hornets to make a nest using the fibre from the books. That would be Nirvana for this."

In the face of genuine originality, there is nothing to do but take the artist on his own terms.

"Which novels have you chosen?" I asked.

"I did *Generation X*," said Coupland, "and *Girlfriend in a Coma* from the U.K. edition first because the paper had a really nice feel to it. Now I'm doing the Japanese edition of *Microserfs*. I worked in Japan, so I wanted to see what I could do with the paper they used there, which is thinner but much stronger."

"Just your own novels, then?"

"It would be nice to chew a Gutenberg Bible or something like that."

"Where do you do your chewing?"

"Right where you're sitting. I watch reruns of *Law and Order* on TV. That's my favourite show."

A little dryness of the mouth was nothing Coupland could not cope with in the comfort of his beautiful home. The price of any good fortune – his, Canada's – is a certain well-founded insecurity. This is why the turn his novels have presented on an old theme is so interesting. His books are anxious, and doom-laden. Apocalyptic.

"Here's a very small haiku about how place affects you," said Coupland. "In my books, almost always things involving death take place at Lion's Gate Hospital, which is in North Vancouver and was where my dad worked. My mom used to be desperate to get time on her own, away from the three kids, so when Dad went into rounds on the weekends he would lock me and my brothers in the X-ray room with all the teaching skeletons. Of course this all registers in your subconscious, and now the Lion's Gate Hospital equals death for me. I can never shake that. On a national level, I think the same thing is true. I think a lot of what Canadians write about is coming from some other place where evil was a really big issue and coming to a land that is a Utopia, really. Yes, it's all great and nice – but all of it could be taken away from us very quickly."

Coupland took me upstairs to his studio and showed me a white plastic replica of the World Trade Center that he'd been making. On the wall was a large photograph of terrified passengers fleeing a burning passenger jet, crashed in a field.

"I was out at the Terry Fox Library in Port Coquitlam recently. I was there to photograph Terry's artificial leg for the book that I'd been working on. Directly across the street Willy Pickton was being arraigned for murder. It was this really binary thing – good on one side of the street, evil on the other. It doesn't matter what you try and do, certain parts of a city are always going to reek of murder and other places are going to reek of hope or family or renewal. The Chinese call it feng shui. You can't deny it."

I asked, "How much do you feel that this 'binary thing' is actually a quality of this place?"

"Okay," said Coupland decisively. "We're in the living room – and look, everything in it is plastic, geometric, and entirely synthetic. And the other side of the window there is green and that's *all there is* out there."

Coupland had the strange but compelling habit of staring at some point perpendicular to my sight of him. I was sitting on the couch, as he was, and he was staring away from me, past the fireplace to the window. Transfixed.

"I grew up not far from here, over where the watershed is, in a suburb that had this same weird binary reality," said Coupland. "There would be some kind of a cyclone fence and on one side you would have the 1970s, and on the other it was one million years B.C. There wasn't even a membrane. There was no osmosis, just this fence that you were not allowed to penetrate, but inside your head you were always trying to break through that wall and get out into a place where human beings never necessarily existed. Ever since, I've always been conscious of the fact that these two worlds are separate. I like the two of them existing side by side, but I don't like them mixing with each other. I don't want a *plant* in the house, not even that."

◇   ◇   ◇

THE THREAT THAT knocked at Coupland's living-room windows lurks in the umbrage of Stanley Park in Timothy Taylor's novel, and has taken seats front-of-house in the terrorized psyche of Zsuzsi Gartner's fiction. The stories of her one collection, *All the Anxious Girls on Earth*, bait the reader with their untoward, sometimes paranoiac sense. Their often comic worry is the toll of living on the West Coast in towering condominiums that defy the landscape they're sitting in. The dream is triumphant – but only almost. Vancouver, Canada's final westward stop, comes laced with apprehension in Timothy Taylor's stories, aberration in Michael Turner's, and a fear of the apocalypse in Coupland's, and reaches levels of neurotic hilarity in Zsuzsi Gartner's work. In her story "The Nature of Pure Evil," a jilted lover phones bomb threats into offices so that she can watch the downtown skyscrapers spill their human contents out onto Vancouver's streets. In another, "City of My Dreams," Gartner's heroine is obsessed by the prospect of an earthquake that will wreck the city. Hers is the Book of Revelations, West Coast–style.

"Before *All the Anxious Girls on Earth* was published," said Gartner, "I went through my manuscript because I needed to put together stories that had come out over a five-year period and that didn't have any apparent relation to each other. I was surprised to find out how many things to do with bombings or explosions were in it, and I wondered if there was some kind of weird, repressed, angry terrorist person living inside of me. They were popping up all over the place."

"In your story 'The Nature of Pure Evil,'" I said, "Hettie is clearly a woman who's very distraught, though she doesn't really show it much – outside her habit of phoning in bomb threats."

"Yeah," said Gartner, sighing. "Her boyfriend goes off to a wedding, doesn't take her with him, and it turns out that it's *his* wedding he's going to. That was a story related to me by my mother. You write something like that and you figure it's just too wacky, and that this will be the moment when people say, 'Oh, come on, that's too weird. That whole story is so implausible.' Except that not a single person said, 'How could that happen?' I've had friends point to *other* things in my stories that they feel are implausible. They say, 'People wouldn't act that way,' and I think to myself, 'Oh, boy, you haven't seen my family.' But no one ever said, 'Boy, that marriage thing just threw me right out of the story.' *Weird, eh?*"

"I enjoy the dread in your stories," I said. "You certainly have a lot of it."

"Dread is something I feel a great deal," said Gartner. "I can imagine dread in any situation."

"You definitely play it up in 'City of My Dreams.'"

"That was my I-hate-Vancouver story."

Gartner, in her early forties now, was born in Winnipeg, but moved to Calgary in early childhood. She worked for a while in Toronto and then moved to Vancouver.

"Do you remember, in the late 1990s, when there was that awful feeling of millennial dread in the air?" Gartner asked. "I felt as if I was channelling all of it and that I was using this place as the idea of somewhere about to blow. In some ways this is a wonderful city, but there are so many *cracks* – you know, a lot of people who are just really *tense*. There's the Downtown East Side, there's the whole Technology versus Nature thing, and then there's Nature trying to take everything back – I mean, the raccoons and the skunks are parading through here and everything grows so *big*."

We were sitting in Gartner's backyard. A few children's toys were dispersed on the patio. Gartner spoke at a clipped pace, the intelligence sharply honed and darting. Occasionally, she would throw a nervous sideways glance, and I imagined that perhaps she was feeling a bit self-conscious about the scattering of plastic blocks and bicycles and wondering how it was that she had accepted this irruption of the querulous visitor into whatever was her daily routine. Except that she was not surveying the toys at all, she was checking the soil around a couple of paving stones that had been lifted at the foot of the low fence that separated her garden from the neighbour's. High bamboo plants towered on the neighbour's side, small shoots were growing in on Gartner's.

"It's like Nature is quietly preparing to burst back through," said Gartner with a kind of brittle disgust. "We've got this bamboo that's not even native here, it's been imported, and once it takes root it bursts through sidewalks all over. *Look at it.* It's taking over the neighbourhood. There's that whole green, benign, West-Coasty thing going on in the city, but Nature's always trying to reclaim the place and underneath it all are these agitated people scurrying around *ready to explode.*"

Gartner looked at the offensive bamboo again.

"That's how Vancouver strikes me," she said. "It's like Paradise being stabbed in the butt with a fork."

✧ ✧ ✧

From Zsuzsi Gartner's "City of My Dreams":

The children at the school for the deaf are the first to sense that something's happening. It's recess and they're out in the playground when they all stiffen for several seconds, even the girl hanging upside down on the monkey bars, her braids dragging in the sand. Then they start signing rapidly, little fingers fluttering, small fists smacking into palms. The birds rise up and darken the sky all over the city.

Carnivores and lacto-vegans cling to each other as tectonic plates shift and groan beneath them. Chum salmon leap through the massive cracks in the concrete at the foot of the Cambie Street Bridge, chum that haven't been seen here since the 1920s, chum the size of raccoons and grinning like gargoyles. The old polar bear, the only animal left in the zoo, left waiting there to die, scrambles for purchase as the warm slab of concrete underneath his nicotine-tipped fur buckles, and he slides into the churning moat, wailing as only polar bears can. The ocean spits deadheads, sending logs rocketing through the city like battering rams to crack open the massive walls of the new library, The Bay, GM Place, St. Paul's Hospital, splitting heads as they whistle by like heat-seeking missiles. All over the Lower Mainland, film sets collapse as the earth heaves and honey wagons shoot into the sky, their contents raining down like some stinking vengeance for a long-forgotten crime.

Piles of baby skulls, smooth as china cups, heave out of vaults below Shaughnessy mansions that once housed convents. Nudists scramble madly up the cliff face from their beach, clutching at branches and swollen arbutus roots, brambles tearing at their pubic hair and genitals, as the ocean roars behind them, a towering inferno of water swallowing pan pipes, arthritic dogs and coolers of dope and sangria. They're shocked, not because the end has come, but because it's so Old Testament when they had thought it would be man-made – a cold, clinical apocalypse so that they could say, *We told you so*.

Part Two

THE AGE OF MAPPING

You can write the history of Canada as one of work, and if you do so the story of the Hudson's Bay Company will be your first big chapter. The Company's navigation of Canada's rivers, and its exploration of new territories when old ones were depleted of the beaver pelts that enriched its coffers, established the limits of London's and then Ottawa's reach. The Company wrestled with Canada as the distribution problem it still is, and its treatment of aboriginals, habitants, its own workers, and gentry laid the way for a class system in this country. The men and women dependent on the Company worked the land and spoke its lore, mapping the territory with their stories just as aboriginals had done. But those who reaped its profits lived elsewhere and wrote the rules and histories. Eventually, the fur trade collapsed, but it had set the precedent. Where there was something to take from land or sea, a Company Town came to be, the farthest promontory of a distant authority that took back with the one hand what it awarded with the other. During work's second stage, many of these towns disappeared because the resource did, and workers roamed the land until they found sustenance again. But a few prosperous ones became trading or industrial towns of a feudal nature, and dotted a map of Canada that might just as easily have been divided into the provinces of families. For a while, Canadians even made things, for Empire and then the Commonwealth, and the boss lived up the hill or around the corner. Then cities ruled, and the relationship to the land that jobs once provided was obscured. Now we are in the third stage of work: Canadians toil in offices, and the land, not the city, is the abstraction. We are the citizens of a globalized age and we're not sure where our boss is or what it even means to have a border.

In Canada, things fall apart. The centre does not hold because the centre was never here.

6

The Company Store

Alberta, October 2004. The Pincher Creek author Fred Stenson and I drove past Royal Oak and then Tuscany on our way to the nineteenth century. The suburbs of Calgary reach Cochrane now, these day-old subdivisions with their Pleasantville names an immense and sprawling banner for vinyl Home Depot hardware that stretch halfway to the Rockies. Le Corbusier had it wrong. The masses were not about to live in great concrete boxes stripped of ornament – no, they would save those for shopping in. Instead, they would live like this – in endlessly repeating streets and faux cul-de-sacs that made them feel like individuals, not ants, in monster homes that managed a semblance of variety through their contractor's random shuffle of their dozen common elements. Roof shingles in three shades. Fake cedar siding in different colours, samples in the brochure. French windows looking out on concrete barriers separating these communities from the highway. The triple-, even four-car garage. How many had nothing in them but weed? The houses appeared as flimsy as stacked playing cards on the grassy hide of prairie ruptured here and there where the rocky ground, the sleeping leviathan, obstinately pushed through. What would remain of these streets, I wondered, after a decently devastating tornado? Rows of concrete foundations, that would be all. *If you want to be remembered, then build your house in stone.* Or write your story down.

That's what the fur trader William Gladstone did. Born in Montreal in 1832 to Scottish immigrant parents, Gladstone led a contractor's life in the West, building flat-bottomed York boats for the Hudson's Bay Company and then lending a hand in the construction of the infamous American whisky post Fort Whoop-Up before dying at Mountain Mill, Alberta, in 1912. In the last years of his life he settled in Pincher Creek, Stenson territory, near the Crowsnest Pass through the southern Canadian Rockies. In 1903, his memoir was published in the local newspaper, *The Rocky Mountain Echo*. It remains the only account of the nineteenth-century Canadian fur trade left by a non-officer, and it was the main documentary source on which Fred Stenson relied for his historical novel of the period, *The Trade*.

"I'm not trying to sound like the worker's poet," said Stenson, one hand on the wheel, "but here was this broad-based, labour-intensive Company, and the story that is told is always about Governor This and Governor That, and how the Company sold Western Canada to the Canadian government and allowed this country to become a nation from sea to sea. The thing is, the Hudson's Bay Company kept records, but to leave records you had to be literate. So it's hardly ever a narrative about the working-man, and it's some of that complexity that I wanted to give back to the story, and the delightful thing is how, if you look at any person below the rank of officer, the story contrasts."

Stenson was taking me west of Cochrane and the Ghost Dam to the site of Piegan Post, the Hudson's Bay Company trading fort that briefly operated in the region in the early 1830s. Piegan Post is one of the principal settings of Stenson's novel, which takes place in the years following the Company's absorption of its main rival, the

Northwest Fur Trading Company, in 1821. It was built at a time when the Hudson's Bay Company, with its remote London head-quarters, was endeavouring to strengthen its hold on territories beyond the farthest reaches of its perversely enormous land grant. (The Company was awarded the 3.9 million square kilometres of land drained by the rivers and streams flowing into Hudson Bay, by Royal Charter, in 1670.) The exact location of so many of the trading forts is still a mystery – but scant remains that impede the historian's work are often an invitation to the novelist.

"I'm fairly sure this is where Piegan Post was during the winters of 1833 and 1834," Stenson said. Several kilometres short of the Rockies, Stenson had stopped his SUV in a clearing at the end of a dirt road in a light forest of pine and larch. It was late October. The air was cold. Many trees were bare, and sound carried easily. There was a stream running nearby. Beaver country.

"At the time, it was a lot easier for the Piegan to go down into the Missouri and trade with the American Fur Company, and it was for that reason that the HBC came here, but the decision to put a post inside the lands of the Blackfoot Confederacy was a serious failure. The Company had decided that it would only trade with the Piegan, but the Indians had always been very smart in the ways that they were able to trade off one Company against the other, and they knew that a monopoly was a disaster for them."

"The Company" established the very foundations of this country on the back of its lucrative hat and felt business, and some of Canada's worst social and political habits too. Canada, the Soviet Union that works. Sobey's, Irving, Air Canada, liquor stores, cable providers, or the Liberal Party – our crippling propensity for monopolies and the habit of dependence they encourage stretch all the way back to the Hudson's Bay Company's system of trading posts – and before. Some aboriginals still refer to the land as "the Company Store," as if our tradition of reliance on an overly power-ful supplier was a fault of the land itself. There was sustenance if you needed it, but most of the country did not exactly offer a *cornucopia* of goods. Long winters and a land that has always dictated cultivation on its own terms made Canadians lousy comparison shoppers right from the start.

The land was our first boss, doling out goods, when the season was right, that with a little good fortune could be traded for something else. More supplies. Another sled. Another trap. Then replenish the cache and start again or get up and follow the resource as aboriginals did. In Canada, you need to know what you are looking for and where to find it – berries behind a rock, salmon in the stream, a Saturday newspaper, booze, or maybe a rifle from York Factory. A diversity of *anything* has never been the lesson here, a choice of employers least of all.

"Writing *The Trade* sure made me believe in corporate concentration," said Stenson. "When Hudson's Bay took over the Northwest Company, the first thing it did was downsize, and now every time I pick up the paper I read of merger after merger, and it makes me think that Karl Marx was perfectly right."

"Do you think that the legacy of the Hudson's Bay Company still impinges on the modern country?"

"Hugely. There is this idea that the Hudson's Bay Company founded the country on the back of all these wonderful English values, but what it also brought over were some fairly objectionable ideas about society and what aboriginals were good for – especially after George Simpson took over as governor in 1821 and put a ceiling on how high the Métis could rise within the Company. The fur trade, the way it was practised in the Hudson's Bay Company areas, was a matter of indentured servitude for working people at the bottom of the ladder, and if you broke your contract with the Company, it was game over. You would never work for the Company again. Your family would be in trouble, and your relatives would have no one else to work for either. That's why, in *The Trade*, Jimmy Jock Bird leaves the Company and joins the Piegan. But it was never something you did lightly."

The rules of the Company directed the Bay men not only in matters of business, but in affairs of morality too. Peter C. Newman, author of *Company of Adventurers: How the Hudson's Bay Empire Determined the Destiny of a Continent*, likened the Company rules to "commandments" operating in the place of organized religion. In Stenson's novel, Jimmy "Jock" Bird, the London-educated "halfbreed" son of a former governor, objects vehemently to the Company's conduct and, in particular, to the racist ceiling it has put on his ascendancy. Harriot, his friend and the troubled Company clerk chosen to participate in the Bow River Expedition's foray into the lands around Piegan Post, asks the missionary Rundle, "Do you think the service of God and the service of the Company can ever be one?" The question is rhetorical. The Company was tactically indifferent towards missionaries, those other great explorers of the continent, knowing God to be its rival, and mindful of the meddlesome consequences a conscience might have on the ruthless practice of the trade. The Company was the first and most impressive example of a very Canadian phenomenon – a distant authority that was all-powerful and often overbearing.

From Fred Stenson's *The Trade*:

> Jimmy Jock picked a stick out of the fire and gestured in the air with its fleshy end.
>
> "My father served your Company his whole life. He thought I could go to England and become a gentleman but they laughed at me there. He couldn't help any of his sons. Now they're all back in Red River hoeing potatoes."
>
> He thrust his stick back in the fire.
>
> "Is that why you're here?" Harriot asked. "Because you couldn't rise in the Company?"
>
> Jimmy Jock looked around the leather room. Something made him laugh.
>
> "You're not the first person to think I'm here out of disappointment. Maybe I'm here for the opportunity."
>
> "If you have influence with the Piegan, you have influence with the Company. I understand that."

"Are you such a Company man as all that, Ted? That you can't imagine opportunity that isn't about them?"

The kettle was roaring and Jimmy Jock pointed at it. Sally looked in the pot but wasn't satisfied with the boil.

Watching her, Jimmy Jock said, "I like this place more and more every day. Part of what makes it so fine is that your Company isn't here."

Oh Canada, sapped by the English before the nation was even started, in a pattern of resource depletion that continues to this day. Take, pack up, move on. How much is our frail patriotic sense the fault of early Canadians seeing the land exhausted bit by bit and watching, as the Inuit did, their souls depart with what's exported. For what? For pocket money. Credit at the Company Store. As the Congo was to Belgium's King Leopold, the land that became Canada was a fantastically remunerative territory, but one that no governor of the Hudson's Bay Company even deigned to visit until 1934. Its people were not brutalized the way the Congolese were, though a host of Englishmen's "country wives" and their Métis progeny might think differently. It was a land held in contempt, the stomping ground of remittance men and then of a colonial administrative class that discovered in the gentlemen's clubs of Piccadilly, as workingmen did more fatally in the trenches of the First World War, just how little kudos achievement in the Canadas garnered. Often it was better, as Jimmy Jock Bird decided, not to ingratiate oneself at all. Forge a success in the new land, away from the class system that kept good men under.

A class system followed, though we do not talk about it in our stories much.

"The myth of a classless Canada is nothing less than that – a myth," said Stenson. "It's as if we believe that as long as we don't *talk* about it, if we don't socialize beyond it and are free to move through it, then class doesn't exist."

"Perhaps our distance from each other is part of what sustains the myth," I said.

Stenson shrugged. "Nowadays, I'd say class division exists

between the urban and the rural. The rural is seen as fair game for any joke, it is automatically inferior. The rural is guilty of all sorts of sins that may exist in the urban areas too, but urban folk imagine they are doing them in a more interesting way. Even the way we speak of multiculturalism has led to the city lording it over rural areas that are thought of as places filled with wall-to-wall white people who see the arrival of immigrants as the ruining of Canada. Small towns are not only thought of as not multicultural, but as *anti*-multicultural. This is nonsense. Small towns would love to have immigrants come their way. They're dying because they don't."

"That must hurt, as so much of Alberta's character is defined by early immigration to the mines and the homesteads in the rural areas." Much of it was USAmerican, a point often overlooked in today's estimation of the province as one with southern ties (and a lot of the point of *Lightning*, Stenson's second novel concerning cowboys' emigration north across the nineteenth-century border with Canada).

"But the rural areas are seen as regressive," Stenson said. "And so is historical fiction. I have nothing against urban literature, but I hope that we never lose the rural and that we retain the literature of *all* places."

✧   ✧   ✧

"When I was first published in the United States, nobody was worried that I was a small-town writer."

In Goderich, Ontario, I had met with Alice Munro in a café in the diminished rural town that has been the source of so much of her work. Handsome brick farmhouses sat in the spring fields of countryside impatient to produce. Change had come slowly to small towns such as Goderich, rural communities that have seen a gradual loss of purpose and the telltale signs of their absorption into the greater economies of nearby cities. A McDonald's, a Wal-Mart. Another, bigger mall.

"I write about the least popular people," said Munro, clearly in agreement with Stenson. She laughed warmly. "I write about *poor country WASPs*. But there is a striving now to see the country as something else – and this is a good thing. The person whose family came from Pakistan is also Canadian." She smiled and laughed delicately again, as if what we were discussing was of no consequence to the estimation in which her stories might be held. They would stand on their own merits. Change was inevitable.

"Mine have been a part of the country for a long time," said Munro. "You just do what you can. There was room for everybody in Canada, but for many who are younger, that seems to no longer be true. Writers of a particular generation will speak to that generation, I suppose."

Work defines our relationship to the land through the ways in which people are gathered – in camps, farms, towns, cities. Jobs define us through their activities, and the duties they demand. They offer ways of understanding character and changing situations. Munro herself remembers how unusual it was for a woman of her generation and working-class background to have decided to write at all. Before we met, she had sent me a typewritten essay about her father, Robert Laidlaw, who had held a variety of jobs before writing a novel based on his own life, *The MacGregors*. At the end of "Working for a Living," the father is caught in a blizzard, trying to make his way home. He almost gives up, but there are too many others that he is living for, too many who depend on his work at the foundry, including "an older girl who was strong and bright enough, but who often seemed to be self-centred and mysteriously incompetent." Too many jobs unfinished, including the clearing of the old fox pens, the detritus of an earlier get-rich enterprise. "Was that all you thought about?" his daughter asks. "Wasn't that enough?" he says. What Munro knows is that work puts all sorts of themes into play – class, certainly, but our very reasons for living and gender relations too.

From Alice Munro's "The Turkey Season":

"Ups-a-daisy." Herb turned the bird over and flexed each leg. "Knees up, Mother Brown. Now." He took a heavy knife and placed it directly on the knee knuckle joints and cut off the shank.

"Have a look at the worms."

Pearly-white strings, pulled out of the shank, were creeping about on their own.

"That's just the tendons shrinking. Now comes the nice part!"

He slit the bird at its bottom end, letting out a rotten smell.

"Are you educated?"

I did not know what to say.

"What's that smell?"

"Hydrogen sulfide."

"Educated," said Herb, sighing. "All right. Work your fingers around and get the guts loose. Easy. Easy. Keep your fingers together. Keep the palm inwards. Feel the ribs with the back of your hand. Feel the guts fit into your palm. Feel that? Keep going. Break the strings – as many as you can. Keep going. Feel a hard lump? That's the gizzard. Feel a soft lump? That's the heart. O.K.? O.K. Get your fingers around the gizzard. Easy. Start pulling this way. That's right. That's right. Start to pull her out."

It was not easy at all. I wasn't even sure what I had was the gizzard. My hand was full of cold pulp.

"Pull," he said, and I brought out a glistening, liverish mass.

"Got it. There's the lights. You know what they are? Lungs. There's the heart. There's the gizzard. There's the gall. Now, you don't ever want to break that gall inside or it will taste the entire turkey." Tactfully, he scraped out what I had missed, including the testicles, which were like a pair of white grapes.

"Nice pair of earrings," Herb said.

"I like writing about work," said Munro. "I like writing about the literal, actual things that you do." "I guess I felt very proud whenever I mastered anything – but then, of course, when I am writing stories that are autobiographical, it's easy for me to remember what it was like, to be a waitress or what it was like to pick tobacco."

Munro looked across the table with a brief quizzical air, answered a question she had put to herself.

"I don't think I've ever done a story about picking tobacco, though I'd like to. I try to give people jobs that would fit in wherever they live, I guess."

"Is work a way to know a place, then?"

"Yes, I think it is."

"In 'Working for a Living,' you remark of your mother's zeal that –"

"There are two kinds of people –"

"Yes, and that if a highway is put through the front lawn, for instance, one kind will see it as the destruction of an otherwise peaceful life, where others will see it as an opportunity –"

"To make money."

"And you suggest that even the change a Wal-Mart brings is not something to cause a frown. In a way, I think of you as a writer who, much like you say your mother did, sees the new road as an opportunity –"

"To set up a stand and sell hot dogs –"

"Or to write some new story."

"Right," said Munro. "Exactly. In my political self, saying as much would get me a horrible mark, but my writer self is *not* political. Everything that is happening, here, now, interests me, but I guess it interests me more because it is something that I can comprehend. I can get around it, because there is also a world that I know nothing about, and I am very aware of this. I don't have many characters who are commodities traders or anything like that. And since I've always been rather technologically shy, there is a whole new way of living that I don't experience – and that I don't *want* to experience. After a while you have simply absorbed more experience than you can handle, so that you are apt to just let yourself sink into what you've got."

"Do you need to be close to your material?" I asked.

"Oh yes," said Munro, "I think I need to see it a lot. I need to see this countryside. I like living in Goderich, though I don't know if I am in tune with the people here. I place them here because I like to see them moving around this landscape, and I like Goderich particularly because it is the kind of town you can deal with. When I write a new story, I place it in Goderich. Why? I just do, even in the changed Goderich, the way the town is different now than it was twenty years ago. What it means, to say that it is different, is that it has become more like everywhere else – people drink cappuccinos and they don't go to church, that kind of thing, and this place interests me more. I suppose Margaret Atwood would feel about Toronto the way I do about Goderich. Maybe what we are all doing is looking for a village."

✧ ✧ ✧

IN CENTRAL NEWFOUNDLAND, the village the young author Michael Crummey knew was Buchans. Deep in the great landmass of Newfoundland's interior, it lies on territory far away from St. John's and the outports habitually associated with the literature of the province. Now the old Company Town is a stop off the road from Bishop's Falls to Deer Lake, not far from the waters of massive Red Indian Lake. You will not find Buchans unless you have business or relations there, and today there is not much chance of either.

At the high end of this late Company Town is the "Old Glory Hole," a deep crater filled with phosphorescent blue water where Lucky Strike, the first shaft of the American Smelting and Refining Company, was sunk in the late 1920s. The hole is a couple of hundred feet in diameter, and it is encircled by a chain-link fence in the middle of the industrial yard that was the nexus of the town's activity until the last boxcar of ore left Buchans in 1984. Only a few buildings – the canteen, the mill and the old Company offices – have not been levelled. The headframe, the one high structure, looms pointlessly. It is a monument to outrageous hope and to the story, approaching the status of legend, of the mine's founding. In 1905, the Mi'kmaq-Montagnais prospector Matty Mitchell lit a fire and the sparking rocks alerted him to the presence of ore in the region. In 1926, ASARCO started operations here and since then several mines have systematically exhausted the local earth of its rich mineral deposits. When I visited with Crummey, the only remaining employee of the vanished Company was there to figure out what to do with six decades' worth of the mine's obnoxious residue. A bit of prospecting still goes on in the area, and there are various small employment schemes – a wildberry farm nearby and a pollution-monitoring project in the woods outside of town, but in truth the town is dead. Slowly, the strangely peaceful site is being returned to the land.

The day I arrived, a few families were lounging on the decks of the row houses, but the streets were uncannily quiet and the sound of a lady on a bicycle cutting across the dirt road beneath the telegraph poles could be heard a few hundred feet away.

In and around Buchans is where Michael Crummey spent his formative years. Nearby Red Indian Lake and its haunting inferences of the vanished Beothuk inspired his novel *River Thieves*, but it was this other disappeared society, of ASARCO and its 7,910 workers, that led to many of the stories of his collection, *Flesh and Blood*. (The company is called ASAMCO in the book, and the town Black Rock.) Crummey's family lived in one of the row houses that his mother still keeps, accommodation granted to the workers once the Company was convinced that it was better off with the men's families around. The Company provided everything, from a basic wage and housing to teachers, doctors, nurses, and, at Christmas, dances, a gift for every child, and carols broadcast on the streets. But the munificence lasted for only as long as the men's labour was useful, and a good part of what was paid in wages was recouped in rents or at the Company Store. It was another incarnation of the Hudson's Bay Company servitude that Fred Stenson had identified.

The absence of wind at the site was eerie, for here the ground once shook. Now the gruff, rumbling sound of a single backhoe starting up was all that broke the air, and the solitary machine set about its work of further obliteration.

"The Company whistle pretty much regulated town life," said Crummey as we stood by the chain-link fence around the Glory Hole. "It marked the shifts at eight a.m., at four, and at midnight, and it blew at noon and at one o'clock. That's how we marked our lives. If we were out sledding in the winter, the four o'clock whistle meant that it was time to head home and have supper. You always knew when it went.

"Everything was operated with money from the Company – the hospital, the fire station, the school, the gymnasium, and, in early days, the rail line too. It carried the ore out, and there was usually a passenger car attached to it, so the Company had absolute control of who came in and out. If they decided that a worker was undesirable, then they put him on the train and instructions were given at the junction that if he tried to get back on he was to be hauled off."

Closer to home, a couple of washing lines extended out into the open alley behind the house of Crummey's mother, Maisie. Sheets flapped in the wind that had been picking up since noon. The quiet beckoned some kind of activity that might have recalled days when the mine was still in operation and these same streets would have been busy with men walking to and from the site, women chatting on the doorsteps, and children frolicking. Birch trees that had been planted decades earlier had matured, and the noise of their leaves whispering was all the wind carried. But with each passing year, the population of Buchans diminishes and another couple of buildings are razed. In Canada's Nowhere, what is really disappearing is any physical memory of the place.

We went into the house and Crummey, in the old family den, looked to me like the apple of his mother's eye, a child that no mother would have wanted to go down the mine. Crummey has shoulders that are slightly narrower than his strong forearms warrant. They are his father's, maybe his grandfather's – a physical tie to the bodies of Newfoundland miners, loggers, and fishermen that had come before; hard labour Crummey had foregone to write instead. That afternoon, listening to him laugh and banter with Maisie as she picked blueberries by the old airstrip, I had felt a

sudden sense of beautifully baffling mystery as I tried to understand the puzzle of a storyteller's origins. How was it that a writer
as eloquent as Crummey should arise out of the mining town of
Buchans, Tomson Highway out of the muskeg-surrounded lakes
of The Pas, or Alice Munro from the Wingham home of a dedicated,
failed fox farmer? Here I was following a writer to the source again,
though what did I imagine could ever authentically explain the
chance miracle of an artist's realized talent?

At school, Maisie told Michael, he was already the one whose
imagination wandered. "If the project was to write an essay about an
orange, then your brother would write, 'It's round, orange, and good
to eat,' but you, you, Michael, you would write a whole long story."

"About the history of the orange," I offered, remembering the
lyrical historical fiction of his novel *River Thieves*.

"Right back to the seed," said Maisie.

"When I started writing at university, I kept it secret," Michael
confessed to his mother. "But I remember I thought I had to tell you
when a poem of mine won a poetry prize, so I telephoned you in
Labrador, and you said –"

"What's it about?"

"Sex, I said. And Ma, you asked, 'Is it autobiographical?'"

Maisie cackled. "'*Semi*,' you said."

The Crummeys' modest row house was one notch up from the
bunkhouses that were the first stop of bachelors winning a job in
the mine and looking forward to making good money, men not
yet worn down by the ways in which it would be taken back from
them. In 1980, I worked in Labrador City for the Iron Ore Company
of Canada until a slump in commodity prices meant that the
entire town was made redundant, and what I remember most is
how the Newfoundlanders in the bunkhouse I roomed in (No. 5)
played cards, shared a bottle, made seal flipper pie – and, as in
Michael Crummey's father's day, the fella to watch out for was the
one who snuck off discreetly and knew where a woman would let
him in.

A bunk, a room, an apartment, a house: the arc of a life – almost.

Home, ultimately, is the place one chooses to be buried in, but for most of ASARCO's rule, there was no cemetery in Buchans, because, said Maisie, "in the Company's view, you were always from away. At sixty-five you were done with. You had to give up your house to the Company because you were of no use." As the mine wound down its operations, the town was finally incorporated in a cynical Company sleight of hand, and it did become possible to own a house or even to die in Buchans. In failing, the town acquired the memorial a cemetery provides to a history that Buchans could only struggle towards while Company rules prevented any real possibility of ownership.

"What affects me most," Crummey said, "is not what's left but what's gone. Every time I come back something else has disappeared, some other building has been torn down. Driving into Buchans is driving into a place I don't recognize."

Outside, in the still air, I pondered how we tend to interpret the world in terms of the short limit of own lives, or those of communities that come and go as a matter of course in Canada.

"All you have to do is look around you," Crummey said, "to see how minuscule human habitation was, and that's true of all of Newfoundland's human enterprise. Compared to the scale of the place itself, Buchans is tiny, and because of that I've always had the sense that human enterprise *in general* is tiny too. There are huge spaces in front and in back of us that have nothing to do with us at all, and that's certainly part of what affects my sense of individual lives as I'm writing. What makes each life so poignant is that it is swallowed front and back by that space without us."

"Are there any physical metaphors that you remember that are particular to this landscape?"

"There is one that I stole not from Buchans, but from a mining town in Northern Ontario," said Crummey. "I think it was Cobalt, where a road was collapsing because a drift had been dug too close to the surface. I loved the notion of it because it suggested that a mine can eat itself into every facet of people's lives, often in a corrosive way."

"And despite all the evidence, the town's certain end was still not accepted?"

"No," said Crummey. "I can remember, as a kid, watching Company planes flying overhead, and hanging from the belly of the planes was something that looked like a bomb. It was a metal-detecting device that the Company was using because they were desperately trying to find other pockets of ore that might have kept the mine running. There was a real sense, as years went by, that it was all over and that the end was just a matter of time, but it was like watching somebody with a terminal illness die, where you go through periods in which there has to be some hope. There were rumours passed around that, yes, they've found this pocket here, or there's more ore in the mine than they thought, and then the rumours would turn out to be false, of course. Eventually you just have to come to grips with the fact that it's done, this thing is going to die."

Work but also bitter contractual disputes and strikes were a part of the Buchans way of life. Folk depended on the Company, but they did not expect fairness from it. This is how it was in so much of Canada, ever since Newfoundland's merchant princes set the price for quintals of cod or – the monopoly that became a country – the Hudson's Bay Company was able to dictate its own terms and purchase fur, the iron of the day, with nearly criminal leverage. And yet the Company was the entity that made life possible in a land that would otherwise have been beyond enduring. It was the distant authority that needed to be tolerated because the nature of the land and its slim pickings gave the people no alternative. It became the model of a *social* relationship, as much as ones of labour, that etched itself into ordinary Canadians' psyche.

"The Company was God," said Crummey, echoing Rundle's words.

"Did it have a face?" I asked.

"The mine managers," Crummey said. "But even as a kid, they felt like functionaries in a pretty big technocracy. I always thought of ASARCO as something that existed somewhere else. Even then I could see that the mine managers were always speaking for someone else, that they were never the big kahuna. We were just a satellite of this faceless thing that operated from elsewhere."

Now the distant authority has retreated, and a conversation that occurs repeatedly, in Buchans, speaks to the people's nostalgia for simpler times when the land provided sustenance and no one was without a job.

At Buller's Place, "Home of the Big Buller Burger," the owner, Gary, remembered Crummey from school days. The restaurant was housed in a building the size of an ATCO trailer. It had a couple of small windows and the door had been left open to catch the summer breeze – and regulars dropping in for a dollar cup of coffee.

"Not many people our age left," said Gary.

"And how's it going?" Crummey asked.

"The shits," said Gary.

Craig, another regular, parked his truck and walked over and the talk drifted to Buchans' prospects.

"What are you up to?" Crummey asked.

"I'm in exploration."

"What are you looking for?"

"Gold's the big thing."

"Really?" said Crummey with a modicum of excitement.

"Ach, there's no gold," Gary said. "You know as well as I do exploration ain't going to find us a goddamn thing."

Later, over a hot turkey sandwich with Michael and his mother at the Red Ochre Inn, the proprietress brought out coffee and disclosed with the semblance of great confidentiality that the Buchans River Mining Company had been prospecting in the woods.

"The same man who discovered Voisey Bay owns it," she said. "His men have been around now, almost a year."

"Oh really?" said Maisie.

The woman nodded her head histrionically. "*I'm expecting an announcement any day soon*," she confided.

"They're always talking about the motherlode of gold here," Crummey said, "about how Buchans will come back."

"They should have shut the whole town down," Maisie said.

Art Crummey left Buchans when his work at ASARCO ran out. He took the family to another, more viable mining town in Labrador – but it is in the small house in Buchans where his spirit still feels most in attendance. Here the three boys would run in and out, Maisie there to look after them, and in the evening he would tell stories – such as the time, he told the boys, that fishing "down the Labrador" with his own father, the cold would get so bad that the only way he could keep his hands warm was by peeing on them. When, in 2001, Crummey's novel *River Thieves* was nominated for Canada's prestigious Giller Prize, his father was Michael's guest at the gala. "It's a long way from pissing on our hands," he said.

"When my father was a boy," said Crummey, "he and his dad's crew would leave the Bay in late May or early June and come back in September or October. During that time there was no word between the people working and the people living back home. That was true for about ten thousand Newfoundlanders who left home every year, and there would be all kinds of stories about men coming back to find babies born that weren't around when they'd left, or of people who'd died and the men not hearing about it for months afterwards."

These seasonal experiences of absence and loss had a precedent of generations, Canadian workers in the Age of Mapping roaming the land for sustenance as aboriginal hunter-gatherers used to do. Long separations were a part of living, experiences in the blood that subsequently infused so much of Crummey's work, from the foraging the author does to understand the extinction of the Beothuk in *River Thieves* to the yearning of his Second World War novel of separated lovers, *The Wreckage*. In Crummey's story "Serendipity," a miner and his family have been separated for so long that the son says, "It should have been no surprise to anyone, least of all my mother, that she was no longer in love when he finally sent for us to join him in Black Rock."

"It's that odd delay," said Crummey, "that not knowing intimate things about people who were so close to you, that always seemed like such a bizarre thing."

From Michael Crummey's "Roots":

What he came back to:

His birth place. A town like a tree with dutch elm disease, something dying from the inside out. The wind across the barrens, whistling through telephone wires, a sound so constant it is often mistaken for silence. His parents' house. Wall to wall carpets. The formica table in the kitchen. Crocheted doilies on the coffee and end tables in the living room. His bedroom. The faded Star Wars bedspread. The window looking over the birch trees in the backyard, their branches almost touching the glass now. Barely visible beyond them, the dirty grey skirt of the mine tailings circling the huddle of mills.

George Neary, the ASARCO mine's long-time manager, spent the last twenty years of his life on the unfinished business of Buchans' environmental cleanup. Before he died, in August 2005, he compiled a history of all the 7,910 who had ever worked at the mines.

✧ ✧ ✧

AFTER THE CLOSING of the mine, in 1984, the search for work resumed and Buchaneers joined the migration of men – and they were mostly men – leaving Newfoundland. The overnight ferry from Port aux Basques is more of an historic route, now that migrating workers take the plane, but on the MV *Caribou*, a chorus of men's snores added to the rumble of the ship's engines. These men were tourists, by and large, though a few would still have been riding in loaded cars, travelling west for work as Alistair MacLeod's Macdonalds do, driving across the Canso Causeway linking Sydney and Cape Breton to the Nova Scotian mainland, on to Canada – and the rest of the world. In MacLeod's story "The Closing Down of Summer," one of the great elegies of work, his shaft miners leave the August beaches to "hurtle in a dark night convoy across the landscapes and the borders of four waiting provinces." As it is with animals, there is a collective, instinctual awareness in these workingmen that the time has come for the next migration to begin. They are miners and shaft-sinkers off to work in Saskatchewan, Alberta, South Africa, Peru. They are hunter-gatherers foraging again, returning with bounty and stories if Death does not take them this time around.

✧   ✧   ✧

"MINERS WOULD DEVELOP the resource," Alistair MacLeod said, "and then the families would come in. The Company Town would be formed, and then the miners would go somewhere else. These people worked in advance of the Company Town. They would be all male and they would travel – they were kind of like a football team."

When MacLeod is not teaching in Windsor, Ontario, he lives in Inverness, the defunct mining town on the west coast of Cape Breton. MacLeod himself was born in North Battleford, Saskatchewan, but this region of the *Île Royale* had been the seat of the MacLeods for several generations – and for Scottish Highlanders generally, since the clearances in Scotland that followed the Jacobites' loss at the battle of Culloden in 1746. The profound relationships that the people of Cape Breton, one of the earliest settled parts of Canada, had to place was forged by the work they did in its land-based industries: the mines, the mills, the fisheries. There are still some fishers who get by, but here as in Newfoundland and all over the Atlantic provinces the sea has been emptied, and men such as the eponymous fisherman of Donna Morrissey's novel *Sylvanus Now* watch as industrial seiners and trawlers and factory ships suck or drag his living and the fish out of the water and toss back the tons they don't want, dead. More conquistadors, their trawlers leaving behind no stories that speak, as myths did, of the ecology as something to be depended on. Another resource depleted, more workers moving on, more land sold as outsiders' second homes.

Outside Inverness, a sign advertising waterfront lots was written in German. Within town, a small museum honoured generations of miners' hard work, housed in an old station of the Canadian National Railway, that other great monopoly, but a couple of new inns as well as a restaurant had been built above the site where the mine had been, overlooking the water. This was a more successful reclamation than was happening in Buchans. There would be a golf course, and more chalets with owners from away. The out-of-towners would enjoy their summer homes. In MacLeod's story "Clearances," a descendant of Highlanders settled in Cape Breton faces being cleared once more – this time in the new country. An end of work means no money and having to sell the land that meant so much.

"You have to be ambivalent about what progress is," said MacLeod. He greeted me on the step of his house overlooking a relative's RV camp and then the sea. He took the bottle of the MacAllan I'd brought in homage and put it aside, not about to be so impolite as to open the gift in my presence. He poured some whisky from the bottle of Glenfiddich that was already open, but when I asked to see his writer's cabin, he declined. Not yet my station. I understood, and even appreciated that I'd been put in my place. Not all things need to be immediate.

"If a developer offers you money," said MacLeod, "and you don't have money, it's hard to listen to others who tell you no, you shouldn't sell your land. There are a lot of people around here who don't have any pensions, especially older people, and for a lot of them the land is a resource. It's like a last cow. There is a big conflict now about this, there is a war between people who want to keep the waterfront pure and people who want to build condominiums, and about fishing and the big boats taking everything or ten smaller boats feeding their families. You can't stand in the way and say, I'm of a certain age and I'd like things to remain as they are. The ownership of the land will change, the ownership of the ocean will change. These are issues that have been in the world a long time."

"My impression is that attachment to place is at its most extreme in this part of Canada," I said. "The sense of the land as a holding, as something that can be farmed and can sustain a family – as something that is for that reason the *essence* of a community – feels, well, almost *Balkan* to me."

"In Nova Scotia, or in Quebec, because people have been in these places a long time, there is a lot more to lose," said MacLeod. His words rolled in his speech as they did in his stories. The Gaelic cadences still applied. "If you said to someone in these provinces, or in Newfoundland, that you can sell real estate in Toronto, then the person would say, 'Yes, but what would I do?' And you would tell them they would get rich, and they would say, 'Yes, *but then what?*' This part of the country has been settled for a long time, and the longer that you're in a particular place as part of a group, the more intensified the experience becomes. You carry your history with you, in what you eat, how you speak, and what you wear. So much of the population of Newfoundland is in Fort McMurray but these people would come back in a heartbeat if they could."

"And yet your characters travel such huge distances for work – and not just to Ontario, Saskatchewan, or Alberta, but to Peru and South Africa –"

"But they're always coming back," MacLeod said.

"Was there ever an effort to keep people home?" I asked.

"A friend of mine," said MacLeod, the mirth rising in his ruddy cheeks, "wanted to leave the Strait of Canso area, where there was a mill, because he wanted to go to Hamilton, Ontario, and work in the theatre. He told people that he wanted to leave the Port Hawkesbury area to work in theatre because there was no work in Port Hawkesbury. But that wasn't quite true. He just wanted to leave Port Hawkesbury. So he got on the train, and about seventy miles from home, the train was flagged down and the conductor got on the train and asked if my friend was on it, and my friend put up his hand, and the conductor said, 'Get off the train – *they got you a job!* You can go back home!" MacLeod chortled. "But he didn't *want* the job and he didn't *want* to go back home!"

The migration west was made for money's sake, or sometimes simply to get away. In Toronto, I'd run into R.M. Vaughan. A contrarian from New Brunswick – his Gothic fiction is a deliberate challenge to more traditional models of Maritime fiction – Vaughan had followed the same path from Maritime obscurity to becoming

a novelist and critic in the country's most bustling and competi-
tive metropolis that Russell Smith, once a Haligonian too, trod
before him.

"Do you go back to New Brunswick at all?" I'd asked.

"Only for funerals," Vaughan said.

And in Halifax I'd found Christy Ann Conlin. The North Mountain
was Conlin's territory, the shoulder of southwestern Nova Scotia
that protects the fertile plains of the Annapolis Valley and, as the
Digby Neck, sinks into the Bay of Fundy. Like Vaughan, she was one
of several notable young Atlantic Coast novelists – Lynn Coady is
another – who had made a comic point of rebutting the stories of
migration and sad return that seemed to be a staple of Maritime literature. "Goin' down the road" was the stuff of cliché in these
Eastern writers' minds, though you sensed that part of the resentment arose from their still being truth in such stories. As if to prove
the point, a hitchhiking kid I picked up en route from Halifax to
Maitland told me he was a carpenter, his dad too, and that the pair
of them were leaving, the following week, to drive out to Alberta. No
work? I asked. Only if you want to work at a call centre, the lad said,
but they don't pay enough. No, the boy said, they wanted to build
houses, and there was work out there, they'd seen the ads.

I'd seen them too, big full-page spreads and even eight-page
colour inserts in workingmen's newspapers, not the *Globe and Mail*
or the *National Post*, enticing labourers and businesses to come
with maps of Calgary's and Edmonton's neighbourhoods and highways and captions reading, "600,000 CARS PASS EACH DAY" and a
dozen pages of construction company classifieds.

I asked Conlin if she accepted that people growing up and going
away was a part of Nova Scotian life.

"I would say that it's an Atlantic-Canadian experience," she said.
"Everybody knows someone who went off to work in Alberta, or on
the rigs. I have friends who died on the *Ocean Ranger*. It's inevitable.
It's a part of our working-class nature."

✧ ✧ ✧

THE VILLAGE OF MAITLAND is home to the writer Leo McKay Jr. It sits at the top of the Minas Basin, on the shining blue waters of the Bay of Fundy. Minas was "les mines" in Champlain's day. The August afternoon that I was driving through, dusk already, the sun made the water gleam, and the northern shore, with its barns and silos and farmhouses, was a far country enrobed in a gentle mist. On the near side of the Bay, the forests were mixed and bushy. Big bear paws of land padded out into Fundy's mud and water. Some of the fields had been cut for hay, and the nearly horizontal light illuminated the patterns made by the tractors and mowers' passes. The corn was high, and water flowed in quiet streams and rivulets through green marshy basins. Along the broader water courses, the Bay of Fundy's dramatic tides had receded and revealed banks and riverbeds of the striking russet mud that colours Canadian shores from here to Prince Edward Island. The farmhouses glowed white, the red barns were more demure. A couple of families were out strolling along the side of the road as if they knew in their bones, though they'd not said it yet, that summer was at its zenith and would not be more congenial than this. Some farmers knew as much and were working late on their tractors beneath a sky that was now purple, with bold dashes of brilliant orange and brush strokes of white and pink cloud.

Around Maitland, where I was headed, many of the houses were grand. Typically they had been occupied for generations and were now abandoned or in need of repair. Once, they had accommodated well-to-do families in the Minas Basin's bygone era of shipbuilding, the largest full-rigged ship ever built in Canada having been completed here, after two years' work, in 1874. Leo McKay Jr., in his early forties when I met him, lived in one of these spacious, dilapidated homes, though he had grown up in Stellarton, a former mining town farther north. The author of a novel, *Twenty-Six*, and the collection of stories *Like This*, McKay was working as a teacher in a local high school. The mining life was at the core of all that he wrote, the tone of his stories rougher than either MacLeod's or

Crummey's work, the style less lyrical because the sentiment was less forgiving.

✧ ✧ ✧

In Stellarton, in May 1992, twenty-six miners died when the shafts they were working in collapsed. The incident became known as the Westray mining disaster, after the company that managed to evade criminal charges of manslaughter even though a provincially appointed Standing Committee ruled the deaths were the catastrophic result of a series of failures in mining practices. The disaster nagged at Leo McKay, who had been working in Japan at the time, and the number of dead provided him with the title of his first novel.

McKay and I drove together to the yard of the Heather Hotel, at the edge of the district he names in *Twenty-Six* and in the stories of *Like This*, and that is still called Red Row. We stopped, and McKay got out of the car and looked around pensively. Behind the motel, at the edge of the short row of workers' cottages where McKay's aunt used to live, was a small depression where the burrowed ground has subsided – a sinkhole such as appealed to Crummey and that you will find in many mining towns.

"I live in this place in my imagination most of the time," said McKay, "to the point that it often comes as a shock to me that this is a *real* place, and just how small it is."

"Stellarton was a Company Town?" I asked.

"Oh yes," said McKay. "My parents were born in the 1920s and 1930s, and 'the Company Store' is still a phrase they remember. It was the Company that provided groceries and supplies for the miners on a credit system."

"Who are the important families here?"

"The biggest name is Sobey, of course. Right on Main Street is where Frank Sobey had his first general store. He started riding his dad's milk wagon and parlayed it into his current fortune. In the 1970s, it was very hard to make any transaction at all without some

of your money ending up with the Sobeys. They owned car dealerships, movie theatres, and let's not forget the grocery stores."

"It's the old Company Store arrangement progressing into something feudal, don't you think? The Sobeys here, the McCains and
Irvings in New Brunswick, the Westons in Ontario, the Siftons
farther West."

"I remember having a big argument with my brother-in-law,"
said McKay. "He's from Saskatchewan, and he liked to say that it
was a great advantage having a family like the Sobeys taking care
of people in the province."

I'd heard as much said in Saint John about the Irvings. "If you
think back to the funeral of Harrison McCain in Florenceville in
March of 2004," I said, "it could be argued that often we *prefer* to be
taken care of in what is actually a paternalistic fashion."

"That's the basis of our being feudal," said McKay. "We believe
we owe everything to this guy, so how can we go against him in any
way. I suppose there are benefits that such a system can offer, but
it's completely unmodern and absolutely not democratic – the
authority has control, and it exerts control."

McKay shifted uneasily, as if the idea was a weight upon his
shoulder. Stellarton was not a pretty town, by any means. A big
functional sprawl, away from hills or water.

"I grew up at a time when the towns and the industries around
which they were built were in a slow state of decline," said McKay,
"though I suppose that *collapse* would be a more fitting word. The
coal deposits here are not dormant, so that the actual process of
mining produces methane and makes working the seams extremely
dangerous."

"And that is what led to the Westray mining disaster?"

"Yes," said McKay. "The story is complicated to tell, because its
tendrils reach out to almost every aspect of political and economic
life in Nova Scotia. At the time, there was a rush for development,
and some businessmen were interested in developing a mine at
Plymouth, where there were just a few farmhouses then. It was
something of a political pet project, so a lot of corners were cut and

the people who were running the mine figured they could do just about anything. The mine was sunk in an area producing methane gas, and even though the administration had a general idea of the precautions that should have been taken, none were. The explosion killed all twenty-six people who were underground at that moment, and eleven of the bodies were never recovered."

Justice K. Richard's 1997 report, "The Westray Story, A Predictable Path to Mining Disaster," assails the industry's lax regulations and "the stage set for Westray management to maintain an air of arrogance and cynicism, knowing that it was not going to be seriously challenged." It was a traumatic and defining moment locally, and towards the end of McKay's novel, the bereaved families raise the issue of whether the two silos at the mine should be left standing.

"They could be seen for miles," said McKay. "As kids, we used to orient ourselves by them, but now they're gone and even someone like myself who has spent ten years thinking about the mine is no longer sure exactly where they stood. They resembled an eleven – the number of dead left underground. There had been a movement to keep the silos as a memorial, but in a very cynical move the provincial government announced that it would be unable to pay compensation to the families for as long as the silos were still standing because they needed to develop the site in order to be able to pay for anything. So the silos were levelled and the government went a long way to achieving its objective of removing any memory of the disaster from the landscape. The government was burying its shame."

A motorcycle roared past, towards a house that had a couple of muscle cars and an ATV in its driveway. Engines can be a fair diversion.

Like Ziv Burrows in *Twenty-Six*, McKay avoided work in the mines. He taught English in Japan as Ziv's girlfriend, Meta, also does. Evidently, McKay was heeding the warnings he laid down in *Like This*. In the title story of that collection, Frank comes home drunk. He is challenged by his son, who stomps on his foot, and then knocked out by his wife, who hits him with a cutting board. The next morning, Frank wakes up with one boot on and remembers nothing. He rises and confronts his son again. The son wants to go down in the mines, he says. Frank lifts his arm, with its half a hand missing, and says, "Do you really want to end up like this?"

From Leo McKay Jr.'s *Like This*:

> He holds his hands out from his sides. I look at his bad hand. The one that's only a thumb. The one that got sheared off in a big set of metal shears at work ten years ago. With a hand like that, you hold it out, a person thinks that's what you're talking about. But he just looks at me.
>
> He needs a shave. He's got no teeth. Big circles loop beneath his eyes. He stands there in an undershirt with one workboot on and one leg cut out of a pair of pyjamas, trying to keep his head balanced on his shoulders.
>
> Mum looks at the Old Man like she never saw him before. Like she was surprised to find him there first thing in the morning, hung over and missing work. She looks at him a while, then turns to me.
>
> I put my head down and take another spoonful of Shreddies.
>
> Mum refills the Old Man's cup. "You ought to take the weight off that hurt foot, Frank," she says. The Old Man sits back down.

"Manual labour takes its toll," said McKay. "It was something that miners and their families grew up with. My father became deaf in one ear, and just as we've been talking, somebody I grew up with drove by whose father was run over by a train. Somebody who lived five or six houses up this street was crushed by a crane. Everybody's father seemed to drag a leg because they had broken it at work or crushed their foot. They had scars, and limps, and bone conditions, and cancers, and lung diseases. I knew someone my age who had to take a hot bath every morning just to be able to get going. And it was not just a question of people's bodies but their minds as well."

"And yet, in *Twenty-Six*, Ziv's father is appalled that his son might *not* work in the mines. He knows all about the hazards but still wants him to be a part of it. What was it – pride?"

"I think that someone of Ziv's father's generation could imagine his children becoming educated as doctors or lawyers. What they could not abide was that work went from relatively high-paying jobs, no matter how dangerous the work was, to low-paying service work. There were several generations who grew up with a particular idea of what work meant and why people were doing it, but the concept of what these generations understood to be meaningful work had changed entirely."

McKay wore spectacles, looked bookish. There was an edge to his speech that was politically charged, though it was evident that his slightly uncomfortable manner was that of someone who was condemned to never feeling completely at home, anywhere. Pictou County was where he had been raised and, after travelling, returned. It was home for him, the material that was his due. In the Amazon, where a seed tossed over the shoulder germinates by noon, the florid literature of "magic realism" was born – in Brazil, with Mário de Andrade's *Macunaíma*, before it flowered most splendidly in the novels of the Guatemalan Miguel Angel Asturias, Chile's Isabel Allende, and Colombia's Gabriel Garcia Marquez. Out of a garden, fecund as Paradise, sprouted the belief that anything can be imagined. In India, populated to the point that human solitude is quite impossible, the prospect of eighty-four *lakh* lives is nestled in her stories of the busy street. But in Canada, the land's meagre provision demanded pragmatism in our character as well as in the stories we told. Even our writers behave in the Age of Mapping as companies do – telling a story as others would mine a lode, and where there is competition, picking up and moving on.

"Certainly, when I wrote *Twenty-Six*," McKay said, "I was conscious that writing about a place is exploiting it just as much as stripping off the trees or digging out the coal, but I was also conscious of naming the place – of saying it *exists*, in all its complications. There's a self-respect that comes out of realizing that where you are is not some bohunk backwater, that the events that occur here are happening to real people and are just as important as anything that happens elsewhere. Part of my job as a writer is to recognize that."

McKay and I drove on to Plymouth and the site of the closed mine. A gravel track beside the road indicated where rail cars used to take the coal away, and a chain was strung across what would have been the mine's entrance. In a field across the road, a young woman in English cap and riding gear was trotting her horse between two gates. The pretty sight was dwarfed by a high slagheap in the close distance, the piled residue of a strip mine. Too vast to remove, it loomed like a giant dozing animal.

"The area all around here was littered with junk. If you wanted to amuse yourself, you scavenged. If you wanted to play baseball, you would just find an odd plank."

"How do you feel about the slagheap there?"

"I have mixed feelings. I know it's an environmental disaster for anybody who lives nearby – there's coal dust blowing off it, and it must be messing up the water table – but still when I come home and see that rather than some shiny new strip mall, the place is easier for me to understand."

"Alistair MacLeod said that for a lot of the Belgian families that worked here, there was not the option of going back to the Old Country, or even farming or selling wood if work at the mine ceased. It was the mines or nothing."

"My impression is that the Cape Breton economy was more mixed than Pictou County's was," said McKay. "The entire landscape of my youth was an industrial one. There was no land that anyone owned, and no connection to farming or fishing. We were all pretty typical people who worked in the mines or did nothing."

The rider in her red jacket was a tease.

"But the lucky few rode horses?"

"One of the things that happens in a place like this," said McKay, "is that everyone is thrown into the same pot. You don't have the segregation or class stratification that you find in places like Vancouver, where there are whole sections of the city that you could map out according to income levels. Sure, I grew up in a place where rich and poor lived on different streets, but we poor kids were in the same school as the Sobeys' children were. I knew families with no floorboards in their houses, where you could drop a rock right through to the cellar, but I can also show you the house where our ex-premier John Hamm lived when he was a doctor. I spent my whole life on Red Row, and I slept over there one night. I went with a friend, and when he stopped outside, I remember saying, 'You don't fool me. This isn't *your* house, it's your *church*.' I followed my friend in and I had culture shock. I phoned home to say that on the wall there was a painting with a light over it, and that its only job was to light the painting."

✧　✧　✧

THE COMPANY TOWNS of Canada's first stage of work became towns proper in the second, industrial in character though often feudal in their arrangements. Authority was still depended on, but the power was exerted by an owner who was local and recognizable. The boss had a face. An address. For a while, the world and all its peculiar pleasures and conflicts and false promises could be found within the limits of these towns. The authority was still distant – though not for reasons of geography, but because of a burgeoning class structure such as had flourished in Britain in the eighteenth and nineteenth centuries. The factory owner was patrician – and, with any luck, benevolent. Thus, in these towns there was still that very Canadian sense of the ordinary man or woman having to endure the authority that was the great provider.

In the many novels of David Adams Richards, the author's attention is not focused on the upper classes explicitly, but the reader senses the thorn that overbearing authority represents for him. The "underclass" Richards says he writes about has none of their power, and in the New Brunswick novelist's work there is a consistent wariness of people with privileges that are bestowed on them, rather than the result of their own hard work – the mill boss and the policeman, but also the social worker with her own agenda, or the academic who wears a uniform of smugness and is otherwise suspect. He is often callous, a philanderer, or fraudulent, and wields his academic credentials over others who are typically less fortunate, uneducated – and brilliant. Readers of Proust and Stendahl, as Sydney Henderson is in *Mercy Among the Children*. Richards's dislike of "sophisticates who would snigger at a failed colleague in a room" is obvious, though his contempt does not extend to those sitting at the top of the local food chain. In a feudal situation, classes must share the territory, and this necessity leads to a social contract that serves both parties, if the worker somewhat less. Richards, an avid fisher whose Newcastle home sits on the salmon-rich waters of the Miramichi, once told me the story of a river guide who took care of a fishing lodge for an American family who never used it. The owners gave the caretaker permission to drink the liquor they kept in the lodge, and the guide became a drunk waiting for the day when they might show. The man knew where all the salmon were but *those* rights he did not have. Not just the salmon was the thing that was owned. So, not without reason, I was surprised that when I asked Richards about matters of class, he was dismissive.

"I didn't know that I wrote about work until people in Toronto told me that I did. To me, they just worked at the mill."

"Maybe the work these characters did was interesting to the people in Toronto because in the cities it has become a more abstract thing."

"I think it was because they worked with their hands," said Richards, "and that put them in a category outside intellectual work. When my first book, *The Coming of Winter*, was published, there was a whole group of reviews that said Kevin was terribly poor, and that he worked with his hands, but it was really that he did a kind of work that didn't need a university education – or the reviewers *supposed* that he didn't need a university education in order to do it – and there was an intellectual reaction to that. You know, he was not university-educated and therefore he *must* be poor. But Kevin probably earned more money than the reviewers who said he was poor did."

Put reviewers alongside those suspect university professors. Urban charlatans, they are. Deejays wielding power that is someone else's.

"Really, I don't write about the 'working class,'" said Richards. "I write about people like Sydney Henderson in *Mercy Among the Children*, who don't have a union card. *Class* was a word I never even used until I read the reviews. My characters were categorized from the first, but not by me, and I thought, 'This is not what I'm doing.' I mean, I don't know *what* class Sydney is, I wouldn't want to be the one to categorize him. Certainly he's as intellectual in his responses to the books that he reads and what he knows about the world as any university professor I've ever sat down with is. He happened to live his life a little differently, that's all."

Richards shrugged and pushed his chair back as if he didn't want to be too close. Richards is one of those authors who speaks of the characters he has written as if they are living, and in the room. He can be pissed off with them too, these men and women who will not leave him.

"All I'm saying," said Richards, "is that work had no greater meaning, when I started to write, than being the work my characters did. I was writing about people whom I'd grown up with all my life."

In the feudal-industrial towns of Canada's second stage of work, authority is in full view. Power has a face and is expected to use it. The governed understand its exercise, and even want to be able to see the human shape it takes. Irving, the man himself, at a town meeting, dressed in rubber boots and speaking with an accent just as the next man does. Or Lord Beaverbrook, who, whatever his English success, did not forget his New Brunswick origins. *One of us.* The fault of Richards's university professors is to stand nebulously outside the straightforward relationship of workingman and overseer – and to be from the cities. Stenson's class paradigm applies in

Richards's New Brunswick too. In *Hockey Dreams: Memories of a Man Who Couldn't Play*, the professors are even worse – unpatriotic, back-to-the-land zealots who *want* Canada to lose the 1972 Summit Series with the Soviet Union and put their bullied husbands in the position of not being able to watch the fabled games. The elite, is the inference, are embarrassed by the vulgar hockey tactics of the Canadian team and cannot see the merits of the authentic, un-college-educated players and fans whom Richards has always known and admired. The influence of the poet Alden Nowlan, born in Nova Scotia but who lived and died in New Brunswick, is huge. In their showdown with the Russians, Richards's hockey players are versions of Nowlan's celebrated soldier of the poem "Ypres: 1915":

> Private MacNally thinking:
> You squareheaded sons of bitches,
> you want this God damn trench
> you're going to have to take it away
> from Billy MacNally
> of the South End of Saint John, New Brunswick.

Richards's stalwarts are good workingmen, or cons maligned by circumstance. His nemeses are the professors and intellectuals, new factors of the distant authority, muddying the neat feudal arrangements that saw, in *River of the Brokenhearted*, the author's fictional Lord Beaverbrook take in the river-soaked Janie McLeary and give her the money she needed to save her fledgling picture house.

McLeary is a tough, resourceful, and hard-working woman who combats conniving rivals, changing circumstance, and the constraints of her gender as she battles to support her family by running a business long before Maritime society was tolerant of the independent woman wishing to make her own way in the world. The character of McLeary is loosely based on Richards's own grandmother, and the encounter with Lord Beaverbrook, in a house where single lamps would have had the sole purpose of illuminating paintings, had roots in real life too.

"The owners could be magnanimous, and I had a little fun with that," said Richards. "When my grandmother needed money for her theatre and she had no one to go to, it was actually a lumber baron who gave her the money, but in the novel I had Beaverbrook do it. My mother was terrified. She had never been in a house like that before. She thought he would refuse, but he said, 'Of course. Sure. No problem.'"

From David Adams Richards's *River of the Brokenhearted*:

Beaverbrook, the little town imp, would one day finance the Spitfire airplane to defend Britain against Hitler's Luftwaffe. But that was still a long way off, in a future he hadn't yet considered – though it was already in the thoughts of his friend Winston Churchill.

At this moment Beaverbrook was trying to think of who this girl was. Perhaps he had seen her as a little girl near the well. But he wasn't quite sure. He smiled, and his eyes narrowed. He had been telling anecdotes about Churchill and Lloyd George, saying that he felt Winston's career was over, an addition to the dustbin of history. It was a very common mistake made that year, and Lord Beaverbrook made his share of common mistakes.

"Although he might make a comeback, I cannot see it," he had ventured, boldly.

Now he shifted his weight slightly, crossed his ankles, and changed his accent to a Miramichi one, which he could affect as easily as a bawdy joke. "A McLeary. I bet you are Jimmy's girl."

She nodded.

"That would be it – Jimmy's girl. Has Jimmy gone to his reward?" Beaverbrook asked.

"Not yet – so the reward keeps dwindling," Janie said.

"Ah yes, a common problem." Beaverbrook smiled. He liked this girl very much. And wanted to know what she did.

He suspected she did not do much. To him, Irish people were fine, but needed taking care of.

"Janie owns a picture show," Eastbrook offered.

"You own a picture house?"

She noticed that he was visibly impressed, perhaps more because she was Irish and a McLeary than because she was a woman.

"Yes, I do, sir," she said.

"Well, I'll be damned. Good going. But don't call me sir."

"Do I call you lord?" my grandmother said clumsily.

"Call me Max."

"I think you have earned sir," she said quietly.

"But that's an *approachable* lumber baron," said Alistair MacLeod. "The resource was owned mainly by a man, or maybe by his two brothers – by, you know, families that are still in the Maritimes and they have *faces*. I know the industries and so do you too, where the resource was locally owned and people go to the owner and say, 'Will you give us an ad for the school yearbook?' and Mr. So-and-So would say, 'Okay, here are your seven dollars.' But now if you go to the Company for an ad in the school yearbook, they say, 'Well, we have to contact Germany!' and they are never going to give seven dollars for the little school yearbook because the Company is a *corporation*."

✧ ✧ ✧

AT THE IRVING gas station in Pokiok, New Brunswick, a stone's throw from the magnificent Saint John River, Debbie waited on the fifteen-odd tables of the Big Stop diner, packed with a few tourists, but mostly truck drivers and mill workers from nearby Nackawic, home of "The World's Biggest Axe."

"How's the hot dog, sir?" Debbie asked, bringing a cola to the table. Not one to waste a trip, she scooped up the plates of the neighbouring booth in passing and then shuffled up the narrow aisle towards the counter, her hips already oversized. She was in her late twenties, I figured. Maybe she was thirty.

"Does the man himself ever come in?" I asked.

"Oh yes," said Debbie. "Eight years ago, he did."

She shook her head from side to side, her eyes stretched in mock relief at having survived the experience. She knew it was an Irving that I was talking about.

"He gave me a fifty-dollar tip," said Debbie, "but, oh jeez, I wouldn't want to go through that again."

"Takes good care of you, does he?"

"Oh yes. Have you ever met the Irvings, sir?"

"No. No, I haven't."

"They're some of the richest men in Canada, but good people, they are."

Ding ding!

✧ ✧ ✧

A JOURNEY THROUGH the wooded province of New Brunswick makes the traveller feel like an intruder, so insistent are the visual reminders that the land and its bounty are the private property of just *a few people*. The Irving name on plates, truck stops, refineries; McCain's on the fries. Is it any surprise that feuds with the First Nations here – over lobster fishing rights at Burnt Church, timber with the Maliseet – have been so extreme? A Canadian in Montreal, Toronto, or Vancouver risks appearing quite mad were he, or she, to talk about the land on which thousands of businesses and institutions and hundreds of thousands of citizens operate as belonging to one native group, but in New Brunswick, where so much that one sees bears the stamp of a couple of families, it seems quite rational to look around and react to it by saying, "Hold on, this land is not *yours*, it's *mine*." The very possibility that such vast tracts of land can be privately owned is an infuriating fact that smacks you in the face – and you either rebel against it, as from time to time First Nations do, or you defer to the order of this family-based organization of monopoly and wealth and choose not to be bothered by the American who owns but never uses the lodge, or when Paul Martin, as prime minister-elect, travels in the Irving Company plane and is *not* reprimanded because the ethics commissioner says, it's okay, it's permissible because the two families are *friends*. Only, hold on, isn't that what an ethics commissioner is *for* – to stop the PM and the Company governor from cavorting?

✧ ✧ ✧

PARIS, ONTARIO, was like Goderich, a rural industrial town that seemed to have been exhausted of any vital economic purpose when I drove there to meet John Bemrose, author of *The Island Walkers*. It is a pretty town, beautifully situated on the river Grand, the waters of which powered the mill that Hiram Capron, an American industrialist and amateur poet, established there in 1829. The Company that provided its *raison d'être* was owned by a "Mr. So-and-So" – Capron was the sort who would have given Alistair MacLeod seven dollars for the high-school yearbook or Richards's Janie McLeary the money *she* needed to run her picture house. Later the Penmans garment factory operated there – becoming, in its day, the largest supplier of knitted goods to the Commonwealth.

Paris is where Bemrose was born and raised. It is an evocative setting that other writers, including Michael Ondaatje, have also used (Ondaatje's errant millionaire, Ambrose Small, flees there in his novel of work in Toronto, *In the Skin of a Lion*). The town becomes Attawan in *The Island Walkers*, and Penmans is Bannerman's. The owner of the fictional mill is one Abraham Shade, and he lives in town just as Hiram Capron did – at the top of Snob Hill.

Shade is an anachronistic figure, one that exemplifies Canada and the Company Town in its new, more elaborate incarnation. The authority on which the workers depend is still overbearing, but the boss is local and the economy is beginning to diversify, so that the critical relationship of employer and worker appears to rest on a social contract in which consensus, and not servitude, is akin to a family value that both uphold. Shade, as Capron was, is a romantic and a philanthropist. He is a benevolent patron who, true to the times, saw not just prosperity but the promise of a modest Utopia in the industrial town that he founded. A poetic sensibility and a commercial one were not at odds, then.

"In writing this particular kind of frontiersman," said Bemrose, "this businessman *cum* writer *cum* poet, I wanted to create the ideal of a businessman who would stand in stark contrast to the kind that prospers today and considers his obligations accomplished something simply by adding to the bottom line. The particular kind of business leader we have today has taken the position that as long as the business runs well, everything else – including the prosperity and well-being and happiness of society – will occur automatically. This isn't true, and some of these men of another era had a much wider vision of their connection to society. Hiram Capron was influenced to put the town and his businesses here because he had fallen in love with the physical beauty of the place – and that in itself is a very uneconomic notion. He became known, affectionately, as 'King Capron' because he took such a deep interest in the welfare of all the people who lived here, and not just as employees. When people found themselves out of work, or if the man of the family had been killed in an accident, then food and money would arrive at the door from King Capron. He felt that it was his duty to take a good portion of his earnings and put them back into the town that was earning him profits. He built schools here, he built a church, he built the YMCA. Whenever someone had a good cause going, then he could turn up at King Capron's door, and he would be ready with his chequebook."

"Did the benevolence of a figure like Abraham Shade have a detrimental aspect?"

"Yes, it did," said Bemrose. "It demanded – metaphorically if not literally – a perpetual touching of the forelock, a doffing of the cap. There may have been genuine affection for such paternalistic leaders, but there is always something in the back of the mind that knows it is merely chance that has put me down here and him *up there*. It is not a question of virtue but actually a matter of chance, so there is a reserve, sometimes, of anger or at least *resentment* in people who, on the face of things, are being cheerful and loyal workers."

Paris, like Munro's Goderich or the Midland that novelist Richard Wright called Huron Falls, was one of a plethora of mid-sized Ontario towns that were largely unchanged from the 1930s through the early 1960s. Often the local department store owner acted as banker too and brokered mortgages, in the way that Canada's leading grocer family, the Westons, is beginning to do again through the "President's Choice" banking card of the Loblaws chain. *Plus ça change*. There was a diversity of trades in these towns and what used to be called the professions – doctors, lawyers, "merchants," and working families, as well as the wealthier ones of Company managers who had often come from away. The beginning of a class structure was evident in these towns' topography – the rich on the high ground, workers on the flats. Schools tended to be public and segregated by faith so that children from all social strata studied together.

"You never thought in terms of being someone 'up there,'" Richard Wright later told me. "It would have been 'beyond my ken.' We were much more modest in our ambitions. A suitable ambition for someone like myself would have been to be a schoolteacher or perhaps to work in publishing. You simply weren't conditioned to look too far. In a way that was a very Protestant thing – a very *Northern Irish* thing. There was probably no barrier there, if you were ambitious enough, but somehow you were conditioned to think that you were not good enough – or it just didn't occur to you to be that ambitious. As Alice Munro famously said, 'Who do you think you are?' Alice's work resonates with me so much, I know her characters exactly, and I think she'd know some of mine too. I don't think I would ever have gone to school with anybody who said, 'You know, one day I'm going to sing at the Met.' It took me a long time to believe that I could ever be a writer, and I had to get out of Midland to do it."

"There's a very moving moment in *The Weekend Man*," I said, "when Wes Wakeham's father, Art, returns from the war. He's been drinking a bit, and there's a scene. He's chastised by the mum and after their argument he resolutely comes down the stairs with a paper parcel in his hands – not with a bottle in it, but his denims, and he goes off to the flour mill to work."

"That's the mentality that I grew up with," said Wright. "You've got to earn your living. You've got responsibilities. You can't walk out the door."

The tidy and deferential arrangements of Canadian towns in the country's second stage of work reinforced an idea of service at home, that was exercised abroad, in military fealty to the Allied cause. The needle of Canada's Commonwealth economy was pointed towards the Old Country then, workers doing what was demanded of them, with Canadian nobility acting as obliging brokers. Jobs were for life, and the reward of good service was promotion, though within strata that were determined in an orthodox class structure. Foremen and managers were workers who had risen through the ranks – but only so far. In the Old World economy such as existed in Attawan, the duty was to family and the social order as it existed. It was a conservative social order based not just on *workers* doffing the cap, but on their bosses doing so too. To do otherwise was to aspire *beyond one's ken*.

"The thing about business is that it is essentially authoritarian," said Bemrose, "and in Canada there has always been a little more deference, a little more fear of authority, than there needs to be. We don't even see an illustration of proud independence of character in our *ruling* class. Really, you should at least be able to look at the *aristocracy* in your country and believe that they are beholden to no one. We look at our aristocracy and see that they are beholden to London and New York."

Bemrose held his hands up in frustration.

"Where is the example of pride that could saturate society from top to bottom?"

Bemrose and I were talking at the Arlington Hotel, on the old Paris main street, named after the famous American military cemetery outside Washington. Bemrose wanted a more Canadian flavour in his novel, and, as Alf Walker's memories of the Second World War are germane, he changed its name to The Vimy House, after the battle of April 1917 in which Canadian soldiers distinguished themselves. At the Vimy is where Bemrose's beleaguered hero meets Malachi Doyle, a union organizer. The Bannerman's factory has been purchased by "Intertext," an American company intent on modernizing, and that must defeat an emerging workers' union in order to institute its plans. As the town finds itself on the threshold of a new, globalized stage of work, Alf struggles at the confluence of two kinds of economies and the rival allegiances they demand.

"Ultimately," said Bemrose, "what distinguishes Intertext from Bannerman's is that the American company has no loyalty whatsoever to Attawan, so when Intertext actually purchases the Company, it treats it as if it were as moveable as a car. The Company can be transferred to some far location with little regard for the effect on the people – and, of course, it absolutely craters the town."

The usurpation of the old post-war economy, by a new "globalized" order with its headquarters in America, is provided a personal tableau in Bemrose's novel, the figure of Alf's son Joe and his affection for Anna Macrimmon. She is the beautiful daughter of one of the Intertext executives posted from afar. Her mother is French. Anna has travelled and is well read. Joe wants out of a community and a social order that he finds stultifying. What he yearns for is opportunity of all kinds – more *culture*, a better job – and falling in love with Anna is one way for Joe to acquire it.

"But in the end, Anna shares the transience of the large corporation that has bought the Company and brought her family to town, and then moves them away," said Bemrose. "Anna is very much a part of this new phenomenon of the mobility of corporations and of capital. She is also an expression of its tragedy, as she too lacks a sense of rootedness in any place. She can't make a commitment, whereas Joe, in his own eyes at least, is a little too deeply rooted."

"The relationship between worker and employer is altered again, because the Company has lost its familiar face."

"Absolutely," said Bemrose. "In one way or another people in every community in this country are dealing with the strange and insidious mobility of international capital. Because it owes no loyalty whatsoever to place, there is an air of indifference perpetrated in the ventures of these conglomerates that means that no matter how much is uttered about wanting to do good things for workers or the community at large, what is said is never quite believed. The workers don't trust that management will always be there for them, and management does not trust that the workers will be loyal to the Company, as they were in the old days. There was a general breaking of the social contract that sustained industry through decades in this country."

Through centuries, in fact.

Attawan is like Igloolik before Parry came, only Intertext is the *Hecla* and the Qallunaat are Americans this time around. In both communities, the local order was upheld by conservative myths extolling values needing to be maintained for the benefit of all. And each stood to be undermined by an invasive foreign order and the new, aggressive morality of the stories they brought. In the battle of stories, it could be said that Bemrose's novel is actually a romance, his Alf Walker a lament for the days when all the King's men could put Humpty together again. Poor Alf Walker is defending an idea of *place*, alongside work as a source of pride as much as livelihood. The new American order – more often said, the *globalized* order – is one in which class deference and fealty to place play no part. Income, and not the type of work one does, is the key to status, and the new boss has spurned the old land-based jobs and feudal arrangements for a territory that is international. The Company has become a *corporation*. In this way, the Canadian town where the boss was briefly local is returned, in Bemrose's novel, to the state of being a satellite governed by a distant authority. Ever since the days of the Hudson's Bay Company, this has been the natural model for administration of this vast country. Canada is at the margins, and the distant authority is in London, then Ottawa, then Washington. But today, in the third stage of work, our alienation is the result not just of geographical and political arrangements, but of the jobs we do. Now the work that is shaping the country's character is done in cities, the final end of so much of the new migration. In Michael Ondaatje's novel *In the Skin of a Lion*, the dynamism lies in the brimming new world of Toronto. Immigrants such as the Macedonian bridge builder Nicholas Temelcoff arrive in Canada and are employed in the construction of the city's infrastructure. The secular temple, on Lake Ontario, of Toronto's Water Filtration Plant, designed by Rowland Caldwell Harris, with its great stone porch, cavernous halls, and elegant detail. Or, the Bloor Street Viaduct, its grand ironwork and roman arches spanning the Don Valley ravine. Work is not so much a way of understanding personal ties to the land but, as a light thrown on the people who are drawn to do it, the demographics altering the very nature of the country and the wonder of its complex cities.

The idea of work has always been important to Ondaatje, whether the Sikh Kirpal Singh's tense defusing of bombs in *The English Patient* or the patient forensic archaeology of Anil in *Anil's Ghost*. But *In the Skin of the Lion* is probably Ondaatje's most famous addressing of the importance of labour, and searching for inspiration he listened to the archival recordings of the true-to-life figure of Nicholas Temelcoff that he found at the Multicultural Historical Society of Ontario. Quite unforgettably, the character of the bridge worker that the Macedonian immigrant Temelcoff inspired hangs suspended from the unfinished viaduct, saving a nun who falls from it with his outstretched arm. Through work, Ondaatje explained to me beneath the viaduct where the fictional incident took place, he was provided a way in.

"There's something ceremonial about the viaduct," said Ondaatje. "Toronto is a city where certain places become landmarks – this viaduct, the water works – just as the cathedrals of Europe are, or the pyramids in Egypt. I'm very fond of such structures."

"Do they represent the spirit of the city for you in some way?"

"Yes, but I'm not sure what that spirit is. Each of us has places that are sanctuaries."

"And they belong to a time when the job of engineer was a more laudatory one."

"It was a time when you were able to build in a way that now you cannot," said Ondaatje. "When I was doing my research, I found a whole bunch of designs for civic structures. There were all these suggestions for what to do with University Avenue that weren't used because they were too weird, too adventurous. They were altering the city around us. The idea that you could choose the kind of place that you lived in seems quite radical today. Now we are locked into thinking about finance and real estate."

"Did it take you time to find your way into the book?" I asked.

"It was gradual. I thought about having some episodes take place on the bridge, and did some research as I worked, but I had no idea that the book was about immigrants and the city, or that there would be the two locations of the viaduct and the water works until much later on."

"How do you find the act of beginning a novel?" I asked.

"It's an act of curiosity," said Ondaatje, "or a search of some kind. The question you start with is, 'How can I begin this story?' Perhaps I have a man walking on a bridge, or I have a boy on a farm eating some rhubarb and walking across a field, which was one of my first images for *In the Skin of a Lion*. Because writing is archaeo-logical, in the way that you are uncovering something, and if I feel – if I *know* – the thing that's going to be uncovered before I start, then the book just doesn't interest me. I'm not going to have the kind of nervousness that I like when I'm writing. I need the mystery of where Ambrose Small is, or who the English Patient is, or what is happening to Anil and Sarah in *Anil's Ghost*. All of these things are behind the curtain. There has to be a mystery somewhere, though I think that with all my writing, I need to find some kind of reality – even though it becomes fictional eventually. I really need to find out who built the bridge, *why* it was built, how it was built, how much sand and how much woodwork was used, what the intention of the bridge was. All these things begin the book. It is like having a series of fragmentary notes that could last you for a while and that you can use later on. The book starts without plot, has no great theme or anything like that, but there must be something in it for me. I have to be learning something, and paralleling that, so must the characters."

"So did you have Nicholas Temelcoff working in a safety brace strapped beneath the bridge *before* you had your group of nuns walking along its windy surface?"

"Yes, I did – or perhaps the nuns were walking along and then I realized that there had to be someone below the bridge, and then I had to find out about Nicholas Temelcoff and he became the solution to the problem that began as I was writing. I was dying to hear this tape, because I was dying to know what it was like to build a bridge and work at night and walk with flares in your hands and stuff like that. And it came down to the question, 'What was it like to work at night?' It was a very dangerous job, and he said, 'It was very difficult.'" Ondaatje laughed. "That's all that he said, and so I was left with this empty space that I had to fill in. The fact that he said nothing was good for me. It was a gift to me because then I had to invent the difficulty."

"There must be some anxiety, when you are researching, for that very reason," I said, "that the facts might make the task more difficult."

"Definitely. You always get frustrated when the facts aren't there, but the *silence* of facts is what frees you to build a whole new room and a whole new situation."

✧   ✧   ✧

CANADA, IN ITS final stage of work, has moved from Company Towns to feudal-industrial ones and now cities, reflecting the progression from prospecting and roaming the land, to settling where the sustenance is, and then taking jobs that have severed their ties to the land completely. The cost is of a commitment to place that is also undermined, as we look elsewhere for income and validation. And yet it would be a mistake not to heed Alistair MacLeod's words that "you have to be ambivalent about what progress is." The new work will explain itself.

MacLeod is the Canadian author who has written most eloquently about the relationship to place that work provides, and work as a source of alienation too – in his story of a reluctant lobster fisher, "The Boat," and in "The Closing Down of Summer" especially. With its rhythmic oral cadences, the latter story is one of the great contemplations of the *physical* side of work and how we've moved away from it.

From Alistair MacLeod's "The Closing Down of Summer":

> I would like to tell my wife and children something of the way my years pass by on the route to my inevitable death. I would like to explain somehow what it is like to be a gladiator who fights always the impassiveness of water as it drips on darkened stone. And what it is like to work one's life in the tightness of confined space. I would like somehow to say how I felt when I lost my father in Kirkland Lake or my younger brother in Springdale, Newfoundland. I would like to say how frightened I am sometimes of what I do. And of how I lie awake at night aware of my own decline and of the diminishing of the men around me. For all of us know we will not last much longer and that it is unlikely we will be replaced in the shaft's bottom by members of our own flesh and bone. For such replacement, like our Gaelic, seems to be of the past and now largely over.
>
> Our sons will go to the universities to study dentistry or law and to become fatly affluent before they are thirty. Men who will stand over six feet tall and who will move their fat, pudgy fingers over the limited possibilities to be found in

other people's mouths. Or men who sit behind desks shuffling papers relating to divorce or theft or assault or the taking of life. To grow prosperous from pain and sorrow and the desolation of human failure. They will be far removed from the physical life and will seek it out only through jogging or golf or games of handball with friendly colleagues. They will join expensive private clubs for the pleasures of perspiration and they will not die in falling stone or chilling water or thousands of miles from those they love. They will not die in any such manner, partially at least because we have told them not to and have encouraged them to seek out other ways of life which lead, we hope, to gentler deaths.

Whoever we are, we are still what we do. MacLeod's dentists have lost the intimate and inherited relationships to the places their parents lived in, as Canada as it was governed by the Company Town and then the feudal-industrial one has given way to a new country in which the location of the firm that we are working for is as likely to be a virtual one on the Web, with call centres in Mumbai or Tucson or Nova Scotia – a fourth-generation miner put to the phones to explain a product's guarantee.

The unanchored character of so much of the work we do goes hand in hand with new doubts about our patrimony. The zealous business communities of Toronto, Calgary, and Vancouver see the chance of new prosperity in serving the distant authority of foreign markets that are described as "globalized" now. Once again, Canadians are subjected to powerful monopolies, only now the economic conditions of this country seem oddly familiar, for the condition of being the farthest promontory of some distant authority has returned in new, more widespread costume. The monopoly is not Canadian any more, the condition not merely Canada's.

"It's funny how work is displayed for us now," said Michael Turner, the day we stood overlooking a fish-feed plant that was still operating at Vancouver's old port. "Around the waterfront it's all heavy-duty work, stevedores and cannery workers, but a lot of what we make in the city now are images. We make films here, we animate. And for years, when the Vancouver Stock Exchange was all smoke and mirrors, we made magic. Now Canada is built on insurance companies and banks and financial capitals and all the myriad arcades that stuff travels around in this mysterious kind of paper pushing. This is really the last of the, quote, *work* that you see in Vancouver – the last, real backbreaking work."

Turner's *The Pornographer's Poem* is a novel rooted in an often sordid, now Web-based industry of casual pornographic filmmaking that could not have a more abstract relationship to the landscapes in which we live. Turner is also the author of *Company Town*, a collection of poems that recounts the imagined history of a bankrupted, family-owned B.C. salmon cannery through the amusingly conflicting memories of four workers he's put there. He has graduated, in his work, from Canada of the Company Town to the new Canada, where ties to place are mostly theoretical and certainly not articulated in work. And yet the old Hudson's Bay tendencies remain, a stubborn expression of the land as it was – and perhaps as it is destined to be. The Company, distant and nebulous, is still something that we endure, without ever expecting much from it, only now Canadians' subjugation before a cartel of overly powerful monopolies is the symptom of a wider, global malaise.

"The model of the Company Store is also manifested at the level of language," said Turner. "So many of the ordinary phrases that we use to describe day-to-day things are borrowed from commercial enterprises. We tell our kids that the *bottom line* is that you must clean your room, and then you get your *allowance*. How is it that commercial language has found its way into domestic space and affected the very way we communicate, even at the level of the family?"

I said, "I'd go so far as to say that our attitudes to government, or to authority of any kind, are shaped by our experience of the Company Town – this dependency, this *enduring* of a distant power."

"But the Company Town is a false notion of a place, insofar as it happens because there is a single business initiative, and everything is brokered by that Company, and it exists, as well, in what you *don't* see. It exists in the ether – in the world's Web, and on the Internet – where there are entities buying and selling without a recognizable address that is in the physical landscape, companies such as Amazon.com and eBay. This is very much the direction in which the world is headed. If nations are reduced to being fairly meaningless in the leverage of power, then the corporations running the world are doing all the brokering, and the Company Town is again the result. We could be in a Company *World* situation very soon. Maybe the solution to the final corporate takeover of the world would be to actually devolve into a feudal situation again, where if you can buy a face to put on your corporation, and a family to go with it, then it will appear a little warmer, a little friendlier, and we won't feel so bad about having to sell our souls to the Company Store another time around."

Turner chuckled wryly, as is his habit.

"Is there any way around the old servitude?" I asked.

"I'd have to refer to myself to answer that question," said Turner apologetically. "The keys to my own writing are production and failure, and you can reduce everything that I have written down to these two ideas. Work is a form of production, but it seems that nobody's ever really making enough money these days to pay off whatever is today's Company Store, so people continue to disparage work as an unpleasant experience. Failure is considered to be the failure to allow work to transform your material situation, but that doesn't actually have to be true. Work keeps me busy. It keeps me producing. I'm probably never paid enough for it, but it's something that I do, and in doing it I create meaning and contest some of those meanings and rethink them everyday. In the end what it means is that my soul is mine, and that the work is not a failure at all."

7

Traces

From Lee Gowan's *Make Believe Love*:

Our farm was an accumulation of many farms: there was
the Vaughn place, the Anderson place, the Davies place, the
Thomas place, and if you walked any of these quarter sections and you knew where to look among the rosebushes and
the wolf willow, you would find a depression in the ground
and maybe a bit of the stone foundation that marked where
the Vaughns or the Davieses or the Thomases had tried to
invent themselves, before the Dust Bowl finally choked them
out. If you dug around, you might discover shards of pottery,
or blackened tin cans. My father had found some scattered
silverware on the Davies homestead and wondered how they
could possibly have forgotten what must have been among
their most valuable possessions, but I liked to imagine Mrs.
Davies tossing the silver over her shoulder as she walked
away forever from the shack she'd called home.

You can think of Alistair MacLeod as a Gaelic highlander from Cape Breton, David Adams Richards as the writer who put the Miramichi on the map, and of Guy Vanderhaeghe as a novelist from Saskatchewan – or you can forget about provincial boundaries and think about the singing of work as a calling these writers have in common. Do so, and our sense of the map of Canada as one of a disparate country is eroded, and in its place another one appears, in which novels arising out of shared experiences wash over the territory just as the people who gave rise to these stories did. The shaft-sinking miners of MacLeod's story "The Closing Down of Summer" leave the beaches of Nova Scotia for work beyond the province and stride into Vanderhaeghe's novel *Homesick*, in which Connaught, an impoverished prairie community much like the author's childhood home of Esterhazy, is transformed by Portuguese workers descending on the place into a vigorous Company Town. Vanderhaeghe is a farmer's son of Belgian stock who remembers when the citizens of Esterhazy didn't want pipes with running water because of the higher taxes they'd be asked to pay. Then the mine came to town and so did prosperity. There were palatial houses with all amenities being built for the managers at one end of town and, in the trailer park, rumours of another kind of woman, "the kind that lived by herself and entertained at any hour."

From Guy Vanderhaeghe's *Homesick*:

> On June 1, with great fanfare, the provincial government and an American mining company had announced that a potash mine would be developed six miles south of Connaught. The choice news was that the town council's gamble appeared to have paid off; Connaught was chosen as company head-quarters. A surge of activity followed hard on the heels of this announcement. Overnight things began to change. Strangers appeared on the streets. The entire second floor of Alec Monkman's hotel became temporary offices for geologists,

engineers, planners, while the third floor became their living and sleeping quarters.

A three-shift crew of shaft sinkers arrived. No one in Connaught had ever seen their like before. To the citizens of Connaught they were a different breed of man, grey-skinned from lack of sun, hard, wild, desperate in the pursuit of their pleasures. Drawn from all over North America, they spoke with every accent, lured by the big money which goes hand in hand with work that demands you risk your life hourly. Their hard-earned wages ran between their fingers like water and they wanted the best that life had to offer and money could buy. They ordered steak and eggs for breakfast, drank Crown Royal. Their cars were big, flashy, expensive, and neglected – Buicks and Chryslers and Oldsmobiles caked in mud or floured in dust. The dangers of the job had made them addicts to excitement so when their shifts were over they made trouble drinking and fighting. There seemed to be no let-up to the noise, the confusion, the disorderliness. Day and night, semis rolled through town bearing huge pieces of earth-moving equipment lashed to their trailers with chains, shaking people in their chairs and in their beds, making the dishes jingle in the cupboard and spoiling television reception. The town council hurriedly passed a by-law outlawing the big trucks from travel on the newly paved streets. Sometimes the drivers heeded the ordinance, sometimes they didn't. When they did, the air was filled with rumble and clouds of yellow dust, and when they didn't, the fresh pavement had to be patched and repaired by the crews of Portuguese.

At the hotel the mining company had started to hire. Men the locals did not recognize caused resentment when they stood in a line that stretched the length of the corridor and slithered down the stairs, each man waiting his turn to step up to the desk and state his occupation – electrician, carpenter, welder, pipe-fitter, labourer. Miners would not be needed for a long time yet.

"Until I was six or seven years old," said Vanderhaeghe, "any work that wasn't on a farm was part-time. Then suddenly people could work twelve months of the year."

"Did the economic boom that you described in *Homesick* last?"

"In Esterhazy, the two mines are still going," said Vanderhaeghe, "but potash is not a renewable resource, and at some point it's going to run out – and then what happens? You don't think about it."

Work today, where there was little yesterday and likely will be none tomorrow. The arrival of the miners from away is good news for Vera, Vanderhaeghe's single mom heroine, who packs them in at the rehabilitated Bluebird Café. The workers will stay until the potash is depleted and then, should the town find no further *raison d'être*, Connaught will go the way of Piegan Post, or Buchans, and become a ghost town instead. Houses sold for a dollar.

"I started school in a place called Mercoal, Alberta," said Alistair MacLeod, "and it was one of those typical Company Towns. We lived in Company houses that were built on skids, and when the price of coal dropped, the town went away. I remember, a number of years ago, driving from Banff to where Mercoal was, and there was absolutely nothing there. I drove into this little clearing and I said to my children, 'This is where I started school.' And they all laughed. They thought, 'Here is Dad being funny.' They were thinking, 'Well, where's the school?' and a woman came out of one of these hunting lodges and said, 'What are you looking for?' and I said, 'Well, I am looking for the school,' and she said, because she had gone to school there too, 'Go over there on your hands and knees and if you crawl around in the grass you will find the foundation of the school.' My father was from Nova Scotia. We had come from a place that was very rooted, and here was this very different kind of place. There are people who come from there who cannot find where they were born, because it was a Company Town that just *vanished*."

The rise of the Company Town and its failure is an inveterate Canadian story, and yet southern Saskatchewan is a part of Canada where the agrarian life was also considered possible. From the days of Louis Riel's failed Métis homeland and the Red River Colony, the Utopian dream had been that crops and livestock raised on the bountiful land would be a *renewable* resource that would see more permanent communities prosper. From the nineteenth century, hopeful families left Upper Canada to spoil the Métis safe haven, settling as their French-speaking predecessors had done. Others came from America, across a border with the United States that was vague until the lawlessness of American whisky-trading posts prompted the expedition of the Northwest Mounted Police to the region. The frontier with America is senseless even today if you consider that land we routinely describe as "prairie" is in fact the tip of the roughly triangular area of the Great Plains extending over some 3.6 million square kilometres south through Texas and into Mexico. Grasslands and rivers and coulees have for millennia been the authentic highways here. The animals and then aboriginal peoples who travelled these paths paid scant attention to the forty-ninth parallel's neat line, though politics affect all territories eventually. In Fred Stenson's novel *Lightning*, American cowboys drive a cattle herd north from Montana and to the Cochrane Lease in 1881. Following the Fort MacLeod Trail, previously the route of the whisky trade, they find the cairn of stones that marks the newly created border and circle it, amused.

Now satellite maps of the area display Canadian wheat fields in wine-dark red and American ones as whites and lighter reds and greens, their variegated colours, on these photographs, the result of different agricultural practices. Canada is entrenched, even though white settlement is recent, the aboriginal presence less so, and the way in which not just humans have passed over Saskatchewan has been ephemeral, mere traces left behind. This is the Prairie Zion, the hard-won territory of visionaries and of workingmen adamantly failing to see how their dreams would be curtailed by arduous circumstance. The province is a land of dodgy harvests, recurring droughts, and, yes, a bit of oil but not much. A plethora of farming communities here are exhausted and empty. Others are being slowly diminished, house by falling house, writing their refrain of spent effort on a land that knows the song too well. Nothing comes easy in Saskatchewan. You work and then, just maybe, you get. Here, the landscape demands to be loved because not to do so is an invitation to despair.

✧　✧　✧

From Karen Solie's "East Window, Victoria":

> Go ahead and think of May,
> how the South Saskatchewan rises
> muddy as a vein to the surface of summer.
> Of pulling crested wheat to suck
> that quick season out
> through the long thick heart of it. The year
> poplar and sage held you in their sunset
> as you fell, leaning into a world
> that did not move away.
>
> But how dare you long
> for those first mornings of frost
> you bit into like an apple, the winters
> skating an unbroken line
> around your small clean body.
> Ungrateful.
>
> Have you forgotten about block heaters?
> Power failures?
> You are lost in the down time of blizzards
> as thin rains fall upon the coast
> and a face that you love
> moves behind the warm window of Vancouver Island

looking more and more
like Mile Zero.

Sometimes writers need to make their subjects strange in order to see them more clearly. The need to assess memories pitilessly is one of the reasons why authors often find it easier to write home from away. The writer sees the place as it is in greater relief from a distance.

In Toronto, I gathered three writers from Saskatchewan who had left the province. Lee Gowan, born in Swift Current, was the author of a couple of novels, including *Make Believe Love*, his story of disrupted prairie small-town life that includes the idea of cinema in its pages. Michael Helm, born in Eston, had been nominated for the 1997 Giller Prize for his novel *The Projectionist*. Like the brooding scholar of his second novel, *In the Place of Last Things*, Helm had moved around some. A strong, almost burly man, he had a habit of looking slightly downward, cagily, as if the strength of his body made him a little uncomfortable and he wasn't quite sure what to do with it. Fights figure early on in both novels and both have smart, uncomfortable outsiders as heroes – men who aren't quite sure what to do with their intelligence. The poet Karen Solie, the author of the Griffin Prize–nominated collection *Short Haul Engine*, was born in Moose Jaw and raised in Richmond in southwestern Saskatchewan. She had left the prairie for the more congenial climes of Victoria, though subsequently she felt out of place there. The pull of home can be an inexorable thing, and ironically, it can be even more so when the living that is remembered is tough. Not to find some way to congratulate yourself for having survived the landscape turns hard years into wasted ones.

"Any place in which you grow up becomes your first map of the world. It defines how you come to think of time, and distance. Everything else is laid over it," said Solie. Young, fair, her thick blonde hair tied up in a tousled bun upon her head, the poet would not have looked out of place at a rodeo or country fair, but words were the dance that she had chosen.

"That first map, that earliest way of understanding the world, doesn't go away," said Gowan. "Articulating what it says is a whole different matter."

"But it's a map of yourself too," said Helm.

"I don't have family left in Saskatchewan," said Gowan. He was tall, lanky, a bit awkward in the city, one sensed, "but when I was setting out on my first couple of books, that's definitely where my subject was."

"But what we do is not just about *naming* the landscape," said Helm. "When we write about a place, we're also writing about the consciousness of that place. Cities are made of fleeting moments of perception and of discontinued moments in the mind, but on farms in Saskatchewan there really is the sense of something very old. There's a sense that the ancient agrarian rhythms still are there, and the question for a writer is how this rhythm works its way into your writing."

"There's a lot more communication that goes on *without* conversation," said Gowan. "Especially in farming communities."

Solie let out a quiet laugh. "Sometimes we grunt and don't even need to speak," she said.

"There are all sorts of unspoken things," said Helm.

In my small kitchen the three sat awkwardly. Almost by definition writers are that way, but the trio seemed particularly uneasy in such close quarters. The landscape of the city is cluttered. It is about the *interaction* of people and things and all of the connections and comparisons and compromises and judgments that such proximity puts into play. But in the hard light of Saskatchewan, people and things have plenty of space to be whatever it is that they are.

"There was a row of teepee rings on the top of the hill near where I grew up," said Gowan. "It was a really windy place to make camp, but because the valley curved there, you could see the game for miles in every direction. If I talk about the sky in Saskatchewan, it's because I'm writing what I know, but still people will say to me, 'Gee, there sure is a lot of sky in your stories.'" Gowan chortled. "Often I'm not even *aware* that I'm using the sky a lot."

"Farmers sure spend a lot of time watching it," said Solie.

"The specificity of a landscape can't help but shape you more notably than the generic nature of a city does," said Gowan.

"In an urban place, almost anything can be of that world," said Helm, "so you can draw freely on metaphor because nothing is alien to whatever it is that you're describing. But out West there are fewer things to make metaphors out of, so that often a description is just saying a name. William Carlos Williams spoke of 'no ideas but in things,' and as long as you know the names of things, you're okay, but I grew up in a small town and not on a farm and because it wasn't easy for me to come up with a lot of nouns, I always felt that I was being left out. If I didn't know the name of a tool and I was writing about it, I had to go find the damn thing."

"Last year," said Solie, "the south saw a lot of rain and down by Eastend there were wildflowers that even some of the oldest people in the town had never seen. That's something else that comes to me when I think about Saskatchewan – these little wonders that punch through the *usualness* of the place."

"When you describe something like that," said Helm, "it makes me wonder just how superficial our memories of the place are. Living in Saskatchewan there is a constant sense of possible erasure. Certainly, you can't have been there through one of the droughts and not have confronted that."

"Landscape creeps in," said Solie.

"It's a landscape that has had a lot of violence done to it because of the farming," said Helm, "and yet there's a whole *other* landscape out there that's still wild."

"One of the biggest differences about Saskatchewan and the rest of the world," said Gowan, "is that elsewhere humans are succeeding in controlling the landscape and changing it. In Saskatchewan, the landscape is winning the battle."

✧ ✧ ✧

LEADER, SASKATCHEWAN, some sixty kilometres from where Karen Solie grew up, is, like so many of the farming communities of the southwest, comprised of a few houses gathered at a crossroads and a gas station (for sale). A hamburger kiosk sells burgers made from frozen patties. Next to it is the Rattler's Café, a one-storey box of a building in which there is a bar, and a dining room with no windows. "Snake Bites" are the specialty – jalapeno peppers stuffed with cheese spread, breaded, and deep-fried. The day I passed through, the room was hot and a couple of overhead fans whirred. At a table in the centre of the neon-lit restaurant, four farmers were drinking coffee and shooting the breeze. One of them wore a pink shirt and a cowboy hat, and was the owner of a vintage Cadillac parked outside. The others wore caps and engineers' overalls.

"I can't tell the City Man his business any more than he can tell me mine," said the elderly cowboy in the pink shirt, "but the money isn't there, and if you have to borrow from the bank, there's always somebody grabbing you by the neck and saying *pay, pay, pay*."

"It's a lifetime of work and for what?" said another.

"It ain't because we're bad farmers," said the third. "It's because the money *isn't there*."

"Gas fields, that's where the money is now," said the man in pink.

"Dad said life in the 1930s was *better* than now," said the third. "The crops of the 1940s and 1950s were good, but that's when the fuel bill started going up, but *now* –"

"But the City Man is goin' to stand out there in the dust and tell you everything's fine."

"It's not easy," said the other.

"Never is," said the third.

"But we're not crying," the cowboy in the pink shirt said.

✧ ✧ ✧

I WAS ON my way to meet Jacqueline Baker in Burstall, near the Sand Hills, the territory that had given rise to the fiction of her collection, *A Hard Witching and Other Stories*, when I realized that I'd been this way before.

In the summer of 1978, I'd worked as a jughound for a seismic crew. My job was to pound the sensors – called "jugs" – into the ground. These record vibrations set off by explosives and give an idea of the stratification beneath the surface. It's the first stage in the exploration and then exploitation of oil and gas. A geologist working in some distant city office draws a grid of lines across a map, with as little regard for existing roads and fields and coulees as Macdonald's government had when it divided up the West for settlement and enraged the local Métis. Surveyors flag these lines that drillers then pursue and perforate at regular intervals. Explosives teams follow in the drillers' tracks and plug the holes with dynamite. Finally, the seismic crew arrives, a modern-day posse spinning out a mile or so of cable from the boxes in the backs of their one-ton trucks, and tossing the loops of jugs to be attached to them. The jughound, last to walk the line, cuts through the roads and fields and water, and drives the sensors into the ground with the heel of his shoe. We'd do this, and afterwards sit in the cab and wait for the field geologist, working from the back of a small mobile laboratory, to ignite the charge and measure the ensuing vibrations with his instruments. Then we'd be given the all-clear, pick up the last half mile of cable, and move it to the front, rolling this way across the prairie for four dollars and fifty cents an hour, time and a half after eight, double after ten, and six hours paid for no work at all when it rained or if the wind shook the ground too much. The days were long, and at the peak of summer, they were very hot. Many times, the six or seven of us waiting it out at the back of the line would get into fights – over who drank the last of the water, a bad joke, or a racist taunt.

The crews in the 1970s were made up of men from Newfoundland, Nova Scotia, and Ontario, mostly. We had drifted west for work, and each of us was handed twenty dollars "hotshot" at the end of the day, ours to spend at diners such as Vanderhaeghe's Vera managed in Connaught, or at the local motel that would promptly jack its rates. I'd started with the crew in Melita, Manitoba, in June, walked through Estevan, Saskatchewan, and then in a line south of Regina and Swift Current, towards Maple Creek, north of the Cypress Hills. In late spring, the fields we'd walked through were freshly tilled.

They'd come alive with green shoots by early summer, and were undulating blankets of golden wheat by the time we'd reached this far. Then it was August, the night air already chilly. The season was turning and soon there would be wind and snow and ice and the roads would be treacherous. Like animals readying themselves for winter, it was impossible, at the time, not to consider the long dark months ahead, and the retreat that folk would soon make indoors. In hamlets with their main streets half boarded up, we'd park our trucks in front of the local tavern, where I imagined cowboys had tied their horses a century before, play pool or shuffleboard, and wait for the barmaid with the change dispenser on her belt to tell us where in the trailer park the party was. There would be a pizzeria, and a Chinese restaurant or laundry, last traces of a people that had put the CP Railway through. Burstall, north of Maple Creek, was a village like this. The streets were quiet and Jacqueline Baker, the writer I was looking for, was waiting on the deck of her mother's house. The fire doors of the local bar were jammed open and a couple of kids were hanging outside the one operating restaurant on the other side of the main street. There was a church at one end of it, a small library at the other. A couple of young men were having a cigarette by their stationary pickup truck. It bore the insignia of the nearby gas refinery, the smoke of which could be seen rising from stacks on the far horizon. The refinery provided some work, but not enough to stem the exodus of young people and so, again, I found myself remarking on the dying aspect of a town that, in the last century, held the promise of a fresh start.

Baker, her dark hair cut short, was an attractive woman in her mid-thirties. She was lean, wore spectacles, the figure willowy but strong. She had that no-nonsense manner of Western Canadian women, where beauty seems an afterthought to the fact of outside living. She was in British Columbia now, at work on a novel, and had returned to Saskatchewan to show me around the area and find the farm on which she had been raised. We travelled east towards Liebenthal, left the paved highway after a while, and drove a couple of kilometres south on a broad gravel road. The dust billowed behind us, and here and there the fields were punctuated by one of a dwindling number of abandoned farmhouses – the ones that had not yet fallen down, that is. I watched a family of antelope bounding in the fields towards the shelter of a clump of trees, or perhaps the cut of a river valley that was below our sightline. Another derelict farmhouse marked the way – abandoned when, fifty years ago, twenty, ten? What had been the home's windbreak of trees had outgrown its first use and become a bushy surround that obscured most of the building from view. Soon it would be swallowed up. When the houses die here, they do so rather beautifully. Their paint peels away and moss takes over their roofs. They take on grey and brown hues before, finally, the roofs collapse and the walls fall to the ground and decay. Why had this house not been levelled, I wondered? To whom did it matter more than the right of way of combine harvesters across the fields it interrupted? Had it been left behind in exasperation, in the manner of Lee Gowan's Mrs. Davies, or was somebody, somewhere, thinking that she might eventually return to the house as Baker was doing with me?

We turned off the gravel road and came to a halt before the Baker home, still standing in the middle of tidy grounds. There were a few trees, a couple of outhouses, some pieces of rusted farm machinery, and three tin sheds that looked as if they were still in use. The window frames of the farmhouse were empty and its doors were knocking.

"This was the original homestead of my stepfather," said Baker, looking up at the window beneath the peak of the roof. "There's an attic up there, and I've been up in it many times, and –"

Baker did not finish her sentence, but the word *ghost* was written across the face of the child she'd once been.

"When did your family arrive?" I asked.

"Around 1908 to 1910, from Maple Creek," said Baker. "It was a long trek, there were very few stopping places and not a lot of water along the way, so that it was quite a journey to come out here and choose the land. In my story 'Sand Hills,' I have one of the fellows staking his claim and then drinking from a slough and dying of a fever in a rooming house in Maple Creek a few days later. That actually did happen to my maternal great-grandfather."

The rooms of the house were strewn with debris and the feces of animals that had made shelter in it, but there was still the poignant suggestion of the lives once lived inside its walls. Some rusted tin cans were sitting on the kitchen counter. The way the window looked out over the garden so practically, one could imagine young children playing on the grass and Mrs. Baker watching them, hands in the warm dishwater. The temptation was to start at the mess with a broom.

"How did you get around?" I asked, looking out at the gently undulating fields stretching away almost infinitesimally.

"I rode a bike," said Baker. "There were two bachelor farmers who lived down the road. One of them is still living there, but almost everybody else gave up a long time ago."

The next house was two kilometres away.

"Do you find it strange to come back?" I asked.

"Yes," Baker said. "It's odd."

Baker pushed her hands deep into the pockets of her overalls. My impression was that she was waiting for me to come to some conclusion that could not help but be unknowing. She was not *really* expecting me to understand what it meant to have a decrepit farmhouse for a family seat. Soon the old Baker home would fall into ground that did not appear to want to retain anything as permanent.

"This land is haunted by all of the events that happened here and all of the people who died to make it so," Baker said. "It sounds clichéd to talk about hard work and dreams and ambitions, but those died too."

"And were you aware of that as a child?"

"Sure," said Baker. "We'd walk across the fields in the summertime, and there was something quite amazing about coming into one of these houses and seeing the peeling, flowered wallpaper, feeling it brush against your arm, and getting those shivers about who lived there and what had been left. These places were haunted.

They're still spooky places for me, though not in a scary way. They're just – well, sad."

I asked, "What strikes you about this place when you return?"

"I look at the sky," said Baker. "It's so much a part of the land-scape that you can't really *not* look at it. There's nothing more beau-tiful than a Saskatchewan sky when there are great clouds travelling across it. The Sand Hills themselves are always moving – literally – and the sunsets are like nothing I've ever seen. It can be spiritually uplifting, but it can also be really, really oppressive. You have this great sky above you and you can't ever really get away from it."

"I remember when I was a young man working on a seismic crew near here," I said, "that I was always looking up. My favourite sky was the one before a storm, when the clouds are a fierce dark grey and resemble the bottom of a cardboard egg tray. The fields would be brilliantly illuminated by light that seemed to cross the fields horizontally."

"That's another one of the things you notice here all the time. The light is so amazing, and so full of changes. Some days can be absolutely clear, and you can see for miles. There's only the sky and the land," said Baker. "That's all there is."

It was like a mantra, this ambivalent paean to sparse elements made through quietly gritted teeth. God's land, it was. Not Eden, this land of yearning, but more testing country such as Job's tor-mentors might have conspired to set him in.

✧   ✧   ✧

WE DROVE BACK to Burstall and walked along a track between two farmers' fields to the edge of the Lesser Sand Hills. The grassy prairie gave way to sagebrush, chokecherry bushes, and wolf willow and then, the other side of a low wire fence, the dunes rose unexpectedly.

"The subtlety and the silence in my stories have a lot to do with the silence of the landscape here," said Baker. "There is the sky, and the wind of course, but when I talk about *silence*, I'm not just refer-ring to the sound of things but to the quiet of the land. The peace in these dunes and in these hills makes me say that." Hills, opines one of Baker's characters, that will reach Maple Creek in fifty to one hundred years. Here was Canada, in all its extraordinary physical variety again. I thought of the white world of Igloolik, of the lush orchards of Nova Scotia's Annapolis Valley, of the magisterial breadth of the St. Lawrence, and now this, the two of us sitting cross-legged on a slope of sand as grains of it were borne by a gentle breeze and tingled our cheeks. Scattered over some 1,900 square kilometres, the aridity of the Sand Hills provided Baker with the stoic atmosphere of her stories, and characters that are often withholding. In the story "Bloodwood," Perpetua contemplates her own – well, it might have been called an *unhappy* – marriage, except that it is not because Perpetua expects so little from her husband, Joe. When she does think about the trials of wedlock, it's her sister Magda's awful union that disturbs her.

"There's a discomfort here, even in talking about oneself," said Baker, "and that's as true of my generation and my mother's generation as it was for my grandparents' generation. Nobody ever really stopped to think too much about what went before. The immigrants who first came here knew nothing of the aboriginal peoples who lived here previously. We'd find buckets and buckets of arrowheads out in the fields, the kids would collect them, and they'd just get chucked out."

"I like that you have a diviner at work in your story 'A Hard Witching,'" I said, "because I think of this as a land of traces and faint clues."

"Absolutely it is," said Baker. "And of patience too – of the *waiting* for something to be revealed. That's why being proactive about life is such a prairie trait. It's about looking for things, it's about putting in the effort, and the Sand Hills are a good example of that. It's so completely dry here. It's a desert. But just below the surface there's water, though you would never think so. It requires work to find that out."

Baker seemed pleased. Nodded. She was talking about herself.

"That's a very prairie thing," she said. "Things slowly revealed, but requiring effort as well."

"Have you ever hated the aridity of this place?"

"Oh, yes," said Baker. "I couldn't even say I like it now. Maybe that's why I have an obsession with water. It's there in all of my writing. In winter, after we had a good snowfall, the snow would thaw and there would be sloughs in the low spots between the hills. There would be this beautiful blue, glistening water stretching out. And really, as a kid, I don't remember ever seeing anything more beautiful than that – but then it would be gone. So yeah, I hated the dryness. Definitely."

In Baker's story "Sand Hills," an itinerant salesman of hand-written Bibles nails the pages of one to the local Catholic church, "flapping away like a million wings, like that old church might suddenly go skyward." I asked if the withholding quality of her characters – and of the people here, generally – was one that could be attributed to the Anabaptist and Lutheran presences in this part of the province, as much as to its austere landscape.

"But they're related, aren't they?" said Baker, her tone of voice betraying a slight astonishment that my observation should merit a question. "You feel so removed, and maybe that feeling of isolation brings you closer to an idea of God. Certainly if you consider what people had to go through to be here, what they met when they did, and what they had to do to live in this place, it seems fairly predictable that there would be that stoic blood in them. Until the 1920s, things were extremely difficult, and even then there were plenty of hard times – the 1930s, well, we don't need to talk about. There was no other way to survive here unless you had an approach to life that said, basically, 'This is what's been handed to me and I'll just get through it.'"

Baker let a handful of sand pass through her fingers. "How else could you stay here?"

From Jacqueline Baker's "Bloodwood":

Only later, much later, did Perpetua realize her loving family had not taught love, but only collected it and stored it selfishly, like the bushel baskets of potatoes and mealy apples in the root cellar. No, they did not teach love. What they taught was this: everything for the family. And just the family. No friends to go visiting on a Saturday afternoon in December, no skating parties, no fall suppers; no group picnics at the river with baskets of other women's roast chicken and pickles and chokecherry strudels; no brandings, as they did not graze their cattle in the community pasture at the Sand Hills. Not even church, for they prayed at home, led by their father in German from the great black Bible brought from the old country. Always just the five of them. Yes, her parents were certainly to blame. When Perpetua thought this, she paused uncomfortably over the word *blame*. But when she considered the effect of their love, it seemed that a little blame was necessary.

For many years, Perpetua had thought this failure to love was something wrong only in her. Then she had received a letter from Magda, poor Magda, alone in Saskatoon with a child, on the edge of her first divorce, who had written, *Tell me how it feels to go to bed each night and wake up each morning beside the man you love* (she had underlined *love*). *I feel sickened and empty. And my child, who is flesh and blood, asleep in the next room, her I can't even speak of, can't even look at some days without shame.* And Perpetua had read the letter twice and wept terribly, big wrenching sobs, her apron up over her face and her shoulders shaking as though her body would break itself apart – wept, not for her husband, whom she did not love, nor for the children she had never had, whom she could not love either, but for poor Magda, whom she did love. She had wept that way until it was time for Joe's supper, and then, seeing him step heavily across the yard, she had slipped the letter into the breadbox, washed her face and greeted him, as she did each day, with a smile and a kiss.

✧   ✧   ✧

LYDIA'S, IN SASKATOON'S Broadway district, is a bar on the east side of the river, across the water from the old CP hotel and the city centre. It was Friday, and happy hour. The dance floor beckoned, but it was still early and the music was not yet booming. The novelist Guy Vanderhaeghe, his painter wife, Margaret, and several others from the small but lively Saskatoon arts community had gathered at one of the long tables at the back, as they did for their weekly ritual of a few beers, the odd plate of French fries, and a boisterous chat before returning home or a dinner at the neighbouring Chinese. Vanderhaeghe, a diabetic, is a tall man of good build who had only recently decided against the punishment of playing hockey with kids twenty years his junior. He spoke quietly, in that soft-spoken but resolute, mesmerizing prairie manner that dictates its own pace and attention from those who listen.

"Esterhazy," said Vanderhaeghe, "where I grew up, was a town of about thirty-five hundred and was largely Hungarian. Langenburg was German, and ten miles away was a Swedish town called Stockholm. There was a settlement called the Finnish colony south of town, and five miles north of us was the English colony. In town, of course, were all sorts of colonies – Poles, Ukrainians, Czechs – and there were approximately three Jewish families that were mostly Eastern European.

"My grandfather came out from West Flanders, around 1910. There was no work in Belgium, and emigrants were leaving for the Congo or Canada. Most of the Belgians were miners, but he was of farming stock and like a lot of the emigrants of that generation his ambition was to own land. He worked in Saint Boniface, on the railway coming out of Winnipeg, where there was a fairly large Belgian community at that time. After that he worked as a hired man to learn dry-land farming practices and met my grandmother, who was of Northern Irish extraction. When he married, he lost most of the Flemish elements of his background, including the language, so that when he returned to Belgium after the Second World War, he couldn't make himself understood."

"You haven't mentioned the French or the Chinese," I said.

"Like every small Saskatchewan town, the Chinese owned the restaurants. Laurie and Benny were two Chinese friends of mine who were great hockey players, and, as you'd expect, the back of the restaurant was where you went to smoke a cigarette. There was a small French community across the river, but they had no presence in Esterhazy. And there were Métis, but no one really thought of them as French. The doctor and the principal tended to be British. They were the dominant class because they were educated, which was a fact of immigration. Ethnicity never determined much, and in no time you had a lot of intermarriage."

Vanderhaeghe put out his cigarette and lit another.

"In many ways Saskatchewan was a melting pot of society because it was so small."

"It's been the United Nations here since 1905," said Margaret.

And then, as if to prove the point, the stalwart among the Friday-night drinkers reconvened at the Vanderhaeghes' house, not yet ready to let the evening draw to a close. Haideh, an Iranian immigrant working as a lawyer in Saskatoon, and Margaret, whose wonderfully oils-splotched studio was in the basement, sat next to each other on the couch beneath one of her large abstract paintings and exchanged Persian lullabies and country-and-western ballads in a melancholy competition of prairie laments.

✧   ✧   ✧

WAGONS, TRAINS, and then planes brought immigrants to the new province at the behest of governments that wished for the Prairies settled, the land an opportunity for immigrants who did not expect to return to the countries they had left behind, in the way that refugees of even the most troubled states now do quite realistically. The novelist Martha Blum was one of these, part of a tide of middle European, mostly Jewish, refugees that reached Canadian shores after the Second World War. Blum, a first novelist at the unlikely age of eighty-seven, was the author of *The Walnut Tree*. It is a fairly auto-biographical novel of Jewish experience in the twentieth century. Blum was born in Czernowitz in 1913. In the territorial shuffle that took place in Europe during the wars and occupations of the last century, the formerly Moldavian city became a part of Austria-Hungary, then Romania, then the Soviet Union, Romania, and finally the Ukraine again. Blum arrived with her husband from the Soviet Union, at Halifax's Pier 21, in 1951. Four years later the couple arrived in Saskatoon.

Yann Martel, then living in Saskatoon, suggested I find Blum. He was at work on the first stages of a novel about the Holocaust, so his referral made sense. I went to see Blum at home, and as I approached the house, a 1950s bungalow on a pleasant, leafy street, I could hear her, ninety-one at the time, playing a Mozart piano sonata. I stopped on the walk, like a latecomer at a concert hall waiting for an opportune moment to take his seat. After a few minutes, I knocked on the door and entered into a house that was the sort of cultural oasis one often finds on the prairie. The white walls were hung with splendid paintings, and various sculptures sat on low bookshelves and on a coffee table. The rooms were immaculate, but tinged with the sadness that comes from knowing that the death of the husband is what has made this tidiness memorial.

Blum offered to show me her Saskatoon, and together we drove along 20th Street, a busy commercial avenue lined with meat packers and food stores and restaurants and pawnshops with vintage neon signs, but also churches of various denominations and an old cinema, these the urban footprints of immigrant peoples who had made Saskatoon their first port of call. Many of the storefront names were Ukrainian, some Chinese, others English. The Barry Hotel. The Diniero Restaurant. The Trio Café. The Tomato

Man sold potatoes, vegetables, some fruit – and, yes, tomatoes. The Odessa Meat Factory sold kielbasa, but also beef jerky. Here was Saskatchewan, without question. The steady flow of people in but also out of Saskatoon keeps the population at best in balance and means that there is little of the razing of districts that occurs in other Canadian cities. The street was a palimpsest, its layers of script the overwritten evidence of a century's passage of peoples.

Blum stared out the window at the passing kaleidoscope of stores. "Here are the pawnshops," she said. "There is one selling old appliances," said Blum. "It's just unbelievable. The people bring their radios and their jewellery and their stolen goods, and these are the things that will tell you stories. A pawnshop shows your discarded life – what you can let go, but also what you steal. These pawnshops have a huge place in the book that I am writing now. They fascinate me because of the cluttered way all these things are collected. You will see a 1920s radio and then suddenly a pair of Chinese vases from who knows what dynasty."

Blum appeared wistful.

"These are the 'traces' for you," she said.

We decided to drive beyond the city limits to the Cranberry Flats, now a conservation area just beyond the city limits, because that was where Blum's decision to stay in Canada had been made. We arrived in the sandy parking lot at the entrance to the park. Blum pushed open the back door of the car, and I sat down beside her and asked how she thought of Canada.

"Canada means the freedom to be myself," said Blum, "the total freedom of not being straitjacketed by others or by their customs. In Canada, you have the vastness of the land, so you don't feel that you have no breath –"

"So the vastness is representative for you? It's not a cliché."

"Absolutely not," said Blum. "In Canada, there is this multi-possibility of existence. From the very beginning, the day we landed at Pier 21, I knew. I looked out and I said, 'I want to be here. I just want to be here.'"

"I came with two children," said Blum, in her thickly accented

English, "one on my arm and the other in my handbag. A friend of my husband drove us here. I was overwhelmed by what I saw. I sat down, we stopped talking, and finally I said, 'Okay, we'll stay.'" Subsequently the river became one of the settings of her novel *The Walnut Tree*, a novel that begins in Czernowitz in 1921 and ends on the Cranberry Flats forty years later.

"The life of immigrants is a reconstruction of their past," said Blum. "Often I will go into a house and know exactly what that person's childhood was like. You will see in the life of every immigrant this desire to reconstruct the shelter that has been lost. You build your house a certain way because as an immigrant you have the constant need to relieve feelings of abandonment. The territory is not your own territory. Everything is new and needs to be conquered."

"And that is what Süssel is doing when she walks the sands of this river in *The Walnut Tree*, no?"

"She wants to reconstruct the river that she remembers from home," said Blum. "She grew up on the river Prut, and wants to rebuild the panorama of her youth, so she's built a house to be exactly like her grandfather's. What she wants is to regain her childhood."

The sight of the South Saskatchewan is breathtaking here. The grassy dunes and the marshes that flank the wide river teem with birdlife. It was late afternoon and the river was glistening. The way it curls through the prairie plays tricks with the perception of distance, and it appeared utterly serene – a great silvery path to "skate away on," wrote Joni Mitchell, daughter of this region.

"What time of the year was it when you arrived here?" I asked.

"June."

"It always strikes me that Canada has a bit of a laugh at the expense of the immigrants who come here in summertime," I ventured. "Nature says, 'See how beautiful I am,' and we go around naming valleys 'Paradise.' Then she socks you with winter."

"This is shifting land," Blum said. "It is not embracing you, as the south would be. You have to love the long, elemental day and want it and then live through it, in the summer as well. It is elemental, and it is very powerful. The blizzards blow you away. The summer dries you out. It's not an easy land. It is there for your taking, but you have to come towards it. No, this is not an easy land."

Blum turned her head away, and it was clear that our conversation was at an end. She pointed me to where the best view of the river was, and asked to remain behind. She sat in the back seat of the car, and I walked to the river lookout on my own. Perhaps she thought that solitude was appropriate, as there was in it the chance for me to be moved, as she had been, so many years before.

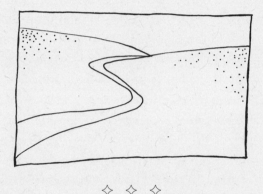

✧ ✧ ✧

"IT'S NOT ARROGANCE speaking here," said Yann Martel, "but the thing is, when you're on a plain, and you're the tallest thing around."

Martel and I were sitting in the front room of the modest Saskatoon home that he had rented, having a pizza. Martel was writer-in-residence at the Saskatoon Public Library at the time, and had charmed not just Saskatchewan but a lot of Canada with his musings about settling in the city. He was off to the Yukon soon. The evidence was that Martel was another body passing over the prairie, but he would return, and in a few short months he had come to be sensitive to the particular properties of the place.

"The plains are elevating," Martel said. "Because of them you look far, and you look *up*, and the openness demands that you fill that space with stories and that you people its flatness with characters."

"I think I've met more writer–painter couples here than any-where else in Canada," I said.

"Everyone in this town seems to be one or the other," said Martel. "Why? I suspect that the great flattish landscape – though it's not really flat at all – does not belittle you in the way that moun-tains do. When you live on a mountain, it's your smallness that is impressed on you. Here the opposite is true."

Surely it was the light – and the frugality of the *things* that Michael Helm so avidly wanted to be able to name – that compelled so many, in their prairie solitude, to form a relationship with the land that was their constant company by painting, writing, or singing it.

"As you move around Saskatchewan and travel roads that are mostly straight, what comes to mind?" I asked.

"I feel like I'm crossing an ocean," Martel said. "Especially around Saskatoon, the undulating landscape makes me feel as if I'm driving my boat over the swells of an ocean. The straight lines don't bother me because ships always travel in a straight line. I'm so amazed at the landscape that surrounds me that I don't even think about it."

◇ ◇ ◇

IN THE SOUTH, the land is immense, an open stage, and the player who sets out upon it is likely to feel alone and an overblown sense of the importance of his thoughts. That, or a harrowing abandonment.

The prairie demands that you fill the grand open spaces with *something* – voices, paint, music, dreams. The promised land of Saskatchewan, vast acres given away for free, was never the grail that immigrants supposed, and yet the "amazing landscape" was time and again the crucible of grandiose imaginings. The Earl of Selkirk and his Red River Colony, the Métis, Mennonites, Hutterites, Doukhobors, Sudeten Germans, Baha'i, and 1960s artists are just a few of those who established colonies in the part of Western Canada that delivered North America its first socialist government and medicare. Some of these schemes were noble, many deranged.

Madness sits on Utopia's perimeter quite comfortably. In Guy Vanderhaeghe's first novel, *My Present Age*, Ed is a disgruntled university graduate, flailing against the banality of his surroundings and the circumstances of his impending ruin. He has a penchant for losing himself in the world of books, films, and music: Huck Finn, his unpublished novel of the cowboy Sam Waters, and Mick Jagger and Jim Morrison. He has no car and is unable to keep a job. The work he has in a library leads to a complete nervous breakdown. And all the while, from the apartment below, the voice of The Beast rages – is it a talk-show radio host or Ed's madness speaking? Ed is angry about many things: His own failures. The hypocrisy of the bygone 1960s. In negotiating the terms of his divorce with Benny, the buyer for his estranged and pregnant wife, Victoria, a set of Balzac volumes has become a sticking point. "Free Balzac!" Ed cries as he is escorted kicking and screaming from the lawyer's office. In the company of the slightly crazed Stanley Rubacek, one of his students, Ed takes to driving around the unnamed prairie city in which the story is set, one that we can safely assume is based on Saskatoon, on the hunt for Victoria. Stanley is Ed's companion mostly because he is the owner of a functioning vehicle, a '71 Grand Prix. The two divide the town into quadrants to make Ed's hunt easier.

From Guy Vanderhaeghe's *My Present Age*:

Moving in a westward, spasmodic flow of traffic that lurches through intersections and bucks along in the ruts worn in the road ice, I cast cautious glances to my right, eyes peeled for motels. It is mid-afternoon, the lowering sun strains behind a fine, crystalline snow which fuzzes the outlines of the signs that picket the roadside. Some of these signs wink and blink with violet or orange neon; others solemnly revolve in the grease-stiffening cold. The majority, however, are megaliths that loom against an ashen sky, pharaonic testaments to hamburger empires. The golden arches of the House of

McDonald are prominent, as is the boast "4.6 billion burgers sold." (A tyrant's brag, "My name is Ozymandias, King of Kings!/ Look on my works, ye Mighty and despair!") The Family Size Bucket of the colonel from Kentucky squats impaled on a sixty-foot concrete pole, sullenly vying for attention with the intaglio of A&W, a mahogany-and-orange blandishment against a pale winter sky. Nearby the huge sombrero and yucca cactus of a burrito palace are rimed with gritty snow and old ice.

It is in the face of all this visual chaos, so opposed to order and simplicity, that I suddenly, perhaps a little guiltily, recall my vow to simplify my life. When I made that promise I had in mind the image of the ancient Greek subsisting on a fragment of pungent cheese, coarse bread, a handful of sun-warmed olives, a little watered wine; a man who discussed the Good, the True, the Beautiful with grave delight, and piped clear music in a sylvan glade. But I feel the absence of hills clothed in myrtle and thyme; of the Great Mother, Homer's wine-dark sea. Good resolutions, it seems, require good scenery.

"The car was starting to dominate Western cities in a way that it hadn't done before," said Vanderhaeghe, "so that even the idea of having to find someone with a vehicle was based on the new reality of the city, but it was also a way of putting Ed into an intimate connection with this other man and of allowing me to have two people out on a quixotic adventure."

Searching is something that not just Vanderhaeghe's cowboys do.

Vanderhaeghe and I were driving through the outskirts of town, placards at the traffic lights advocating the child's right to life. We followed the banks of the Saskatchewan River that have been preserved so presciently and passed the Mendel Gallery, established by Fred Mendel, a prosperous Jewish immigrant who had meat-packing plants in Europe and Australia and fled Germany, with his art collection, for Saskatchewan. The open green campus of the University of Saskatchewan was in view on the river's far side. We crossed the 25th Street Bridge and drove along Saskatchewan Crescent past the houses of professors and into the Broadway district, past Lydia's and the small stores and coffee shops that made this once Bohemian district of hippies and students a desirable quarter now. When, in the 1960s, Vanderhaeghe attended university here, he wore jeans that were too short as they were the clothes he had and not because they were the hippy costume of the day. The cynicism he acquired regarding the fads and hypocrisies of the time were behind the agitated comedy of *My Present Age*. He did so here, while living in the three-storey Maple Manor apartment building a few blocks behind Broadway Avenue. Some twenty years after the novel's publication, the odd literary tourist still rings apartment doors on the third floor looking for Ed, rogue hero of the novel and a bit of a cult figure now.

"Like Ed," said Vanderhaeghe, "I couldn't abide the idea of the few professions that might have been open to me – the civil service, the law. So I threw the dice and decided to become a writer. I'd always been a great admirer of black comedy – humour that had an edge to it. What lies behind a lot of comic novels is anger, and already I was angry about what I considered to be *my* failure. At that point in my life I bristled against any authority, and especially authority that I considered to be relentlessly stupid. In my mind, that was true of the hippy ideas of the 1960s and 1970s and it was a part of my rage, no doubt about it."

"But Ed almost relishes the downward steps that he takes."

"Ed was what I feared would happen to me," said Vanderhaeghe. "I've always had a feeling, for as long as I can remember, that I'm one step away from disaster. Now I never sank as low as Ed did, but I always felt that I certainly had the potential to do it. I knew that if my will was weakened at all, then on the bottom steps would be where I'd ultimately find myself."

The hard work required of a landscape that demands, according to Martha Blum, that you "come towards it," encourages withholding in Jacqueline Baker's characters and provides madness a seat at the table of a number of Guy Vanderhaeghe's novels. In *Homesick*,

Vera's younger brother, Earl, hears voices and suffers for it, and in *The Last Crossing*, Simon Addington teeters at the edge of insanity brought on by syphilis. In *My Present Age*, Ed's frenetic companion Stanley Rubacek fibs about his life constantly, and Ed's own breakdown leads to his hospitalization at one point.

"My mother had a long history of mental illness and so I lived with that," said Vanderhaeghe as he flicked his lighter and brought the flame to another cigarette. "In saying so, I'm not trying to sound like a victim, but obviously the idea of madness does reside at the back of my mind. Sometimes I think that I am attempting to suppress it, and to keep these characters out of my novels, but they won't seem to let me do it."

"One of the things I enjoyed about Ed's searching," I said, "is that it heightens the sense of Saskatchewan, even in the motel strips of the city, as a landscape that only yields its clues reluctantly. Perhaps this part of the country has a history that is inherently not obvious."

"It's not that a place like Saskatoon has no history," said Vanderhaeghe, "it's that we don't think about it enough, so that the unencumbered geography of the place – the geography of a place that has not been marked by man-made objects – is much more easily confronted than a city that's only one hundred years old. The timeless quality of the Prairies is something in which you can lose yourself."

The fact of the city of *My Present Age* not being named emphasizes Ed's condition and contributes to the novel's "psycho-geography," the imaginary map each of us imposes on the grid of a place, and that speaks as much about our subconscious as it does the real world. The dynamic is one that works in two directions. Geography and its attendant "sense of place" affect the way we think, and we are also prone to *choosing* landscapes that reflect our psychological condition. What we are thinking finds a way of expressing itself in the world as it is, though what we are thinking is frequently the result of activity that the land invites. So any one of Graham Greene's lost souls seeks solace in leper colonies or dissolute failing states, as Ed does his slim chance of redemption in

Vanderhaeghe's abstract Western city. His wife is out there, some-where, though she will not be located on any mere map. The streets and malls of Vanderhaeghe's setting is the author's way of mount-ing what's outside as a dreary, lost opportunity for which Ed has no appetite.

Vanderhaeghe and I stopped at a coffee shop on Eighth Street, a road that had not changed much since Ed's day, though it had since been absorbed into the greater city, and other, bigger malls and big-box stores farther out of town had given the street, in Saskatoonian terms, an historic aspect. More traces.

"As a writer who lives here I use the features of the place," said Vanderhaeghe. "Saskatoon has no real mythology to speak of, and countless writers from around here have dealt with the visceral impact that the prairie imposes on the human being – the weather, the sky, are parts of the landscape that are talked about a great deal, but Saskatoon is so new that it's mostly unwritten, and it's very dif-ficult for the writer to fully engage with a place without the guide of a preceding literature. Maybe the psycho-geography of a place is something that can only be written about after several generations have contributed to its memory. Today, for instance, we've been travelling through parts of the city where buildings from thirty years ago have been taken down. Those parts are better for the writer because you have something to react to. If you're in London, England, you have plenty to react to. There's the written record, the architectural record, and maybe Canadian cities like Toronto or Montreal are getting to the point of having sufficient generations of writers who have written about them for there to be a literary char-acter to those cities, but in Saskatoon there's not much to write about other than the city as a record of where you live. Saskatoon was very much a city of malls. There was this older, commercial part of Saskatoon, and something of a main street and shops here, but it was the psychological geography that I was having to work with."

✧　✧　✧

THE PRAIRIE TAKES its toll. At Wanuskewin, a provincial heritage site outside of Saskatoon, prayer wheels and other traces of the aboriginal presence of the Prairies have been preserved. At the foot of a buffalo jump, a couple of centuries of the bones of animals that stampeded to their deaths are ingrained in the soil, a bit of its history. I sat with the poet Louise Halfe – who told me about her mixed-race status, and the death of her brother after he was dumped by Edmonton police outside the city on a "Starlight Tour." She wept. So had Sharon Butala done, in a cabin in Cypress Hills Interprovincial Park. "I'm not usually so open," said Butala, composing herself, "but this is a culture that oppresses women, and it seems not to know how *not* to do that. There are days it angers me so much that I wouldn't care if every single farmer on the Prairies went broke." It was tough being Ed, it was tough being native, tough being a woman, and judging by my driving companion's hollow stare forward, it was plenty tough being a white man on the prairie too.

Michael Hetherton, author of the short-story collection *Grasslands*, was taking me over the Cypress Hills, a topographically anomalous set of uplands located in the southwestern corner of Saskatchewan. The hills are their own ecosystem, an erosional plateau that was created in the Cretaceous period and precedes the Ice Age. We were travelling the Gap Road that cuts through the Hills and its forests of Jack pine, and Hetherton was driving very slowly. The road was a gravel one in perfectly good shape, but I was getting used to these subliminal displays of sadness. His mother, Hetherton confided, kept the blinds in the living room down rather than have to look out over the prairie, lonely as a doldrums sea.

"I'm told there's not much true grassland left," I said.

"It's a small area," said Hetherton, "but when you're in them it feels awesome. It feels as if they go on forever."

"As someone who's accustomed to living here, what is the feeling of place that you have?"

"Well," said Hetherton, "I'll try and relate it to my fiction."

"Okay."

"When you try to connect with other people in the landscape, you feel this longing. But that longing amounts to a lot more than just what we feel in the landscape. It connects us to a higher sense of ourselves – to a sense of divinity and loneliness. As you try to connect with other people, that's what you feel, that sense of longing."

It was hot, midday, and I suggested we step out of the car. The grasslands below the hills stretched away like a giant rumpled blanket.

"My characters are struggling with their connections to people and so they all have that longing," said Hetherton. "That's what my whole book is about."

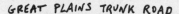

GREAT PLAINS TRUNK ROAD

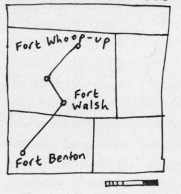

The breeze was light and felt good against the face. We were looking west towards Alberta and the site, in 1873, of the Cypress Hills Massacre, where twenty-two Assiniboine were murdered by a bunch of drunken American "wolfers" who claimed that the Indians had stolen their horses. It was one of the most notorious of several violent incidents in the Canadian West at that time, and it helped prompt the formation of the North-West Mounted Police by then prime minister John A. Macdonald and the construction of Fort Walsh for a barracks. The massacre was used by Guy Vanderhaeghe as a part of the panorama of *The Englishman's Boy*, his novel of the West and Hollywood's romancing of it.

"Can you see Fort Walsh from here?" I asked.

"No," said Hetherton, whose stories were, in a sense, typical of the region. The tale of a love affair that could only end badly, set against an abandoned house, a ferry crossing, or the bar of a hotel in Maple Creek.

We got back into the car.

"I write about people trying to get by in a harsh landscape," Hetherton said. "They feel longing because they're searching for love in this landscape and not doing it successfully."

Hetherton started the engine and turned the vehicle around. We headed back down the road and north towards Saskatoon.

"All great art comes from longing," Hetherton said, slumped over the wheel of his beaten red SUV and muttering, like a displaced character from an E.M. Forster novel, about the need to connect.

"We have to connect if we want to be in touch with our higher selves," Hetherton said.

◇ ◇ ◇

DRIVING BACK TO Saskatoon along Saskatchewan's no-nonsense highways, we passed through one dwindling community after another, even their landmark grain elevators now under threat. It seems a certainty that those who remain in a place are affected by the departure of those who do not, and I wondered just how different our national psyche might be were it possible to travel the country in some kind of loop and not straight lines. In Canada, we proceed along one of the compass's two axes, and then turn 90°, or 180°, and return along exactly the same path. Our journeys have built into them an unavoidable component of failure. Imagine if you will, that Macdonald's and then Sir Wilfrid Laurier's push west had taken the more northerly route that, among others, the CPR engineer and time wizard Sir Sanford Fleming advocated. Fleming's suggestion for a route traversed the northern "fertile belt" of Saskatchewan and Alberta, through Edmonton and the Rockies just south of Jasper. And imagine that development had occurred in the central and northern parts of the provinces along this route and had not been stymied there by the building of the CPR along Canada's frontier with the United States – land where the development of towns would have occurred anyway. It would have been possible, today, to travel Canada in a circle, as fur traders did. A traveller could leave Montreal, head north towards Hudson Bay (or out the St. Lawrence and over Labrador and into the Bay) and travel south from York Factory along the Nelson or the Hayes and the North Saskatchewan to Fort Edmonton, south to Rocky Mountain House, Piegan Post, and then east along the South Saskatchewan and back towards Montreal along the border-hugging route in use today. It would be possible to travel the heart of the country without the metaphorical backtrack of returning the way one came. How much more whole, more realized, and more in touch with our history would we feel were it possible to travel the country this way? Instead, Canadians are fated to cross the country in straight lines and come back the way that they left – or not at all. In each case, the journey is a failure and our psychological baggage weighty. In each case, our country defeats us. Who wants to travel in reverse? Who wants to be left behind? In Canada, it is not so much the land as our *plotting* of it that has impeded the nation. Without the holistic succour of the circle, in our geography, we do not feel even our *history* collectively, but rather as stops along a journey that leaves us stranded in one part of the country or another.

✧ ✧ ✧

SHARON BUTALA'S TERRITORY is the ranch that she and her husband, Peter, keep at Eastend, south of the Cypress Hills and straddling the border with the United States. This is the part of the province where Wallace Stegner lived and wrote – a strip of the country that Scots and English would liken to "The Borders," as differences between Americans and Canadians are as slight here as they are in the neighbouring English and Scottish counties of the Old Country. Stegner was to this part of the country as the music of Ian Tyson is, or as Russell Banks and Jim Harrison are to points farther east; an artist whose province lay on both sides of the frontier, his "regional" provenance more telling than his national identity. The same can be said of many southern Saskatchewan writers, including Guy Vanderhaeghe, whose two historical novels are set in times prior to the creation of the frontier with America along the forty-ninth parallel and the defeat of Louis Riel at Batoche, in

1885, that truly established the reach of the Canadian nation here.

"Everybody came with the wrong idea," Butala said. "This was going to be a paradise, the streets were going to be paved with gold, and every little prairie town thought that one day it was going to be a great city. Now all those places are ghost towns, and the people are dispersed. The original myths that brought us here were calculated. They were *lies*. Their purpose had nothing to do with freedom and liberty for the peasants of Europe. It was no way to found a country."

"Have you ever hated your physical surroundings?" I asked.

"Oh, yeah," said Butala, "most days I do. I remember reading about Sylvia Plath – I think it comes up in Ted Hughes's *Birthday Letters* – travelling with him through New Mexico on a honeymoon or something. The landscape is just like that around where I live, and Plath said, 'This land is *evil*.' She was so stunned by its rawness, and its bareness that she transposed her own fears and anger and all the rest of it onto the ground. But the ground is inhabited by spirit. The *ground* is not evil."

"But, there's not much *there*, is there? It's just land. It's just earth and sky. So you have to mull other things. Otherwise, you have nothing."

From Michael Helm's *In the Place of Last Things*:

> "Tell me about the prairies."
> "They're flat."
> "C'mon. Something must account for your small-town charm."
> "You want alot of dust and wind, enduring hearts and all that. I'd rather stick a cattle prod in my eye."
> "So tell me what to want. Places have characters."
> "Only broadly. What they have are minds, and minds are beyond my powers of description."

✧　✧　✧

DRIVING WEST TOWARDS Medicine Hat, and then north to Edmonton, it was hard not to regard the abandoned homesteads as emblems of the province's changed fortunes. Neither was it easy to ignore the sadness that you meet in people who live so close to the bone here.

If space and the notion of the border are the metaphors that Canadians live by, then topsoil is another that matters here – its thin layer, its tenuous grip. In Saskatchewan, the wind blows dust and seed and humankind over country that may never have been meant for the kind of habitation Agricultural Man has striven to impose on it. It changes the course of rivers, the shape of the Sand Hills, and blows away the earth that permitted so many places of settlement that are shadows now of the communities they once were. The great agrarian machine still works the tired soil defiantly, and more of the old homesteads collapse. More of the men and women go, young and old, but the land that has had so much violence done to it endures. Still, the effect of the place is so particular and so strong that it is very hard to leave its sensibility behind. The elemental relentlessness of Saskatchewan writes itself in the habits of those who were raised here, and after a while, you learn the obvious. Place is manifested, most of all, in the way that people speak, when they do so at all – and in their gait. In their language. In that prairie reserve. In nods of the head that often do as well as words. This is a land of messages discernible only to the patient few, of subtleties of character burnished by what Michael Helm described as the "constant sense of possible erasure." Grunts are enough, because so much does not need to be said.

✧ ✧ ✧

IN EDMONTON, I sought out Gloria Sawai. Born in Minnesota, she grew up in Saskatchewan near the Albertan border and Medicine Hat. In 2002, at the age of seventy, Sawai won the Governor General's Award for Fiction for *A Song for Nettie Johnson*, a collection that included "The Day I Sat with Jesus on the Sundeck and a Wind Came Up and Blew My Kimono Open and He Saw My Breasts." That story was much anthologized, and for more than its title – a funny one, true, though at the root of it was a dialogue with faith that is a leitmotif in the work of so many prairie writers. We met in the Edmonton Public Library. Sawai, her silver-white hair cut in a bob, was dressed in a sky-blue skirt and smart jacket chosen for the occasion. She appeared stiff and cautious, perhaps unsure of why she had come. It was that prairie wariness again. You could see it written on her face – this man from Toronto, what was he up to? What did he really want?

"What did Mavis Gallant say?" asked Sawai. "'Place exerts itself through childhood, imagination, and memory.' That's what I believe. Everything I write comes out of the land. Well, my childhood memories are prairie. They're dust, they're wind, they're odd people in little towns. They're just kind of desolate actually, partly because of the religious nature of my upbringing, and partly because of the communities that I lived in."

Sawai's voice was dry and gravelly, true to the climate that she was remembering.

"The land just sifts into my pores somehow," she said.

"Do you believe?" I asked.

"I do belong to a religious community," Sawai said. "It's Lutheran, and I have a kind of love-hate relationship with it. This is not our home, the land says. The earth leads you to heaven and to hell, and we are just sojourners. That's the message I got."

Sawai fiddled with the purse she was holding.

"My faith is like my family of origin," Sawai said. "I wish it were more *impressive* in some way. I wish home were a place I'd like to take my friends to, and that I could show it off to people. That's not so, but still, it is my faith. Its basic teachings – grace, mercy, forgiveness, resurrection, new life – are part of my bloodstream, and I would like to think of it as having helped me be open-minded and questioning. There's a quotation I like from George Eliot. It's in *Middlemarch*, I think. 'The religious enquirer, unless overcome by fear, will not stand still.'"

"Have you been back to Saskatchewan at all?"

"Hardly ever," said Sawai. "I remember going back years and years later to the town of Admiral, where I lived. The house I grew up in was gone. It was just a little hole in the ground. Weeds were growing out of this hole. It was just so *desolate*."

Sawai was quiet for a moment as she scrutinized her visitor.

"People leave Saskatchewan, don't they?" she said.

"Yes, they do."

"It was just so desolate," she repeated.

"What about the wind?" I asked. "You write about that."

"Oh, I like wind," Sawai said, relaxing a little. "I like *weather*. In every story that I've written, there's something about weather in there someplace – and that has to do with the land, doesn't it?"

"It does."

"Yes."

"What is your base mood? I think of it as the sediment at the bottom of the river. As we work our way through the day, all sorts of other things wash over us, but underneath it all is the mood that we begin with and that we return to. My mother says hers is despair. Mine is to feel baffled."

"Mine's a combination of the two," Sawai said. "I don't know where else my melancholy came from. There's an awful lot of dark stuff that comes to me because there's so much *silence* down there, so much isolation – but no matter how much crap's down at the bottom, there's a foundation of grace, and love, and all that good stuff."

"What do you mean by 'grace'?" I asked, wondering, again, about the tenacity with which religious ideas and ones of punishment often take root beside each other on the unforgiving prairie.

"Oh, the undeserved little blessings that come upon us every day. We aren't even looking for them, and they just come and lift us up. The unconditional acceptance and unconditional love, maybe, that's at the heart of things."

Sawai stared at a woman reading at a nearby table, then turned to me quizzically.

"I haven't been there," Sawai said, "but people I know who have gone to Italy, or Greece, they have these wonderful exotic experiences of flamboyant people who are open-armed and bold and festive and lead wonderful lives. Well, that's not Saskatchewan," she said, letting out a cagey half-laugh.

It was affecting, this habit she had of halting her candour in its tracks. Sawai seemed nonplussed by the strange contingency of life – Russian, really, in the face of the more flamboyant ways of living she had encountered, and in her querulous anguish about the lot that had been dealt her. It was not *regret*, but it furrowed her brow, this emotion.

"When you go back," I said, "does Saskatchewan feel more familiar to you because you've written about it, or, if by writing about a place you make it imaginary, do you become a stranger to the place that it really is?"

"In the imaginative story, you make the place *more*," said Sawai. "You send up the parts that are dramatic to you. I remember that last summer I was in Moose Jaw, I had driven up to Saskatoon, and I just wasn't as *moved* by the landscape as much as I remember having been moved by it as a child. The imagination colours it, I suppose."

"Do you prefer the place as it is, or as you ended up representing it?"

"I like Saskatchewan as I ended up representing it better," Sawai said. "It's more *interesting*. It's more vigorous. It has more of a profound effect on the characters – and on me. It's Saskatchewan as I remember it, but I was a child then, and everything has a stronger effect on you as a child."

"In Saskatchewan," I said, "I think of the effect of place as being so strong that I really do believe it is a region unto itself."

"I'm pleased that you have had that experience of Saskatchewan," said Sawai excitedly. "I had thought that you were probably *totally urban Toronto*."

Now it was my turn to laugh. "No, no, no," I said.

"Well, I think that too," said Sawai, cheered now. "I think I'm *lucky* to have come from Saskatchewan. I think that I'm *blessed* having come from Saskatchewan. It was a *grace* to be there. It was a grace to know those people, a special gift. Really, I do think so."

Sawai shifted, looked away, and then fixed her gaze on me.

"I'm not as *excited* writing my new stuff because I've tried to move to Europe," she said. "Why'd I do that? Europe and Asia. I thought that it would be sophisticated and not so – well, not so *regional*, huh? But it's not quite as *interesting* to me.

"I'm not taking it out of my own bone," Sawai said.

✧ ✧ ✧

After seismic work of the kind that I had done years before was completed, the data is analyzed, and if the prospects are any good, an oil well is sunk. At the stage of drilling, industrial activity creates a huge gash and an open sore upon the land. But then the well is capped, and a simple pump sits at the top of the wellhead. In southwestern Saskatchewan, land that Baker and Solie and Helm and Gowan and Sawai had left behind, you see these pumps all over the place. They look like mechanical horses gracefully bowing down, taking some water, and then lifting their heads again. They are silent, and from a distance, they are even beautiful, these minimal traces of the colossal activity that went before. In the spring, when the fields around them are tilled, arrowheads and flints and other mementoes of aboriginal activity that occurred on these plains are brought up to the surface. The landscape itself is one of traces and the wellhead is just one more. Here, the land is constantly conspiring to wipe you out without trace. As much as the Inuit North, this land of subtle clues is one that demands to be read. There is no ornament here, no fuss or affectation, and the iconography of southern Saskatchewan is slight and meaningful for that reason. The imperative is to divine where all things are. The arrowheads and stone circles are testament to an almost vanished aboriginal presence, just as coulees indicate the subterranean existence of vital moisture. Nothing is immediately apparent. Its landscape demands that you scrutinize it more closely for the stories that wind, rain, and erosion reveal in the prairie's economical language – traces of history beneath grasslands that have been altered by modern agriculture into other ground entirely. But, if you let your eye settle on the prairie for long enough, then old truths will raise themselves discreetly. Even the odd and miraculous phenomenon of seeds lying dormant for scores or even hundreds of years before sprouting again is an indication of the character of a land where deep-seated sentiments are carried close to the bone and the eternal verities are only slowly revealed.

Here, not only buffalo came and went. The Saskatchewan landscape is one over which all things passed – water, plants, animals, people. Aboriginals followed herds across the land, and then settlers tried to farm it but did not fare much better. The land is beautiful and strangely haunting. Its message is one of dreams, and failure – but also effort.

Here, Man tried. Not for the first time, not for the last.

$$\diamond \quad \diamond \quad \diamond$$

FROM SHARON BUTALA'S "Gabriel":

He found a large rock, one that came to mid-thigh with a depression in the bare soil all around it where cattle had once stood to use it for a rubbing stone, and before his cattle and his father's and his grandfather's, buffalo had used it. He leaned his buttocks against it, half-sitting, and was surprised to find it was warm, still radiating heat from the sun. He wondered how far inside it the heat had penetrated.

The rock was granite and that peculiar shade of pink with minute points of light in it and other, equally small points of black. He swivelled and ran his hand over its hard, rough surface and noticed for the first time how it was almost covered with patches of ivory-coloured lichen and patches of the palest green.

It struck him then that the rock was a beautiful thing, miraculous, and that it had sat in this spot for a very long time, so long that he couldn't imagine all the years it must have been there. He stood, then squatted on the ground beside it, put his arm around it, and lay his head against the bulge of its side.

And then he saw how it would be.

The hills would turn to hoodoos, were half-way there already. His land would lie fallow, he couldn't tell for how long, but a very long time. He and Frannie would move to the city. Frannie would recover, she would get a job sooner than he would; she was younger than he was, smarter than he was in a quick way, she would regain her old determination, and a woman, she would not mind taking orders. They would have children and the children would be fine. By then he would have a job as a mechanic or a construction worker or a mainte-nance man in some high-rise building. They would live both better and worse than they lived now. Evenings, he would sit in front of the television with his feet in their grey workman's socks up on a footstool, his muscles aching pleasurably from his day's labour. He would grow sleepy, he would doze, and from then on, for all the rest of his long workingman's life, his dreams would be of the farm.

✧ ✧ ✧

AT CALORIES, a restaurant by the repertory cinema on Broadway, Guy Vanderhaeghe and I decided to have lunch before my plane out of Saskatoon. A local publisher recognized Vanderhaeghe and joined our table. "Why do you think it is," he asked, "that there is so much great historical fiction coming out of Saskatchewan?"

"Because we've got no fucking future, that's why," said Vanderhaeghe.

8

Our Myths of Disappointment

Novels make sense of the news' meaningless little bits.

DOUGLAS COUPLAND, in conversation
with the author, 1992

All societies, not just aboriginal ones, tell creation myths. Every incarnation of a society has them because the job of the creation myth is never quite done. Certain of these stories, like the myth of Canada as a peacekeeping country, are shunted aside or pass into the realm of history, their vigour undermined by new historical circumstances, at which point other stories rise to take their place. Sometimes these stories are totally new – as when war or an invasion has fundamentally altered a society. Or, in a peaceful country such as Canada, where political evolution tends to be subtle and slow, new myths may just be revisions of the old ones. The ones that endure are often called "founding myths" and bind the society nationally.

In Canada, before First Contact, the creation myths of the Iglulingmiut explained a country without Europeans in it. Then

269

these stories were adapted to explain the monstrous reconfiguring of the world once the Qallunaat arrived. As these settlers sought to establish themselves in the not altogether congenial land, stories of the kind that Margaret Atwood discussed in *Survival* flourished. In their mythic way, the stories honoured Nature and all the wild things in it – "Bad Mommy Nature," nasty Indians, Americans too. (Fear is a form of honour.) And as still happens in parts of Canada, Vancouver being one such place, these stories mollified the anxieties and aspirations of the land's new tenants through their evocations of Canada as Nowhere, of the country as a previously vacated house, and no doubt other models for stories I have not identified here. They addressed the question of how the new society came into being, and what forces it needed to contend with in order to entrench itself.

Each generation requires stories that meet its particular needs so that new creation myths are born that suit the age. The myth of multiculturalism, notably, pushed aside the ideas Margaret Atwood had put forward in *Survival* in 1972 – the belief, more than thirty years old now, that intimidating Nature made Canadians see themselves as victims.

The survival myth endured for nearly one-third of a century because it was a story perfectly suited to Canada's Age of Invention – a time when the land itself, and also the behemoth of USAmerica, threatened the nascent country. The survival story depended on the belief that the bush was scary and either uninhabited or inhabited by scary things – just as the ravines around Don Mills were. In the Age of Mapping, Canadians appropriated the country and stories set about describing *what* was on the territory and no longer its viability. The great discovery of the Age was that the country was full – of people, stories, and history. The dominant question was no longer Northrop Frye's "Where is here?" but "*What* is here?". And so the survival myth died, usurped by a myth that was infinitely more suited to the requirements of the country in its Age of Mapping.

Multiculturalism, the powerful myth of the country's second narrative age, was the logical end of an argument that says the bush is *not* empty but occupied. And if it was occupied, then it was therefore habitable and safe – and the towns were not "garrisons." Recognizing, in particular, that aboriginal peoples were living in spaces Northrop Frye and others of his generation had previously considered wild, dangerous, and empty of culture if not of people, was the spur of a creed of ethnic and cultural sensitivity that was learned in the bush and then transferred to the cities.

Technically, multiculturalism was the government's way around the pressing political problems of *biculturalism* in Quebec, but the policy would not have taken root had there not been some truth to the idea it proposed: a country composed of many ethnicities able to recognize one another and share the territory in an atmosphere of mutual respect. This was the lesson of the Age of Mapping: that many peoples already shared space, though not in circumstances so crowded that they had yet to learn just how to live with one another. That question belonged to the future Age of Argument. In the Age of Mapping, what was required was a story of discovery, and of celebration, and the myth of multiculturalism provided it.

In Canada, the rise of the myth of multiculturalism, and the importance that our novelists and storytellers have, are related. Multiculturalism was in its genesis a story that extolled the achievements of ordinary Canadians over their leaders. It was inextricably tied up in what novelists and storytellers were managing when – as Fred Stenson chose to do – they told stories in contravention of the official version of history to "see how they contrast."

But they were also stepping into a void that was incumbent upon them to fill. In Canada, the young country, there have not yet been many of these, and so novels of historical fiction hold a special place.

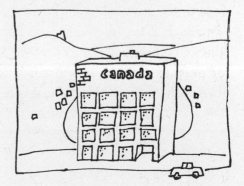

In Canada, we hold our storytellers in high regard for

this and a variety of reasons. The country is young, still unformed, and without the sheer accumulation of stories that, over time, makes the nationally binding myth unnecessary. Canada is still in that extraordinary but ephemeral instant when, as the American writer F. Scott Fitzgerald wrote in "The Crack-Up" of his own exhilarating youth, "the fulfilled future and the wistful past were mingled in a single glorious moment – when life was literally a dream." The past, present, and future of this country are, for the short and thrilling time we find ourselves in, all wrapped up in the gorgeous moment of an enigmatic question: "What does it mean to be a citizen of Canada?" or, by extension, the citizen of any country? Think on it too long and the gorgeous moment will be ended, but for the time being we are poised on the brink of an incalculable future – calamitous or exciting, we don't know. What is certain, what *does* make it thrilling, is that our fate is one that each of us can help determine. This is not the case in Britain, where the sheer amount and long train of history means that most aspects of society are set and, if fiddled with, only by an elite few. Nor is it the case in the United States of America, where the search for a viable founding myth is unnecessary as the country already has one that works quite brilliantly and their nation-building has been done.

✧ ✧ ✧

ACCORDING TO THE American Dream, anyone in the United States can prosper – in the next generation, if not this one – regardless of skin colour or background or economic fortune, through hard work and the sense of fair play that is enshrined in the country's constitution. It is a dream that is acted out in the spheres of business and government constantly. The Dream is a lie, of course, but the attraction of a tale, and not what meagre truth may be behind it, is often the power that makes a good story viable. And so, from Dallas to New York, Mexican dishwashers with no benefits and lousy pay wave USAmerican flags at demonstrations and do not want the rich to pay high taxes because they wonder what might happen to *their* savings account when they run into the money. The

American Dream, as a myth of personal success, is sold time and again in entertainment and in sports. USAmericans *win*. They do so through plucky effort, knowing that character and not social privilege, or steroids – well, so the story goes – makes the difference. (Where Englishmen, the legacy of Dunkirk, lose through plucky effort, but feel good about it anyway.) So it is the kid from the wrong side of the tracks who turns out to be the math whiz, the neglected athlete, the Wall Street tycoon, the one who gets the pretty girl. F. Scott Fitzgerald's *The Great Gatsby* was the dream for sophisticates, as it painted all the lies and deceits and the cost in lives of what good old USAmerican ambition entails, though we tend to remember the lavish parties of Jay Gatsby and the light upon the dock more than we do nasty, and entitled Tom getting Daisy back or Gatsby's own pitiable end.

The Great Gatsby is the closest that the United States has come to achieving the Great American Novel. No other novel will come closer, as Fitzgerald's emblematic story belonged not just to USAmerica's Jazz Age but to its Age of Mapping. This is the period when the Great Novel of Anywhere is most likely. The limits of the country had not yet been emphatically defined. USAmericans, as Canadians have been doing more recently, expected novels to address questions of identity, and some sort of consensus, at least among the dominant class, was still possible. But the truth of any great story, or of a "classic" novel such as Fitzgerald's, is that it changes the age because it exhausts any possibility of improvement. It satisfies its purpose and its readers so completely that the only thing that can follow it is contradiction, comment, or something wholly new. This does not mean that great novels cannot follow, only that Fitzgerald's *The Great Gatsby* was so brilliant an encapsulation of the hopes and aspirations and flaws of a country in its gorgeous moment that it put an end to USAmerica's Age of Mapping and ushered in its Age of Argument. Richard Ford is a novelist who has taken on the job of writing America every bit as ambitiously as Fitzgerald did, and speaks, through his character Frank Bascombe, the journalist and then real estate agent of *The*

Sportswriter and *Independence Day*, of America in its "middle age," for good reason. The Age of Argument in which he, Don DeLillo, Jonathan Franzen, and others are writing is one of constant debate and revision. Consensus of the kind that *The Great Gatsby* attained is no longer possible in USAmerica. And yet the Dream is resilient. It is a New World myth that is so fantastically powerful and pervasive that no matter how many times it appears to have been exposed as a sham – recently by the sight of tens of thousands of impoverished, needy, discriminated African Americans wading through the squalor of New Orleans after Hurricane Katrina hit – USAmericans take no notice. The Dream is a very, very good myth.

Canadians have no such binding story, or at least not one that is as obvious and clear. We are in need of such a myth, and in the 1960s the Canadian government developed one, the story of multiculturalism, as a way of keeping the country's "two solitudes" together and simultaneously appeasing the rest of the country's united nations. The policy succeeded because it coincided with a bunch of stories already being told that expressed Canadians' *resentment* of government. Where the rebellion that spawned USAmerica gave business and government validity in that country, and made their theatres suitable venues for the Dream's long-running show, in Canada, the situation was opposite. For centuries here, business and government were the same thing. In many ways they still are. The country that was built on the legacy of the Hudson's Bay Company persists in state-owned liquor stores, airline, oil companies, and the mimicking habits of private enterprise and its plethora of monopolies, some still commanded by single families.

This is the main reason, specific to this country, that Canadians hold their storytellers in high regard (and it is why the American purchase, by Jerry Zucker in 2006, of the Hudson's Bay Company meant so little.) Historically, Canadians have looked to their poets and novelists for myths that might explain the country because business and government were for so long patrician and intertwined and disqualified from providing them. The Company and the merchant princes; the families that administered the country before (and during) Confederation; London, then Ottawa, now Washington, were all incarnations of an oppressive distant authority. The regime of the Company meant to be Canadian was to have to endure the central powers on which one's livelihood depended. *Canadian*, as the word was used in the early years of the territories' settlement, described *les habitants* of the land and not its gentry. The land was where the Canadian expressed himself. Although the sheer necessity of a central authority made him "doff the cap," the Canadian did not settle here to be ruled. Sure, he was grateful to the ruler for being there as, most weeks, his days were filled with need, but he learned not to expect much more than a meagre stipend from governments that tended to be overbearing and indifferent. What he asked of his stories was to counter this authority.

So, in the Age of Mapping, Canadian novelists and storytellers provided quasi-factual lessons in the Canadian experience over the annals of Governor This and Governor That. And they answered the question of what it was to be Canadian. Today, there is sometimes quite invidious scoffing at the debate about identity, as if to have it or listen to such stories competing with an essentially white, Protestant, and anglophone history of this country were an indulgence or a sign of weakness. If only we recognized our history, goes the argument, if only we *knew* it, then the diminution of what it means to be a citizen of Canada would cease. The fiercest critics of Canadians' search for a meaningfully binding national myth – one that reflects the country as it *is* and not just as it has been inherited – believe that identity politics of this kind have *killed* history. Often these advocates of a more conservative view of history look to the current strongman of America for models to imitate, as earlier generations of the Canadian administrative classes did England, thinking that they will find more vigorous examples of national character and gumption there. They do so without acknowledging that as historians they too are in the business of myth-making – every bit as much as the peddlers of multiculturalism and peacekeeping they heap such scorn upon. They forget that America, Canada's slightly older brother, went through the same narrative stages of Invention and Mapping. And they rely, as demagogues have always done, on the handy shots of adrenalin that stories of accomplishment in war (and sports) provide. Rejecting epic thinking of this kind does not make Canada an "anti-national society," but actually a more sophisticated one. Historical conservatives choose not to see that Canada's unusual history underpins the country's generally pacifist nature and many Canadians' turning away from "official" histories of the textbook kind. Discomfort, not ignorance, is at the root of it.

Distance from the centre, and his subsequent distrust of it, made Canadian Man a fairly proletarian creature in a country that, ironically, does not believe class matters much. Even Quebec, where language and colonial defeat enshrined a different cultural sense, did not evade this pattern completely. Lousy leverage at the Company Store has ingrained an ambivalent wariness of concentrated authority that is almost atavistic in Canadians, inordinate governing power seen as something that must be tolerated if only for the sake of the country getting by. Stories that can be considered Canadian creation myths express a distrust of whatever is the prevailing power at the same time as they extol the virtues of the ordinary, modern, and racially sensitive Canadian who has been let down in some way. They assert a national sense of self, but where stories of war do so through the celebration of triumphs, these stories rally their listeners around an implicitly stated sense of collective injury. The Canada that these stories uphold is the equitable, multicultural version of the country that was the discovery and the banner of this country's Age of Mapping. The stories fostered in this second age can be described as the country's Myths of Disappointment. The progenitor of these myths, the story of the prior Age of Invention that satisfied its purpose so completely that the only thing that could follow it was contradiction, comment, or something wholly new, was the story of Sir John Franklin and his third, ill-fated expedition of 1845–47.

◇ ◇ ◇

ErEBUS BAY, NUNAVUT, August 2004. Beechey Island, named after a lieutenant on William Edward Parry's first polar voyage, of 1919, lies off the southwest tip of Devon Island, some eighty kilometres east of Resolute. Three sailors from John Franklin's third expedition are buried there, in the slate and gravel. All their companions aboard the *Terror* and the *Erebus* later perished. The bodies of these three unfortunates constitute the only human remains of Franklin's third expedition of 1845–47 to have been discovered.

I had made the journey to this desolate spot, all granite greys and browns or the dull white of wet snow, because of the importance of the Franklin story to the Canadian psyche in the Age of Invention. It was summer, but the day my Zodiac landed ashore, the sky was cloudy and foreboding and there was a silken feel to the chilly air that came off the water, playground for polar bears that could be spotted swimming twenty kilometres out to sea. I kept watch for any ones on land that might have been curious, but saw no living thing. To sailors of the nineteenth century, South Sea cannibals must have seemed a bawdy entertainment next to this dour panorama. "How is it possible to live here?" is the question that any first-time visitor to the Arctic asks, even in summer. More so, "Why would anyone want to?" The idea that English explorers and their crews managed, almost two hundred years ago, to survive one or two or even three winters locked in the ice in wooden ships, and that they planned to do so, is still extraordinary to contemplate. So we remember Franklin's last Arctic foray as a disastrous failure, but also as an example of extraordinary fortitude. That snowy August morning, I stood by the graves and their bleached wooden markers and paid homage to the three men and the expedition of which they had been a part.

The sailors' makeshift cemetery has become, over time, a memorial to a moment of Empire that the English were not much interested in. There is a modest commemorative plaque in London, "Erected by the Unanimous Vote of Parliament" on the southern side of Waterloo Place near the Athenaeum Club, but the sailors' true monument is here, on Beechey, at the site where the crews of the *Terror* and the *Erebus* buried their young mates in this shallow graveyard and in the story and the song that remember their mysterious end, including the Celtic ballad "Lady Franklin's Lament."

> Through cruel misfortune they vainly strove
> Their ship on mountains of ice was drove
> Where the Eskimo with his skin canoe
> Was the only one that could ever come through

But the English had more successful explorers and colonists to celebrate, and were embarrassed by some of the stories that exited the Arctic, the one concerning cannibalism especially. Yet the story "concerning Franklin and his gallant crew" has been inspiring to a host of Canadian artists, songwriters, novelists, and poets. Stan Rogers remembered Franklin in his song "Northwest Passage." Gwendolyn MacEwen wrote about Franklin's third expedition in *Terror and Erebus*, a CBC Radio play. Rudy Wiebe wrote about Franklin's first expedition in *A Discovery of Strangers*. The Montreal poet David Solway wrote about this "story/ beyond the imagination/ of the present moment" in his collection *Franklin's Passage*. Margaret Atwood wrote about the importance of Franklin's expedition critically in "Strange Things: The Malevolent North in Canadian Literature." My late father, the novelist Mordecai Richler, used the third, fatal expedition as a way into his most ambitious and self-consciously Canadian novel, *Solomon Gursky Was Here*. And on the evidence of the story "Franklin's Library," published in a 2005 issue of *The Walrus* magazine, the Kingston novelist Helen Humphreys is one of the more recent writers to be intrigued by the mystery of the captain's two ships. In all of these accounts, the Arctic is a formidable landscape, but where, in the earlier ballads and imaginings of Canadian writers, Franklin is an heroic figure, his noble memory still present in the Arctic, somehow, from about the 1980s, Franklin dies as a result of some kind of shortcoming on his part. This was the scientific conclusion of a Canadian archaeological team led by Owen Beattie and John Geiger that disinterred the three sailors' bodies and performed autopsies on them a century and a half after the fact. The corpses offered a wealth of material to interpret, as the three crew had been effectively freeze-dried. Beattie and Geiger had argued in their 1987 book, *Frozen in Time*, that lead from the badly soldered tin cans in which Franklin's expedition carried food poisoned the sailors and affected their judgment.

Poor Franklin. In 1854, the Englishman John Rae encountered Inuit who told stories and possessed relics of the Franklin expedition, and five years later Francis McClintock found more, including knives, watches, pistol shot, medicines, a sextant, and *The Vicar of Wakefield*, an Oliver Goldsmith novel. The stories Inuit told, and the bizarre remnants of Franklin's expedition, suggested that members of the crew had tried to drag boats stocked with provisions and a few luxuries south before dying. The conclusion that Rae reached, and that McClintock seconded, was that the sailors, in the face of death, had resorted to "the last dread alternative" – cannibalism. It was a hypothesis that enraged, among others, Charles Dickens. The odd and useless cargo McClintock found only served to corroborate Beattie and Geiger's theory of the sailors' madness.

It is instructive to compare how Canadian writers have interpreted the Franklin story with what their counterparts from continental Europe, the United Kingdom, and the United States have written. In the German Sten Nadolny's 1983 novel, *A Discovery of Slowness*, the explorer is an outcast but resolute and deliberate man, someone who belongs to an earlier time. The book applauds the "slowness" that is a part of this imagined Franklin's qualities, ones that are to be admired as a kind of laudable anachronism. The book can be read as a precursor of the "slow" movement and a lament for what Europe of the late twentieth century has lost. In the Englishman Robert Edric's *The Broken Lands*, Franklin is one of several dedicated Admiralty officers tenacious (as good Britons are) in the face of the deaths that will become them. And, in the Californian William T. Vollmann's *The Rifles*, Captain Subzero, the author's alter ego, is obsessed with Franklin and dreams his way through a contemporary Northern panorama and the vestiges of an Inuit culture hopelessly eroded by European contact. Captain Subzero is a symbol of invasive Empire, and also of the author's own priapic irruption into the North – the author conquering, as the explorer had intended to do, if in his idiosyncratic, stumbling way. In Canadian accounts, the message is quite different. The Arctic landscape is the daunting figure, and the Inuit are generally wise. The John Franklin of Canadian stories – in novels and Beattie and Geiger's scientific account – is an icon of English failure and imperial insensitivity. Franklin makes bad judgments either due to his consumption of lead or because he is something of a slow-witted remittance man. Either way, Franklin fails to mingle and therefore to learn from the Inuit. He relies on the technology he has imported from outside. It fails him, and he dies.

His death is essential. Had Franklin survived a couple of winters on the strength of his own wits, then there would have been no benefit to Canadians in the recounting of his adventure. The land and ice would have been no less terrifying, and survival would still have been the issue. But with Franklin alive, the story would have been just another about intrepid British explorers and their imperial conquests, and not the first and most important of a long line of stories of the daunting North. It would have been a story about England, another nice piece of *their* glorious history, not Canada's.

The Franklin story is a Canadian creation myth because it explains and upholds our ideas about the country that we live in. The lesson of *Canadian* versions of the story is that Franklin would have survived had he depended less on *technology* and more on Inuit Qaujimajatuqangit – worn the furs, eaten the raw meat. It doesn't matter at all, in these tellings, that there was not enough meat to go around even for the few Inuit who did frequent the area, or that no sensible Canadian now heads North without a GPS and thermal insulate. No, the point of the Franklin story as it is told today is that the modern Canadian is so attuned to our vast land and its panoply of peoples that he would have *related* to the Inuit and recognized their long and venerable history of Northern living. The Canadian would have respected the Inuit as a wiser people habituated to the strange Arctic landscape and listened to their advice, taken their cues.

Had the explorer subscribed to these *Canadian values* – had he been as enlightened as we Canadians imagine ourselves to be currently – then he would have lived. The inference of these tellings is that Franklin died because he was *English*, not Canadian. In mythic terms, he needed to die for Canada to be born.

Our modern notion of multiculturalism had its roots in sentiments like these. The Franklin story was exemplary, both as a creation myth and as cautionary tale, and, as the mother of all Canadian creation myths it carried the seed of the subsequent myths of the Age of Mapping within it. Britain is a distant authority in the story – and it *fails* John Franklin, through a lousy course in native studies and a cargo that should have sustained his men but poisoned them instead. In this way, it is the prototype of Canada's Myths of Disappointment, stories that allow Canadians to rebuke the authority on which they depend and foster a sense of homegrown identity in so doing. The relationship that exists even today to power, in which Canadians depend on the centre but expect little from it, and have subsequently acquired a view of themselves as hard done by, was learned in the era of the Company Store and was the foundation of the Myths of Disappointment. The message of these stories is of ordinary Canadians having been neglected or exploited by an overbearing and usually distant authority that is never as enlightened as ordinary Canadians are, and that holds even those who do its good work in contempt.

"The sheer distances that separate most Canadians from the centres of power," John Bemrose said, "have an effect that is simultaneously oppressive and liberating. It's oppressive because Canadians have learned not to expect too much from power – it's too far away – and liberating because they can shrug their shoulders and say, 'I'm going to do it on my own. This has nothing to do with me.' And yet the centre remains, and every once in a while it reaches out at a critical moment, or fails to, and new grounds for resentment arise. You can see this in Alberta, where people who have discovered their own vigour, and their own independence, expect to have the kind of power that they have felt emanating from Ontario all these years. While there has always been an energy in the country at large, suggesting a wider project that we must connect to, many Westerners have not been able to figure out what that wider project is – it's Canada, of course, but to say 'Canada' is just too vague. The phenomenon of Western discontent is merely the latest and most dramatic example of what so many communities all across this country have been feeling for many years."

✧   ✧   ✧

"IF YOU GREW up in a world like the one that I did," said Rudy Wiebe, "then you had a very strong sense that there were authorities in different places – Regina, Edmonton, or wherever it be – that would tell you what to do and what to learn. But what they told you very rarely reflected the life you were living – especially if you were from a non-Anglo-Saxon minority, right?"

Rudy Wiebe, the prolific, nearly frantic Mennonite novelist who was born near Fairholme, Saskatchewan, in 1934, lives in Edmonton now. When we spoke, his manner was tense and full of consternation, as if the world was on his shoulders and it was surprising that I could not see this weight of Atlas on his back. Wiebe's work is not a triumph of style, but he is important to the Canadian canon, if only for the voluminous assault his books amount to, on what the author feels have been abundant oversights and misconceptions concerning the history of this country. If the historian Pierre Berton set out to narrate Canada's neglected stories, then Wiebe saw his novelist's job as fixing the ones already on offer. This he has done with a zealous fervour, inspired by an identification with the beleaguered and a keen interest in Canada's litany of alternative heroes – Louis Riel in *The Scorched-Wood People*, Big Bear in *The Temptations of Big Bear*, and in his non-fiction, the convict Yvonne Johnson, much abused and serving a twenty-five-year sentence for murder, in *Stolen Life: The Journey of a Cree Woman*. (Wiebe co-authored with her.)

John Franklin appears in *A Discovery of Strangers*, the novel Wiebe set in the time of the explorer's ominous map-making Northern expedition of 1819–21. On that first journey, Franklin lost half his men. In Canadian eyes, the English captain had already proved himself a worrying incompetent. Franklin is not a central figure in the novel, but nevertheless the author entrenches the view of Franklin's arrogance and costly stupidity by juxtaposing his misadventure with the aboriginal wisdom and experience of the Yellowknives. Wiebe was upholding the multicultural idea of Canada that was beginning to flourish by deploring the power of the distant authority that resided with Franklin.

"The canoes are dragging all this *stuff* into the country, right?" said Wiebe, bringing himself to the edge of the low couch he was sitting on, hands in the air, gesticulating to make his point more clear. "There's power in all this industrial stuff, but in Franklin's journal, he writes about every single axe breaking because the wood was frozen solid. In the end, only one of the voyageurs, who is careful enough to know how not to break the axe, can use it – but they destroy about forty or fifty axes, because they splinter in the cold. I found that incident to be a wonderful metaphor."

Wiebe laughed and shook his head in disbelief, as if he had just driven by this display of English ineptitude on his way home from work that day.

"You don't even have to make these things up," said Wiebe. "They're already there in the story."

✧   ✧   ✧

COLONIAL POWER WAS killed in the Franklin story, and the land came to be held in awe. In its promotion of the "Idea of North," the tale of Franklin served the Age of Invention perfectly. Now the authority at the centre is Canadian, not British, but it's still the thing we blame.

Canada, in the Age of Mapping, required something more of its fundamental stories. It needed myths that would explain not so much the vagaries of the land but of its *polity*, stories that would explain the extraordinary nature of a territory settled by peoples whose primary challenge was no longer surviving Nature but the country's administration. It needed stories that would uphold the virtues of modern Canadians in the face of a government and a powerful patrician class inherited from the colonial period. Myths of Disappointment did the job, and if you consider that Quebec's "*mythes de défait*" are loosely related, then the nature of these stories attest to a unity that spans all "solitudes," even if our dispersal and fragmentation prevents us from seeing them as such. You can be a beleaguered aboriginal, a disenfranchised Acadian, an oil-rich Albertan hoarding his spare change, an Africadian haranguing that there was slavery here too, a disgruntled Quebecker wanting more Ottawa payola, or someone from Labrador who thinks that Newfoundland, not Canada, is the distant authority, because insisting on this sort of low-grade resentment is actually a *Canadian* trait. It is expressed in stories emanating the length and breadth of the country, from Newfoundland's cod moratorium (blame Ottawa, and not the industry stupidity of overfishing), to the Arctic and its Northern peoples' litigious recollection of the residential schools. On the one hand, this tendency to feel betrayed is a result of the land – of its sheer dimension, of the hard work demanded merely to get by, and the fact of our being so few. But subsequently, it was also the fault of the way we organized ourselves, using a business model instead of a nation-building one. The legacy of the Company Store was ruinous – Canadians' tolerance of monopolies, our reliance on subsidies, the constant sense of being mildly injured, and the allegiance of government and a few families' cartels (rather than Ottawa defending citizens against their excesses) are just part of the story. Even the burgeoning absurdity of Canada's aboriginal land claims – the Métis now claiming Winnipeg, the Lubicon that they were never a part of the country at all – can be seen as a lesson of the country's early formation perfectly learned, the blueprint of aboriginal ambition being the land claim that was granted to the Hudson's Bay Company of Adventurers in 1670.

The subjugated ape their masters. During the long colonial period, the centre of power was in London (and in Versailles, for a few years here and there). Then power was transferred to Ottawa, the Brasilia of the north. The capital did London's bidding through two world wars, before the country deferred to the greater economic engine to the south. Real power in Canada has rarely been local, and so the country's Myths of Disappointment ensued.

Consider a few.

The story of residential schools, Canadians' participation in the First World War, the internment of Japanese Canadians, Diefenbaker's cancellation of the Avro Arrow jet-fighter project, the Acadians, the alleged failure of Canadian historians to adequately report the history of black slavery in Canada, the cancellation of the fabled CBC news program *This Hour Has Seven Days* in 1966, the disastrous National Energy Policy of then prime minister Pierre Trudeau in 1980, and even the 2004–5 NHL strike all fit into a common mould in which good Canadians are let down by institutions they serve and that should protect them.

The Myths of Disappointment are as old as Canada. The die was cast on Beechey Island, but it was refined at Batoche, in Saskatchewan. That was where, in May 1885, Louis Riel and the Métis made their last stand against Canada's first prime minister, John A. Macdonald. In November of the same year, Riel, rebel leader and an elected member of Parliament, was tried and exe-cuted and he's been the Ned Kelly of Métis folklore ever since. Novels, and most recently Chester Brown's artfully imagined *Louis Riel: A Comic-Strip Biography*, have remembered the rebel and dual citizen – he became an American in 1883 – for his democratic qualities and, in particular, for his championing of the rights of the Métis minority to enter Confederation on their own terms, after the Hudson's Bay Company's sale of Prince Rupert's Land to Canada, in 1889, led to the annexation of the Red River Settlement. A movement to honour Riel as a Father of Confederation periodi-cally recurs – Riel having acquired mythical status for his Canadian values, which is odd as he sanctioned the execution of the pris-oner Thomas Scott and was ready to ally with the United States at one point.

Sometimes we have to go through real paroxysms to make the stories fit, but good myths are agile. The story of Riel has become one of a community leader's struggle for local empowerment achieved by peaceful means. The Métis, in the story imagined this way, were unfairly coaxed into resistance, having tried all other avenues made available to them by the Hudson's Bay Company–controlled politicians of Assiniboia, in 1870, and then, in 1885, a Canadian government operating in bad faith. Riel, so the mythic story goes, merely wished for the Métis, their land divided by Canadian surveyors in contravention of their traditions and the water courses that made their settlements viable, to be responsible for their own affairs, to be educated in French and as Catholics, and to be free of the interference of the distant authority. Riel became a hero, and his story another Myth of Disappointment, because the Métis leader's death is regarded as an injustice in the Canadian folkloric imagination, and thinking of the story along Robin Hood lines helps conjure the modern *compassionate* country into existence.

From Chester Brown's *Louis Riel: A Comic-Strip Biography*:

"When you read the defence Riel made for himself, it's impossible to think that this man was worthy of death," said Wiebe.

"But technically he was a criminal," I answered. "He executed Thomas Scott after a sham trial."

"Technically, yes, he was a criminal," said Wiebe, "but they didn't execute Gabriel Dumont, did they? And he shot at least forty or fifty Canadians *by himself*. He was the best shot. At the Battle of Fish Creek, Métis kept handing Dumont a loaded rifle and he kept on shooting. And yet Dumont died a comfortable old man telling stories to children – so *killing people* was not the thing that was wrong, right? Having certain *ideas* was wrong. They executed Riel for having *ideas*."

"And what do you think Riel's ideas were that so irked Macdonald and Ottawa?"

"That his people had a right to place, and that they could have their own kinds of communities the way that they had always done, and that they could live and worship and teach freely. They wanted the authority to rest with *them*, and not with someone who was two thousand miles away telling them what to do."

◇   ◇   ◇

"CERTAINLY THE WHOLE peculiar, messianic, latter part of his career means that you have to pick and choose very carefully what you approve of in the figure of Louis Riel," said Guy Vanderhaeghe.

It was May when I visited Batoche, the same month that Gabriel Dumont manned the Métis barricades and the lunatic Riel, who fancied himself a prophet by then, resorted to conversations with his God. I was in the company of Vanderhaeghe. His *The Last Crossing*, with Fred Stenson's *The Trade*, is one of the best historical novels ever to have been published in Canada. The Saskatchewan he was writing about still had a good decade to go before Riel and his band of Métis made their brave last stand upon its stage, but a disconsolate Gabriel Dumont appears in "Cafe Society," an early short story from *The Trouble With Heroes*. (Vanderhaeghe's first book, it was published after *Man Descending*.) In it, Dumont is in Paris at the

Paris Exposition of 1889. The Métis rebellion is behind him, and the sharpshooter is a part of Buffalo Bill Cody's travelling Wild West Show. From his café table, he looks up at the Eiffel Tower and mulls the advantage that such height would have provided him "against fat old Middleton," the Canadian general, during the most significant battle of the Northwest Rebellion at Batoche. Today, the plains appear quite different – they have been cleared, for a start, though there are still shallows behind clumps of bushes where the Métis were able to snipe from trenches, and in the walls of the white-painted church that stands about a kilometre away are the pock-marks of Canadian bullets.

"Some wind," I said.

"It's been howling for a week," said Vanderhaeghe, lighting a cigarette in the cup of his hands. "And it'll likely howl for another week. Get used to it."

"The way in which our conception of what Louis Riel stood for has evolved alongside Canadian needs is quite remarkable," I said.

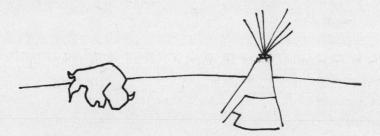

"In this part of the world," said Vanderhaeghe, "the transformation has been a reflection of the guilt that European settlers felt in putting down the Métis resistance. At least in terms of the first rebellion at Red River, in 1870, Riel divided the country along French and English lines. The second rebellion of 1885, the one that occurred here, has taken on the significance of being a regional attempt for us to have asserted ourselves. White Europeans in this part of the country have started to look on him with a great deal more sympathy than before the 1950s, as people have begun to attach to him some of the mythic symbolism of Western resistance to central Canadian domination. At least locally, Riel became a statesman-like figure, culminating in the attempts to have him decreed a Father of Confederation because of his role in the establishment of the first Manitoba government in the early 1870s. It was, of course, our Métis selves – our indigenous selves – who acted against the controlling central force, and so Riel is always going to be most important to that part of the community, but since then he's attained a wider stature and become a symbol of the regional concerns of Western Canada over a one-hundred-and-twenty-year period."

◇ ◇ ◇

THE LESSON OF Batoche was that the Nowhere of the Red River Settlement was not far enough. With French Quebec to his east and the restless United States to the south, Macdonald was not about to allow the newly formed Dominion to be pincered between hostile francophone societies, and so he rubber-stamped the railway and sent out the troops to put down the Métis rebellion. "Just watch me," he might have said.

Riel was a lost man, a crazy man, a papist who thought himself a prophet and gave himself the name "David." And, an affliction of political demagogues from Ancient Greece to West Africa and the Balkans, he fancied himself a poet. His lyric condition offered Ottawa advantage – he was committed to an asylum in 1876 – but what mattered was his charisma and that Macdonald feared his plans for an independent nation possibly allied or even annexed to the United States. Riel's was a legitimate threat to the fragile knit of a country that had only just reached the age where it could order a drink. Canada, then, made even less topographic sense than it does now. In 1867, the only hope for the country lay in a strong centre having the guts and sheer audacity to undertake the business of colonizing its corner of the continent. The case for Riel as a Father of Confederation can certainly be made, though more for what his actions prompted Macdonald to do, rather than anything he himself stood for. Indeed, there is a sense in which Canada, the bona fide nation, ends ninety-five kilometres east of Lloydminster, along the line made by the battle sites of the Northwest Rebellion – Batoche, Cut Knife, Frenchman's Butte, and Loon Lake. These were the westernmost points at which Macdonald's soldiers fought for the country. (The rest was just police work.) The vast territories that lie north and west of this line and, to the other side of Ottawa, beyond Ontario, Montreal, the Eastern Townships, and the old Maritime provinces, is a territory that old-fashioned European cartographers might well have described as "Greater Canada" – a lot of Quebec, some of Saskatchewan, most of Alberta, and all of British Columbia and Newfoundland too. These are places where the silence of Canadian guns meant that *story* needed to accomplish what the capital's armies did not. The historian with a sliver of ice in his heart could argue that, unlike the expelled Acadians or the only moderately defeated French Canadians, Albertans were *allowed* to feel distant, as, west of Batoche, there was no rebellion or its military aftermath to convey the message that Ottawa, no matter how perversely, cared.

◇ ◇ ◇

IN THE STORY of the Métis defeat at Batoche, Ottawa is the culprit that makes a martyr of that troublesome Canadian, Louis Riel. Canada's new status as an independent country means that the distant authority, the power at the centre of the story, has shifted from England to Ontario, but the dynamic of the story is the template of all the Myths of Disappointment that ensue. Good, ordinary Canadians – here, Louis Riel and his Métis – have been let down by the institutions of a country whose better values they exemplify. It doesn't matter that these values are later ones. Historicity is not the business of the Canadian creation myth, or those of any nation for that matter. Finding common causes is.

Less than thirty years later, with the outbreak of the First World War, the eminent Canadians are many. More than sixty thousand of them will become martyrs to the Allied cause. The story of Canada's contribution to the First World War effort counts both as history and as one of our most enduring creation myths. The Canadians, we are taught, could have served Britain no better. Under their generals, Sir Arthur William Currie and the Englishman Sir Julian Byng, Canadian soldiers and their engineers scored costly but important victories at the Somme, at Vimy Ridge, Passchendaele, and Amiens. It was the moment, it is often argued, in which a true national spirit was forged, Canadians, if a lesser number from French Quebec, fought together side by muddy side in the trenches of Europe – most exemplarily at Vimy Ridge in 1917.

What Canadians also remember of that bloody time – a good thing too, because the English and Americans don't – is the waste of soldiers' lives by English officers, General Douglas Haig the most notorious among them. The "Butcher of the Somme," Haig sent thousands of Canadians out of the trenches and on to senseless deaths. As he did not expect the Canadians to accomplish much at Vimy, he did not even bother to plan for victory, undermining the Canadians' advance and allowing the defeated Germans to retreat unscathed. The result of the Canadians' superior tactics was that they were sent into battle again and again, and even resented for their success. The story of Canada's participation in the Great War is one of this country's creation myths because the heroism and stoic camaraderie of the men in the trenches explains our modern country from sea to shining sea, and shows Canadians in a courageous and sympathetic light. It's one of our Myths of Disappointment because, once again, the authority in question – here the sum of Britain's generals – did not hold the lives of these valiant Canadians in any meaningful regard.

In Jack Hodgins's novel *Broken Ground*, the disappointment is reiterated at home as the demobbed veterans are given the dubious reward of some desultory allotments on Vancouver Island. The land, previously clear-cut, must be rehabilitated by the men in order that they might keep the parcels and maintain them as farms. In this passage, one of the returned soldiers, Matthew Pearson, remembers the execution of the shell-shocked soldier Hugh Corbett, "shot by us for not being shot by the Germans."

From Jack Hodgins's *Broken Ground*:

"My God, it was a terrible thing to watch. When he started to gag and retch, they loosened the gas helmet long enough for him to heave the contents of his stomach onto the ground. Then they yanked it back down and got out of the way of the guns.

"They didn't even do a proper job of it. The medical officer said he wasn't dead, so the Colonel they'd sent from H.Q. to make sure everything went according to regulations walked over in his shiny boots and fired a bullet into his head. The assistant provost-marshal looked at his watch and recorded the time of death."

"My God," Taylor said.

"Some of the boys were sick afterwards, though they tried to hide it. You heard vomiting. You heard muttered curses. 'Get a headache in this army and they blow your bloody brains out to cure you.'"

We ought to have mutinied, was the common opinion. We should have refused to let them do it. We should all have marched off in protest. "Why didn't we think of this before it was too late?" I let them say it. There was no harm in it now. But eventually I had to remind them that the army would only have planted a few more posts against the slaughter-house wall and done the same to the rest.

Private Berry, who had a way of knowing peculiar facts unknown by the rest of us, announced that Hugh Corbett was the twentieth Canadian shot for desertion since the start of the War. "Not a single Australian. If you're inclined to headaches or confusion you should have emigrated down under while you had the chance," he said. "The Aussie government refuses to let them do it. Not ours. Not Borden and his generals kissing London arse. Anything for bloody old King George!"

"Our history is a series of disappointments by the people we count on to look after us," said Hodgins, whom I'd first met during a literary festival in his hometown of Victoria, where he also taught creative writing at the university until his retirement in 2002. We sat at the end of Cook Street, in a pseudo-English pub full of faux leather-bound books and soccer memorabilia. Victoria is the city where Sir Arthur Currie was born. Even more than its pubs, the town's gardens offered the chance of anglophilia. You can retire here, and you can grow roses without the wicked mainland Canadian winter hacking away at your nostalgia for the Old Country. Beyond the pretty capital, it was a different story, and so the Canadian prime minister Robert Borden's government saw advantage in allowing the soldiers returning from the Great War to have a go at land that had previously been logged but was otherwise useless.

"There was disappointment because the British did not treat us as we deserved," said Hodgins, "but there was also the disappointment of coming home and being rewarded with farms that were unfarmable. The land that they had been awarded was virtually impossible to cultivate, and I'm sure that the blasting of the stumps, as much as six feet wide and ten feet high, would have been reminiscent of being in the trenches of the First World War, and occasionally as dangerous. There must have been many times when it felt to the men as if it were just a continuation of the same."

Hodgins grew up on a "stump ranch" in the Comox Valley, near the Campbell River on Vancouver Island, where, in 1922, a fire ravaged the island.

"When I was looking at photographs of First World War battlefields after a fight had been lost or won, and then at photographs of this community after the fire had gone through, it struck me that one could exchange some photographs and nobody would have known the difference. They showed blackened dirt, burned trees, and broken stumps and desolation as far as the eye could see. 'My gosh,' I thought, 'these people no sooner got back from living in that hellish landscape, and the next thing they know they're looking at one that's identical to it.'"

"Would you consider this story an example of a Myth of Disappointment?" I asked.

"Yes," said Hodgins, "because there was also the feeling that Canada, unlike the United States of America, was based on the concept of 'good government.' This apparently causes us to be more consistently willing to *bow* to authority, but it also means that we expect more from those who lead us. We expect that we will be shown the way, that our heroes will be treated well, and that people will be rewarded for the hard work that they do building the country. Maybe our disappointment stems from discovering that the best we can hope for is to cope. Our heroes tend to be people who manage well in the face of terrible tragedies, rather than people who *triumph*, as Americans tend to do in that country's stories and myths."

The story was not always told this way. In Timothy Findley's 1977 novel, *The Wars*, the author's emphasis is on the horror of war as it applied across the board. It is probably Findley's best novel, filled with images of the freedoms his soldiers left behind, of the pointlessness of young men's deaths and injuries, and the impossibility of human relationships in their wake. But Findley was a Canadian ensconced in monarchist Ontario's aristocratic class, one that was the agent of the distant authority. He was close to, if not at, the centre of power in the country at a time when Upper Canadians were quite content to do Empire's business.

In the very different Canada of nearly three decades later, far-flung communities and regions of the country were asserting themselves, and the story of Canada's participation in the Great War was modified to reflect these altered needs. In what is possibly one of the consummate stories of Canada's Age of Mapping, *Three Day Road*, the writer Joseph Boyden quite brilliantly interwove the country's aboriginal story with the larger and more widely accepted white Canadian one. The novel is based, in part, on the story of Francis Pegahmagabow, a Cree sniper from Northern Ontario who became the most decorated aboriginal soldier of the Great War but returned home to poverty and bigotry. Boyden's pair of native sharpshooters, Xavier and Elijah, take their rightful place alongside men such as the New Brunswick poet Alden Nowlan's Private Billy MacNally of Saint John, the forest workers of Jack Hodgins's *Broken Ground*, and the soldiers of the Newfoundland Regiment. (The last were not Canadians yet, but their stories of disappointment were running in parallel.)

Boyden's first aim was to explore man's easily savage nature, so he places the story of Windigo, the Cree man-eating spirit and human nemesis, in the desecrated and mustard-gas poisoned fields of France. But he was also exploring issues of race relations, and just as the Canadians were often condescended to by the British, Xavier and Elijah are not altogether welcomed by the settler Canadians, despite their superior sniping skills. The story is a Myth of Disappointment that replicates Hodgins's one, although it is told, this time, from the native point of view. Boyden's novel puts their story at centre stage and, as all good Myths of Disappointment do, upholds the neglected Canadian and wishes the modern, polyphonic nation into existence.

"War is the Great Equalizer," said Boyden. "Plenty of native men told me that despite the horrors they faced overseas, these were some of the better times of their lives because for once whites treated them as equals. An eighteen-pounder or a machine-gun bullet makes no distinction between skin colours. In war, you all *live* beside one another, you die beside one another, though you can only go so far in trying to make disparate worlds one. As Peggy tells Elijah and Xavier in an estaminet in France, 'If we return home, they will just treat us like shit once again.' Elijah believed that if he proved his talent as a sniper, others would treat him as an equal, even in peacetime – but I think he would have been proven quite wrong. My desire in this novel was not to say to the reader, 'Hey! We're all the same! Can't we just get along?' because we *aren't* the same. Therein lies our beauty but also our continual misunderstanding of one another."

"How much," I asked, "was the point of *Three Day Road* making the Myth Worlds of aboriginal and settler Canadians one?"

"At first, integrating the mythic aboriginal story with the Canadian creation myth of the Great War was a very unconscious thing," said Boyden. "Really, as is true of any writer, I just wanted to tell a good story but, at the same time, introduce Ojibway-Cree culture of which the reader might not have been aware. But the further I explored the legend and the psychology of a windigo, the more I realized it made perfect sense to explore ideas of rabid hunger and greed in the context of the Great War. The mud of France and Belgium became, to me, the perfect breeding ground for a windigo – and especially a *native* windigo in the shape of a young man who was displaced from his home in the bush of Northern Ontario to the bloodbath of Flanders and Arras."

Novels have a place in society because the good ones change it. Now the story of Francis Pegahmagabow, or of Tommy Prince, Canada's most decorated aboriginal veteran of the Second World War (another Ojibway from near Parry Sound), is known. There can be no going back, on a Canadian creation myth that used to be exclusively white.

From Joseph Boyden's *Three Day Road*:

> This Vimy Ridge is quiet compared to what we endured at the Somme in the autumn. And I'm glad for it. Fritz's line runs along the high ground to the east. The Canadians sit hunkered below him, our every movement visible. Troops must move at night or be pounded by Fritz with great accuracy. This is the place where the French army was nearly wiped out two years ago, and the British last year. Although the Canadians are not supposed to hear of it, word is that the French lost 150,000 men in the fighting here, and the British 60,000. Those numbers are impossible to keep secret. They are impossible for me to understand. I ask Elijah, "How many does that mean?"
>
> He smiles. "A very difficult question to answer," he says.

I can see that he has the medicine in him. His lips curl at the edges in a slight smile and his eyes shine. When he is taking the morphine he forgets all about his British accent.

"Think of all the trees we passed canoeing to the town. Think of how many trees the fire ate. That many, maybe."

✧   ✧   ✧

CANADIAN MYTHS OF Disappointment are versatile and robust and constantly adjusting themselves to recognize whatever is the current seat of the distant authority. So, just as the angle of deference of the Canadian economy has, since the 1960s, oriented itself away from London and the old colonial master towards Washington and the new seat of Empire, so did Myths of Disappointment correct their bearings. What remains the same is the story's rebuke of the powerful centre. The deaths of four Canadian soldiers from "friendly fire" in Afghanistan in April 2002 is the perfect example of a Myth of Disappointment that reflects the shift in the nature of the distant authority, the power to which Canadians defer. Canadians are disappointed, this time, not by Britain's generals but by their *American* governors. The U.S. Army becomes the power Canadians were serving and that should have been their protector.

Or, stepping back only a matter of a decade to a time in which Canadians thought of themselves as peacekeepers – the power, then, in Geneva and New York (how distant that rallying call seems now) – consider the way we have chosen to recount the story of Roméo Dallaire, the Canadian lieutenant-general, later the author of a best-selling memoir, *Shake Hands With the Devil*, a book that sold a lot better here than in other countries that had cause to be concerned about the history it raised. Dallaire was responsible for the United Nations peacekeeping forces in Kigali, Rwanda, when, in June 1994, the Hutu-perpetrated genocide of Tutsis started. The lieutenant-general is a vaunted figure in Canada, though not especially in America nor in certain corridors of the UN – and neither, for more sinister reasons, in Belgium or France. (Rwanda was a Belgian colony. France was alleged by Paul Kagame, the Tutsi leader of the Rwandan Patriotic Front, to have played a helping hand in the likely assassination of Rwandan president Juvénal Habyarimana, the event that triggered the genocide of the Tutsis.) Dallaire, the story goes, urgently notified the UN, warning of the catastrophe that was about to take place in Rwanda. His cable was ignored.

I call the Dallaire story a myth because it is not an unopposed version of events, and yet it is the one that Canadians most like to hear as it supports the Myth of Disappointment's requirement that Dallaire was an exemplary Canadian let down by the authority that should have been his steward. And, true to its higher purpose, the story also upholds the modern nation's idea of its unimpeachable multicultural self – this time on the international stage. In keeping with its aggrandized view of our place in the world, the distant authority that disappoints the eminent Dallaire – and therefore all Canadians – in this version of the myth is the UN's leadership in New York.

This is definitely not the story that Gil Courtemanche, a French-Canadian journalist and occasional documentary maker, tells in his bitterly impassioned novel of the Rwandan genocide, *A Sunday at the Pool in Kigali*. The major-general in Courtemanche's account, a character clearly inspired by Dallaire, is a peripheral, culpable, and pathetic figure, though his conduct is no less reprehensible than the ineffectual Canadian diplomatic corps who lounge around the pool of Kigali's Hotel Mille-Collines. The novel was less successful in English Canada than it was in Quebec, or in Europe, perhaps because of an incident early on in Courtemanche's story. Méthode, a friend of the French-Canadian journalist Valcourt, is dying of AIDS. He is celebrated with a party *before* he dies, rather than with a wake, during which his mother holds his hand and entreats a prostitute to "Give him a nice big one before he leaves for heaven, my girl." This scene may have irked prissier English-Canadian sensibilities, though it is more likely his portrait of the feeble UN major-general and the morally corrupt Canadian diplomats were the things that offended. The Canadian major-general,

Valcourt decides, is "a miracle of mimesis, a perfect incarnation of his country and his employer too, rather the way masters who adore their dogs end up looking and behaving like them. Unassuming, apprehensive, ineloquent and naive, like Canada. Meticulous, legalistic, a civil servant and exemplary bureaucrat, as virtuous as 'Le Grand Machin' itself (as General de Gaulle was pleased to call the UN)." *A Sunday at the Pool in Kigali* is a novel, of course, but the reckoning in Courtemanche's fiction was informed, and it has been corroborated by other actors in the Central African drama. The implication is that a tougher soldier would have acted without the necessary New York instruction, but that was not the story Canadians wanted to hear.

From Gil Courtemanche's *A Sunday at the Pool in Kigali*:

The general had done everything to justify his present passivity and future impotence. Had asked another of his own kind, a public servant, for permission he did not need and knew would be refused. Had written reports asking for more troops, knowing that no country wanted to send more troops to Rwanda, but knowing also, which was more serious, that with the several thousand soldiers he already had he could neutralize the extremists of the presidential guard and their principal accomplices in a few hours. Like the general, Valcourt had watched the Rwandan army's manoeuvres and exercises and had barely managed to keep himself from laughing out loud and offending his hosts as well as the French military instructors, who looked the other way while their pupils floundered like Boy Scouts on their first outing in the woods. A few hundred professional soldiers could take control of the capital in a matter of hours. The UN didn't need reinforcements, just a bold leader on the spot. All the Western military experts knew it, and in particular the UN general himself.

The geographically varying impact of *A Sunday at the Pool in Kigali* suggests that French Canadians may have different requirements of their "national" stories, but certainly in the rest of Canada the myth of Roméo Dallaire persists. Myths fill in gaps left by history that falls short of the mark.

"Every country, in some unconscious way, wishes that its history was heroic," said Courtemanche when I visited him at his home in Montreal's Mile End. It was the end of Courtemanche's working day, and the irreverent writer and social critic had opened a bottle of good white wine and lit a cigarette, as was his habit.

"The French *patrimoine* is built on the idea of a glorious history of wars," said Courtemanche. "Theirs is a history of victories and defeats and of *le roi soleil*. We could say the same thing about Great Britain, with the Battle of Trafalgar and all the rest of it. But Canada's history is almost devoid of any of that. We are probably the only rich, complex, contemporary, modern nation *without* a glorious history. We have a history that is a bit like we are, a history that proceeded slowly, and without great drama – and it's the same thing in Quebec. For years our little history meant that in Canada and Quebec we invented heroes out of people who were mere normal, little persons like Dollard-des-Ormeaux or Marguerite Bourgeois. She was a good missionary, but she was not a *saint*. She was not a Mother Teresa. And we did the same thing with Rocket Richard, the hockey player. We need heroes to create the impression that we live in a great country. Oh, there were some crazy people. There was General Colborne, who defeated Les Patriotes, and Lord Durham, who wanted to forbid the teaching of French – but these were really small incidents in Quebec's history. Colonialism was actually quite *indulgent* towards the French Canadians. The net result is that colonialism didn't succeed, and that we're still talking about Quebec sovereignty. Well, countries can be great *without* the kind of cruel and fantastic history that makes for a lot of novels and a lot of books, but we can't understand that we don't need those sorts of stories to be a great country."

"Perhaps," I said, "we look for instruction from our storytellers because we don't have any of the simple national myths such as you find in the United States – myths of victory or of the American Dream –"

"And we don't have the Civil War or the building of a nation from slavery. There are a lot of things that I'm quite *happy* we don't have," said Courtemanche, coughing smoke as he laughed.

"The way I see it," I continued, "what explains our reliance on storytellers is not so much that we do not know our history, as an historian like Jack Granatstein would argue, but that we don't really care for our history much. It doesn't provide us much excitement –"

"Because we tend to dwell on what are 'traditional' historical events," said Courtemanche, "like the date of a new king, or the year of a war. We don't write about our social history that is actually quite interesting – like how come in Canada, or in Quebec, there is a trade union movement that is so strong no matter what happens in the United States? Or how is it that we still have a leftist party in Canada? Instead we discuss treaties, or how people got thrown out of New Brunswick and Nova Scotia."

"You said earlier that you don't mind – you're almost *relieved* – that we don't have a grand history in the manner of other, older nations. Perhaps one of the virtues of being Canadian is that history itself is often a pointless idea, as we now have so many peoples from elsewhere that there is no easy agreement even about our fundamental myths."

"There's a big difference between French-Canadian and English-Canadian thinking there," said Courtemanche. "The loyalty to Canada is not a loyalty to *history* – not to the way the state has been edified and constructed. It's a loyalty to equality, and some kind of security – to some kind of a midsummer night's dream. Quietness. Peace and good neighbourliness. Not too much arguing. No conflicts – or just small conflicts that can be resolved by shaking hands. It is a loyalty to *values*, but values don't make for great novels."

◇　◇　◇

AND THEN, TROUBLE.

"If you start talking about Canadian history, then you're generally talking about history that had nothing to do with Newfoundland up until about 1949," Wayne Johnston said, "so that Newfoundland is already outside whatever patterns there may or may not have been in Canadian literature up to that point."

The Newfoundland author Wayne Johnston emphatically rejects the arbour of grand ideas and views even multiculturalism as a Canadian idea with no real application in the province. I'd met Johnston a few times over the years, and had always admired the pointed comments he was able to deliver with a wry, deadpan expression. In Toronto, we talked one afternoon – effectively his morning, as his working pattern is to write through the night. His masterful novel *The Colony of Unrequited Dreams* imagines the life of Joey Smallwood, the newspaperman who became Newfoundland's first premier after he tabled and won the referendum of 1948.

"I have no interest at all in where my books fit into a way of interpreting Canada," said Johnston, who, comfortable on the couch, stared unflinchingly as he resisted any of my attempts at including him in any greater literary endeavour. "I'm much more interested in how historical forces affect the characters in my novels. I'm someone who, like Shelagh Fielding in *The Colony of Unrequited Dreams*, believes that history – even recorded history – verges on chaos. The attempt to find patterns in history, the need for those patterns, and the *imposition* of those patterns on life and on art interest me because they are the tendencies that destroy a lot of people. *These* are the things that I write about, but I am not trying to put forward any of those interpretations myself. In my novel *The Navigator of New York*, for example, there is a place beyond what can be known or will satisfy armchair explorers. The idea is that the North Pole is a fake, but once they get there they discover that their quest has nothing to do with the North Pole at all. The Pole is always moving. It doesn't exist. They're chasing shadows. So let's just say that I'm against all big ideas – in religion, history, philosophy, it doesn't matter. I'm less interested in the question 'Does God exist?' than the fact that people are asking it. Given the climate, it seems to me that the big ideas don't wash."

Born that year, Johnston can remember how Smallwood's victory divided families. In his succinct and quite wonderful memoir of Newfoundland, *Baltimore's Mansion*, the tension of the referendum is played out through a cast of reticent Johnston family men. In *The Colony of Unrequited Dreams*, the journalist Shelagh Fielding is an entirely fictional character he introduces into the novel, and her discussion of Judge D.W. Prowse, the author of *A History of Newfoundland*, is tinged with regret and enlivens the controversy of Newfoundland having become a part of Canada. The threat of secession, from any part of the country, is the ultimate Canadian response to feelings of political disappointment. The 1948 referendum prompted heated political argument when it was contested, and it was still able to do so on the occasions I visited Newfoundland. It remains a paramount concern for Johnston.

"If you read Smallwood's autobiography, *I Chose Canada*," Johnston said, "then you quickly realize that he had no idea *what* he was choosing – which is not even to say that there was something in Canada that he didn't understand. Smallwood was sometimes obsessed with the idea of Newfoundland as a nation, and sometimes he was obsessed with the idea of Newfoundland as part of a Canadian dream, but he couldn't define either one."

"But just as you describe historical forces exerting themselves on your characters," I said; "it must be fair to assume that historical forces also exert themselves on the way *you* choose to tell a story."

"Yes," said Johnston, "but the difference is that I don't look at those forces as being easily identifiable, and so the question of whether the author struggles with those forces in the way that my characters do really doesn't make sense to me. The things they are struggling with are things that I do not believe exist. Within the novel, the history Fielding is writing is a parody of Prowse's *A History of Newfoundland*, and one of the things about his 1895 history is that it is a completely formless eight hundred pages. It has some really fascinating anecdotes in some places, but he couldn't give it a shape. His one conclusion was that he hoped Newfoundland would join Canada one day. So when Shelagh Fielding says that after the referendum, there will always be the people and the place of Newfoundland, it is a way of countering historians trying to fit the place into patterns."

"But don't you think it's actually preposterous to believe that you can separate yourself entirely from the context in which you're writing? You are, nevertheless, a novelist working in a particular age, and you're probably channelling something, no?"

"If I'm channelling anything, and I'll admit that as a person alive in 2005 and writing about Newfoundland, I'm probably channelling something, it's the natural attempt of people to try to find a form in the formlessness. I sympathize with my characters' preoccupation with finding a shape and a form and a purpose – but that doesn't mean that I think that the shape and the form and the purpose are there. I'm surrounded by people trying to find those patterns, and I don't think that I'm unusual other than in admitting to it."

"I'm under the impression that you consider it *suitable* that Prowse's endeavour should not have succeeded."

"Yes, I'm glad that it didn't," said Johnston. "Prowse was a very good example of a New Worlder who needed to prove something, who needed to forge an identity for Newfoundland – and if you read his history, as very few have done, you'll see that it's a gigantic failure. I'm glad that he didn't find an idea for people to ride for a hundred years."

"But isn't that what story does?"

"I don't think so. It doesn't assert that individuals are representative of other individuals except as human beings. It doesn't say that here is a representative Newfoundlander and that through this person's experience you can see reflected the experience of all Newfoundlanders."

Wayne Johnston was right, but then again so was I. The stories that I have chosen to characterize as Myths of Disappointment – the measure of an attitude, really – did not emanate from Newfoundland until *after* Confederation with Canada in 1949. The irony was that

Johnston's *The Colony of Unrequited Dreams* was, to my mind, the story that came closest to being the "Great Newfoundland Novel." It addressed the essence and core questions of Newfoundland so completely, as Fitzgerald's *The Great Gatsby* had done for USAmerica, that only revision or comment could ensue. Effectively, the novel Johnston published in 1998 ended the province's Age of Mapping and ushered in its Age of Argument. It reflected the Rock as a robust and assertive society in a way that much of Canada was not. And it deflected the necessity of Myths of Disappointment, stories of the second Age that assert a society's worth through a certain haplessness. No wonder he was giving me such a hard time.

"Look, I wouldn't be completely relativistic. I don't think any-thing goes. I don't think there are three and a half billion interpre-tations of equal value. I wouldn't go quite that far. But I do think in 2005, after so many ideologies and so many schools of philosophy have been erected and overthrown, that it's pretty apparent that these all-informing big ideas, whether they're for Canada or for the world or for literature, don't work. And that's not the way to look at things. Don't throw out common sense altogether, but know that big ideas don't wash. I'm writing against the idea that history has any kind of formal shape. Either consciously or unconsciously, all fiction writers are doing that."

From Wayne Johnston's *The Colony of Unrequited Dreams*:

> For a few seconds there was nothing in the world but sound, the continuous blare of the whistle, the chugging of the train. The conductor saw me and waved his hat as he went by, grin-ning gleefully as if he hoped I was an independent. To spite him, I waved back. I saw his mouth form the words *We won*.
>
> What did he imagine we had won? What, had he "lost," would he have imagined he had lost?
>
> I watched the train until it disappeared from view, the sound of the whistle receding. Something abiding, some-thing prevailing, was restored.

I've often thought of that train hurtling down the Bonavista like the victory express. And all around it the northern night, the barrens, the bogs, the rocks and ponds and hills of Newfoundland. The Straits of Belle Isle, from the island side of which I have seen the coast of Labrador.

These things, finally, primarily, are Newfoundland.

From a mind divesting itself of images, those of the land would be the last to go.

We are a people on whose minds these images have been imprinted.

We are a people in whose bodies old sea-seeking rivers roar with blood.

✧ ✧ ✧

AT THE BEGINNING of my journey, I had considered Evangeline, the heroine of the nineteenth-century American poet Henry Wadsworth Longfellow's invented story of lovers separated by *le grand dérangement* of the Acadians from Nova Scotia in 1755, to be another example of the country's Myths of Disappointment. The story had been grasped not just by the Acadians, but also by a zealous Maritime tourist industry spearheaded by the Dominion Railway (a company later absorbed by the Canadian Pacific Railway). Subsequently, the name Evangeline has appeared on everything from chocolate bars to washing powder to a contemporary brand of fair-trade coffee. *Evangeline* was the first feature film ever made in Canada, and it was the subject of the Nova Scotian novelist Alfred Silver's *Three Hills Home*. Its message of a people let down by their governors, and its commendation of our current Canadian humanitarian sense of self appeared to fit the Disappointment schema. The inference was that Canadians, peacekeepers *extraordinaire*, would never have been involved in this early example of British-orchestrated ethnic cleansing. Except that the Acadian story is a proud one and might well have been of a different character. So, in Montreal, I went to see Antonine Maillet, the Acadian novelist and playwright from Bouctouche, New Brunswick, who won the Prix

Goncourt in 1979 for her novel of the Acadian diaspora, *Pélagie: The Return to Acadie*.

Maillet, diminutive in stature but august in manner, received me at her house on the Montreal street that now bears her name. She is a literary celebrity not just to Acadians but to francophone Canadians generally, even if the political views her people held *envers Canada* were infinitely more tolerant than those of Québécois *indépendantistes*. Indeed, the kindness of the Acadians and the *absence* of the resentment to be found in Canada's Myths of Disappointment, even in the face of all the punishments their history has meted out, was one of the things that interested me.

There is one extraordinary account of the Acadian expulsion by an eyewitness. Lt.-Col. John Winslow of the New England Volunteers was one of the English officers who, with Col. Robert Monckton, carried out the deportation orders of Lt.-Gov. Charles Lawrence in 1755, and he recorded it in his diary. It was Winslow who read the edict towards the assembled Acadians and then, like a lesser Sidney Carlton, proclaimed that "The Part of Duty I am now upon is what thoh Necessary is Very Disagreeable to my natural male & temper as I Know it Must be Grievous to you who are the Same Specia." His elegantly articulated but really only mild discomfort was very English and, from the Acadian point of view, tragically ineffectual. The Acadians were loaded onto boats and transported to the Thirteen Colonies, where many of the colonial British subjects but soon-to-be Americans bullied, enslaved, or incarcerated them, not least because they were Catholic. The Acadians' long trek home, from the Thirteen Colonies to new settlements in New Brunswick and along the part of southwestern Nova Scotia that was subsequently called the "Acadian Shore" – the country's most industrious farmers having been transformed into fishers by historical circumstance – was the subject of *Pélagie: The Return to Acadie*. The return, in the novel, has a nearly biblical quality. Pélagie dies as Moses did, within sight of the Promised Land.

Land means a lot in the Acadian psyche. The name Acadia suggests either some quasi-Canadian place or an Arcadia that is by definition vague. At first the territory was hard-won from the salt marshes of the Annapolis Valley and rendered fertile by virtue of Acadian hard work and their ingenious invention of a system of drains and sluices. Then it was stolen by the English who, with imperial nerve, later founded Acadia University in the middle of the plundered farmlands. Memories of the land came to matter more to the Acadian sense of identity than the idea of a formal state did. Their "nation" was effectively founded, that fateful year of 1755, in the exile that was the result of their refusal to take an oath of loyalty to either of the warring governments, English and French. The Acadians had no state they were able to call their own, and then no land to put their houses on.

From Antonine Maillet's *Pélagie: The Return to Acadie:*

> Acadie, tossed from one royal master to another, had managed to slip between the two and fool them both, going about its own business right under the old-country noses of Louis and George, still sniffing the wind for spices. And without breathing a word, the little Atlantic colony had let the kings of France and England send back and forth their revised and corrected maps of Acadie and Nova Scotia, and had gone on happily cultivating its garden. It wasn't to last; the harvests were too good to be true. And the English soldiers, dreaming of a few country acres, began to covet these Acadian fields.

"Exile," Maillet writes, "is a hard chapter in the book of history. Unless one turns the page."

What the Acadians did have was story. Their not declaring themselves beholden to either imperial cause did one other very un-Canadian thing that allowed the incipient nation to break the ties with the distant authority that kept all other communities in the territory in abeyance. Their necessary self-reliance meant that the stories were *not* Myths of Disappointment but more transparently edifying ones.

Maillet's fabular story – an epic more than it is a novel – chronicles the long journey the exiled Acadians undertake to make the idea of their homeland real again. *Pélagie: The Return to Acadie* is an "epic" not because the journey takes a long time, but because its mythic aim is to celebrate and enshrine the history and the culture of the Acadians in a way that distinguishes the Acadians as a people. It chronicles the Acadian battle to survive in the face of all sorts of enemies – from the people they meet along their journey to the obstacles Nature presents. And yet the story is not one that seeks redress. Pélagie's cart carries the living, but also, metaphorically, the dead. The long march home, northwards up North America's eastern seaboard, is what provides the novel its narrative thrust. The lesson of *Pélagie: The Return to Acadie* – a universal instruction, really – is that story, not war, ultimately binds a nation.

"Myths," said Maillet, "are universal because they answer the great philosophical questions of humankind. Where are we going? Where are we coming from? What are we doing here? Who are we? Myth is very strong in Acadia because we are a part of the myth. The myths came from legends and the legends started in reality, and in our case the reality is a history of deportation, of our return to the land, and of our hiding in the forest. These experiences gave birth to a series of legends about giants and strong, brave men, that enabled us to be able to survive as a people. All these stories were told orally, and when I write, all these ways of telling a story meld into one another to create a book."

I said, "The possession of land, and all the ties of belonging that possession creates, comes up a lot in your work. In Acadia, the relationship to the land is so much more impassioned than in the rest of Canada, don't you think?"

"Acadians are living paradoxes," said Maillet. "They are always the opposite of themselves. Land might be their wealth, but it is also their tragedy. From the very beginning, they searched for territory because land is what represented their sense of belonging to a nation. They had come to Acadia from afar, and they needed to secure their language, culture, and oral traditions – but they were deprived of all of this almost as soon as they were able to plant these memories in the soil of Acadia and become a people again – and I must say that they were a happy people. Acadia, before the deportation, was a success story. The first settlements prospered, but then they uprooted from the land and experienced something close to a genocide."

I explained my notion of Canada's Myths of Disappointment to Maillet, and then my suspicion that the story of Evangeline had a different quality – that Acadian stories, as she or even Longfellow expressed them, did not follow the model. "For a start," I said, "there is not the ambivalent relationship to power that lies behind these other Myths of Disappointment. Acadians depended on themselves, not Britain or France. They were an autonomous people."

"I think that your analysis is correct," said Maillet. "It's true that we have never been dependent upon a central power – until perhaps today, as in the last years we have realized how beneficial it can be as a minority group to have the support of a sympathetic government. But in reality, the Acadian people have always had to manage on their own. The *grand dérangement* was the first case of ethnic cleansing in North America, and the reason why the English deported the Acadians was that, for the very first time, well before the American and the French revolutions, there was an attempt on the part of the French settlers in Acadia to create a republic, a land of freedom where we could shake ourselves loose of the King of France. We did not want a King. We were self-sufficient. We were the first to elect our patriarchs. We were the first Republicans, though we do not want to say as much out loud. Ours was a form of democracy that was well ahead of its time, and so the anglophones – those colonials from Boston who were not American yet – became afraid, and this is the reason why the English tried to nip the Acadians' freedom sentiment in the bud. They were afraid of anything new, as it was a threat to the established order that was, at the time of the King's rule, a kind of feudal system. So they crushed the Acadian endeavour as it started. They rooted out the Acadian people by deporting them, and in so doing they prevented the realization of a great modern project."

"Why are the Acadians not more angry as a people?" I asked. "You are not like the Métis, the aboriginals, the Newfoundlanders, or Quebeckers – not even like *Canadians*, constantly demanding more, constantly feeling short-changed or hard done by."

"To that," said Maillet, "I would answer the way that I have already to the Québécois who ask me why we did not strike out and punch the English. *Because we would have broken our wrist*, I tell them! The Acadian people became as cunning as a fox because they were not as gifted as the wolf. When you are strong, you attack. When you are weaker, you wait. You use tactics, you do not charge. You move forward but always carefully, on the sides. Acadians have a sense of timing. Sometimes it fools them. They wait too long, they lose the opportunity, but I always say sniff like a dog, wait for the *bon moment*. Do not act for revenge's sake, or for the sole purpose of a fight. Unfortunately, it can be said that Acadians have used these careful tactics too often. At one point, they could have said, 'That is enough now' – as some people did. I have said this, Louis Robichaud has said this, Clément Cormier has said this. There were no Acadians left behind, and so we had no teeth left with which to bite the aggressor. What were we to do? Perish – or come home in Pélagie's cart and gradually rebuild our nation from the start, knowing that it would never be the same? Acadians had to establish a relationship with their native soil, only they had to do it throughout the diaspora, because returning to the land as it was would have been suicide. The English who had deported them were still living in the country that had been theirs, and so the Acadians had no choice but to return to other land than had been theirs in the first place. So they went deeper into the forest, farther north towards Quebec, and towards the part of Nova Scotia that became New Brunswick as we know it today. The Acadians hid for one hundred years in the forest before they asserted themselves, and it was another one hundred years before they felt at home again. The link to native soil is a very old memory – that is my interpretation, anyway. It is the inveterate memory of a lost paradise that we are still trying to recapture in some respect, and yet we know that it will never be fully regained."

Maillet looked across at me from the deep leather chair in which she was sitting. It seemed a kind of throne.

"In the end, our land has become a vase in which we are able to put our dreams, our memories, our culture, and maybe our hopes. Do you understand?" she asked.

"I think so."

"Fighting has never been the Acadian way," said Maillet. "We have two centuries of submission behind us and we have learned, with time, that we needed to achieve more than other people have done because we carried this millstone of trauma around our necks. The syndrome of the deportation has always weighed heavily upon us. It was an integral, inescapable part of our lives. I remember as a child, the way my generation used to talk about the *grand dérangement*. It was the page of history we carried with us, and the only way to get out of that situation and triumph was to use the tool of humour. Often the French have asked me how it is that a tragedy such as my play *La Sagouine* can make the Acadians laugh that much? 'Is it because Acadians feel it only superficially?' they asked, and I said, 'No, we laugh so that we won't die.' Humour was the only way out of our misfortune. With laughter, my generation finally turned the corner as a people. We put the *grand dérangement* behind us. It was then that we became living human beings and not just survivors."

The experience of the Acadians was instructive. In time, I thought to myself, the rest of the country would learn the confidence and rootedness of this first Canadian tribe, a nation whose authority has always rested with themselves.

· Part Three ·

THE AGE OF ARGUMENT

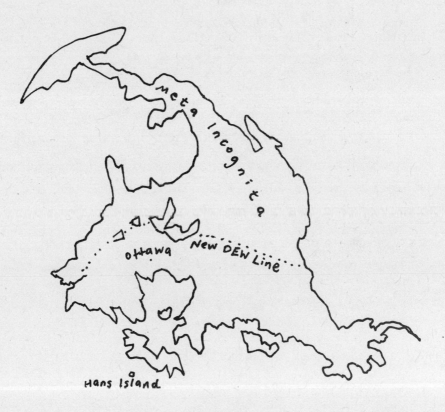

The trouble with the great country that proceeds without a bloody or eventful history is that it is challenged to collect the overarching stories that allow its citizenry to think of itself collectively. A dearth of such stories makes the task of national unity less straightforward. So the Myths of Disappointment achieved what more bellicose stories do by promoting a collective sense of having been injured, and that will do but is a passing phase. Canada, the young country, will in the end accumulate a past, though it may be one of fragmentation and not glory if the values that constitute the character of the country are not agreed upon. With frontiers that, until recently, appeared infinite, or absurd, historically it has been difficult for Canadians to conceive of their country as a whole and "distinct society." Borders, real or imagined, are the catalyst and the sine qua non of a national endeavour and robust ones serve a society in its Age of Argument. The job of stories in the Age of Mapping is to plot the extent of a country and what fills it so that we can think about the territory as a coherent entity. But once this mapping is done, there is no longer the expectation or the necessity of a unanimity of views. The point of stories becomes to inform and contradict and add to one another, and in this way the community evolves. The task of stories is one of arguing versions of the society in question. The litera-ture of the Age of Argument is the canon at its most secure.

Three regions of Canada's atlas are distinct societies already. In each, the role the border plays is instrumental. Newfoundland, Canada's most recently confederated province, has a natural border with the sea that long ago entrenched the island's distinct sense of identity. In Quebec, the ersatz border of language defines the territory and pro-vides a boundary within which all the constituent parts of a community of many tongues and origins argue their idea of la belle province. *The third distinct society is the City, har-binger of Canada's destiny, because its borders are limits that no longer matter.*

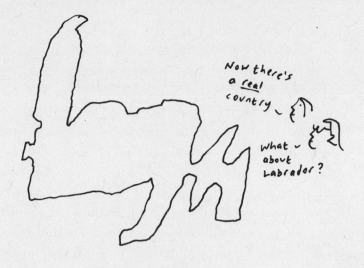

9

Making Things Up

*When you describe an experience, what you are recounting is your memory of the act, not the act itself. Experiencing a moment is an inarticulate act. There are no words. It is in the sensory world. To recall it and to put words to it is. to illustrate how one remembers the past, rather than actually experiencing the past. Keep this in mind as you read the words of others as they remember an incident.**
MICHAEL WINTER, *This All Happened**

Air Canada and not the ferry now carries most Newfound-landers to and from the island, though even the new high-way of the skies has not changed the island's unalterable fact. Newfoundland is a place you drift towards more easily than you part from it. In its very genesis, this landmass, with its fantastic grasping shape, was born of "chunks of three continents fused together," wrote Michael Winter in his debut novel, *This All Happened*. Newfoundlanders wait for what comes their way because they know that home is a place where most things, including themselves, wash up eventually. The artist Rockwell Kent in Winter's second novel, *The Big Why*. The baby in Joan Clark's novel *Latitudes*

317

of Melt. The drowned passengers of the *Titanic*. The jet-born human flotsam of the planes diverted to Newfoundland's safe haven after 9/11, and the Russian refugee and cruise ships of Lisa Moore's novel *Alligator*. Bad news from fishing boats, or the oil rig *Ocean Ranger*. So Newfoundlanders have seen all they have to see and are surprised by little. The place is contained, and the newest generation of writers free to write about whatever they please – to benefit from the island's history and not be seconded by it. The word that most Newfoundland writers were using on the visits that I made was *now*. "This is the moment," said Winter, "but don't think about it long. As soon as it's familiar, then it's something that's been and gone."

A popular T-shirt (boxer shorts, if you wish) supports the "Newfoundland Liberation Army" – and shows the silhouette of a gang on the crest of a hill brandishing not guns but flutes, guitars, and fiddles. A wealth of colloquial expressions, and a body of lore tied to the land every bit as directly as are the stories of First Nations, emphasizes the integrity of the place.

In Newfoundland, the role that culture plays in a vigorous and confident society is understood. Stories are *in the bone*. In this island that still bears the marks of an oral society, songs fishermen used to sing contain in their lyrics directions around the difficult shore. The names of towns and villages here – Heart's Content, Heart's Desire, Heart's Delight – are among the most poetic in the world – a song in their own right. In the way that they relate the memory of a place, rather than using the name of some Old World monarch to stake a claim, they are closer in nature to aboriginal names than to settler ones. Newfoundland even has its own lexicon, it has its own book. *The Dictionary of Newfoundland English* is to the province as the Mahabharata is to India, or as Shakespeare's plays are to England – work that contains not just the words but the soul of the place. Idiom is proof of Newfoundland's difference, and of the unambiguous nature of the place as a *nation*, this sentiment as strong for the islanders as it is for francophones.

In St. John's, the off-the-shelf ugly red-brick buildings of the federal ministries, the distant authority, carry the insignia of the

Canadian government and suit the landscape least of all. They are an imposition, for there is no historical project of the kind that Quebeckers scoff at in English Canada needed here. Newfoundland is where folk gather in kitchens, sing songs, recite poetry, and read to each other, in a part of the country that was, for too long, ridiculed. Newfoundland was the colony that went bankrupt and that asked to be governed by Britain; the island on the sea that had to be told not to fish. And yet the effect of the island's isolated character – of living in outports that were even smaller coherent worlds, and of the fiercely individualistic nature of the fishing industry on which so many depended – was the development of a self-reliance that is extreme. Being an island helps. An authentic border gave Newfoundlanders the sense of a nation that Acadians had to discover in exile. Here, to describe a person as "independent" is one of the best things a Newfoundlander can say of someone else.

Newfoundland knew its own Ages of Invention and of Mapping, and on the Rock you will hear Harold Horwood and then Kevin Major described as novelists who proved that it was possible to be a writer from Newfoundland – *and make a living by it*. That you did not have to leave the island unless you wanted to. You will hear other novelists described, as happens across the water, as writers who were not ashamed to name the place and set their stories on the Rock. And now, in its Age of Argument, you will hear some wonder about stories that no longer seem to *need* to be set in Newfoundland at all. This is a far cry from the period that immediately followed Confederation, in 1949, and culminated in the morally devastating cod moratorium of 1992 – bad years for Newfoundland, in which the shock of annexation made the province forget the *cultural* borders that had made the society distinct.

It was this forgetting of the island's distinct character that made a second mapping of the province necessary. In the period now remembered as Newfoundland's cultural renaissance, new stories charted its history, championed its culture, extolled its dialect and manner of speaking. Poetry, song, comedians, and the novels, to name a few, that Horwood, Major, Bernice Morgan, and Robin

McGrath wrote, put Newfoundlanders back on the map – for Canadians but also for themselves. The movement, at its peak in the 1970s, was the hard-done-by territory's fight back against the cultural erasure put into play by the process of Confederation that almost half of Newfoundland voted against in 1948.

"If you asked people whether it is possible to have a nation *without* politics, most would probably say no, but I think that Newfoundlanders would say that you can," said Robin McGrath, the author of *Donovan's Station*. "In part that's why we didn't resist giving up political control to the British, in the 1930s, when we had Commission government – our connection to where we live was so strong that it didn't change anything."

McGrath's novel is a narrative of the province told through the old woman Keziah Donovan's recounting of her life. McGrath is a cultural chauvinist – a nationalist, really, whose fiction, essays, and even printing reflect her love of home. Hers is the political purpose of a generation that fought for recognition, the attainment of which allowed a subsequent generation of Newfoundland writers to enter freely into the province's Age of Argument. Even her quiet house on Portugal Cove is an exhibit in her defence of Newfoundland, its extraordinary hearth a tribute to local architecture and ingenuity. The chimney of the house is an enormous funnel, its stone foot large enough to accommodate the fire, a baking oven, and short benches on two sides.

✧ ✧ ✧

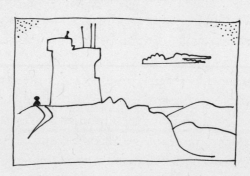

"OUR NATIONAL ANTHEM – not the *Canadian* anthem but Newfoundland's – is one of the few that glorifies the land, as opposed to nationhood," said McGrath. A matriarch.

"Was *The Dictionary of Newfoundland English* significant?" I asked. McGrath smiled.

"I love the *Dictionary*. I even wrote a young adult novel about it. In 1966, I was at Memorial University, and one of the first things I had to do was to go home with these enormous forms about English usage in Newfoundland. That was the basis of the *Dictionary*. It was a really empowering thing – that's an ugly word, but that's what it did. It gave us a sense that our lives were *serious* and that they mattered."

"How much do you believe that writers of the current generation – such as Lisa Moore and Michael Winter – are following on the success of the cultural movement of the 1970s of which you were a part?"

"I certainly grew up overwhelmed by the consequences of Confederation," said McGrath. "It was a time of phenomenal change and a phenomenal loss of pride. Schoolbooks were being taken away from us and replaced by ones that were totally unfamiliar. To have grown up in Newfoundland during the 1950s and to have been mocked and jeered at and made fun of – to be constantly reminded that you're inferior and to find yourself the butt of a national joke instead of being welcomed – that was a struggle. It was like being the adopted child in a family. In some ways it allowed us to burst out of the other end with things like CodCo – but I can see that people of my generation were probably a bit too obsessed with the 'Newf' cult. It would have been a good idea to move beyond it, but our younger writers are doing that for us."

✧　✧　✧

THE SAME TRAITS that make a place distinct can make it stifling. Wayne Johnston left Newfoundland because it was easier for him to write outside the narrow confines of the island province. In "Catechism," a short story published in *The Walrus* magazine in 2004,

Johnston portrayed a novelist from the Rock who has taken up the position of writer-in-residence in Regina and is handed a brick to put on the accelerator of his car to keep it idling and warm during the deep subzero temperatures of the prairie midwinter. He is escaping the fallout of an affair he had at home, though it can be read, too, as the story of a novelist wanting to escape the Newfoundland Telegram – a network of gossip and rumour that works faster than hi-speed Internet and monitors the actions of Newfoundlanders and their friends – whether from "around the Bay," Toronto, Ross River, or Fort McMurray. The cable is historic. "A man and his acts cannot be separated for long," declares Rockwell Kent in Michael Winter's *The Big Why*. "Newfoundland possesses a circular wind that carries information." Kent, an ornery American artist who left Manhattan in 1914 to take advantage of the isolation of Newfoundland, settled in Brigus (the outport that was the explorer Bob Bartlett's home) and became the subject of so much misinformed gossip that he was deported from the island in the following year, under suspicion of being a German spy. Johnston left too, though by choice, evading the pesky wind by moving to Toronto (or its gusts, at any rate). Winter, one of a younger generation of novelists that looked to Johnston as a mentor, chose instead to confront the wind head on. In his first novel, *This All Happened*, he makes a banquet of it. The novel is a warm, touching, and highly amusing story of Gabriel English having to come to terms not just with the end of his relationship with one Lydia, but of his coterie of St. John's friends, a time of life.

✧ ✧ ✧

I TRAVELLED TO Newfoundland to meet Michael Winter at home. His relationship to his material was such that he needed to visit it, and so he returned to the island periodically. A tall, slightly lanky, affable fellow, he took me first to a house overlooking the harbour of St. John's. It was here that he had written most of *This All Happened*, running drafts of it to his close friend Lisa Moore, who, at the time, lived a couple of streets away. We had driven past Mount Pearl, a nondescript suburb of St. John's, Winter explaining that he rarely took his jalopy past the overpass that separated downtown and historic St. John's from the rest of the Avalon Peninsula.

"Do you know anybody who is actually *from* Mount Pearl?" I asked. "I've been told that it's technically impossible to be *from* Mount Pearl as the subdivision is only thirty years old and in Newfoundland you can't be from anywhere until your family has been around for at least one hundred years."

Winter understood. He was a one-year-old when his family made the move to Corner Brook from Newcastle-upon-Tyne, in England. Nearly forty years later he was still often regarded as being "from away."

"People have this idea that Elizabethan folk were tilling the same soil for five hundred years," said Winter, once a geographer. "New research indicates that only *sixteen per cent* of people living in England during Elizabethan times inhabited the same plot of land as their grandfathers did. In fact, the society was quite mobile, but in Newfoundland that was usually not the case. Newfoundlanders were growing up in communities separate from one another, and it was hard to travel between them. The point your friend was making is that Mount Pearl has not existed for long enough for the parents not to have been from somewhere else. The *somewhere elses* are where the people in Mount Pearl are from."

"In *This All Happened*, and in the earlier stories, your main character is Gabriel English," I said. "Did you invent the name to address a feeling of strangeness despite having spent a life here?"

"It was completely intentional," said Winter, breaking out into a typically generous grin. "I could have called him Michael Winter, but that seemed too easy a joke."

Winter raised a finger in the air to make a further point. "But you know, the names are quite close," he said. "Both Gabriel and Michael were archangels." Names, in Newfoundland, matter. Winter, no surprise, had taken issue with the American writer Annie Proulx changing the names of local communities for her novel *The Shipping*

News – to protect the innocent, she said – the very idea that Winter deliberately set out to subvert in *This All Happened*.

Winter is part of a writers' collective, the "Burning Rock," the name of which is known now across the country. The bunch were close friends – still are – because to live in St. John's is to be part of an astonishingly close community. Winter left – though, a writer who understands the arc of a life, he did so not without having paid tribute to his circle of chums, as well as to the curiosities of his craft. In his title *This All Happened*, Winter was playing with the question of what in a novel is true to life, and what is not. He was asking what it means to be "making things up."

"If your last name is *English*, it means that you're the foreigner in a community that's mainly Irish," said Winter. "It makes you the outsider. I grew up in Newfoundland, and it's my home, but because I was not born here my life was so different from the other people that I grew up with. My family was so distinctly opposite from other families that there was no way to feel except as an outsider."

"Maybe you should have lived in Mount Pearl," I said.

✧   ✧   ✧

WE ARRIVED AT the Ship Inn, a third of the way down the steps that lead from Duckworth to Water Street. It was a popular bar, music most nights, that Winter helped give renown when he used it in his novel *This All Happened*. It seemed an appropriate place to begin, in the writers' hothouse of Newfoundland, a discussion of the ethics of making things up.

"I'm going to read you the first part, okay?" said Winter, still standing outside the Ship's heavy door.

"Go ahead."

"'Gabriel English was the protagonist in a book of stories I wrote entitled *One Last Good Look*. Let me tell you about Gabriel English. He's a writer. He's supposed to be writing a novel. Instead, he writes a collection of daily vignettes over a full calendar year. These small windows onto moments follow the evolving passion and anguish Gabriel feels for Lydia Murphy. The vignettes also document the desperate relationships that blossom and fail around him. Gabriel discusses his friends, confesses his failings, copies overheard drunken conversations, declares his dreams, reports gossip, and charts the ebb and flow of his love affair with the people and geography of Newfoundland – in particular, the port city of St. John's. *This All Happened* is a literary tableau of Newfoundland life, for better or for worse, seen from within.

"'Caveat: This is a work of fiction. Any resemblance to people living or dead is intentional and encouraged. Fictional characters and experience come to life when we compare them with the people and places we know. New experience is always a comparison to the known.'"

"That's it?"

"That's it."

"Shall we head on in?"

"After you."

It was a brisk and sunny afternoon in St. John's, late spring and still a time for heavy coats. I had arranged for a few of Winter's close friends to be inside – the filmmaker Mary Lewis was one, Lisa Moore, the author of *Degrees of Nakedness*, *Open*, and the novel *Alligator*, and Michael Crummey, the author of *Hard Light*, *River Thieves*, and most recently *The Wreckage*, were two  others. A few more members of the Burning Rock, the literary collective that Moore and Winter (though not Crummey) belonged to, were also inside: Mark Ferguson, Larry Mathews, and Claire Wilkshire. The group was founded in 1986 after some of Mathews's creative writing students at Memorial University decided they wished to continue their association.

Moore was waiting at the long table just inside the door. "Coming in?" she asked.

"My pleasure," said Winter.

They're affecting, this bunch from Newfoundland. Moore was a painter who had studied at the Nova Scotia College of Art and Design before she became a writer. She published stories in both *Burning Rock* anthologies, *Extremities* and *Hearts Larry Broke*, and her second collection of stories, *Open*, was nominated for the Giller Prize in 2002. She had been a sensation that first year, flashing across the room at the Four Seasons as if it were a dance floor and doing it again in an emerald green dress when, three years later, she was nominated for the Giller a second time for her first novel, *Alligator*. Winter, sitting at the same table, demonstrated the group's close nature when he cried as the winner was called and Moore had not won. Her novel, like the earlier short stories, was so filled with energy and characters that it was possible to be skeptical about the sheer amount of life the book contained – as if it was not plausible that Newfoundland could be busy and crowded and sophisticated and modern, and not the dour, windswept place of its Age of Mapping. The first time I met Moore, she had taken me out to Cape Spear, Canada's easternmost point, driving badly and talking animatedly all the way. We had grabbed some sandwiches from Auntie Crae's, and whiled away the afternoon sitting on a rock beneath the lighthouse discussing unwritten plays and her impending novel, *Alligator*, not written yet. Perhaps you have the picture in your mind: grey water, crashing waves, green grass blown flat by the wind above a steep fall of rocks. A solitary figure on the cliff and a tilting house or two.

Only that wasn't the Newfoundland we were looking at. A steady stream of visitors on the banks did away with the idea that Newfoundland was far from anywhere. A cellist played at an art exhibition that had been installed by the old Second World War gun placements nearby, and all the while a helicopter was hovering above the blue sea in front of us looking for the body of a teenaged suicide. Someone Moore knew, of course. For an afternoon I had been able to see the world Moore's way, the Newfoundland of her books that was vital, febrile, and close. I found myself wide-eyed, though Moore was not fazed, of course, grilling me intently with all manner of questions, as I came to learn was innately her manner.

"Come on in, old buddy," said Crummey.

"Hi, Mary," said Winter. His companion during the writing of *This All Happened*, Winter had known Mary Lewis for years.

"How are ya?" said Lewis. She smiled. Electrically.

"I'm great," said Winter.

"Hello, Michael," said dour Larry Mathews, a short story writer in his own right, and the creative writing teacher who had seen promise in this lot.

"Good to see you all," said Winter.

"Well, that's a relief," said Claire Wilkshire.

Newfoundlanders can use a few simple words, as Wilkshire did, to bring a fella strutting a little down to earth. The ribbing is part of the island's generations-old tradition of trading teases and verse and anecdote and songs at kitchen parties called at the drop of a hat – more likely, after a pub's last orders. "Do you have a song in you?" asked Winter the first time we met – or was it the second time? Somehow, it was always at a party. One had the right not to be certain.

I was encountering these novelists as their reputations were spreading across Canada and a few were distinguishing themselves, though before the deviating fortunes that come on with the thirties had started to pull them apart. These friends were still dedicated and collegiate. They had embarked on an adventure together with little expectation of the success they had come to know. It was in the nature of their vocation, but also because of the place that culture has in the politics of the island, that they were so routinely and passionately discursive. As much as francophone Quebeckers, Newfoundlanders understand that culture stands at the vanguard of any society's effort to define itself. The belief here is that art is rife with possibility. One of the great entertainments of Winter's *This All Happened* lies in the conversations about form and technique that Gabriel English, the author's alter ego, has with his writing friend Maisie Pye. The avid talks the pair have sound much like those that

Winter and Moore habitually do. It is a relationship, in the novel, that competes in its intensity with the distressed love that Gabriel still harbours for Lydia, an affection that has seen simpler days.

The beauty of Newfoundland is that the job of the writer, singer, playwright, comedian, or painter is just another trade to go along with fishing, mining, or work in the shops. In their social inclusion, and in the boozy and charismatic camaraderie of literary pals who cannot quite believe their good fortune, St. John's is the closest Canada gets to Dublin. But the thing that distinguishes the generation of Newfoundland writers to which Winter, Moore, and Crummey belong is that crucial fact of theirs having been the first to be relatively unencumbered by the politics and lingering controversy of the referendum of 1948. They are a confident lot, able to shop and choose their influences from the island's proud and reasserted history – and also from elsewhere. You get the sense that writing is a real adventure for them, steeped in both revolution *and* tradition. Their being such good friends, as well as their interest in the actual process of writing, is what had prompted me to gather the bunch of them to discuss, most of all, the ethics of fiction. Because when you are such good friends, and where the immediate territory you draw your material from is so small, then it's quite likely that interaction with the ones you love is what will sow the seeds of your stories – if your short story writing or filmmaking pal hasn't used the same exchange already. This, after all, is the way writers work.

In London, working for BBC Radio at the time, the Indo-British novelist Salman Rushdie had contributed an interview to a documentary I was making about the ethical dilemmas a writer often faces. The date was Monday, February 13, 1989, and the conversation that Rushdie had in studio turned out to be the last the author gave about his novel *The Satanic Verses* before a fatwa was declared on him by Iran's Ayatollah Khomeini. Islamic fundamentalists were a mostly undeclared enemy then, and what had preoccupied him during the interview were not any of the offences that the mullahs were in the process of accusing Rushdie of making, but

THIS IS MY COUNTRY, WHAT'S YOURS? | 329

transgressions the author did not realize he had made towards his family. The novel had made him realize that the *family* stories that had contributed to the novel were not exclusively his to tell. What he regretted was that he had upset his family.

The usual disclaimer on a novel's copyright page is a lie – but also not. Fictional characters often do bear more than a passing resemblance to people living or dead, but something magical occurs in the transformation. Just *what* happens in that transformation, and how it comes to pass, is what enticed Michael Winter to throw down the gauntlet. *This All Happened* is, by and large, a young man's book, and a very funny one, but the questions that Winter raises in it are serious. He is asking when it is fair for an author to appropriate experience that belongs to someone else – a close friend, perhaps, a relative, or lover. Fiction owes as much to the real world as it does to the imagination, and he is asking if an only slightly altered record excuses the hurt it can create. These are quandaries all writers face. The disadvantage in Newfoundland, where even a walk to the bar can be a revealing public journey, is that the writer is less able to hide from the people who may have been his sources in the way that novelists in big cities are able to do. Eventually, if you don't take that job in Saskatoon, you'll be found out. You'll run into real-life characters uncomfortably close to the ones that you say you've created.

✧ ✧ ✧

EARLIER IN THE DAY, at the Duke of Devonshire, another of the pubs off Duckworth Street, I met up with a couple of the Burning Rock collective, a pair who attended more as friends than as writers with any real ambitions. The two were waiting on stools, beer in hand. I had been told that Max, one of the characters in Winter's *This All Happened*, had been closely modelled on one of them.

"Which one of you is Max?" I asked.

"I'm Max," said one.

"Oh?" said the other, looking surprised. "I thought you were Jack, but you're Max?"

"Yeah, but you're Max too."

"Yeah," the other said. "We're both Max."

"Max is a *composite*," said the one.

"And not just of us, I think."

"No," said the one. "Max is not just us."

"You were a part of the Burning Rock at one point?" I asked.

"Technically we still are," said the other, "but we're definitely errant at the moment."

"So you must both have a fair understanding of what goes into a writer making things up," I said.

"Sure," said the one. "There were a lot of things in that book that were *verbatim*."

"Yeah," said the other. "They were *absolutely, totally verbatim.* Right out of my mouth."

"And mine."

"Yeah," said the other, taking a swig of his beer.

"Yeah."

"What Michael did brilliantly," the other said, "is that he put so many of the St. John's characters and experiences into the book and yet never has anyone ever felt kind of like – well, *the next time I see him . . .*"

"The next time I see him, what?"

"The next time I see him – *you know*."

"Nobody feels that," said the one.

"I mean, there were lots of lovely moments in that book, especially from gatherings. Some of the things that people said and did in the party scenes were very funny. But I think it's pretty much *universally felt* that nobody feels that," said the other.

"The book was well observed," said the one.

"I wasn't expecting it to be documentary," I said. "But one of the things that strikes me about fiction is that good novels do arrive at a kind of poetic version of the truth."

"Yeah."

"Yeah."

"So they don't have to be *true* –"

"No."

"– to arrive at a picture that is actually quite real."

"There's a great Mike Jones scene –"

"You know him, the actor?"

"Yes."

"I don't remember which character says it in the book –"

"Wilf," said the other.

"– but he says that there's a certain time when you go into the Ship, and the walk from the door to the bar is really difficult to do because –"

"*It's the loneliest walk in the world*," said the other.

"Yeah. That was a Mike Jones line."

"Yeah."

From Michael Winter's *This All Happened*:

Wilf walks into the Ship looking uncomfortable. Then he sees us and relaxes. He is in a suit he wants to wear in Lydia's film. He looks like a Beatle in it. Wilf, at the age of fifty-two, has become a promising actor. That word, promising. Wilf buys a pint and sits with us and sighs with relief. Wilf: When you open up the Ship Inn door all by yourself. Youve walked downtown alone. You dont want to be alone. You feel like a dog and you want a bit of company. Well, you open up that door and you steel yourself. It's got to be all one motion, no hesitation. Open the door and stride in, but a slow stride, maximum exposure. And you make your way to the bar. And all the way there you keep your eyes on the bottles and the mirrors and youre hoping, youre hoping there's someone in there who knows you. You hope you dont make it to the bar before someone waves you over, grasps your arm, says, Hey Wilf, how's it going? Yes, sir, that walk to the bar is the loneliest walk in the world.

At the Ship, I ordered a round for the table and pushed my copy of *This All Happened* over to where Winter was sitting, the gathering a reckoning before his friends – and material.

"Okay," said Winter. "This is the caveat. I'll read it nice and slow."

"Okay," said Moore.

"What does 'caveat' mean again, Michael?" asked Mathews, goading him.

"*Beware.*"

"Well, I knew that."

"All right, then," said Winter, "here we go. 'Any resemblance to people living or dead is intentional and encouraged –'"

"Okay, that there," said Moore.

"Jesus, what's wrong with that?" asked Winter.

"That's *tongue-in-cheek.*"

"Yes," said Winter, "because every book says the opposite, right? It's not a disclaimer. It's more of an *acclaimer.*"

"So, you don't really mean that –"

"– you're going to find these people in the book," said Crummey.

"You're making fun of readers who think the disclaimer in a book is true."

"No, no," said Michael, "I'm making fun of people who think they can *write* a book and then say, 'Oh. But I made it all up.'"

"Really?" said Moore. "What I thought was that you were making fun of people who think that people in a book are *real*. I didn't realize you were making fun of people who think that the people in a book *aren't* real."

"He was making fun of *you*, Lisa," said Mathews.

"So you mean it."

"Yes."

"But you've gone on record and said that your characters weren't real people," said Mark Ferguson. "And then you say that comparisons to the real –"

"*Hang on*," said Winter. "I haven't finished my caveat yet. I say, 'Fictional characters and experiences come to life when we compare them with the people and places we know. New experience is always a comparison to the known.'"

Winter closed the book.

"Well, come on, you've got to give me that."

"I'd say that's true," said Ferguson.

"*New experience?*" said Crummey. "What's that?"

◇ ◇ ◇

THIS ALL HAPPENED started out as a diary that was funded in part by money from the local arts council after Winter argued that a year in the life of the new city would be an excellent way to commemorate the five hundredth anniversary of John Cabot's discovery of Newfoundland.

"I said, 'Look, fellas, John Cabot, when he came across the water –'"

"In 1497, was it?"

"'– he wrote a diary,' and I said, 'Well, here we are five hundred years later, and what I am going to do is I will map the emotional terrain of the province.'"

"So in the beginning," asked Wilkshire, "you were committed to making the journal true, is that right?"

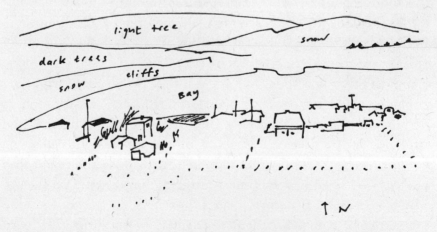

(the illustrator's home)

"Yes, yes – but then I had the three hundred and sixty-five days and I had three hundred characters and nothing happened and it was really, really boring."

Said Moore, "Well, you should have just gone with that!"

✧ ✧ ✧

FROM LISA MOORE'S "Nipple of Paradise":

Already I remember the summer in short-hand, distilled, made up of only a hundred or so specific images intermingled; meals, sex, nights on the fire escape, hours in the office, the birth, the affair. And by next summer I won't even remember it that clearly. But for now it has reached the half-dissolved stage, the separate gestures of the summer exaggerated like the colour in Polaroid photographs.

After I found out that Cy had slept with Marie I sat on the fire escape with my foot on the railing, and a spider crawled over my foot, my toes tensed, each toe stretching away from the others. I could feel the spider make its web, lacing my toes together. It struck me that I had never felt anything so sharply before. That's how a story should work. Like that Chinese ribbon dance. They turn off the lights so you can't see the dancer. All you see are two long fluorescent ribbons, drawing in the dark, like the strokes of that summer.

Knowing too much about writers and their lives, about who they are and who their friends are, can get in the way of a story that is fiction, after all, if only because the events in it have been edited and selectively arranged. Even doing only that takes skill. Do it well enough and fiction can seem like fact again, with the result that readers and friends sometimes confuse characters with people whom they know. Even writers and their families are not immune to making such mistakes themselves, but it was a surprise to learn that this category of error had been made by the luminaries of Burning Rock.

At a Larry Mathews class that I attended at Memorial, Lisa Moore had been the invited guest.

"In my first collection of stories," Moore told the table of graduate students, "there's a story of a woman who is pregnant, and while she's pregnant, her husband has an affair. Michael Winter is a very good friend of mine and because he lived here at that time I would speak to him every day on the telephone. Often we exchanged pages, sent them back and forth – not by email, because he lived just up the street. I would send him four or five pages, and he would send four or five pages down. So we were in very close contact, but somehow Michael hadn't read this one story of mine that won an award. I had moved to Toronto, and Michael had to phone me and tell me that I'd won. Now I don't know why he was the person that was phoning me, but he sounded completely depressed and I thought, 'What's wrong? I won an award. *Come on.*' Finally he said to me in a grave voice, 'Lisa, I'm sorry, I didn't know what had happened. I didn't know that Steve had an affair when you were giving birth' – and I was completely stunned because my husband *hadn't* had an affair – at least not that I know of."

There was a collective groan from the students.

"Many of the images in the story of how the birth happened were true," she said. "Those physical details were so vivid and so dramatic and so fresh that they worked perfectly. But then when I was writing it, I thought that there needed to be more tension there. Something bad had to happen. As a writer, what you need to do is to take characters and put them in moral situations that the reader can sympathize with and understand – and then you have to make the worst possible thing happen. So it wasn't enough that this woman nearly died in childbirth. 'What could be worse?' I asked. '*Could* it be worse?' And yes, I decided it could have been. Her husband could have had an affair – and Michael, who actually writes fiction and who is completely aware of how a writer takes details that are absolutely true and then changes them, believed the story so much that he was hardly able to speak to me about it. My husband was actually the one who answered the phone in

Toronto and he looked baffled and said that Michael had been rude to him and that he hadn't said hello or goodbye or anything. So Steve said to me, 'What's going on?' And then when I told him, Steve said that he would definitely be having an affair if I ever got pregnant again because many people were asking him about it and wanted to know if the story was true."

"And how did you feel about your story after that?" a student had asked.

"I think all the fuss indicated that it was damn successful – for me," said Moore, laughing. "But it wasn't so good for Steve."

✧ ✧ ✧

"I NEVER THOUGHT that for a second," said Winter.

"*Michael!*" said Moore, "what are you saying?"

"No," said Winter. "This was somebody else who said that to you, and you've applied it to me – just like the time when I made you a Bruce Springsteen cassette tape, and there was room to spare, so I put some Otis Redding on the end of it. About five years later I was in the back of your car with you and Steve, and the cassette was playing and at the end of it Otis Redding came on. You turned around and you said, 'Isn't it great?' And I said, 'Yeah, it's good, it's really good,' and you said, 'This is the guy that Springsteen discovered in New Jersey. He had room on the end of his LP, and so he put this unknown guy on the end. Isn't it amazing he did this?' My jaw was dropping! I couldn't believe it! I'd made the cassette for you!"

The bartender looked up as everybody at the table roared – except for Moore, who looked positively demure.

"That's an interesting story, Michael," she said, "but it has nothing to do with what really happ –"

"It just goes to show how you fabricate," said Winter. "How you make interesting stories out of completely bogus details –"

"Or how Michael does," said Moore. "Why believe Michael over me? *Guys?*"

✧ ✧ ✧

From Michael Winter's *This All Happened*:

> In nature you see only half of a thing at a glance. But in writing
> you patch together bits and sides. More than is natural. It's a
> full map of the world, but in two dimensions. A flat map is not
> the globe. Something is lost in seeing it whole. Or too much
> seen gives the wrong impression.

The axiom the best writers go by has always been to write what you
know. It is not so much an instruction to give the thorough details
of a trade – as, say, Herman Melville might – as it is an exhortation
to be emotionally authentic, to be true to the story and the characters that you create and not to compromise. In Lisa Moore's work,
as in Michael Winter's, the authors are writing fiction derived
from their *sense*, as much as the experience, of St. John's – the port
city chronicled not for the first time, but with enough vigour and
enthusiasm that it can feel like the first entry into a room. In *This
All Happened*, Gabriel English chronicles the year by writing a brief
daily entry about the disintegration of his love affair with Lydia
and the slow distancing of himself from Newfoundland and his
coterie of friends. Although Winter takes time out to pay homage
to the topography itself, the foibles of characters much like his
own friends are his preferred subject. Within the novel, described
by its publisher as a "journal-à-clef," the trouble Gabriel gets into
for writing his buddies, and Lydia, so closely is remarked upon.
Winter went so far as to show drafts of his work to his friends, a
habit the USAmerican writer William T. Vollmann shared when he
would write about skinheads, prostitutes, and pimps. Easier to do
among friends, you would think. Winter even showed his developing novel to his partner at the time, the filmmaker Mary Lewis, and
she gave him her imprimatur. But it's odd what the printed word can
do. A book published is an object out in the world. It has its own life,
one that can come right back at you.

"As Michael was writing his book," said Lewis, "he did show me
drafts, and I actually took part in the editing of it, so I knew what

was in the book when it came out. I was well aware of everything that was in it, and the implications of it all."

At Coffee and Company, on Water Street, I had an espresso with Mary Lewis. The barista's face was stretched from cosmetic surgery, her breasts obviously doctored, and the tan curiously out of season. She looked Russian. I wondered how much at home she felt in St. John's. More human flotsam to animate the place.

"In fact, Michael did at some point say to me, 'I'm thinking about having the Lydia character be a filmmaker and an actress, what do you think of that?' And my initial response was, 'I think she should do something else.' So we thought, what could she do? We were thinking a lab technician, or maybe she's a florist, and everything rang so false. So I said, 'Do what you want to do, I don't care. She can be anything you want her to be,' so that's what he ended up having her as, a filmmaker and an actress.

"That was the fatal error, in my mind, and after the book came out, there was a turning point with regards to my relationship to that book. The CBC Radio program *Talking Books* was on, and Michael and I were home for Christmas. We were in my parents' kitchen when we heard, '*This All Happened* by Michael Winter,' so we turned up the radio and all the ruckus in the kitchen came to a halt so that we could listen to the program. The host, Ian Brown, put a question to one of his guests, who had been a professor of mine and also of Michael's at different times, so that we both knew her quite well and were very friendly with her. He asked her to describe the book and how as a woman living in St. John's did she relate to the story. And, of course, the questions the book raised were, 'How do fiction and reality meet?' and 'Where does that blend happen?' It's in the title, *This All Happened*, and the disclaimer that 'Any resemblance to real-life characters is fully intended.' The professor said something like, 'Well, *This All Happened* is a book about a character living in St. John's named Gabriel English. He's a tall, somewhat reclusive, aloof, artistic character who's a writer and who's remarkably like Michael Winter, the writer of this book. And Gabriel English is in love with a woman who is a filmmaker – a beautiful, elusive, yet somewhat annoying woman, who's remarkably like the woman Michael Winter happens to be in love with.'

"Michael and I looked at each other, and we looked at my parents, and the two of us just blushed completely, and Michael kind of caved in the middle of it all, and his face died, and that was the turning point for me. Up until then, I had thought, 'Oh, this is fiction, it's not me – people will understand that.' But at that point I realized that even people whom I count as friends could not help but draw the comparison and see the direct relationship. And so we went on as though nothing had happened, as people can do, until about a week or so later when it all came up in a big, long discussion between us about the whole issue of, well, 'To what degree did you try to make this character read as me? You and I know where the fiction is and where the reality ends, so I don't have any problem with the book because I have the necessary knowledge,' I said, 'but to what degree did you deliberately try to fool all the other readers into believing that all this was actually real? To what degree were you responsible to me as a friend?' And that was a big question that we both discussed passionately, but I don't know that we arrived at any final answer."

$$\diamond \quad \diamond \quad \diamond$$

"You don't believe, then, that language and the writing down of things alters the truth," said Moore.

"Of course it does," said Winter. "In the attempt to write something down, you're saying to yourself, 'I wish to portray this person or moment accurately,' but you know that that's a lie. If you draw a portrait of a person's face, you don't get the jawline correct but it's similar."

"But do you really say to yourself, 'I wish to portray that person accurately' or do you think, 'I want a beautiful character, an interesting character, an enigmatic character,' and then you see someone in a bar turn around in a way that strikes you as interesting and then you write that down?"

"No, this is what happens – and you do this, Lisa, a lot of us keep diaries. That person turns around in the bar, and you write that down as accurately as you can in your diary, and then later when you're writing a story, you say, 'Oh, yes, there was that face in the bar. I'll use that here.'"

"I'm often wary of you pulling out your pad and scribbling down notes," I said.

"I'm honoured when he pulls out his book," said Crummey. "I think maybe I've said something interesting."

There was a general round of chuckles.

"Now, I'm not supposing for a moment that you're related in any way to Maisie Pye," I said, "but I wonder, Lisa, if you'd be so kind as to just read this little paragraph from page twenty-nine of Michael Winter's wonderful novel."

"Sure," said Moore, taking the book. "Michael writes, 'I meet Maisie Pye to discuss our novels. She's making a novel about what's happening now. It's a thinly veiled autobiography, except she's pushing it. The Oliver character has an affair, and her friends, when they read it, think Oliver's cheating on her. 'He's not,' she says. 'People believe if you write from a tone of honesty, conviction, and sincerity. If you capture that correctly, then readers will be convinced it all happened that way.'"

Moore stopped reading. Looked up.

"Keep going," I said.

"Gabriel says, 'I'm having great fun with my characters because it's all set in the past. I described Josh and Toby and Heart's Desire, the research I've done on the American painter and Bob Bartlett's trips to the North Pole. I'm using Max and Lydia and others as these historical characters. Max is going to be my Rockwell Kent. My father might be Bob Bartlett. That way, I can be present in the past.' Maisie said, 'So, who am I?' 'I haven't used you – *yet*.' And she's disappointed."

The table erupted into laughter.

"I'm sorry to expose you like this, Mike," Moore said.

"I can't believe that's in the book," said Winter. "I wrote that in 1997. I didn't realize I had any idea about *The Big Why* so far back."

✧ ✧ ✧

THE CAR WAS borrowed from Stan Dragland, and Crummey and Winter, the two Michaels, were in the front seats as we drove to a small summer literary festival in Salvage. At Whitbourne Junction, the parking lot at the Esso station was almost full. We sat at a table in Monty's Place, the restaurant behind the gas bar, and ordered some lunch. Toutons and molasses for Crummey, a Sharonburger for Winter and me. Back home, I'd seen Winter sing songs on the guitar at a Toronto novelist's party, but the awkward Ontario sing-along had made Winter and his chorus of Newfoundland chums seem like a couple of Tomson Highway's beavers on Yonge Street. Winter had left Newfoundland, but it was clear that he was perennially restless for it. The way he jumped from story to story about the caribou hunting he did in Newfoundland each September, the way he smiled and kept his mouth shut as others talked about experiences that were obviously dear to him, the way he would point to the icebergs in the water or a car parked perpendicular to the highway with jars of bakeapple jam on its hood, or the way he laughed as he told the punchline of an anecdote, cried out that this place was still most like home for him. Such affection there was.

"He's a sweet fella," I'd once said of Winter to a mutual writing pal.

"Not at all."

"He has the sliver of ice."

"Absolutely."

"But he loves his *characters*."

"Sure."

Considering this love of his, it occurred to me what a useless emotion moral indignation is to the novelist. The journalist relies on it for pronouncements on the way the world has gone wrong. But for the novelist, all indignation does is get in the way of that imaginative leap that needs to be made.

The endearing way Winter looked at Crummey, or merely the road, radiated the pleasure he was taking in the world that surrounded him, as he was doing with the tale of Brigus and Bob Bartlett, a story that had been much on his mind. He recounted another, of Dorothy Wyatt, once mayor of St. John's, and then a candidate for city council, who was so popular with the electorate that after she died during the 2001 campaign, her constituents voted her in anyway.

Winter asked Crummey if he had ever met John Baird, a descendant of the bullying settler John Peyton Sr., whose violent antics and unsavoury character were at the heart of Crummey's novel of Newfoundland in the last days of the Beothuk, *River Thieves*.

"No," Crummey said.

Winter nodded to himself, something on his mind, then raised that finger again. "The funny thing is that I wrote a lot about my brother Paul," he said. "The character of Junior, in my stories and in *This All Happened*, is often based on him, but not always. Paul hadn't really looked at any of my work until a friend of his said, 'You should read Michael's stories 'cause they're all about you.' And so Paul read them, and he said to me that he was hurt. And I said, 'Well, I'm sorry, but I feel like the character is always portrayed with love and affection. Even though you're a bit wild, you're interesting, and the people that read these stories will be curious about the character that I draw from.' And Paul said, 'Look, if you write about me again, I will deliver a punch to your head from which you will never recover.' So I've since agreed to that, and I won't write about him any more, but I did say, 'What is it, exactly, that you're upset by?' And he said, 'Well, when you say that my dog was in the cab of my truck and that he would press his snout against the windshield and leave snout marks on the glass, I'm not happy with that. I feel like you've exposed me and my dog there, and I don't like that you've written about that.'"

Winter laughed. "Now, I've written a thousand things about my brother that are much more insensitive than that, and it just goes to show how you can never know what you'll write that somebody might take offence to."

I said, "But what if someone approached you in the Ship Inn and said, 'That's outrageous!' and – let's assume this person thought he was Max – tells you, 'I'm a far better canoeist than you intone in that shitty novel. I would never have taken my canoe over the rapids, and I would certainly not do so with my wife, whom you call "Daphne," if she was *pregnant*. What kind of idiot do you think I am?' How would you respond to that?"

"I'd buy them a drink, for one thing, and then I'd sit them down and say, 'You're right. You're absolutely right. What was I thinking? I must have been temporarily insane. Can you ever forgive me? Here, have another drink.'"

"When I first started writing," said Crummey, "I really struggled with the very emotional questions of 'Who owns stories? Who owns a person's life experience?' How much right does a writer have to take these things and set them down in a way that can be, or at least can feel, disrespectful to the origins?' I realized that everybody's experience of a particular event is slightly different, so one person setting it down on paper and saying, 'This is the way it happened,' is almost necessarily going to be a denial of some part of other people's experience of the same event. That can feel like some kind of violation, I think."

"But I'll tell you," said Winter. "I've had people come up to me and believe that certain lines belong to them, and I've kept a master copy of every line that's in that book and who said what in real life so that I know, for instance, if this guy Mike, let's say, *didn't* say a line but is embracing it. He knows for sure that he said it, and he's telling everybody, 'That was my line and Michael Winter wrote it down.' I'll just let him go on and believe it because there's no point in arguing with that. But if somebody feels like I've written about them in a disparaging way, and I know it's not them, then I'll try to explain that and who I lifted the line from."

✧　✧　✧

WHAT SERVES THE writer best is a climate of purpose, and Newfoundland had it in the 1970s cultural renaissance, during which artists and musicians and actors used Antonine Maillet's comic medicine to transform themselves from derided and demoralized Newfoundlanders into "living human beings and not just survivors." The remarkable thing was that the impression of Newfoundland as Confederation's new but impoverished partner, as an endless recipient of handouts with nothing to contribute but a dwindling cod harvest and its young "going down the road" to look for work, was altered by its *artists*, not its politicians, into the realization of something fresh. Now Newfoundland is understood to be a society with a rich and singular heritage that is utterly its own – "a distinct society." The theatre that was founded in the building that had previously been St. John's hall of the Longshoremen's Protective Union, and studios such as those at 77 Bond Street, also in St. John's, were kettles of impassioned artistic activity. Art was being used to make highly charged political points that would, in turn, allow a younger generation of artists and writers to be assertive and confident as a matter of course. For Winter, Crummey, and Moore's generation, confidence was not the objective, but a point of beginning. Moore walked me over to 77 Bond Street to acknowledge the debt she and her peers owed their predecessors.

"There was a photographer's dark room, a pottery studio, and all kinds of painting going on," Moore said. "There were life-drawing classes and big dusty windows that let the light in dramatically and all these old easels set up. The floors were spattered with paint, and all those smells that are art smells, like turpentine and oil and developing chemicals from the photography studio. And all over the walls there were nude paintings from the adult drawing classes that took place in the evening."

"And you attended classes here?" I asked.

"I did. I came here as a child. We would drive in from Hogan's Pond, and my father would drop me off. It was during the 1970s when the cultural renaissance was going on in Newfoundland. For the first time, artists were going back to the outports and gathering songs and fairy stories and folk tales that were sometimes as many as four hundred years old. The band Figgy Duff was making music with those stories and preserving the complex melodies that those songs were about and giving them new life as rock music. Pamela Morgan, who was the lead singer, told me once that she felt the band was born as a response to the sort of cultural inferiority complex that might have existed in Newfoundland in the 1950s and 1960s, when Newfoundlanders felt a sort of shame about the way they dressed or the way they spoke or the way they fished. It was at this point in the 1970s that people were recognizing that ours was a really unique and interesting culture, and there was an authenticity and a desire to celebrate it for the first time. It was a really exciting place to be."

Lisa Moore was a true stylist. Her stories brimmed with all sorts of barely contained energy – the sexuality of the pregnant, was how I had come to think of their atmosphere. Some of these stories approached the claustrophobic – although there was certainly no sense, in her fiction, of wanting or having to be anywhere else. Even in stories that peregrinated to St. Pierre and Miquelon, or to Toronto – where, in a moving scene in the story "If You're There," she watches Jeremy, a man very much like Gabriel English, who has left Newfoundland two years previously, walk off never to be seen again – there is no sense of needing to be anywhere else. The island is everything. It is complete.

"I can remember the first time I saw my own experience reflected in literature," said Moore. "I think it was with Wayne Johnston's *The Story of Bobby O'Malley*. There's a high school in it that I recognized as a high school I had been in, and that was a very powerful experience. Up until that time, I had read about Trafalgar Square in Virginia Woolf, and I knew all these different cities and places by reading about them first. They were mediated through the literature that I had read. Of course, there was other writing, like Percy James's, but it was set slightly further in the past. I hadn't seen my contemporary experience written down. And when it is, it makes the ground more solid underfoot. It validates existence. It also provides permission to write about your own experience."

I asked Moore, as well, if the 1948 referendum was no longer the first and foremost political event and principle around which her generation was writing.

"I see myself as a Canadian as well as a Newfoundlander, although it's true that the question of Newfoundland independence is certainly still in people's minds in some strange way."

"But isn't it possible that you grew up in an atmosphere in which the political destiny of Newfoundland was settled, so that it was fair to think of Newfoundland as a distinct society – the integrity of which you are no longer having to question?"

"But I also think that Newfoundland identity is a changing thing," said Moore. "It's something that is always in flux, as all identities are. Though what I would certainly add is that I don't feel any anxiety about an *archival* process in writing fiction, or the need to capture the past in order to provoke nationalism or to validate our existence here. What I'm interested in is capturing the changing moment. I'm interested in what's happening *now*."

"If you read Don DeLillo or Richard Ford or Raymond Carver," Michael Winter had said to me, "then you think, well, to write a world-class story, you have to write with a kind of modern language, so you sabotage or kibosh the whole fishing culture that might be yours because you realize, oh, that's *old*, that's the Old World, and the modern world is avocadoes from Chile and flights to Cuba and that international scene, and that's where my story is. But the thing is to achieve a balance and say, 'The new Newfoundland includes *all* of this, and we must reflect this external situation as artists.' But the writer must also ask, What is it about how we talk to each other, about how we live, and love, that is uniquely Newfoundland?"

✧   ✧   ✧

FICTION, THE ART of making things up, is far more than the pasting together of real-life incidents. Writers depend on what they see and hear, and the pinching of material is restricted not just to friends but done at the family table. Borrowing stories and their rhythms is the way the whole culture has been passed on in Newfoundland for generations, although the legacy is more likely to be communicated on the page now than in impromptu recitations usurped on the Rock, as in Igloolik of Inuvik, by television and the Internet. At dinner one evening, with family and friends of Michael Winter's in St. John's, the television was not on. The entertainment was a recitation by Leah Lewis, Mary's sister, of "Jigg's Dinner," one of the thirty-two "little stories" from Crummey's volume *Hard Light*. Ostensibly the poem conveys instructions for the traditional Sunday meal, and how to prepare it and also attend Mass, but what it really honours in its few lines is a whole bygone world of Newfoundland living. The tone of the evening had been set, and the master of the house, Dr. Lewis, who travelled not only to Newfoundland's outports to take up "locums" – temporary medical posts subbing for doctors on leave or otherwise absent – but to Africa (he was off to Arusha, Tanzania, the following week), followed his daughter's spontaneous recital with a bellowing celebration of the last whale from the final verses of E.J. Pratt's "The Cachalot."

> . . . Then, like a royal retinue,
> The slow processional of crew,
> Of inundated hull, of mast,
> Halliard and shroud and trestle-cheek,
> Of yard and topsail to the last
> Dank flutter of the ensign as a wave
> Closed in upon the skysail peak,
> Followed the Monarch to his grave.

"It was just the way people entertained themselves," said Crummey. "That was how information got passed on. That was how people entertained one another when they were sitting around having a drink.

"When I was away at university, I had a real sense – but it was a false sense – of Newfoundland culture being something that existed in the past, and of whatever Newfoundland was now as being something lesser. But since I've moved home, I've had to change that view quite a bit. There's certainly no question that there have been huge changes, and that as a result of those, some things that were once part of just about every Newfoundland community have been lost, but I myself am constantly surprised at how much of the old world has carried forward."

"Is it fair to say that you are part of a generation of writers for whom the referendum of 1948 is no longer the most overarching issue?"

"I think so," said Crummey. "As far as I knew growing up, Newfoundland was a part of Canada and therefore I was Canadian. I never questioned it. It was not something that felt like a grievance or like something that needed to be redressed. I know it's still a hot topic, but for most people of my age, it's almost a non-issue."

"But as with so many communities in Canada," I said, "the idea of secession can still be brandished as a threat."

"Sure," said Crummey. "I had a conversation with Joel Hynes, a Newfoundland writer who is younger than me, and he said that he would actually like to see the province separate. He said that he had a three-year-old son, and he would love the boy to grow up a Newfoundlander. And I said to him, 'You were born in Newfoundland when it was part of Canada,' and he said, 'Yes.' And I said, 'Did that make you feel like any less of a Newfoundlander?' I wasn't trying to be facetious, and he thought about it and then he said no, it didn't. Certainly I do not feel like less of a Newfoundlander because of the fact that I have some connection to Canada as well. There are all kinds of problems in the relationship, and many things that could be changed for the better, but I don't have the sense that Newfoundland is less of a nation because it has become a part of this larger confederacy."

"What about the phenomenon of people leaving? Is the idea of exit as critical an issue for your generation?"

"Yes, that is still a huge thing. When you leave for work, you're usually not flying back the next day, and the communities people are leaving are usually small so that the impact is huge – particularly places like the Northern Peninsula, which have been hit hard by the cod moratorium. You have communities now where everybody is fifty or older because the young people have all gone. They may come back for summer holidays, but that's not the same as living here. The rural part of Newfoundland and the urban part of the province – as in St. John's – are two different worlds right now, and the situation in the rural areas is approaching crisis. I don't know if there's a solution on the horizon."

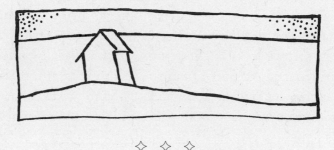

✧ ✧ ✧

FROM MICHAEL CRUMMEY'S *River Thieves*:

John Senior set the bag on the ground between his feet. There was an amused look of surprise on his face. He reached a huge gnarled hand and closed it around the skull of the Indian man. He lifted it clear of the frame and then gathered up the jawbone as well, holding the two together at the joint. All the teeth but one were still in place. He flapped them back and forth and spoke under this mime in a low-pitched voice. "Just a dead Indian," the skull said. "Nothing to bother your head about."

Peyton stared. He could feel the violation in the act, putting words so carelessly and callously in the mouth of the dead.

To be writing in the moment does not preclude novelists setting their work in the past, just as setting a novel in historical times doesn't exempt writers from present issues (otherwise most novelists just wouldn't bother), nor from the ethical issues the Ship Inn writers had been discussing. Michael Winter's novel *The Big Why* used the time the American painter Rockwell Kent spent in Newfoundland during 1914–15 and integrated it with the author's own experiences to comment on the present day and, implicitly, the sometimes constricting, sometimes deceptive habits of historical fiction itself. Michael Crummey's *River Thieves* is a beautiful story more conventionally told, an evocation of the period of the disappearance of the Beothuk and the role that the Peyton family might have played in their extinction. In the novel, Peyton Sr. is not an altogether savoury sort. He is implicated in the death of the husband of Demasduit, otherwise known as Mary March, and one of the last of the Beothuk. The Peyton family's descendants still live in Traytown, a place they are most definitely "from." En route to Salvage the two Michaels and I had visited them. In the close confines of Newfoundland, blood runs thick and the memory of centuries is somehow recent, so that even history offers little sanctuary to the writer grappling with the tenterhooks of making things up. Inevitably there was going to be a moment when, as had happened to Winter with the people who inspired the characters of *This All Happened*, Michael Crummey would come face-to-face with real-life folk who could claim blood ties to characters the author would prefer to think that he had imagined without offence.

"People are going to read into the writing anyway," said Crummey to Winter and his pals at the Ship. "My favourite story about that collision of fact and fiction has to do with Wayne Johnston and his novel *The Colony of Unrequited Dreams*. Claire Fielding, who's Joey Smallwood's fictional alter ego, sort of –"

"Shelagh *Fielding*, you mean."

"Yes, sorry. Shelagh Fielding."

"Who's Claire Fielding?" asked Moore.

"The writer."

"Claire *Wilkshire*, I believe," said Mathews.

"Okay, okay. *Shelagh* Fielding."

"But Claire's one of the major inspirations for the character of Shelagh, you realize," said Moore, enjoying a laugh at Crummey's expense.

"Along with several other women in St. John's," joked Winter.

"At this *table*," said Moore.

"How about we hear Michael tell the story?" said Wilkshire.

"So Wayne said that Shelagh was a completely fictional character – that there was no Fielding in Smallwood's life. But since his book came out, there have been at least three women who have come up claiming that there was a Fielding character – and they were it."

"And they walked up to him with a cane and a silver flask –"

"And a wink."

The friends at the table laughed – mirth, at the Ship, in abundant supply. "The odd thing," I said, "is that even writing in history is no defence from this. You had an amusing encounter after *River Thieves* that I was witness to. Michael Winter set you up, I think."

"I was set up, yeah."

"But what do you think, boy?" said Moore. "That you're going to write about the Peytons and *not* have to meet any of them ever in your life?"

"And not have a gun levelled at your head?" said Winter.

"No," said Crummey with a grin. "I fully expected to meet them. But I didn't think that my friends would drag me into the lion's den and –"

"You didn't know where you were going?" asked Moore disbelievingly.

"He had no idea!" said Winter.

"– and say, 'This is the guy who wrote the book?'"

"Winter didn't tell you where you were going?" asked Wilkshire, loving the ruckus.

"No, he didn't," said Crummey. "We were out in Salvage, doing the Winterset Literary Festival, and Michael had been dealing with John Baird, who is the great-great-great-grandson of John Peyton Jr., who figures in the novel. Michael introduced me to John, and John said, 'You might be interested to know, I'm Peyton Jr.'s great-great-great-grandson. I haven't read your book, but I gave it to my father, and he's read it.' His father was ninety-two. Baird said, 'He inhaled the book. He read it in two days.' And I said, 'Oh, what did he think of it?' Then I stopped right there, because actually I didn't want to know. 'I don't know what he thought of it,' John Baird said and then asked, 'Would you like to meet him?' And I said, 'I don't want to insult you or anything, but if it's all the same to you . . .' and he said, 'Oh, all right,' except that he and Michael had a little conversation and decided that –"

"We'd been talking for two days about how to get you down to meet him," said Winter.

"And I remember that we scrambled down the hill from John Baird's house to the one below," I added, "and there was Mr. Baird Sr., out on a patio in view of the water. It was a sunny day, and he was discussing 'Joey' as we came in. A serious fellow."

"A whole bunch of people were sitting out on the patio," said Crummey, "and introductions were made. I didn't know how good his hearing was, or that he was sure who everybody was, so John had to reintroduce me, and then I could see the look of recognition in his face. He said, 'Oh. You. You sit here next to me.' And before we'd gone down the hill, John had shown the lot of us a couple of artifacts from John Peyton's day, including a huge copper pot that had been taken out on the expedition to bring Mary Shawnadithit's body back down the river, and that they had dumped to get rid of some weight. Thomas Peyton, John Peyton Jr.'s son, had recovered it later, and there it was in the house and being used as a flowerpot. Then John brought out a musket that the family believed had belonged to John Peyton Sr., and for whatever reason, when we went over the hill to see Mr. Baird, John brought the gun with him. He brought the gun down the hill, and finally Mr. Baird noticed that his son was carrying this musket around on the patio, and he said, 'John, what did you bring that gun down here for?' And then he said, 'If you want to shoot someone,' he said, *'shoot this fellow here'* – and he was pointing at me! Now I wasn't going to have a drink, because we were driving back to St. John's that afternoon, but I quickly asked for one."

Good writing depends on degrees of ruthlessness, and if you're going to write, then you're going to have to get used to that notion.

If you're worried about being *nice*, and if you put that quality in front of the art that you're making, then you'll need to face the likelihood of some kind of compromise. That "sliver of ice in the heart" must exist alongside the warmest love an author keeps for his characters and friends. Otherwise, the writer condemns the writing to being second-rate.

"There's a useful debate to be had about limits there," said Crummey, "which is why I put the scene in *River Thieves* about Peyton Sr. holding the Indian skull, which I don't think I would have been comfortable publishing the book without. John Peyton Jr. recalls the moment when he was a boy and he and his father came upon a Beothuk grave, and his father, in a jokey way, picks up the skull and uses it as a puppet. He speaks through the skull of this dead Beothuk, and the son realizes that the same thing can and probably will happen to him in the future – that someone a couple of hundred years from his own lifetime will raise his bones up from the grave and put words in his mouth. And I know that what I was doing in that scene was letting the real John Peyton Jr. step out of the book and point at *me*, because *I* was the stranger two hundred years later putting whatever words I liked into his mouth. There was always going to be a certain amount of violation in that act, and as a writer I wanted to acknowledge that."

"I think if you want to have friends," said Winter, "there's a code. I remember, very early on, showing my first book of stories to Jane Urquhart and she said, 'Michael, I can't write about the things that you're writing about until all of my family is dead, but you don't seem to have the same compunction.' She wasn't judging it. She was, I think, amazed that I would choose to write as I was doing. But the older I've become, the more I've come to realize that there's an awful lot that can be hidden, so that you don't actually have to betray whomever it is you're writing about."

"One of the things that I really enjoy about your writing is that you seem to write out of love," I said. "Love for your characters and whoever, I suppose, might have inspired them. What do you do with those that you don't?"

"That's interesting because in the more recent book, *The Big Why*, what I liked about the character Rockwell Kent was that he seemed to be quite different from Gabriel English. He appeared, to me, to be much more outraged and angry about people and institutions, and he could never fit in. He was always pissing people off, and I thought, 'Well, I want to write about an asshole. I want to make an asshole interesting because I've done the Gabriel English thing. Now I want to try to do the opposite.' So, as the author, every time I was imagining something that Rockwell Kent would do in Newfoundland, I would think to myself, 'Okay, so what would I do?' and then I'd think of Kent doing the exact opposite. I made a complete alter ego to Gabriel English in the new book."

"But even the way you explain it shows that you can't get around your essentially lovable character. You said, 'I want to make the asshole interesting.' Does that excuse 'making things up'?"

"Writers like Philip Roth write about interesting assholes, these antagonistic protagonists who are lovable in the end – well, perhaps not *lovable* but attractive. But you see, the thing is, when you're writing, you're devoting a large amount of your energy to making the actual sentence interesting to read. You run the risk of becoming complacent and thinking, 'Oh, but maybe that sentence will hurt so-and-so, and people will see that it's them,' but you're so tired from actually making the sentence live that you forget the other responsibilities."

"The question of ethics," said Moore, "is something that writers learn to be more conscious of as they mature and as they get a firmer grip on their skills. The difficulty is that sometimes the emotional truths are in the texture of a moment, and if you try to write it some other way, then those emotional truths are not there."

"So that occasionally you need to portray the real, even at the cost of crossing those boundaries and offending people you know."

"No," said Moore emphatically. "Because for me, the people in my book are never real people. Though I do believe that the *places* are probably real."

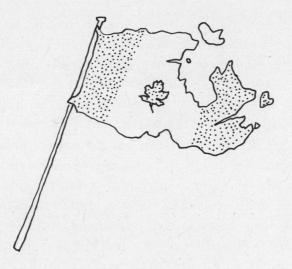

IO

Je me souviens – de quoi?

Trois-Pistoles, Quebec. June 2004. Beyond the chest-high garden fence a bearded man appeared, pushing a wheel-barrow full of compost. He was naked but for a floppy sun hat, gumboots, and minuscule tight black underwear, the stomach of a man in his early sixties generously protruding. It was possible that the man had been drinking – and why not? The rural afternoon was not just sunny, but downright gorgeous. The man's garden was high and in flower. Beyond it, the St. Lawrence, flanked by fields tilled since seigneurial times, was broad and placid and blue. It reminded one of just how *big* everything on this continent is. The man seemed a little surprised, though he had been expecting me. I explained who I was, and that I had a court date in the area (true) and that I had not meant to intrude (not true).

"Pour un meurtre?"

No, I said, sorry to disappoint.

Facing me was Victor-Lévy Beaulieu, the staunch separatist. A prolific author known in Quebec writing circles simply as "VLB," he has written voluminous essays on Melville, Tolstoy, and – his contemplation something of a Québécois rite of passage – Jack Kerouac. He was the founder of Éditions VLB, the publisher of the *Dictionnaire de la langue Québécoise*, as well as some forty-odd books of fiction, poetry, and memoir.

Of the village of Trois-Pistoles, VLB has written that it is where "my grandfathers were blacksmiths, and my father a butter and cheese maker. It is where I lived out the days of my childhood, running over the Fatima in high summer, swimming in the river in view of the Islets d'Amour, and gathering clams in front of the Île-aux-Basques, running along the railway tracks to find the lumps of coal that we needed once in a while at home, all the while avoiding Little Canada because, it was said, bad Maliseet spirits still lived there. I have never been able to tidily file away the memories of these past times, because this is how the culture of a people is carried – in your beginnings. They live in you, pursue you, and oblige you to remember them unceasingly because, in your very core, what they speak of is your destiny."

In Quebec's healthily European tradition, culture is the continuation of politics by other means. Hence, in the spring of 2006, the vitriol that VLB and others of Quebec's separatist old guard heaped on the iconic playwright Michel Tremblay when he dared to suggest that he "did not believe in sovereignty anymore." The movement, in Tremblay's view, had become beholden to "money, money at all cost." "It was a beautiful dream," he said, "and one must respect such dreams, but it will never be more than a dream if we keep looking at it in economic terms." A masterful playwright capable of being tremendously funny and heartbreaking in turn, Tremblay had been a Québécois cultural hero for his explicit depictions of the Boulevard Saint-Laurent's working nightlife, and for mounting *joual* upon the stage, most memorably in *Les Belles-sœurs*. He was the author, in 1989, of *Making Room* (its other title, *The Heart Laid Bare*), a prescient novel of a male homosexual couple in the controversial and then unusual position of raising a child. André Pratte, the editorials director of *La Presse*, and Robert Lepage, the brilliant theatrical director and filmmaker, had also expressed, if not doubts about separatism, a willingness to debate the merits of federalism again – as Francis Chalifour, the prize-winning young adult author had also chosen to do. Lepage, with little inhibition, declared that he "felt Canadian" when he travelled. He was thinking of buying a condo in Vancouver someday.

So the beleaguered VLB was livid, abandoned on the battlefield. While Bernard Landry, the former PQ premier, was declaring that he would no longer attend Tremblay's plays, VLB accused the playwright of premature senility. "Go back to Florida," said VLB. "Eat shit. You're an asshole." Calumny that led Marc Cassivi, a columnist for *La Presse*, to remark that, "These days, it would seem more of a taboo for an artist to come out as a federalist than as a homosexual. The fact that Michel Tremblay is gay hasn't been an issue for thirty years. But the moment he renounces his faith in sovereignty, there are those who bellow for his excommunication. Being a federalist, in cultural circles, is something to be borne in silence, an ignominious vice."

Tremblay, VLB announced, had changed his mind for "insignificant reasons." A messianic ideologue, VLB might well have pronounced of these renegade Québécois artists, "Forgive them, they know not what they do." It was easy to understand why Michel Basilières, a Quebec author of mixed linguistic parentage, left the province for Toronto and wrote *Black Bird*, his mordant Gothic comedy of Catholic Montreal and the 1976 Parti Québécois victory, out of town. There was no freedom to be satirical there, he told me.

The existential ease of younger writers is more than irritating, it is terrifying to some of Quebec's literary old guard. In any society, urban centres are cauldrons of debate, and the variety of opinion that had been gathering in French-Canadian ones had for some time been seen by VLB as undermining sovereigntist ends. Cities are by nature cosmopolitan and inherently less interested in erecting borders, Montreal in particular. Home to former PQ premier Jacques Parizeau's "ethnics and those with money" – and to anglophones of course – the most alluring city in the province was never going to be a bastion of *indépendantiste* support. Anticipating the betrayal of the cause, VLB left Montreal, the fount of so much of the new Quebec literature years ago, and returned to the rural part of *la belle province* that he claims to have been his family's seat for four hundred years. The Trois-Pistoles home that Beaulieu lives in is typical of the area, with a gabled roof and a covered veranda that spans the old wooden farmhouse's front. It sits just outside the village, north of Rivière-du-Loup and south of Métis, on the main road that runs along the south shore of the St. Lawrence River towards the Gaspé. The views are stirring here. Evening sets the sky ablaze, the valley a dramatic canvas of reds and blacks. Gazing over the St. Lawrence towards the North Shore and the Saguenay, the revelation of this river having been the first great avenue into this part of the continent is humbling. Basque fishermen set up camps here in the Strait of Belle Isle and along the northern St. Lawrence in the early sixteenth century, and would have encountered First Nations with little inkling of the change that was headed their way. (The joke in anglophone Montreal high schools was that the name Quebec came from standing on the shore and yelling at the first French ships, *"Go back! Go back!"*) Samuel de Champlain sailed down the St. Lawrence in 1608 and negotiated with the Algonquin and the Huron, founded the city of Quebec, and eventually small *habitations* and seigneurial strips replaced the Indian camps and lined the river's banks. The road along the shore, below and out of view of today's Highway 20, is named the Rue des Pilotes after the river guides who still board freighters and occasional passenger ships wanting to avoid shallow waters and the outcrops of weathered rock that are a distinctive feature of this, the Kamouraska region. In Quebec, and in the Acadian-drained valleys of Nova Scotia, is where you feel Canada's old soul.

✧ ✧ ✧

FROM TORONTO, I had tried to arrange a meeting with VLB. Finding him was never going to be easy, as English Canada was simply not on his radar. The sometimes cantankerous, strangely charismatic author had been congenial over the telephone but, as the date of our rendezvous and the necessity of confirming it approached, he stopped returning calls or replying to emails. A few days before I was due to leave for the province, a message arrived saying that he was sorry to have been out of touch, but his cat had broken the answering machine and he had not received my voicemails. Apologies, our date was no longer convenient. But I had bought my ticket and rented my car, and my suspicion was that no matter what the date had been, this cancellation would have been forthcoming. So I did not acknowledge his message and travelled anyway. In Trois-Pistoles, without an address, I asked around for VLB with no success and subsequently found myself sitting in a quiet restaurant across from the cathedral, flipping the pages of the telephone book until I found a number that matched his. I drove out of town and turned into the driveway, where a vintage 1960s American convertible was parked. The voyageur's new canoe. I walked up the wooden steps and rang the bell, but there was no answer. Around the side, a young man was sitting on the steps of the neighbouring house, observing me.

"Je cherche Victor-Lévy Beaulieu," I said. "Il habite içi?"

He nodded. It was the set of *Deliverance*, the Québécois remake.

"Vous savez où je pourrais lui trouver?"

"Là," he said, gesturing towards the back gate.

Which is when the man in the black briefs appeared. VLB and I had already sparred at a literary festival in Montreal, cordially enough, and my calculation had been that VLB would have noted the effort I had made and would be gracious enough not to turn me away at his door. This proved correct, and we arranged to meet the following morning. The next day VLB received me, sober and dressed, letting me into the house by the side door where several yapping dogs but also a goat and a small sheep had the run of the kitchen. His house was as handsome inside as out, its walls of panelled wood dark with age. The kitchen window looked out over the vegetable garden and the St. Lawrence. VLB returned to his seat at a long antique table at which a dozen people might have eaten comfortably. Before him was the twelve-hundred-page manuscript of his yet-to-be-published book on James Joyce, its pages written in longhand and single-spaced. The sheep bleated and, leaving a trail of droppings, nudged my arm as a dog would do. VLB explained that the animal's mother had not been feeding and so he had been giving it milk.

The previous afternoon, I had visited the magnificent Jardins de Métis, a villa and gardens established by George Stephen and his niece Elsie Reford on a splendid property in the Gaspé. Stephen had been the president of the Bank of Montreal from 1876 to 1881 and then a railway baron who made his fortune with the fledgling CPR and enjoyed a regent's lavish lifestyle. He built a railway line from Montreal to Métis-sur-Mer, a popular spot for country residences at the time, so that he could make the journey to the massive fishing lodge that he built there effortlessly. There were salmon runs nearby, and the small promontory on which the lodge was built benefited from its own gentle microclimate, and Elsie Reford imported shrubs and rhododendrons and then the blue poppies for which the gardens are now famous. The lodge, constructed at about the same time that VLB's house was built, offered up a contrast that could not have been more symptomatic of the now-mythologized ways in which the French Canadians regarded themselves as workers of the land and English-speaking settlers as its natural overseers. Here, within a few kilometres, were the palatial summer homes of the English, but also a sheep and a goat sharing the hearth of this modern-day French-Canadian *habitant*. There was, *chez* VLB, the sense that all details were opportunities for political statements. Even his letting the outside animals in was one more way of making the point about tribal belonging. To an extent I agreed with him. After the Parti Québécois victory of 1976, most of the comfortable Anglo-Saxon progeny of Lord Mount Stephen and his lot fled Westmount and the province for Toronto and the security of their bank accounts more quickly than Lebanese do failing African states. See the profound difference in the loyalties to place that land-holding and liquid capital foster. VLB seizing upon his roots here had been the reason why the onus was on me to go find him in Trois-Pistoles. VLB was staking a claim to the *patrie* of Quebec in a way that he'd publicly alleged younger writers of the province were not.

VLB lit his pipe and we started. I asked him about the importance of place in his work and immediately he referred to one of his late compatriots, the novelist Jacques Ferron. The author of *Tales from the Uncertain Country* and other well-regarded, if eclectic, fictions, Ferron was a doctor who had been a Jesuit, a communist, and, during the October Crisis of 1970, a negotiator between the FLQ and the federal government. He was also, in 1968, the founder of the Rhinoceros Party, a satirical political invention that promised, among other things, to pave Manitoba and create the world's largest parking lot; repeal the law of gravity; and move the Rocky Mountains one metre west as a make-work project.

"Jacques Ferron," said VLB, "addressed the question of place with a phrase that I believe to be quite fantastic. He said, 'When I write, I draw the geography of my country.' What he meant by that was that if you wish to portray this landscape, then you're going to need to know it first – and knowing the geography of your country is not merely a question of knowing the *history* of a place, but of living it through the experiences of people who know it already."

At first, VLB spoke with the sort of quiet, slightly menacing severity that one might have encountered in a father who, having repeated himself too often, is one admonition away from administering a beating. Yet I had made a point of speaking to him in French, and after a while it was evident that I was not in Trois-Pistoles to question the legitimacy of the Quebec separatist movement, but to understand the political role and even capability of the novel as it was perceived by him.

"When I read William Faulkner," said VLB, "what I find striking is that here is this American who has invented a fictional county in which he has located all his work, but we are able to recognize the southern United States quite easily –"

VLB drew on his pipe and stared at me coolly.

"– and without question," said VLB, "Faulkner's influence on me was huge. What I've wanted to do is to reinvent this region of *le bas Saint-Laurent*. And so I have reinvented a town called Trois-Pistoles, in which all my characters live, a beautiful part of my country that has not been discussed in our literature for all sorts of reasons."

I asked, "Do you have a manifesto when you write?"

"Writing for me is like resuscitating the spirit of a place. The role of an author, wherever he or she is living, is to make characters come alive, but saying this presupposes that authors have a vision and an understanding of the society that is surrounding them. What I have criticized in some of my contemporaries –"

VLB corrected himself.

"What I have criticized in my contemporary *fellow* writers –"

Whatever VLB actually thought of their novels, still he regarded his deluded compatriots as necessary comrades on the journey towards independence.

"– is that this vision has been erased for the sake of an aestheticism that amounts to nothing if the rest is not there."

On previous occasions, Margaret Atwood, Wayne Johnston, and David Adams Richards had been among those who had virtually leapt out of their seats when I had spoken of the obligations of the writer – *should* being a word that one is better off avoiding in anglophone Canada, anyway. Political aspects of the novel that would eventually recede into irrelevance were, in VLB's estimation, of the essence. But, the wily VLB was too clever to believe that the politics of a novel lay in the merely literal details of anything it recounted. For him, the novel had a biblical quality, tying stories and therefore a people to the landscape, as the Old Testament does Jews to the Promised Land.

"I live in Trois-Pistoles," said VLB, "so my skills and ambitions as an author are going to prompt me to want to describe the features of this particular landscape, for no matter where we are, the sensations of childhood are going to be the strongest that we know. The importance of a particular landscape is derived from the fact that our birthplace is usually the one for which we retain the most affection. One of the tasks of an author, I believe, is to give back this history to the people – but imbued with a vision of what a society is currently. The territory where I live is *mine*. It's a space that I want to describe because it belongs to me. It belongs to *me* even though I share it with others, even if this territory is collective by definition. A sense of place is all wrapped up in this notion. It's a bit as if I were some kind of animal marking my own territory with the tracks and paths that I have made. It's a way of *possessing* the terri- tory – of saying that it belongs to me and nobody else. Certainly, given that I am a separatist with an expectation of independence, I would expect to be the master of my own backyard – and I can't be that if I have no territory of which to speak."

VLB's insistence that the territory "belongs to me" was impres- sive. It was tempting to excuse him and reason that VLB was taking the view that for any writer, a territory is personal – a ter- ritory that is conceived of and belongs to each and any writer in the singular way that he or she has "reinvented" it, but this was not what he was saying. VLB, an historical dogmatist and a bully, was excluding anglophone Canadians with his separatist's sleight of hand – his proposal of a Quebec that was, in its name and essence, francophone. His espousing of the writer's need to chart territory that "belonged" to him was a way of laying claim to *la belle province* in a manner that he was not willing to see disputed. His Quebec was an atavistic society in its Age of Invention – busy determining its borders, its "truths" and its ideology, the accla- mation of a society that is still insecure. It was a throwback to the 1960s – the years after *la Révolution tranquille* in which VLB him- self flourished, and there had been a proliferation of novels with an explicit political purpose. The French-Canadian situation of being the "nègres blancs d'Amérique," in Pierre Vallières's unfor- gettable phrase, meant that an appeal could be made then, through the novel, to expose and address the situation of the hard-done-by francophone Quebecker, as aboriginal novels were doing for the country's First Nations.

Of all places in Canada, it has always been easiest to describe the novel as political in Quebec, its power keenly felt during the first period of Québécois assertion, when *indépendantistes* were not yet describing the separatist goal as one of "sovereignty-association." The political program was an ideology because it was the narrative of a community that still felt tentative and vulnerable. To question any part of the dogma then, no matter how significant or trite, was to be perceived as having criticized the whole. This was the period during which my father, the novelist and essayist Mordecai Richler, almost single-handedly among Canadian artists took on the separatists and their excluding vision. His fight for a more democratic and inclusive society was viciously attacked. This was the period during which even ordering an espresso, and not *un espress*, was taken as a provocation, and so it is hardly surprising that as fierce and effective an attack on the separatist movement as his *Oh Canada! Oh Québec!* should have engendered such a furious response.

Even anglophone Canadian apologists joined in the effort to mollify my father's arguments. The complaint that he did not address English Canada's anti-semitism was reiterated – as if that excused its long tradition in Quebec. The silly, risible argument that "Richler was able to use the international platform of *The New Yorker* to vent his mockery and scorn, leaving them unable to reply" was made – as if any self-respecting writer in the world would refuse such a commission, or that the platform of *government* was not enough for the Péquiste side. The irony is that no matter the fury of the separatists, or the timorous discomfort of his anglophone detractors, my father's essays took much of the bad wind out of the sails of the independence movement in a particularly ugly period and, just as great stories exhaust the age and usher in the next, introduced a new period of discussion in which a polemic such as *Oh Canada! Oh Quebec!* would have been less necessary. Today, this ugly, ideological period has ended, to the point that even Biz, the iconic leader of the sovereigntist pop band "Loco Locass" was able to shrug his shoulders and agree with some of the points my father made about Bill 101 ("Of course Mordecai Richler is right when he says it's a theatre of the absurd to have people measuring signs . . ."). This, and the vitriol heaped on Michel Tremblay, last gasps of a diminished franchise, are indications of a more reasonable age. For a funny thing happened on the way to the New Canada. The Manitoban Cree leader Elijah Harper's eloquent reminder, in 1990, effectively scuttling the Meech Lake Accord, that the French and English settlers' quarrel was occurring, in fact, on aboriginal land, and the calamitous error that Jacques Parizeau made when, in 1995, he blamed the loss of the referendum on "ethnics and those with money," forced the separatists to re-examine their political tactics and to be more tolerant and discursive in their pursuit of a "sovereigntist" agenda.

Two other things happened.

Firstly, the politics of the *world* changed. The debacle of the former Yugoslavia, beginning in 1991, was the first of several nationalist wars that had tremendous international repercussions and put the comparably petty Canadian quarrel in an altered context. No longer was it possible to be quite so morally aghast at Pierre Trudeau's quick containment of the 1970 FLQ October Crisis, or to be unimpressed that the resolution of one of Canada's fundamental disputes was being settled at the ballot box. The lesson of the October Crisis, and of the democratic exercises that followed, is that it is simply not permissible in Canada to kill anyone for their political beliefs, even when the integrity of the nation hangs in the balance. Indeed, anyone who argues that the notion of "Canadian values" is a euphemism for an undermilitarized nation not willing to test its mettle, or that multiculturalism is the naive doctrine of the nice, is obstinately forgetting this most important and sophisticated nation-defining moment and the principles it taught.

Secondly, the constant grappling with the separatist question has had the ironic effect of educating the rest of the country in the absurdities of separatist politics but also the case for them – a course in civics that was simply taught more effectively *outside* Quebec, where discussion was open and not an "ignominious vice." The Canada that Quebec *souverainistes* picked a fight with in 2006 was a more seasoned society than the one it challenged in 1976, and in the referendums of 1980 and 1995. Nor is Quebec the same nation that VLB came of age in either. Tremblay was right. The disappointing conclusion of the election of January 2006, in which Stephen Harper promised Quebec that he would address the problem of fiscal imbalance without any of his predecessor's grovelling (and in which Gilles Duceppe, cavorting with village ice-fishers, suggested there was still place for a sponsorship program of the kind that led to Liberal scandal and their defeat), was that even in *la belle province*, as has been true of the rest of the comfortable country for so long, politics has been reduced to questions about accounting.

In Canada, the country "without a bloody and eventful history," there is finally consensus of a kind. Few reasonably doubt that Quebec is a "distinct society" any more, and many Québécois have taken note of this. But sure, say many, Quebec society is different – but so, in principle, is everybody else's. A kind of nullification has taken place as a new generation of Canadians, including Quebeckers, has become politically engaged with the world under grossly changed conditions of globalization and a massively various immigration affecting *all of* the country.

Today, Quebec is a more sophisticated society, and VLB's voice is but one of many disputing it. After the years of nurturing that the false border of the province's language laws provided, after a couple of referendums and three decades of considerable power, the French-Canadian voice cannot convincingly claim not to be heard. The province is distinct, but this alone makes it no different from any other part of Canada. Because of Quebec, the notion of citizenship and what it entails has been under constant and skeptical review everywhere in Canada. This ceaseless necessity to revise the principles of civic participation, as much as any demographic fact, is what makes the country "multicultural." And the skepticism that this doctrine has ingrained is a strength, not a weakness. Canadians have more in common than they know.

✧　✧　✧

From Nadine Bismuth's *Scrapbook*:

> I wondered how publishing a novel would change my life. For
> example, what confidences would I bestow on the hordes of
> journalists who would call me at home eager to know more
> about the novelist Annie Brière and her sombre, yet touch-
> ing, world view. Would I tell them about my crooked teeth
> and the kilo of metal clamped upon them and how, because
> of it, I couldn't imitate my mother saying, "She sells seashells
> by the seashore"? Would that be why I started writing? A
> more attractive founding myth would be necessary. Perhaps
> a serious disorder of the immune system that kept me
> bedridden for months at a time or an unhappy childhood as
> part of a dysfunctional family?

The work of a new generation of Quebec writers, one that includes
Nadine Bismuth, Mauricio Segura, and Guillaume Vigneault among
its members, is confident, engaging, and not ostensibly political.
On those occasions when the work is overtly so, the point is not
one that applies singly to Quebec, as in the urban multicultural
concerns of Segura's novel, *Côte-des-Nègres*, or it is fresh and laughter is being solicited. Either way, the signal is that Quebec's French-
Canadian community has surpassed its testy, ideological stage and
is ready to satirize itself. In Bismuth's *Scrapbook*, Marcel Jolicœur
is an obviously *indépendantiste* writer who has written one highly
successful novel, *Bras de fer*, for which he has famously refused a
Governor General's Literary Award. But he has yet to complete a
second and has since become a hack of the university lecture cir-
cuit. When Jolicœur does take the stage, he is drunk. A novelist's
genius, Bismuth's aspiring novelist Annie Brière concludes, lies in
his knowing how to alert the waitress that his glass is empty.

Jolicœur could be VLB, one of those foot soldiers of the Quiet
Revolution who has felt, like a plane circling above its destination,
on the verge of obtaining the sovereigntist dream for a tantaliz-
ing three decades now. Despite what I have said, political volatility

means the dream may well be within reach. In VLB's mind, that day cannot come too soon – it *must* come soon – as there is change and decay in a lot of what he sees. In particular, he sees it in young writers who have forsaken the literary politics of independence for novels that francophones describe as *autofiction* – the literature of the self. All fiction is that really, but in Quebec, "autofiction" describes a kind of indulgence, as if to partake of stories that do not comment on society directly is an act of literary negligence. In February 2004, in an article in *La Presse*, VLB attacked younger Quebec novelists for failing to occupy Quebec in all its spaces. "In 1969," he wrote, "Jacques Ferron said of our literature that it was in a state of boiling over because there were so many young novelists and so numerous were the issues they were discussing in their works." VLB proclaimed that for the first time Quebec literature was imbued with *style* and that it borrowed freely from (his heroes) William Faulkner and Jack Kerouac and was better off for doing so. "The overarching preoccupations of the hour, collectivities and individuals, were at the meeting: from the subjects of terrorism to the independence of Quebec, the refusal of the too-numerous family to material and cultural poverty, the rivalry of

town and country, from religion to sexuality, *everything* was discussed." Thirty-five years later, the desultory VLB despaired, the province's young writers had abandoned all seriousness, forsaken their forebears, and the ties they represented between the old nation and the new.

✧ ✧ ✧

AT LE MAS DES OLIVIERS, on Avenue de la Montagne below Ste-Catherine, I gathered three writers of the new generation so irksome to VLB. Nadine Bismuth was one. Mauricio Segura, a Chilean-Québécois author whose first novel, *Côte-des-Nègres*, had taken a gritty look at multiculturalism in practice in a Montreal high school was the second. Guillaume Vigneault, the author of *Necessary Betrayals*, completed the trio. They were attractive, this lot. Guillaume, with his young man's beard and wavy collar-length hair pushed back Byronically, was playing the young troubadour's part. Segura had a boyish face that was chubby and round, and a thoughtful, slightly dolorous expression – *sympathique*, is how the French would describe him. There was consternation in his eyes, and where Vigneault sat back with Gallic ease, smiling, shrugging with such *insouciance*, Segura was in the habit of leaning forward and sharing his thoughts as if each one was deeply troubling and he might learn something from the others. Bismuth, the child of a Québécoise mother and Tunisian father, was an alluring young woman with an aura about her that was patient and poised. She was an observer, her elegant silences an invitation to others to speak. In her first collection, *Les gens fidèles ne font pas les nouvelles*, she proved herself a tender judge of character who was able to imagine herself into the lives of young and old to equivalent effect. She had the light touch of a pastry chef, a wry ability to create stories from seemingly insignificant moments – hence, scanning so rhythmically in the French, that first collection's playful title, *Faithful People Do Not Make the News*. Her novel, *Scrapbook*, its title revisiting the author's interest in life as a tapestry of moments, is a comedy of manners set in the publishing community and the cafés, university campuses, and apartments of the new Montreal. The Ritz-Carlton is a landmark. The place that she was charting; the distressed city that Segura was chronicling; or the continent that Vigneault was in the romp of his novel around America had little to do with the Quebec that VLB was interested in naming.

"If I'm a Quebecker," said Vigneault, "and decide to write novels taking place on the moon, then there's no reason I shouldn't do that. It's not so black and white. The more germane question, it seems to me, is not about failing anyone's mandate, but why we have been given one at all."

"True," said Bismuth.

"Do I fail my country if I don't meet it?" said Vigneault. "That's ridiculous."

In *Necessary Betrayals*, love fails Vigneault's young hero, Jack, and so he takes to the road and travels out from Rouyn-Noranda into the continent of North America and back. The road novel is a classic French-Canadian genre. The trip Jack makes is in the tradition of the one Jacques Poulin made in his novel *Volkswagen Blues* and that which the first Jacques, Jack Kerouac, made in *On the Road*. Kerouac, about whom VLB has written, is something of a folk hero in Quebec because of his French-Canadian ties and because he is regarded as having acted out a journey that has an archetypal quality in the French-Canadian imagination – the pioneering forays into the continent of the first *voyageurs*. Quebeckers have always been at ease in America, to the point that anglophone Canadians have often misconstrued the relationship with the United States, as if it was hypocritical of separatist French Canadians to campaign against English Canada while cozying up to a country with an anglophone population ten times the size and that would all the more easily swallow it. But Quebeckers feel no such fear. History put the French Canadians at the fluvial opening of a continent that at some fundamental level they still consider theirs. Not without reason. The journeys that explorers, missionaries, and then traders made, paddling others when they were not leading expeditions themselves, sent French Canadians as far as Louisiana and the Mackenzie Delta. The francophone reach, in America, is the "Ghost Empire" of Philip Marchand's parlance. The continent, in this Québécois frame of mind, already *is* French Canadian, so why would they not feel kinship with it? True, Quebec no longer *owns* these lands, but its writers revisit them in the romantic explorations their literary characters periodically make, and there is a way in which, at the bottom of it all, the American and Canadian states seem like frivolous activity that has followed the *voyageurs'* pioneering work. In the Mediterranean of North America, Quebec is Athens to the United States' Rome. French Canadians, moreover, identify with Americans as Republicans. (When, in 1882, Louis Riel was in exile in Montana, he campaigned on behalf of the Republican Party there.) They had been monarchists once, but were rendered Republicans by virtue of having been defeated by their enemies, the infernal monarchist English.

So the Quebecker is more free in America, land that was once his backyard, and does not share the English Canadian's trepidation of the greater economy to the south. (As much as the "Idea of North" is touted, the fear that is Canada's "Idea of South" is actually what defines much of the country – from Inuit afraid to venture into Indian territory, to white Canadians worried about America dictating the terms of "free trade," its cultural invasion, etc.) The difference is that the generation of which Vigneault *fils* is one is also free in Canada. I had met him once in the Canadian West on a book tour, and there was none of the animosity or posturing that I have encountered in older French-Canadian novelists, obstinately making interaction hard for anyone who did not address them in French but who, like Bismuth's Jolicœur, take the government's subsidy anyway.

Still, I did not assume Vigneault's ease within the territory of Canada to be evidence of his politics, only an indication that he was the child of a time in which separatism was no longer the agitated ideology it had been – and remained for a doctrinaire old guard. Unlike in the young VLB's day, today's Quebecker has little trouble travelling or doing business in contemporary Canada, and there is no question that *la belle province* has been reclaimed by francophones. Many younger Quebeckers even share the wider, Canadian sense of the absurdity of the nation-state, now that one is possibly closer at hand. What is the necessity of another army? Where do the proper borders of an independent Quebec lie? Are the aboriginal territories of the North, never a part of the French colony, to be included? What defensible steps can be taken to prevent Westmount or Sherbrooke, say, defecting from Quebec in turn? How is the community authentically defined? The last is *the* Canadian question, a preoccupation across the country. And yes, answers to it are sometimes wonderfully contorted. In Montreal, arguing with a young separatist about the long-term absurdity of aboriginal land claims, he suggested to me that it was a mistake to think of the state as a static entity. Quebec was a nation founded on language, he said, and I should imagine, instead, a fluid state such as France or England was in the Middle Ages, with their limits morphing constantly. Today's Quebec might include the aboriginal North, tomorrow's, the state of Maine, reflecting the spread of the tongue.

Debate is the lifeblood of the province, no matter how occasionally absurd. It is a part of the Gallic legacy, and so I knew that Bismuth, Segura, Vigneault, and I would have no trouble discussing the political obligations of the novel. We had started by addressing the charges VLB had made.

"I don't see where VLB's been getting the idea that writers have a duty to explore Quebec in all its places," said Vigneault. "When I write, there's no checklist that I'm working with."

"What makes a novel Québécois," said Segura, "if it is genuinely necessary to insist on a story's Québécois aspect, is its point of view. But in today's globalized era the discourse is much more universal than it ever was in the 1960s. When VLB makes this accusation, it's as if he wants us to explore Quebec in every nook and cranny, but even then writers did not travel into these hypothetical places much. If you consider the famous novels of the day – Hubert Aquin's *Next Episode*, for instance – well, the story takes place in Switzerland. The *point of view* is Québécois, and surely that's what matters."

"You talk about the 1960s," said Vigneault, drawing on a cigarette, "but when I think about those years, stories that take place in cities come to mind – the novels of André Langevin and Réjean Ducharme, or of Jacques Poulin hitting the road. I don't see a lot of stories taking place in Abitibi."

"The specific place is not that important," said Segura. "Is the reader of Poulin's *Autumn Rounds* even aware of where the story takes place?"

"Quebec City," said Vigneault, "but you would have to know that beforehand."

"When we write," said Bismuth, "we're conscious of our position in a certain tradition – I am writing today, in Quebec, in 2005. That said, I am not about to lie prostrate in the face of it, as the literary tradition is so very young here."

Bismuth makes her claims gently and graciously, a hazard in a province where *not* being overtly political can get you into trouble. In *Scrapbook*, Bismuth had written the city of Montreal as so many English writers routinely do London, or the French Paris – which is to say affectionately and well. By naming it, for a start. In Montreal, storied city, the truth is that not only Québécois novelists have been occupying the city in all its spaces, but francophone and anglophone and now "allophone" writers are lighting the territory. Stories *do* battle, and in Montreal there has always been a gamut of novelists declaring that "the territory where I live is *mine*." The more magnanimous, *pace* VLB, understand that in the Age of Argument, it is incumbent upon the writer to counter one set of maps with others. That is the excitement of the place.

"Quebec literature is recent," said Bismuth. "It isn't weighty in any way. It's actually quite astonishing that any of us should feel humbled by the tradition as it stands. For my part, I feel that whatever is the Québécois legacy remains to be determined and, personally, when I'm writing, my literary models are much more likely to be American or Anglo-Saxon than they are French or even Québécois. Really, what's unusual about being a writer in Quebec is that one is free to be able to write and feel one's way from the confluence of a *number* of traditions. Here we are in a francophone country that is at the same time influenced a lot by America. In effect, we're in French *America* and what's interesting is to be able to mix and play around with these various models."

"Do you see the city as an abstract place or one that has its own identity?" I asked.

"I see the city as a concrete place," said Bismuth, "and Montreal especially, though I play with the symbolic connotation of places as I think that this is part of a novel's universal quality. In *Scrapbook*, the Ritz-Carlton hotel keeps cropping up because the narrator goes there and imagines that it's a very prestigious place for her to be. All great cities have spaces with positive or negative inferences, and I like to make my characters travel inside the city through whatever are these symbolic common places. Whether the story takes place in Quebec or in America, often I will focus on the setting of a restaurant, a hotel, or a house, more than I do the specific geographical or political aspects of the places that I'm working with. For me these settings start as voids, and the challenge that I present myself is to render these places inhabited, if only because what is human is also very chaotic, and location is what allows me to situate the conflicts my characters have."

"Having come from elsewhere," said Segura, "I don't have quite the same history of concerns. Looking back at Jacques Godbout and Marie-Claire Blais, and other writers who flourished in that time, it's probably true that we have more elbow room today. We can do whatever we want – and, sure, the novel doesn't have to be strictly political, as seems to have been the requirement then."

"And yet," I said, "*Côte-des-Nègres* is certainly a political novel, at least in a social sense. Have you ever asked yourself why multiculturalism would be more or less of an issue here than it is in Chile?"

"I wrote *Côte-des-Nègres* trying to explore that issue," Segura said. "For me, the novel asks the question, 'How can we live together?' or even, 'Is it *possible* for us all to live together?' So I place my characters in conflicting situations, and then I follow them and see how they react. But does a novel ever really supply answers? Is a novel an essay? I don't think so. As far as multiculturalism goes, my novel raises issued that were on my mind, but I'm not sure that I have any particular message to impart. What a novel teaches us in relation to place is that there is a tremendous difference between events happening in some neighbourhood of Montreal and whatever is occurring outside the city – even elsewhere within this same province. And what is interesting for the writer is that there is a set of completely different identities within this place we call Quebec – I wonder what it is that links me to Abitibi, for example. Obviously, there are regional similarities, but there are many ways in which I feel much closer to someone from Toronto, or France."

Vigneault laughed. "My novel starts in Abitibi," he said.

From Mauricio Segura's *Côte-des-Nègres*:

Spit balls rained down on the principal's jacket. He looks out at the teachers lined up like soldiers by the podium, then exhales slowly into the microphone. "Friends, colleagues, if you please, we've made this decision for the common good." The students begin to clap their hands and stamp their feet. Above the uproar, he pushes on. "One more thing: My friends, please, listen to me." In a single voice, the room resounds. "No! No! No!" Yet he perseveres. "I've been informed that these tensions have been caused by so-called 'ethnic conflicts.' On that subject, I have just one thing to say. Would you mind listening?" Once more he turns towards the teachers, purses his lips and runs a hand angrily through his hair. For a moment, he feels as though he's about to fall. The loneliest man in the world. "Bunch of stupid, little fucks." The teachers glance at each other shocked. The students are bent double in laughter. They pound their thighs. "Now, that's the best one of all. Ha-ha-ha-ha!" Barbeau tries another explanation. "For the last several months, a few individuals have been trying to separate us into ghettoes. We won't let that happen. What we have to remember, my friends, is that there aren't any Italians or Haitians or Latinos or Jews or Asians or even Quebeckers. Do you hear me? There are just students here, students who want to work and who want to learn. When it comes down to it, we're all brothers." At the back of the gym, a row of them take out their imaginary violins and begin playing sentimental music. Some of them hug one another melodramatically. Others exclaim "Brother!" and dissolve in tears and convulsions. The principal leaves the podium without a backwards glance. The students are triumphant.

Quebec, like the rest of Canada, is becoming a region of cities empowered demographically, if not yet through fair political representation. The same twenty-first-century questions that need to be addressed from Halifax to Victoria are being posed here. The cities of Quebec had become places in which a multitude of communities argue their own versions of society and subvert, in Vigneault's words, issues previously "black and white." The rise of urban concerns made VLB's assertions appear quaint or, worse, retrograde. For only in corners of Quebec that were as white and *pure laine* as Trois-Pistoles could one quite so easily claim that "the territory where I live is mine. It belongs to *me* even though I share it with others, even if this territory is collective by definition."

✧　✧　✧

"EVERYTHING IS POLITICAL. Even saying that something is *not* political is a way to define the place of that phenomenon in a society – and society is inherently political."

The necessity to the real estate agent of sufficiently distinct societies, a.k.a. neighbourhoods, trumps the politics of language. As property values in Montreal have skyrocketed, the East End district of Montreal where the novelist Gil Courtemanche lives is now called "Mile End" again. Sitting with Courtemanche in his living room, I had a view through a side window of the house that prompted me to ask about one beautifully extraneous moment in his novel, *A Sunday at the Pool in Kigali*, in which the enraged journalist Bernard Valcourt, contending with Rwanda's imminent genocide, thinks back to Quebec and remembers the year's first snow. It is a placid caesura that has the abutting quality of a dream within a story that is otherwise a genocidal nightmare.

"That's the only beautiful time of winter," said Courtemanche, "the first snow."

"Did that scene sit comfortably in the novel when you first wrote it?"

"No, and it surprised me a bit. I knew that at some point Gentille, Valcourt's lover, would ask questions about winter because she was

African, but I really didn't want to talk about Quebec at all. Valcourt was simply *there*, in Rwanda, a Quebecker by accident, so I was quite surprised at the appearance of this *petit passage*. But I wrote the novel here in Quebec and the room I was writing in was angled in such a way that there was a lot of light. The only beautiful moment of winter that I ever saw *in my life* occurred while I was writing the novel in that room. The light was so bright, the sun was *so* dazzling. I looked at the snow that afternoon and I knew I had to write about it."

"Do you think of yourself that way – as a Quebecker by accident?"

"We're all what we are by accident. We're Canadian by accident, we're Quebeckers by accident, or French by accident. Except for some immigrants, I'd say. I have a lot of friends who left France to live here, or who left India to live here, and to my mind these are the only Quebeckers and the only Canadians, in the true sense of the word, because they *chose* their country. We didn't choose a country. We choose in some sort of passive way by remaining here, but most people who stay in their own country do so not out of love of country, or fidelity or loyalty. They do so out of necessity."

One of those immigrants who did choose Canada was Rawi Hage, the Lebanese-Christian author of *De Niro's Game*. A stunning first novel, it tells the story of Bassam, a young man inevitably involved in smuggling and concomitant thuggery during the lawless long years of the Lebanese civil war. Pressure mounts on Bassam to join the Christian militia, though he escapes Beirut for France after the Sabra and Chatila massacres of 1982. Canada does not appear in the novel, except as a promise of refuge that turns out to be illusory. The man who offers Bassam a Canadian passport in Marseilles is a Mossad agent, and the inducement is a trap. Bassam is in his early twenties when he leaves Beirut – as Hage was – and he travels to Rome instead. The novel is bold for a variety of reasons. It demonstrates the sheer amount of violence that wears the team colours of battling faiths, and that is actually the result of having a surplus of young men in a wartorn city with nothing better to do and no other means of getting by. Hage's novel also dispels the elevating but patently false Canadian creation myth that would paint all new-comers to the country as benevolent. Canada, trusting Canada, may end up making a saint of Bassam, but the likely existence of Islamist terrorist activity in Toronto, and proven Tamil Tigers cells, as well as many other rebel groups in exile is a sign that Canadian novels have some catching up to do. "Part of nation-making," says Dionne Brand, the Toronto novelist and poet, "is the creating of a story that *everyone* can believe in – but that's not how individual stories are made. The official myth needs to be a pleasing one, because that's how the story is kept afloat. The myth must always be a story of rescue."

Hage, who was a student in Beirut, speaks Arabic, French, and English. In 1984, he emigrated to New York, where he lived for nine years before moving to Montreal. In his new enactment of the Canadian story, USAmerica is the railway siding. Canada is the des-tination of first choice.

"I had just left my country, I barely knew any English, and I struggled," said Hage, a photographer as well as a budding novelist, working four nights a week as a taxi driver when, in a bookshop café near St. Joseph's Oratory, we discussed his novel. Some of Hage's photography had been a part of an Arab-Canadian exhibi-tion scheduled for the National Gallery in October 2001, suspended in the aftermath of 9/11. A small man, Hage wore a black leather car coat and had the slightly rounded shoulders and steady watchful gaze of someone in command of his animal reflexes, so that when the reaction did come, it was to the bomb that *was* close, or the stranger whose body language spoke messages that I, in my inno-cence, would not recognize. I, the comfortable Canadian. I, the Canadian by accident, the one who did not choose his country but was born here.

"New York was a horrible experience," said Hage. "This is why I love this place. I don't feel as alienated here as I did in New York. What was really hard was that Lebanon was cut off. There were no working telephone lines, and the Internet was not a fact of life yet, so I wouldn't hear from my family for months, and I could only get news about Lebanon from TV. Looking back, I don't even know how I survived. It was very traumatic, and I don't know if I'm still dealing with that trauma or not."

I would have said yes to that. Working for companies, Hage later told me, was something that he was loath to do. "Organized hierarchies lead to violence," he said.

"What did you know about Canada before you came?"

"I had an uncle in Ottawa whom I used to visit, and I was working on having papers in the States, but that would have taken five or ten years, and I heard that Quebec was accepting Lebanese because they were francophones. I heard there was this Lebanese program – that they wanted Lebanese for some reason – but this was all community talk. You know how it is. Immigrants speak to one another and know more, I think, than the government knows. They will say to you, 'If they ask if you want kids, say Yes.' Someone told me that there is a chance to get in because you speak French and you're a certain age. Immigrants instruct one another."

"And so you applied from New York?"

"Yes. I applied and was accepted, and it was a great feeling to know that you are equal to the people you come to. It's a feeling of relief. I remember coming here when I had my papers and just walking on the street. Feeling secure, feeling safe. It was a conscious decision. This is where I want to be. I'm accepted. I'm *legally* accepted, and that is a fantastic feeling."

Hage was a part of an orchestrated francophone immigration into Quebec that has turned a city once known for the cultural contribution of its Jewish community into another one entirely, with an Arab population that is now numerically greater. And yet the politics of language devised to aid the French language, in Quebec, are now undermining the separatist cause as these communities' concerns are often concentrated elsewhere and indifferent – even intolerant – of Quebec's secessionary politics. To wit: in Albania, in 1997, I sat in the yard of the National Film School with a Tirana colleague, an engineer by profession who was working during the country's civil war as a BBC fixer. His wife wanted to emigrate to Canada, he said, but the Canadian embassy in Belgrade would not process the couple's application.

The pop-pop-pop of small-arms fire could be heard from the streets outside the compound, and I suggested that, as he and his wife both spoke French, an application to Quebec might be more expedient than the leads he was pursuing.

More gunshots went off.

"Quebec?" he said. "Why would I want to move to Quebec?"

In *De Niro's Game*, as in Courtemanche's *A Sunday at the Pool in Kigali*, the racial pedigree of his principal characters is never "pure." Valcourt's lover, Gentille, was a mixture of Tutsi and Hutu; Hage's Bassam and his unfortunate friend George, co-opted by the Christian Phalangists, are also mongrel. A Middle Eastern cocktail to confound the extremists. To the civilized, and I would count enlightened Canadians among that number, proselytizing nationalist politics are vile, and these two authors use mixed bloodlines to say so. Blood makes a mockery of the Rwandan genocide and of the civil war Hage shows to be a game of bandits, thugs, and demagogues.

"I'm the ultimate existentialist," said Hage. "I strip my characters of their families, of their country, and I make them as marginal as possible. George is half-Jewish and half-Lebanese, and Bassam is half-Lebanese and half-Armenian. And both their mothers and fathers have died. I have stripped them to the bottom. And in spite of all this, they confront life as much as they are able. The means are questionable, but this is what they do."

In Paris, Bassam wanders the streets in a state of utter estrangement. His gun, the thing he has much depended on, has lost its purpose, and he throws it into the river. Like an addict trying to kick an obstinate habit, he goes back for it at one point; at another, he plays the eponymous game and stares down its loaded barrel.

"When you describe yourself as 'existentialist,'" I said, "is it because *anomie* is your base feeling?"

"I don't want to say that I'm alienated," said Hage, "but because of my experiences – having lived through war, then as an exile and as an immigrant – there is always the sense of being estranged. I can't get away from it. I think I feel at a loss – yes, I feel loss. But I've come to terms with that now."

"Louis Hamelin, a novelist and literary critic here, equates language with country," I said. "Even though this notion excludes those who are not francophone from feeling that this province is their *patrie*, that is how many Québécois feel."

"I've lost languages and gained languages," said Hage. "And I don't even know if I'm capable of writing in Arabic now. I hope I'm more universal than being limited to a language."

Hage took a swig of beer. The proprietress of the bookstore, a white French-Canadian woman with an adopted black child, introduced herself enthusiastically.

"Canada is not a homogeneous society," said Hage, "and Quebec is not homogeneous either. We tend, as immigrants, to stay understated and not to want to offend anybody. It's not in the interest of such a multicultural society to be too nationalistic, but there is much we should take pride in."

"Would you write a novel set here?" I asked.

"Yes," said Hage. "I feel very Canadian. My second novel is almost done and it's set in Montreal."

✧   ✧   ✧

"THERE ARE ALWAYS people suggesting that the novel has been depoliticized," said Guillaume Vigneault, "but that is something that should really be judged case by case. It's possible that there is less political *necessity* today, but I don't think that translates into a withdrawal from the political sphere. Merely as a citizen, I am politicized, so just because things in a novel aren't named, or because issues are not treated as black and white as they were in the 1960s, it does not follow that the novels we write are empty of political content. I would say that there is a sort of micro-politics all over today's writing."

"In *Necessary Betrayals*, when your character, Jack, makes his expedition out into the continent – and there's a certain tradition of that kind of road trip in Quebec literature – what is the space that you think you're occupying?" I asked.

"The relationship to place in my novels is quite different from my own connections to places," said Vigneault. "Like Mauricio, I am urban, though I am urban by choice because I come from the country. But curiously, I have trouble making my characters *stay* in the city. I deal with space as a kind of negation. It's as if they have a need to visit exceptional places because they are in situations in their *interior* life that are exceptional, and so they travel. They're on a quest to find peace – but somewhere else."

I explained my notion of the country's Myths of Disappointment and asked if there were equivalent stories in Quebec, of folk let down by the authorities that should have been their stewards, told in ways that emphasized today's modern, culturally sensitive Canadian pedigree.

"To my mind," said Vigneault, "there's still a sense of the colonized nation in the air here. We have, in *our* founding myths, this idea that we are destined for little more than a meagre loaf of bread. I've been criticized because the characters in my novels know too much, they travel too much, because they have too much freedom in the way they choose to live their lives. With regard to *Necessary Betrayals*, I've even been told that Jack's sorrow is not credible because he's such a *talented* photographer."

"All this sounds so terribly familiar," said Bismuth, whose *Scrapbook* tour had only recently ended.

"Nobody in France ever told me anything quite as stupid," said Vigneault, "but here you have to create likeable losers for your narrators – they have to be missing an arm or have a clubbed foot."

Perhaps a serious disorder of the immune system that keeps a writer bedridden for months at a time –

"There's a long-standing tradition of sordid realism here," said Bismuth. "Our founding myths are stories of failure or of aborted revolutions."

"*Les mythes de 15 février* and *les Patriotes*," said Vigneault, recalling the story of the rebellions of 1837–38 and the defeat by Generals

Colborne and Monckton of the first *indépendantistes*. Martyrs in the view of contemporary separatist extremists, some were hanged, others banished, and in the following year Lord Durham's report proposed the assimilation of the conquered French and "responsible government."

"Depressing myths," Bismuth repeated.

"Or how about the story of the Plains of Abraham," said Vigneault.

"*Precisely*," said Bismuth. "We have no founding myths that allow us to turn a page and actually to *build* something. All we have are these myths of failure."

"Yet for my part," said Vigneault, "I prefer myths like these."

"Why is that?" asked Segura.

"Because they're *our* myths," said Vigneault. "True, the stories can be depressing, but there's something pleasing in them nonetheless."

"Something comforting?" asked Segura.

"If we failed before, then we can fail again," said Bismuth, her tone rising to one of impatience now.

"Well," said Vigneault, "I prefer to have been defeated on the Plains of Abraham than to celebrate having killed lots of people there."

Segura was perplexed. The province's literature, the Québécois social critic Robert Sauvé has charged, often concentrates on male figures as "losers." The myths are not quite ones of disappointment because in them, Quebeckers are failed by themselves – by their own authority, or the lack of it. In early 2006, Sauvé told the *Toronto Star*'s Graham Fraser that defeat on the Plains of Abraham has led to a history of "failed fathers" in the province's literature, and that "masculine characters on the big screen have been alcoholics, suicides, rapists, cowards or, of course, dropout fathers." Montcalm, Papineau, Laurier, Lévesque, even the FLQ – kidnappers of the British diplomat James Cross and murderers of Pierre Laporte – were, in Sauvé's estimation, "loser terrorists."

"My impression," Segura said, "is that there is definitely a difference between the Québécois and Canadian worldview."

"I don't think that we worry about defining ourselves quite as much," said Vigneault. "I watched that Molson Canadian television commercial – you know, the one that says, 'My name is Joe, and I am Canadian!' – and I asked myself, What is this?"

"But it was intentionally ironic," I said. "It was aimed at that part of the Canadian character that used to wonder how we were different from Americans. The fact that the ad was lampooning those old anxieties about identity showed that we are not worried about our seeming lack of difference any more. We can laugh at it. Now the Nowhere that we occupy is in the American imagination, not ours."

Vigneault shrugged. Had another puff.

"But here," said Segura, "the challenge is one that concerns the survival of the French language and of Québécois culture in a continent that is predominantly anglophone. The situation is adverse, but it's one that stimulates us to try to find solutions, and this is what makes me think of Quebec's literature as different from what is being written in the rest of Canada. The conditions that we are facing are quite particular."

Vigneault concurred: "Language sets us apart."

"But the political agenda in Quebec can be so burdensome!" Bismuth said.

"*C'est vrai*," said Vigneault. "Here we are constantly made to feel that literature has a mission –"

"That attention must be paid," said Bismuth.

"That's right," said Segura.

✧   ✧   ✧

"WRITERS HAVE AN obligation to the times," said VLB, "and if they do not honour it then effectively they are living *beside* the world they inhabit. I have trouble accepting, in the time in which we are living today, that the novel should concern itself with simple psychological questions rather than political ones. Much of our present literature appears feeble to me exactly because a lot of writers disregard the social and political dimensions of the novel – it's actually quite extraordinary, reading so many of our contemporary novels, to see the extent to which these books' authors are essentially absent. I think of these writers as tardy in assessing changes in our society so that in this sense, these writers hobble along instead of advancing things. It's as if, on the imaginary plane, writers have found refuge in bygone values because they do not know, or *want* to know, the future that is approaching. This lack of curiosity is a shame. It gives us a literature that is often retrograde – a literature that just should not exist any more."

I had brought up the position of several young Québécois writers, a number of whom had contributed to a collection of responses to VLB's attack published in the literary review *Zinc*, in which he himself had been characterized as the retrograde dinosaur. VLB responded in the same, measured tones. *Diminuendo*. The blow would follow.

"There is no question that the political situation in Quebec has been a major preoccupation of our novelists since the 1960s," said VLB, "but our politics fluctuate. One day we believe that we'll have a country of our own, the next day we're not going to, with the effect that the political consciousness of the *literature* vacillates as well. We have proceeded from novels that were urban, and at the same time revolutionary – such as Hubert Aquin's *Next Episode* or Réjean Ducharme's *L'Avalée des avalées* – and, after that, a period that spawned novels of desperate and despairing characters, such as you'll find in Marie-Claire Blais's work. This is normal in a society such as Quebec that feels *menacée* – threatened – and contending with these vacillations can be hard work for an author, as Hubert Aquin's own end demonstrated. A novelist as talented as he was does not commit suicide without reason. Aquin used to talk about the 'cultural fatigue' of French Canada. Jacques Ferron spoke of the 'cultural fatigue of an uncertain and an ambiguous country.' It is hard for a writer not to be dragged down by these feelings."

The 1960s and 1970s were a golden age of Québécois expression, whether in music, film, or literature – a not-so-quiet revolution. But a door has closed upon this period. It is, after all, much more inspiring for a person to pine after something he imagines he does not have, than to possess whatever it is that he imagined he needed. The Quebecker can think himself short-changed, maybe (and what Canadian does not see himself as that?), but oppressed, certainly not.

I asked VLB if he thought that the political consciousness of Quebec literature had ebbed because the battle at home had been won.

"There is certainly a danger of disengagement looming over Quebec," said VLB, his resolve utterly undiminished, "and that the likelihood that there will ultimately be separation has prompted Quebeckers to be complacent. This has happened in many other parts of the world where independence has been gained and the people have receded into a kind of cultural fog. I know that there are very few examples in the world where countries that have won their independence have then gone on to produce great works in the years that follow. That's a risk we take on – and the risk will be much less if there is already a cultural foundation that we can build on. Independence will demand of Quebec writers that they exert themselves far more than they do presently. It's *what must be done*."

VLB spoke calmly, but his measured manner did nothing to disguise the commandeering nature of his agenda. If I'd had any doubt about the dogmatic nature of VLB's cultural program, then it was squashed in this reminder of the chilling Leninist phrase. In *What Is to Be Done?*, the first chairman of the Council of the People's Commissars of the Soviet Union brooked no criticism and upheld the mission and instincts of his communist party over the base, catch-up instincts of the masses. Like Michel Tremblay, the poor sods knew not what they did.

You could see, in VLB, a nostalgia for more "interesting times," when the grandfathers and fathers he was lionizing occupied the front row of social and cultural movements in the province. But when people know the dreams for what they are, and can finally speak them without inhibition, then they fall out of the realm of the excited and more lyric imagination and into the domain of the real. The "cultural fog" descends because there is no longer any urgency in these stories' political revelations, no longer any of the oppression that inspired these stories in the first place. In the decades following *la Révolution tranquille*, writers in Quebec cannot be blamed for drifting away from the literary purpose that arose out of their desire to reclaim the contested space they inhabited. Now the old stories had become tedious, familiar – *stated* – and to repeat them was unacceptable for writers of Bismuth's generation as it would be for writers from any part of the country or the world, for that matter, as the novel's first obligation is to be new. The *souverainistes* have not won a referendum yet, but Quebec is a comfortable society, and it is becoming harder and harder to construe the sort of subjugation that might have goaded new writers into taking up the mantle of a Hubert Aquin or a Jacques Ferron. VLB was impatient for a canon that would have supported his orthodox view of Québécois culture, but the younger writers whom I spoke with were merely impatient to be able to get on with their art.

✧ ✧ ✧

"To suggest exactly the spaces and particular places that writers should have to visit in their work," said Nadine Bismuth, "that's very *romantique*, but it's not our reality."

"My feeling is that VLB is imagining mythical places from forty years ago," said Guillaume Vigneault.

"I certainly don't think he's referring to cities," said Bismuth.

"No, and neither is he thinking of places with massive modern tractors," said Vigneault. "He's talking about places where there's still the chopping of wood, he's talking about rhyme. That really is romanticism."

✧ ✧ ✧

Place has made Québécois and Canadian anglophone writers compatriots even if demagogues would prefer to categorize them otherwise. The metaphor of the house – to be found in the literature of English Canada from Nova Scotia to British Columbia – appears as often in French-Canadian novels. In *la belle province*, the house is its own protected world and the last resort against forces that are vaguely threatening. The Québécois version of this very

Canadian metaphor is the intimation of a culture that feels surrounded in the continent – and yes, often menaced, although the
perceived threat is now likely to originate in lands beyond Quebec,
or even anglophone Canada.

In the novels of Élise Turcotte, the house, the ordered house,
appears often, as does that of the human body as a kind of frail
last sanctuary. It did not demand a great leap forward to see how
Turcotte's notions of the vulnerable house might have stemmed, in
North America, from a Québécois sensibility such as VLB had
described it – of the province, in the old master's words, as *une société
menacée*. Except that Turcotte saw these metaphors as symptomatic of broader aspects of the human condition – no one of us ever
truly being safe.

"To me," said Turcotte, "a writer is someone sitting on a wobbly
chair. A writer is in a state in which she is always ill at ease vis-à-
vis her own life – and, therefore, towards her own culture, her own
country, and the world that surrounds it."

The empty house is at once an extension of the body and the
shrine of any person's profound existential anxiety, for these are difficult times all around, in which it is irrational – forgive me, Jacques
Ferron – to be certain or unambiguous about anything. Larger
questions than those pertaining to the independence of some nar-
rowly defined community have seeped into the "social vision" VLB
thought was lacking in the work of younger Québécois writers.

Turcotte, in her forties, started her writing life as a poet. Prose,
she told me, came to her along with the sense of impending mortality that motherhood had brought on. Her novels are delicate
things, their careful writing only serving to bolster her sometimes
oppressive suggestion of these unarticulated threats. They have
an atmosphere of unsettling contingency and do not support the
explicit politics of place that VLB would prefer, but they're political
all the same, even more so in their quiet etiolation. Turcotte is
one of a new generation of writers that senses Quebec as VLB
would have it, as a small pond. She wants to get out into America
and make the trips the Jacks did – making their forays into the

country and coming back *with profits*. If the Hudson's Bay Company had been the model for not just economic but also social transactions in English Canada, then the greater free enterprise spirit of the Northwest Fur Company's free-traders (swallowed up by the Company in the merger of 1821) provides the template here. Still, it can be hard for a Quebecker to reconcile her French roots with the pull of America, even in the wake of the "Ghost Empire." Turcotte describes herself as "*une Nord-Américaine qui parle français*" – a "North American who speaks French."

"Like many others of my generation, I knew that we needed to define ourselves as a people existing within *both* the French- and English-speaking North American worlds," said Turcotte.

We had taken a table at one end of the numerous cafés on Avenue Laurier, in Outremont. A street of taverns and druggie hangouts when I went to school at a French high school nearby, it was now a chi-chi avenue of eateries, elegant boutiques, and upmarket shops. Sometimes, *ça change. Vraiment.*

"The preceding generation struggled to accept, much more than mine did, the duality of their French roots and their attraction to America," said Turcotte. "In my case, the duality was much more focused in our imaginations. I know that growing up, I learned to define myself by looking at myself as someone that I was not. I knew that I was not a French woman, and that I was not an anglophone any more than I was an American. I understood that I was a Quebecker – but what did that mean, to be 'a Quebecker'?"

Explicit descriptions of landscapes do not occur much in Turcotte's novels, and so I asked her if she regarded herself as writing out of a particular time and place or from some more universal position. Turcotte, gamine, scrunched up her forehead. Thought about it.

"When I'm writing," said Turcotte, "I feel as if I'm in my own house and removed from the world, but I still feel connected to it in some way."

"The house appears often," I said. "Are you aware of that?"

"I don't actually read myself much," said Turcotte, "so I have to rely on other people's views regarding the landscape of my stories, but people tell me that there is always a certain tension between the interior and exterior world in my work. Perhaps that explains the houses in my books. In *The Sound of Living Things*, the people live in a house, and are separated from the world, but all the chaos of the world outside enters their house anyway, through the television and the newspapers. That's the feeling that I have when I'm writing. I'm experiencing the solitude of the writer, so I'm outside the world – but I'm still open to it. I have a window, and I'm looking out on the people who are passing by. And in my last novel, *The Alienated House*, life simply cannot go on as it does, and my character Elizabeth has to find some way to be able to manage both her solitude and to show compassion towards the rest of the world. I suppose the question I am posing is, 'How can we live in a world which is so terrifying, and so threatening, and not feel guilty about it?' That's how I often feel myself, and all my characters are like that. We're caught between two worlds – and I find that to be true of Quebec's literature today. In a lot of recent novels, there is that same tension between all that we are experiencing inside ourselves, and events occurring in the outside world."

Turcotte was a sprightly figure, filled with sinewy and excitable energy, so that it was odd listening to her allude to doom in so many ways – to feel her so *afraid*. At times she was capable of sounding as filled with dread as the West Coast's Zsuzsi Gartner, though in a more poetic mode – proof of the universality of novelists' concerns, nonetheless, and of the greater world bearing down upon Quebec.

"Often I've tried to depict a world in a process of disappearing, and I've done so again in the novel I've just finished," said Turcotte.

"I'm not even saying this to be funny, but I suppose I believe that the feeling of our ultimately disappearing is one of the major themes in today's literature. There is a real feeling that humanity will just be done with one day – and the threat is constant. Nowadays, every-thing is so fragile, so fleeting. We read a lot of novels in which characters experience feelings of anxiety for no evident reason – I see as much in the work of a lot of today's young writers. This, I think, is a new development. There is a theme of disappearance that exists even more than the theme of death. There is a lot of *wander-ing* in these novels, and the atmosphere they convey is of a world of terrible fragility that has already started to flounder."

Turcotte sat back in the wooden bench, as if spent by the force of her own alarmed vision.

"I have these images of ships sinking, of all kinds of catastro-phes," she said.

From Élise Turcotte's *The Body's Place*:

It's over, she thinks.

She has put away her school books. Run a damp cloth over every piece of furniture. Now she is looking at her bedroom, satisfied.

Hélène likes things to be finished – a family supper, a month, a year. She likes the worst to be laid out behind her. Today, the worst was extinguished, along with the last hour of the last day of school.

Every piece of furniture, every object in her room repre-sents a part of herself, a clean, smooth section of what is in her soul.

The inside of her body must be like that: a square chamber containing invariable geometric forms. A bed, a chest of drawers, a bookcase. No dirt. Nothing glaring.

She runs her hand over her face, then along the full length of her body.

Is it me? Is it absolutely me?

She goes to the window, opens it, and leans outside to look at the river. After that, she turns her head towards the street.

It's such a small street.

If you look too quickly, you could misjudge and think that it's a street in a nearly dead neighbourhood, frozen in another time. You could imagine that everything is quiet and straightforward there, and filled with normal stories. A young girl could stop in front of the house and shout: Are you ready? Hélène could then hurtle down the stairs, go outside, and hop on her bicycle. But it's not that. Nothing is really joyous, and nothing has died yet. Everything is just a little bit missing, vanished, faded.

✧ ✧ ✧

ÉLISE TURCOTTE SUGGESTS that all novels are political if only "because life seeps through." Life does so via language, primarily. Alongside the fight against the English, and the Catholic Quebecker's own clergy, the great achievement of VLB's generation was to be able to stand up and reclaim as their own the French language as it was spoken in Quebec. Yet, much like the smoker who's still an addict because he can't ever risk having a puff, the generation of the Quiet Revolution remained beholden to the nemeses they fought so hard against. The young writers who followed in their steps were less antagonized. They were free to have *good* pastors for characters, to hang out at the Ritz and order an espresso and not *un espress*, and play with the language in any of its permutations and not just *joual*.

The proof of VLB's intolerant views concerning the purpose of fiction and its lack of present style lies in numerous places but specifically in the extraordinary work of the novelist Gaétan Soucy. Both language and religious ideas matter to Soucy, who also teaches philosophy, enormously. To my mind, Soucy was one of the most exciting writers working in Quebec, France, Canada – or anywhere, for that matter. In his slim, pitch-perfect novel *The Little Girl*

Who Was Too Fond of Matches, two children have grown up in utter isolation in the country with their father, deceased as the book opens. The result of their isolation, and proof of Soucy's own love of language, is that they are morally unanchored and speak a confusion of vocabulary ranging from what had been the demented father's expletives to arcane terms picked up from his library of old books. The historical and topographical setting of the novel is befuddling and mysterious. Place is archetypal, and something that "seeps through." Nothing is certain – to the pair of siblings, or to the reader – not even his characters' gender. I met Soucy at Byblos, a teashop in Montreal's Plateau district, and the sensation I had was that this confusion extended to his very sense of being, the man wondering if his aspiration to write was itself a fiction. Soucy's conversation was wrought, the torment of a Catholic philosopher at the confessional – another, evidently, who, like Turcotte, thought the world terrifying and felt guilty for living in it. It was affecting, this trepidation of such a highly intelligent man who, it probably was the case, needed to create some sort of obstacle – here the possibility of "writer's block" – in order to begin at all. Doubt is where the artist's true thinking starts and with Soucy, it had a sacred aspect.

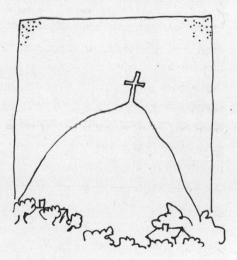

"I'm speaking off the top of my head," said Soucy, "but I think that what is manifested in my work is a basic culpability of existing – guilt really, a feeling of being ashamed. I suppose this is related to the idea of original sin, and of our need to *expiate* this sin in order to be saved. That's the reason why the idea of *le pardon* – forgiveness and the act of forgiving – is so important in everything I write.

In each of my four novels, there's that same theme of forgiveness. Often I wonder if, as a writer, I was not also trying to expiate the sin of existing myself."

Soucy drew deeply on his cigarette, put his elbows on the table, and rested his chin on his hands. He looked skyward, the answer possibly up there. The round face. The intense eyes and copious white hair casually flopped over to the side. Soucy was only in his late forties, was it deep thought or fright that had turned it that colour? The first time I met Soucy was in Turin. The two of us were part of a Canada Council delegation to the Northern Italian city's book fair. Gordon Platt, a bureaucrat, welcomed the writers over drinks in one of the meeting rooms of the hotel in which everyone had been billeted. Platt spoke. "Any questions?" he asked. The man across the room, the one with white hair, the round face and scrutinizing gaze, had been visibly pacing and now he could contain himself no longer. "*Ce que j'aimerais savoir,*" he said, "*c'est qu'est-ce qu'on fait içi?*" What did he mean by *ici*? Was that here in the room, in Italy, or in life? Later Soucy and I had a meal together. He was forthright and curious, one of those urgently inquisitive people incapable of having a flippant conversation. His tendency was to appear "nonplussed," as Dostoevsky's characters used to be described in the old Penguin translations I had read as a child. The novel, he told me, was beyond nations. Our politics are defined by the communities that we decide we belong to – the town, the province, the state, the family of man. Our sense of time is important too, he said. If we think in terms of the arc of humankind, I offered, then we are less likely to be upset by the rise and fall of governments – and Soucy, it was clear, was of this ilk, someone who measured even his agnostic objections against Catholic notions of eternity and absolutes. Truly, his struggle was Russian.

"Often we choose to believe that a novel offers some kind of truth about the world," said Soucy, "or that a book opens avenues to different ideas and so helps guide us. The novel clarifies the spaces that we live in – but I wonder if what a book also does is to reveal some idea of our shortcomings to ourselves. Surely, what is invaluable in a novel is that fiction makes errors explicit. It displays to each of us our false ideas about the world. And maybe we can learn something from these observations."

Soucy drank the rest of his red wine and offered me a cigarette.

"Every great writer – and I'm not saying that I'm one of them," he continued, "is a person who bears some sort of grievous failing that is presented in a novel. These false truths create a chasm between me and the world. I certainly don't believe that any of us needs to justify our existence philosophically, but I know that I'm writing in order to bridge this gap – and consequently I'm giving expression to whatever is that fundamental sin."

"Do you believe that fiction is essential?"

"*Mais*," said Soucy, "if you think about it, we're all living in a fiction already. We live in a world of the imagination. The relationship I have with my daughter belongs in that world. The relationship to my father is the same. The relationship to the woman I love and to my friends, these are all fictitious relationships. We can't come to terms with the worlds we live in without fiction because we're all *made* of fiction. The image is perhaps grotesque, but in my novel *Vaudeville*, the main character is made up of different fictitious parts, as Frankenstein's monster was. Our life is sewn up of different kinds of fabric, every stitch tangled up between them. What I believe is that the fiction we write or read or see on the movie screen helps us. It makes us aware of these fictitious relationships that we have with ourselves."

Soucy raised a hand to draw the attention of the waitress, and we ordered more wine. The café was filling up, noisy with Montrealers drinking tea, coffee, liquor, reading the day's papers and playing checkers and backgammon.

"Maybe it was wrong of me to have wanted to write," said Soucy wistfully. "It's delightful that my books sell, but they might just be different lies. I have to admit that I find the whole idea of being a writer less and less credible."

Then Soucy became morose. He confided that it was taking him a while to find a way in to his new novel and wondered if there was any real necessity for him to write any more. Eoin McNamee, a young and talented Northern Irish writer I used to know, was someone else I remembered meeting in this state – enervating for the writer, but illuminating for those in their company. The writer's angst can be intense, and often it takes its toll on the writer's loved ones. It expunges the bilious bad feeling and is cathartic for the writer who remains young because of this expulsion, while those around him age.

A young woman came into the teashop. Soucy gave her a bundle of keys. His marriage, he told me, had recently failed.

"I've been going through something of a crisis for the last couple of years," Soucy said. "It's been extremely stressful because all of my life I have been engaged in the idea of being a writer and now I feel less and less that I am one. I don't believe in what I do, and this is terrible – because now, at forty-six, I should be at the peak of my writing life. This is the time in which I should be most creative."

"What is stopping you?" I asked.

Soucy frowned again. Such trust. Such *interest* in the other, such impassioned curiosity, where VLB had none. So much more human, even his befuddlement.

"It's not a fear of language or even writer's block," said Soucy. "I just don't believe in *me* any more. The feeling is just not there."

"Perhaps writing is not appealing to you any more," I said.

"I would say that we are no more masters of our being writers than we are of our sexual orientation. The problem is that I just don't believe in the idea of my *own* writing any more. I'm a person who has a certain aptitude for happiness, but, at the same time, I feel a fundamental despair. Perhaps I have been expecting too much from literature. Basically, I have been asking it to save me."

Soucy offered me another cigarette. I ordered two more glasses of wine.

"Yes," he said, in a dialogue with himself. "I was expecting too much," he said.

Salvation is a tall order for any book, but Soucy understood the novel as a tool in the ontological business of existing, and there was merit in that. It could be argued that reading the novel is a luxury of peacetime, but that it rises to its greatest heights in times of conflict, when social tensions imbue it with higher purpose. In the consensual society, it flounders, as in South Africa *after* apartheid, in the Soviet Union *after* the fall of the Berlin Wall – or in Quebec *after* French Canadians won unassailable standing. But if the struggle is with the mystery of life itself, then the novel that addresses it cannot lose its vigour.

✧ ✧ ✧

"WE'RE TALKING ABOUT adversity," said Mauricio Segura. "Does a social situation of no conflict produce novels that are as urgent or as stimulating as they would be in a situation of civil war, for example? Well, I'm not sure. It could be said that in Quebec, or even in the whole of Canada, that by and large what we have is a literature of dull peace."

"Of a 'vast' landscape," said Bismuth, laughing softly.

"Of course," said Segura, "and if we want to make a caricature of it – well, like in Quebec, or Canada, *c'est beau*. It's *okay*."

"Do you ever, as writers, worry about keeping pace with the society around you?" I asked. "Our world is changing pretty quickly."

It was a point that the American critic and occasional novelist Walter Kirn had raised, having suggested that the uncanny pace of technological and social change in contemporary society meant that the novelist was better off conceding the "new" to the news.

"I'm connected to the world in my own way, with my own particular rhythms," said Vigneault. "Maybe one day I'll be told that what I am doing is outdated, and no doubt I'll be a little surprised, but it's not like I'm a computer scientist who needs to learn the latest version of Windows because otherwise he can't work. I'm a writer."

"Gaétan Soucy speaks of fiction guiding us," I said. "He says that it 'clarifies the spaces that we live in.'"

"I know what he means," said Vigneault. "I remember a university professor of mine once asked if I really needed to write, and the answer to that question is that I wouldn't go *crazy* – I wouldn't be miserable if I wasn't writing – but I would feel a certain lack of definition."

Segura appeared startled. "You can live without writing?" he said.

"It's a luxury," said Vigneault. "Yes, I could live without it."

"Really? You could live without writing." Segura had to digest the comment.

"Sure," said Vigneault. "I'm not a graphomaniac. My need to write comes from a sense of having to make order of my life, to specify things, to put words to things. It's a compulsion. It's like being a clean freak and needing to wash your hands eighteen times a day. If I see a particular kind of light, I think to myself how pleasing it would be if I could name it, if I could describe it – but, my God, I wouldn't die if I didn't. I would *die* if I had no water."

There was a silence around the table. Nobody was making a fortune. Segura had an infant child and Vigneault had started writing for television. Bismuth did not want him to lose his way – or not to be lost to the literary community, in any case. Youthful exuberance loses its energy, can be sapped by the necessities of the day to day. There is a graveyard of third novels by writers whom circumstance compelled to stop at two. For as long as one is responsible only to oneself, it is easier to entertain ideals about writing as art and questions about the political ends it can attain.

"How do you achieve the 'new'?" I asked.

"But we are, each one of us, 'new' already," said Vigneault. "I myself am a unique accident with my own perception of things, my own memories, my own life. Because of all that I am, the path that I take is going to be, by definition, unusual, and it will result in something peculiar. I don't feel the need to be original at any price. The novelty will come as long as I'm genuine, I would say."

"Writing reflects reality," said Bismuth. "We choose elements from it and create something 'new' in a character's point of view. Still, that doesn't mean a writer should be denied the right to revisit ideas or choose literary influences –"

"Absolutely," said Segura excitedly. "We're a community. We interact. There are bridges that span the spaces between us and so it's normal that we should influence each other's work. Myself, I am always taking things in – in movies and in books, in the news. All the time."

"It's what we *do* with the things we take in that makes the point of view new," said Bismuth.

✧ ✧ ✧

"'WHAT IS MY contribution as an author?'" VLB said, "or 'Am I providing something beyond what already exists?' are questions that, without a doubt, any author asks, even if a lot of them would prefer not to."

And then, the dogma again.

"I'm convinced," VLB continued, "that every author is writing a chapter that belongs to a great text that we could call a National Book. I'm in agreement with Jacques Godbout and Jacques Ferron on this score, both having said it before me. Naturally, there are some writers who will not have as big a part in this National Book because of their lack of curiosity or because they are not asking themselves the pertinent questions. For me, there are those who write – and then there are *authors*. The difference I see is that a writer scribbles a story, but an author creates a work of *art*. An author uses scope to add something new to what already exists. This is true for Quebec, as it is for the world in general, and if writers do not have such a goal in mind, then maybe these writers should be doing something else. They'll be happier, so will their readers be – and the culture will be much better off."

✧ ✧ ✧

"BUT IT'S A profession that's completely fortuitous," said Vigneault, laughing. "When I call it my job, it's always with the uncomfortable feeling that I'm telling a lie. It's not so much a job as it is a disposition that, with some luck, *transforms* itself into a profession."

"I'm not expecting the writer to behave as a journalist does," I said, "but I do think that *Côte-des-Nègres* was a novel of *témoignage*, Mauricio."

"But it's not *only* that," said Vigneault. "The book has other dimensions. It doesn't have a mandate."

"That's right," said Segura. "The writer has a certain responsibility to facts and to what's real, but I don't think that we are witnesses. I don't believe that we're in the business of having to write affidavits. We write *novels*. We're in the business of stimulating the imagination. That's what we do. We stimulate the imagination."

"If we decide to write," said Vigneault, "then we have to be convinced that our imagination is interesting and that it's interesting enough to invent something new."

"But VLB would like us to return to the novelty of the 1960s," said Segura. "He would like us to deconstruct the language – to write in *joual* and without commas."

"That's not new any more," said Bismuth. "It's been done."

"Well, there you go," said Vigneault. "*Voilà*."

From Guillaume Vigneault's *Necessary Betrayals*:

> There's nothing magic about takeoffs. You just give the plane her head, let her do what she was made to do. Other than compensating for her excesses, you let her be. The plane's speciality is generating lift, leaving the ground behind, climbing. That's its specialty.
>
> Landing is another matter. Landing is unnatural. Landing is like quitting – quitting in a calculated, preferably precise, delicate fashion – but quitting all the same. It's not just a question of flying slowly to an altitude-ground level of zero then turning off the ignition on touchdown: you would rebound, not a good idea. According to the rule book, landing is a question of getting the plane to fly level, ten centimetres above the ground, on the verge of stalling, then killing lift: betraying the plane's trust, her soul, in one sure, integral gesture. Landing is a betrayal. But with her tanks almost empty, the plane won't hold it against you for long. There are necessary betrayals.

I I

Home and Away

We manifest ourselves through stuff – the knick-knacks we collect, the cars we drive, the music that we listen to, and, if we're fortunate enough, the houses that we build. Go to Liberia and you'll see the mansions nineteenth-century freed slaves built in the style of the American plantation owners that once oppressed them. Travel to Montreal and you'll find houses that Scottish immigrants built in the fashion of Edinburgh's upper classes – society to which most of them were not admitted. In Vancouver, you'll find the same phenomenon of obsequious replication in the posh district of Shaughnessy, where the precedent is English, in the Tudor style.

Canada was a part of the British Empire, and then the Commonwealth. Why should this story of received ideas have been any different in this country than it was in India, during the Raj, Kenya, Trinidad, or New Zealand, for that matter? True, Canadians never bothered with cricket (those who have arrived here since, knowing how to play, are the characters of a different story), but we were exemplary colonial subjects in other ways. Even today, we seek approval from our past and present masters. The country's dwindling number of anglophiles want a nod at the club and Britain's cultural imprimatur: a Booker nomination, a review in the *Guardian*, or the *TLS*, an art competition as exciting as the Turner Prize, a pat on the head from the BBC or the LSE. Others, acting out old genuflectory habits in new guise, look to America's marketplace and its cultural arbiters for moral and economic vindication. So much of the political quarrel in Canada, a satellite still, has really been about which imperial arse to kiss – England's or America's? In today's globalized world, the class differences that Fred Stenson identified in the chasm between rural areas and the cities is replicated on the international stage. Canada is the country bumpkin. England and America are the metropolitan swells.

Of course, even recognizing the many ways in which this country behaved like a colony is an awkward first step. Stuff and those houses provide all sorts of clues. In Toronto, for so long the city that *wanted* to be British, some of the city's well-to-do even cultivated the accent – another accessory, another way to imitate the old masters. The architecture of the city contains a record of Canadian colonial servility – and not just in its civic and commercial buildings. Visit Wychwood Park, a salubrious housing estate situated in a leafy enclave in the city's west end, and you'll be reminded of the persistence of old colonial ties. I went there with Russell Smith. The *Globe and Mail* columnist, whose family moved from South Africa to Nova Scotia in the 1960s, was in his early forties, the author of a couple of collections of short stories and a novel that dealt with what it's like to be young and clubbing in Toronto. More recently, Smith wrote *Muriella Pent*, a rich and entertaining fictional satire of artsy Toronto society and the city's multicultural aspirations.

Muriella Pent is a decent woman, a widow not quite ready to retire or be retiring. She would like something interesting to happen in her life. A volunteer with the city's Action Council for the Arts, she offers to host a writer-in-residence. In the petty cultural politicking that ensues, the radical or perhaps merely dysfunctional council proves itself as parochial as the Residents Committee of Stillwood Park, the gated community in which Muriella lives – and with which she is at odds. The novel's Stillwood Park is modelled on Wychwood Park, an estate that once included Marshall McLuhan among its residents. Wychwood Park has a tennis court, a pond, lots of greenery, and many of Toronto's most distinctive homes.

"In the book," said Smith, "I have one of the older residents complaining about how the character of the park is changing. He hints heavily that it's because of all these new ethnic names coming in, like Shirley *Melnick* and Ralph *Poziarski* – new money, obviously – and that's why nobody's playing tennis as they used to or taking care of things like the goldfish or the swans."

"The place has a fantastically English air," I said.

"Yes, it does," said Smith. "I pictured the back of Muriella's house looking like this one here, with all its little leaded windows poking out from beneath the shingled mansard roofs, and with its fireplaces and turrets and balconies."

Marmaduke Matthews, a landscape painter in the employ of the CPR who purchased the land with a view to creating an artists' colony, founded Wychwood Park in the 1870s. He named it after Wychwood Forest, a park in the part of Oxfordshire, England, where he grew up. Wychwood Park has been designated an Ontario Heritage Conservation District, though an artists' colony it is no longer. The disparity between the original intentions of the estate and the reality of living in it provided Smith a lot of grist to play with in *Muriella Pent*. Lexuses, Mercedes, BMWs, and various SUVs parked in the driveways hint at the true nature of these houses' far-from bohemian ownership. Matthews's utopian exercise was doomed to fail just as the famous English experiment that inspired it had done.

"Many of these absurdly large mansions date from the 1890s," said Smith. "They were built in the Arts and Crafts style by a disciple of William Morris called Eden Smith. Morris was interested in neo-medievalism. Throughout the nineteenth century, there was a fixation in Britain with medieval architecture and medieval styles.

Here is Morris's disciple bringing to Canada a colonial copy of something that was already pastiche in the nineteenth century, so that what we have here is a twentieth-century copy of a copy." Smith chortled. "That strikes me as very Canadian."

"But it's not just the architecture that's English," I said. "As I walk through the estate, past chestnut trees, the leaves of which are twice the size of those in Cabbagetown, the once Irish part of Toronto I live in, it strikes me that this abundance of flora is the result of decades of imitations of English gardens."

"Someone's come and fixed this garden up. It used to be really quite rundown. Now it's a descending, tangled, leafy glade with terraces of flowerbeds and little grass patches at the bottom, such as I imagined belonging to Muriella. But you're right, there's none of this modern nonsense about using indigenous plants, no, sir. This has to be brought from the Old Country."

Somewhere near us, a gardener clacked a wooden gate shut.

"The park is all about English rural life being duplicated in downtown Toronto. The idea was for these houses to look cottagey – but *massive*," said Smith. "This was exactly the thing that William Morris was doing in Britain in the 1860s. Morris had this naive and very romantic notion of an organic rural life in which there would be little distinction between the lives of a peasant and of a wealthy middle-class person. The movement was doomed to fail because the only people who could afford his artisan-made work were extremely wealthy."

"I don't imagine there are any gentry mixing with peasantry in this particular enclave –"

"No, just as Morris's idea of the organic community was lost when they started, so is this now a very exclusive place for the elite. In fact, one of the things that fascinates me about this place is that very close to here – just a couple of blocks north – is a seedy strip of St. Clair that is a place of arrival for new Canadians from all over the world. We're not at all far from a Caribbean quarter that is the stomping ground for a lot of recent immigrants from the West

Indies. As a result, the park seems even more isolated and barricaded against the contemporary reality of Canadian life."

Muriella Pent is a portrait of a curmudgeonly artist and various sycophants and hangers-on, privileged and not, who see gains to be made in the lofty business of art. Muriella Pent dabbles at well-meaning but sentimental fiction of her own. She would like to be a bit closer to talent – and, frankly, someone interesting. When the Action Council for the Arts offers the post of writer-in-residence to Marcus Royston, a Caribbean poet, it is Muriella who provides lodging for him in tony Stillwood Park. Muriella's decision puts all sorts of comic shenanigans into play – some of them are sexual, there's a disastrous party, and plenty of opportunity for her Stillwood neighbours to snoop. One of the novel's wry turns is that Royston is hardly the young, dub-reciting rebel that the liberal arts council had imagined it was getting, but a cantankerous and culturally *conservative* poet of an older generation, whose caustic, tongue-in-cheek grant application wins over the council duped by their own parochial agenda. Royston knows a thing or two about Empire, more than the council ever will, and enough so that he recognizes the behaviour of a society that does not want or even know *how* to think of itself as having been colonized. When, early on in the novel, Muriella drives Royston to her home in Stillwood Park, she recounts the history of the estate in passing and describes one of the houses as "authentic."

"When you say 'authentic,'" says Royston, "what do you mean?"

"Royston is of mixed race and dark-skinned," said Smith, "and so he's very conscious of being from a colonial background. He comes to Canada and immediately starts seeing traces of the same colonial culture in which he was reared. He sees the military architecture, and he's fascinated by its resemblance to the British-built forts on his island. He sees neo-British architecture and is intrigued by it. He wants to talk to Canadians about their being colonial, but they're all shocked. They don't want to consider it. It's a very strange thing. It's a blank spot in our thinking that may exist because of our proximity to the United States. We believe that we're a lot like the Americans, but we're not."

Royston bears a certain moody resemblance to Derek Walcott, the St. Lucian poet who won the Nobel Prize for Literature in 1992. The verse Smith makes up for Royston is steeped in European classical references, even as it utters urgent cries on behalf of the colonized. A volume of Walcott's collected poems sat in the library of Smith's Toronto home alongside novels that gave away the South African provenance of his family, and that could not help but recognize the foibles of a previously colonized society.

"All white South Africans feel guilty about being from where they're from," said Smith, "and all of them feel a very conflicted relationship to what was their homeland. Some are very defiant about defining themselves as South African. In my family's case, my father wanted us to get away because there was a great deal of political strife and violence going on there, and so we ended up in Canada – with our funny accents and different cultural mores. We drank tea instead of coffee. We didn't know how to ski or skate. Although I feel Canadian now, and miss Canada very much when I'm abroad, I understand that feeling of always being a stranger no matter where you are. It is a typically colonial feeling that I wanted to exaggerate in the novel by embodying it in a person who is of such a mixed background and education that he doesn't really know where his greatest affinity lies, or even where home is. And Marcus, of course, surprises everybody because they are all expecting that they have brought a political writer from an underprivileged developing nation to this very prosperous place, and that he is going to be full of leftist rage and indignation. In fact, he turns out to be much *more* of an elitist, in so many ways, than they are. His education was much more British than a Canadian one was ever likely to be. He's steeped in history and classical mythology – and he's certainly more of a snob than any of the people hosting him are."

✧　✧　✧

EMPIRE AND ITS residue teaches all sorts of bad habits. The white Anglo-Saxon Protestant inhabitants of Smith's Stillwood Park, with their strangulated accents and their rules and their bewilderment that the times in Toronto are changing, insist on belonging to a class that once lorded it over them. Their assumptions about Toronto and their own legacy of entitlement are descended from the stranglehold that York's nineteenth-century Family Compact had on the land and legislature of the old Upper Canada in the half-century before Lord Durham's report of 1839. The Upper Canada Rebellion, and Baldwin's subsequent reforms of 1841, put the undemocratic power of these Ontario families in the shade, but the die had been cast. Even today, in Toronto, you can hear the names of the Family Compact whispered in the way that New England Americans might describe this or that person as being descended from the pilgrims of the *Mayflower*. Except that our brave forebears were a bunch of landed aristocrats and British stooges with only pilfering commitments to the place. As it is in Afghanistan, and was in Sicily after the Second World War, so it was here – the receding colonial power installs, in the country, those it is able to negotiate with: PLUS – people like us.

The mostly Anglican governing stratum was loyal to the monarchy and quite liked a class system and the social distinctions that went with it. York became Toronto, though unlike in Delhi, there was no *Times of Canada* in which young Canadians of the upper classes might solicit one another as the children of Hindu Brahmin families do with marriage notices, still published, in India's newspapers. Still, there are ways of sorting the wheat from the chaff. The Granite Club accepts Jews for members now, but it was not always thus, and a couple of Toronto's more exclusive schools still have lists at dances restricting colleges from which eligible dates may attend. And, of course, there have always been Balls and a selection of places in which to see and be seen. One spot that was popular in Toronto during the 1930s with businessmen and the "ladies who lunched" was the Arcadian Court, a splendid art deco dining hall that sat on top of the old Simpson's building, now The Bay, in the heart of the city's downtown. This was the era of Margaret Atwood's novel *The Blind Assassin*, in which labour unrest, the freedom of the motorcar, and the advent of the war in Europe augured tempestuous change for the book's well-to-do families. Iris Chase, sister-in-law to one of them, uses the Arcadian Court on occasion. It is a large, airy ballroom with the separate section of a mezzanine balcony, where, much like a segregated synagogue, the women sat apart. The Arcadian Court has high pillars, tall plants, and the cream colours and French-window motifs of an English Orangery. The day that Atwood and I had lunch there, a woman at the baby grand provided "piano stylings." The Court was not at all full, but the room was cavernous, so the murmur of voices and the sound of cutlery on plates carried far.

"If you were mingling with those kinds of people in the 1930s," said Atwood, "this is where you would have lunch. Toronto was very different then. It was quite stodgy."

"'Those kinds of people' being what?"

"The upper bourgeoisie," said Atwood. "There was a thin layer of aristocrats imported from England, but mostly people with money. There was a whole social system, and you can find it if you go back and look at newspapers, because there you will find all of the weddings, the engagements, the accounts of tea parties, the accounts of entertainments, the accounts of charity balls. Malabar, the costume place, got going at that time. It was where you could get your outfit for the costume ball – and they just *loved* giving costume balls in the 1920s and 1930s."

"There was a loyalty to Empire that operated with more strength here than in the rest of the country," I said, "and that made sense, I suppose, as this was the seat of the colony's financial administration."

"During the war that loyalty was very strong everywhere, except in Quebec, where conscription was not popular. Everybody was very into the Royal Visit. That was why we were in Canada, as far as I was concerned. We got to see the King and Queen, although that enthusiasm wasn't limited to people from a British background."

"I'm fascinated by the story of the Family Compact," I said. "Frankly, why it doesn't piss us off more."

"The original Family Compact," said Atwood, "was a beginning of the nineteenth-century, end of the eighteenth-century construction, and it went through various heights and reversals. It was originally Anglican, but it lingered on in various enclaves. The people who took them on were reformers who brought in the temperance movement and the idea of education for all. They were more democratically inclined. They wanted to spread the benefits and have a large supply of educated clerkish labour to keep the accounts. That was the struggle that went on in the nineteenth century, and by the time you get to the twentieth, there are still the old families, but it's not just they who are running things. The franchise had been extended, and as more and more immigrants came into the country, the old families lost power. They couldn't control the vote."

"Sometimes I wonder why it is that more novelists haven't taken the Compact on."

"Robertson Davies did," said Atwood, "and, to a certain extent, Timothy Findley did in some of his stories."

✧   ✧   ✧

"A NOVEL ABOUT the Family Compact? But they were so *boring*," the St. Catharines writer Richard Wright said. "Who could possibly want to write about Jarvis and Munroe and all those people?"

Wright's epistolary novel, *Clara Callan*, is, like *The Blind Assassin*, a story set in Ontario during the 1930s that also uses a pair of sisters to relate its story of imminent war and changing times.

"I think that one of my ancestors – a man named Nicholas Heggerman – belonged to that group of robber barons," said Wright. "There's a street named after him, right behind Toronto City Hall. The only time I ever touched on any of that was in my picaresque novel, *Farthing's Fortunes*, when Billy meets up with this rich young woman who happens to be crippled. He lives on Jarvis Street or on Sherbourne in the days when the fashionable people had their houses there. There's a lot in that book about Toronto and the poverty of the 1890s and how it ran on into the early years of the twentieth century. Talk about the homeless, now – *forget it!* Go back and see what had to be put up with then."

"But doesn't it stun you that the well-to-do in Toronto still refer to families as having been a part of the Compact, or even that schools and streets are named after them?"

"I suppose so," said Wright, one of the authors in Canada who writes most effectively about the white-collar workingman. "At Ridley, the private boarding school where I teach, there's a Gooderham House – named after the Gooderham of the distillery – and at Upper Canada College or at Trinity and Bishop Strachan you see the old names recurring all the time."

"They were the names of an entrenched aristocratic class."

"When I arrived in Toronto, in 1956, it was very much an Orange city," said Wright. "There were some good jazz clubs, but it really was very stuffy and constipated in those days. You had Rosedale, and you had Forest Hill. You had the merchant princes, and they were the people who controlled the city and went to Upper Canada College and to Havergal and Bishop Strachan and Ridley and Trinity. They belonged to the Granite Club, and emerging middle-class people went to the Boulevard Club."

Some of the mansions that the families built are still standing, though their fortune has been of varying degrees and reflects the expeditious priorities of the city they built. The Massey mansion on Jarvis Street – now a busy city avenue, once a handsome residential street lined with trees – is a Keg restaurant. The Gooderham home, north towards Bloor, was until recently Angelina's, another steak house. Another, once the home of Sir Oliver Mowat, a former Ontario premier, is a part of the glass front of the National Ballet School. Other mansions, on Jarvis and Sherbourne, are boarded up, or boarding people, and waiting for the day when their decrepitude means that preservation orders will be impractical and developers can build more of the drab high-rises that dwarf these historic roads now.

In Toronto, the souvenirs of history do not count for much.

On nearby Parliament Street is the site of Upper Canada's first legislature, sacked in 1813 by the USAmericans. It lies beneath a Porsche dealership and a car rental agency. Somewhere, apparently, a plaque marks the spot. Toronto society has always been more complex than that of towns and settlements more visibly in the grip of the Hudson's Bay and other powers, but the lesson is the same. Citizens turn to storytellers to resuscitate their history because few businessmen and politicians are interested.

Beyond the streets where the mansions of the Family Compact crumble was another Toronto of slums, hotels, and rooming houses that flourished through the turn of the first half of the twentieth century – a period that is occasionally described, in neighbouring USAmerica, as "The Age of the Bachelor." The rooming houses were the emblem of a Presbyterian culture in which itinerant workingmen came to Toronto to see how their fortunes unfolded. In Wright's *Final Things*, Charlie Ferris is on the slide, and one day his twelve-year-old son, Jonathan, goes missing, allowing Wright the opportunity to investigate streets and the people Ferris and the boy would have known.

"Charlie is a sportswriter," Wright said. "Early on, he's separated from his wife, and the boy's going to a boarding school. Ferris wants him to see another side of life – it was a way of getting back at his wife too, for being such a snob. He takes Jonathan to Allan Gardens, on Carlton between Yonge Street and Cabbagetown. I had always loved Allan Gardens because you used to have a few older, more refined ladies who were seeing out their last years in apartments on Carlton Street, and there was the conservatory, of course, where you could go in and see all these lovely flowers in the middle of winter. But there was such a mix there. Because of the rooming houses and old hotels, you could live fairly cheaply. I wanted Charlie in a seedy but not totally decrepit building, and I found one just north of Carlton off Sherbourne. Mind you, there were also respectable people living in those places, guys who were called 'old shoehorns.' They didn't make much money, working in the shoe department of Eaton's or Simpson's – hence the name. They lived over in places like that. Bachelors."

"What happened to the rooming houses?"

"They were going out by the early 1960s," Wright said. "People had more money. The wages were better and apartment building was going on. Workingmen could afford to move into Rosedale, where the townhouses were mostly split into apartments. I took my first apartment in Toronto in 1964. It was on Rose Avenue, tucked in behind Bloor and Sherbourne. It was a brand-new building and it was just great. From there, I would go over to St. George Street, Huron Street – the rooming houses in those places were all gone by the early 1960s. My God, I wonder what the cost of a house would be there now."

Wright shook his head in disbelief.

"I was born towards the end of the 1930s – but the 1930s hung on. In those days, things just didn't change as much. A house looked much the same in 1946 as it did in 1936 because of the war, and because there weren't as many goods on the market. Even growing up in the 1940s, I was surrounded by the 1930s. I would hear the stories of the awful times that people had, so that the earlier decade was all still there with me, right through the 1950s."

In Vancouver, the house is a place that was previously occupied, and in Quebec a defence against what threatened from outside. On the prairie, an absence of opportunity meant that the house was falling down. And, in stories from one end of the country to the other, the house is a repository of memories that reach back generations – a vessel of stories gathering in a country that is often amazed that it has any history at all. But the thing about the rooming house is that it is not a house at all. It's a *room*. There is not even the pretence of occupation. Possessions are few, and what history there is in it is denied by the rules of the establishment posted in the corridors and the impossibility of storing much that is not essential. The city can be such a damning place and often crushes those who come to it. In Alistair MacLeod's novel *No Great Mischief*, Alexander MacDonald takes his older brother, Calum, out of a shoddy Toronto rooming house and back to Cape Breton, where his home and history are. If you were from the Caribbean, as novelist Austin Clarke's boarders are, there was no such option.

✧ ✧ ✧

"THE ROOMING HOUSE," said Clarke, "was my first habitation. It provided a sense of community and, at the same time, a sense of isolation. I would say that my characters in rooming houses were stunted people – people of no hope, people who are judging the society based only on casual encounters with people they meet going downstairs and on the way to the bathroom."

Clarke and I met at the bar of the Grand Hotel on Jarvis Street. He had forgone his penchant for three-piece wool suits and was instead dressed casually – in a denim shirt, his silver-tinged hair twisted into short dreadlocks. He was a regular here, and clearly in his element. The bartender knew him, and so did the maître d'. So did a woman from a Caribbean embassy whom he crossed the floor to greet with outré nineteenth-century charm – a bow, a kiss of the hand. Then back to his martinis. Clarke arrived in Canada from Barbados, where he had been a student at prestigious Harrison College. He came to Toronto in 1955 to attend university and became an acute observer of West Indian society in the city. In a lot of his early short stories, conflict arises from the gulf between life as it was in the new world of Toronto and life as his landed Caribbean immigrants imagined it would be, given that they were playing by the rules – acquiring the car, the bank account, the new suit.

"Commanding the rooming houses," said Clarke, "was always the immigrant's wife imposing her rules of morality on the people who lived in them – one bath on Fridays, no women in the rooms, and no food cooked of a pungent nature. You had certain freedoms, but your freedoms could not compete with the lifestyle of the land-lady, so that the apartment gave you back your freedom. It was as if you were put in solitary confinement, but it was a very happy experience in another sense. In the rooming house somebody would say, 'Oh, I just got a job and the boss is looking for other people.' You had a lot more reliable information from women that you were seeing at the washing machine, or at the table that was shared in the kitchen, whereas in the apartment you had greater freedom but you were cut off from information that might be helpful. Lots of people in rooming houses ended up getting married, especially in the 1950s and 1960s."

The city Clarke arrived in was Toronto the Good, where the Family Compact was history but its habits were not. It was a town of anglophilia and "bluebloods," in which it was (and is) still possible to speak of "Massey Culture." The city, as Clarke remembered it, had not exactly been welcoming.

"I was not shocked in my effort to be integrated into Canadian society," said Clarke. "Of course, it is more proper to speak of *Toronto* society, as even then Toronto took itself very seriously, and considered itself the centre of *Canadian* society. The colonial experience in Barbados gave me a sufficiently broad education, but I was completely lost when I came here, not having a history of knick-knacks or of little framed pictures that would allow me to trace my ancestry and say, *This is me at the cottage.* So I realized a great, serious bout of rootlessness. It was a tremendous burden that took me years to overcome. I was rudderless and did not know how to stop the drift, or how to let the drift take me someplace. This was caused by my sudden possession of freedom. Here I was, at nine o'clock every morning of the week, dressed in a jacket, trousers, and waistcoat – but with no place to go."

Who, I wondered, would tell Austin Clarke and Russell Smith just how much the black man from Barbados and the white man from South Africa had in common? Clarke would have understood Smith's disgruntled poet, Marcus Royston, each without quite the right trinkets and customs that say, *We belong*. In so many of Clarke's early stories, his characters are struggling to assert their place in the newfound country. Some are broken by the effort, others become dandies turned inside out by customs they believe might help them belong.

"Barbados was a very structured society," Clarke said. "At Harrison College, it was understood very quickly that one could not go out with a girl unless she was from a particular school. A person without success in the new country would go back to the idea that he had been to Harrison College. He would depend on this history of pedigree in precisely the same mean-spirited way that the English had used theirs against him in Barbados, and this would have brought about depression. When such a boy came to Toronto, he looked for people of the same social class – in other words, someone who had come from a high school like his own. This made sense in Barbados, where there were hundreds of such people, but not in Toronto, where, out of loneliness, women chose men they would not have settled with in any circumstances back home. So he would live in a world of double indemnity, because his status was just not measured as it was in the old society. It was measured in how great was his bank account or his car."

"Why do you think it is that we write so few explicitly political novels in English Canada?" I asked.

"Perhaps we do, but do so not always understanding the meaning of politics. If I write a sentence in a short story – let's assume that it's a West Indian talking – that says, 'It is damn cold outside, it is dark when I wake up, it's dark when I come home,' then you should realize that it's a political statement that the character is making. He is expressing bitterness, anger, and frustration about the two lives that he is living. Once, he was in the warmth of the Caribbean. Now he is enduring the cold, and that this cold is associated with the temperate countries of the First World and its apples and grapes, and not the warm climate of mangoes and swordfish that he knew. This is a political statement, and if writers do not understand that, then these writers do not have a political consciousness."

The bartender replenished our drinks. On the television above the bar, a news item featuring Perdita Felicien played. The hurdles runner from Pickering, Ontario, had been a favourite at the Athens Olympics, but crashed to spectacular, awful defeat and now the footage was being broadcast for the umpteenth time that summer. I reminded Clarke that in the Kenyan novelist Ngũgĩ wa Thiong'o's masterpiece, *A Grain of Wheat*, the athletic race that ends the novel is an allegory for the beginning of his country's adventure of independence. Clarke looked up and watched the news item. "When I was in Barbados," he said, "I ran a race in my last year at high school that I had to win. I could not come second. I thought I could win, even though I was up against a conspiracy of pace setters from other schools. I made my move and for five minutes nobody could catch me, but then I saw another runner over my shoulder and I panicked. I am saying this because I do not accept Felicien's explanation that she does not understand what happened. I believe that she was overwhelmed by the responsibility that was put on her shoulders, and I wonder why she did not adopt another strategy and hide herself at the start."

"The pressure of racing, not the race itself, is what you think made her stumble?"

Clarke lifted his glass and swallowed the last of his drink.

"Come on, Richler. I'll feed you some of my plantain and fish. What do you say?"

◇ ◇ ◇

WE WALKED THROUGH the parking lot behind the Grand out onto Shuter Street towards Moss Park. This, in Hugh Garner's day, had been Cabbagetown proper, but the district was levelled in the 1950s to make way for the housing developments of Regent Park. High hopes were held for the residents of these mostly four- or five-storey apartment buildings that replaced the slums and rooming houses of the old Irish working-class district. A better life was in the offing. The housing blocks were surrounded by green spaces and divided by dead-end streets that would, it had not been anticipated, end up isolating the area and make it a den of crime. Clarke lived across from its southwestern edge, the other side of the street from the high apartment towers of Moss Park. His was one of the few remaining Victorian homes on the block. The houses in his row had bars on their windows, a curious *oubliette* in a rough, changing downtown. Inside, Clarke prepared a couple of plates of akee and ushered me towards a couch and coffee table between walls of bookshelves painted black. The phone rang and Clarke excused himself.

"I'm sorry," he said, "that was a call from London – Ontario."

Clarke chuckled.

"Interesting that we have to say 'London, *Ontario*' in this country," he said.

Literary magazines were scattered on the coffee table and on the floor. Neither was there any shortage of knick-knacks – photographs, awards, posters, first editions of his books. Finally, Clarke had the stuff. In his early stories, and in the upstairs-downstairs atmosphere of his "Toronto Trilogy" of novels – *The Meeting Point, Storm of Fortune*, and *The Bigger Light* – stuff counts for a lot. Clarke's Toronto is mostly written from the point of view of an underprivileged black class that lives either in rooming houses, far from the mansions of Rosedale and Forest Hill, or in those mansions but down the stairs. What Clarke was interested in, then, was how the pressures and disappointments of trying to be a success in the new society affected his characters' behaviour towards themselves. In some of his best stories – such as "Griff," "Canadian Experience," or in *The Meeting Point*, where poor Henry adds a zero to the balance in his savings book and, he figures, much-needed status in so doing. Clarke's characters are wont to put the colonizers' ways before those of their own oppressed blackness. Some put a nearly impossible emphasis on the suit, the bank account, the automobile and the woman – as Calvin does in "The Motor Car," proudly taking the white lady out for a drive on the Don Valley Parkway in his shining new vehicle. Stuff makes belonging. Stuff proves the man.

From Austin Clarke's "The Motor Car":

> But Calvin gone up Danforth with new motor car and white
> woman beside o' him, like if he going to a funeral – "Got to
> break she in gently, man" – and the Canadian thing not too
> please that Calvin didn' listen to her advice as a woman
> should advise a man, and buy the Cadillac; but she still please
> and proud that Calvin get the Galaxie. She sitting in it like if
> she belong there by birth. And Calvin don't really mind, 'cause
> he have the car, and it driving like oil 'pon a tar road back
> home. He make a thing along Danforth as far as Bloor, turn
> 'pon Yonge and tack-back as far as Harbord – the intinerry
> ain' exactly as he first think it out, but it would do – make a
> thing along Harbord and meet up with Spadina, and continue
> according to plan. And in all this time so, not *one* blasted West
> Indian or black person in sight to look at Calvin new car and
> make a thing with his head, or laugh, or wave. When he make
> a right 'pon College at the corner o' Spadina, a woman with a
> bag mark HONEST ED'S start walking through the green light,
> drop a tomato, stannup in the middle of the road and bend
> down to pick it up, and Calvin now, whether he looking for the
> woman tomato or he looking the wrong way, nearly run over
> she. Jesus Christ! *Blam!* Brakes on. The Canadian thing nearly
> break she blasted neck 'gainst the windshield. Calvin rattle
> bad like a snake. Police come. Police look inside the car.
> Police see Calvin. Police turn he eyes 'pon the Canadian thing,
> who now frighten as hell, and the Police say, "Okay, move
> along now, buster!"

"The thing about possessions," said Clarke, "is that you are successfully an owner of material things only if people recognize them
as your precious possessions, and what really disillusions Calvin is
that when he brings home the new car, nobody is there to see him
exude his pride of ownership. I remember that when I wrote the
story I was living on Brunswick Avenue. My study was in the front

room on the first floor, so I could see everything, and there were two Jamaicans who had just bought two new cars. The cars arrived on a Thursday, and Friday, Saturday, and Sunday, they were under the cars, repairing them. And I said to myself, What are they doing? You don't have to repair a new car! They were exuding the spirit of possession – and, of course, that kind of ownership is only significant if people are aware that you have a new car or if they are conscious that you have a new suit to wear on Friday nights or Saturday nights. Calvin is robbed of that, and in the same way he is robbed of his ambition –"

"The woman whom he is driving in the car dies. She's a white woman who sings calypso, and that offends him."

"Calvin is a man who wants it known that the woman he's going out with is sophisticated," said Clarke, "only she can't be *too* sophisticated. It is not cool that his woman not only sings calypsos, but that she knows the lyrics to this particular calypso, that has a very obvious sexual connotation."

"So singing it destroys the idea that she has any class. Is that what bothers Calvin?"

"Yes. Of course, this is presumption on his part. It's a very unfair way of judging character, but he is doomed to behave the way he does, because of a colonial upbringing that does not allow for any freshness of thought. It has applied on the psyche of the colonized person a severe and almost suicidal conservatism."

◇　◇　◇

CALVIN'S CAR, that consummate bit of stuff, was a symbol of material change, of getting ahead, and of a sometimes reckless life spiralling out of control. It was a literary vehicle that Austin Clarke used as effectively as F. Scott Fitzgerald had done and that Richard Wright used too. In *Clara Callan*, the train trips Clara takes to Toronto from her small Ontario hometown put the affair she's having in danger of discovery. In his later novel *Adultery*, set in contemporary times, Wright provides his lead a car and the possibility of sex and secrecy.

"One of the great contributions of the automobile, for good or ill," said Wright, "was the creation of *privacy*. The privacy to go somewhere on your own without anybody knowing where you're going. The privacy to make love. The car revolutionized sex, I think, particularly in the 1930s and 1940s."

Wright's adulterer is discovered, the woman's murder an unforeseen corollary event that puts his affair under the glare of the media's bright lights. Still, all things considered, the car was an improvement on Clara's 1930s situation, that staid decade desperate for social liberties. In New York, at the end of it, the 1939 World's Fair offered a vision of progress through technology, its promise cruelly and ironically vindicated by the coming war.

"What a wonderful thing the World's Fair was!" said Wright, who declared that he'd been reading a terrific book about it. "The fair was a celebration of progress, the last summer before the war, a magical time for people to see these wonders of technology – televisions, radios, refrigerators – which had been around, but not everybody had them. That to me was the marvellous thing about the 1930s. We're all into the Internet now, but the really big, big, technological changes occurred in the first fifty years of the last century."

✧   ✧   ✧

IN TORONTO, BARRY Callaghan, son of Morley, was one of those keen to chronicle the city in its new variety. His family lived for a while on Walmer Road, in what was then the working-class district of the Annex. The family's was a "railroad apartment" – so named because the rooms were all appended off one long corridor, front to back, like berths in a railway carriage. The city in which Callaghan was born, in 1937, had been the uniform place of which Wright had complained. There was a mix of classes, and faiths, but not many ethnicities. There were Chinese and Catholics and Italians in his Annex neighbourhood, and Jews near the Christie Pits. The riot that took place there after a baseball game in 1933 has since become fodder for novels by Lauren B. Davis, Karen X. Tulchinsky, and Steven Hayward. There were the seeds of change, but the city was still waiting to be squeezed out of its straitjacket of conformity. That change would occur with the 1960s but, for the time being, there was still no shopping on Sundays in Toronto, there were curtains drawn on the mannequins in the window displays at Eaton's, and there was certainly no public drinking. Callaghan, however, was enamoured of the blues, and as the author of *The Black Queen Stories*, he wrote portraits of a variety of underground-city characters – hookers, tailors, reverends, gamblers, and failed blues singers – with the cumulative effect of identifying a city with the augmenting ties to the United States that soul music offered. At the junction of College and Spadina, as Callaghan remembers it, there was a sprouting of nightclubs that were the first port of call, in Toronto the Good, for musicians and the changes they brought. Today, streetcars trundle and screech noisily down the middle of the avenue, and computer shops and fast-food joints have sprouted beside the low-rent lawyers' offices at this high end of the street. A city, as it grows, becomes several things.

"The cars would angle-park, and in the space between the cars all the bookies would do their stuff," said Callaghan, the two of us standing on the noisy corner. "There was a poolroom near here and there was the Show Bar in the Waverly Hotel. The bars would close at eleven or sometimes twelve – always by one – so that life in the wee hours of the morning was hard to find. If you knew the right people, you could get whisky in a teapot in parts of Chinatown. There were after-hour joints around here. They were illegal, of course, but they were here and everybody knew they were here, including the police."

From Barry Callaghan's "Crow Jane's Blues":

> Crow Jane, who was a singer in the local after-hour clubs, was walking down Spadina Avenue, her hands in her pockets. There were chrome studs on the lapels and cuffs of her jeans jacket. It was nearly midnight but there were five bandy-legged boys playing stickball on the sidewalk in front of the Silver Dollar Show Bar and across the street, in the doorway

beside the Crescent Lunch, some immigrant women, probably cleaning-women, were huddled around a homeland newspaper. Their warm laughter touched the loneliness that Crow Jane had felt all week, a loneliness that left her with a listless sense of loss, but she wasn't sure about loss of what, and that was why she was out walking her old haunts, looking into the show bars from the old days, threading her way through the late night street hustlers who were standing half out in the street between the parked cars, and for a moment she felt good, seeing herself years ago the way she used to slow-walk down the street knowing where everything was, the upstairs bootlegger who kept the beautiful Chinese twin sister hookers who put on a show every midnight, and over on Augusta Street, behind the fruit stalls, there was heavy-jowled Lambchops, the Polish-Jewish giant who hired himself out as muscle to the after-hour clubs.

"Great street, eh?" said Callaghan, laughing as a police cruiser cut around the corner with its lights flashing and siren wailing. A couple of pedestrians jumped back up onto the curb as a souped-up purple Honda with a tailfin and blackened windows took advantage of the cruiser's wake and accelerated through the traffic.

"On this corner, there used to be a little guy named Charlie Carter, who died of a heroin overdose," said Callaghan. "He would see me coming and would do that walk toward me, what they call 'pimp walking' now – that walk with the little hitch in the hip. He would come walking at me with his hand out and say, '*I'm cool as the breeze on Lake Louise 'cause I ain't no square from Delaware. I got lard in my hair. Give me five on one 'cause the other four are sore.*' The 'five on one' was a signal to attach your thumbs together. That was shaking hands. All that signifying was a part of the images and rhythms that were coming into this world. For Toronto, Spadina was a very wide avenue indeed."

◇　◇　◇

IN TORONTO OF the early 1960s, the old social ties to Britain persisted, as well as certain habits of class, but out of sight of the Presbyterian version of Toronto that Atwood and Wright were chronicling, the city was being changed by these tides of influence from the United States and the West Indies, in particular. The fight for civil rights, in USAmerica, meant that the Underground Railroad had never been completely retired, the novelist Lawrence Hill's family just one that rode it. In the United Kingdom, the racial tensions that prompted the Conservative MP Enoch Powell to warn Parliament, in April 1968, of "rivers of blood" were the immigration of coloured people from the former colonies not halted, had the effect of diverting many West Indian and Commonwealth emigrants to Canada instead. People's aspirations, the way they dressed and spoke, the music they listened to, were changing. In the third novel of Clarke's Toronto trilogy, *The Meeting Point*, there is a telltale moment in which Estelle visits a coffee shop in Yorkville, and Clarke is able to use the fabled hippie strip to mark the city's evolution into something more polyglot. Nightclubs paved the way for not just music but also ideas travelling from the United States into Canada, this ebullience one of a series of phenomena undermining the old status quo and fundamentally altering the character of the country. During the 1960s, Canada's long-ingrained deference to Britain was eroded, as a series of geopolitical events, at home and abroad, shocked the country into occupying its proper position on this continent. The rapid-fire sequence of the civil rights movement, the Cuban Missile Crisis, and then the war in Vietnam coincided with Diefenbaker's nuclear recalcitrance and the Quiet Revolution in Quebec to force Canadians' attention upon their own geographical position in North America and away from the old colonial relationship – one that had already been diminished by the deleterious effect of the Second World War on Britain's economy.

The poet and novelist George Elliott Clarke, who was living in Toronto when I met him, grew up in Three Mile Plains, outside Windsor, Nova Scotia. His father was a self-made man who drove a taxi in the last years of his life and who was renowned for his reading knowledge and for providing local historical tips to his customers, two discreet reasons why his son might have written *George and Rue*. The novel tells the story of the murder of a New Brunswick taxi driver in 1949 by two alienated Africadians, George and Rufus Hamilton – whom Clarke discovered to be his mother's cousins. One of them needs money to pay a doctor and get his wife and child out of hospital. Clarke, who has made it his work's calling to bring attention to the ways in which Canadians were not exemplary with regards to race, will remind you that slavery existed in Canada; that Angélique, a black slavewoman in Montreal, was cruelly scapegoated, tortured, and executed in 1734; or that Viola Desmond, a black woman, was ejected from a movie house in Nova Scotia as recently as 1946. The argument for universal health care was advanced, in Canada, partly as a consequence of the Hamiltons' case.

Clarke is part Mi'kmaq but also of United Empire Loyalist stock. His activism was learned from the United States, which is why he chose to teach there for a time, though while at Duke University he learned that Africadians are as invisible in the eyes of African-Americans as Canadians are to USAmericans generally. So much for *North American* "négritude."

Clarke has a wonderfully ebullient manner when he speaks, as if his excitement cannot be contained. There's no dour fight for survival going on in this writer's psyche. The lush cornucopia of the Annapolis Valley, not the hard rock of Al Purdy's Belleville, explains his heady, even *lusty* ideas about Canada. Attitudes he learned from the music he listened to. As a Haligonian schoolboy, the competing loyalties Clarke knew to monarchy and to Detroit were communicated on the radio.

"It was a frustrating time because one was always being pulled in different directions," said Clarke. "For example, I can remember the Queen's birthday. When I was a kid in primary school in the 1960s, the Queen would make an announcement, and it would be played on the radio and over the school's PA system. All us kids would wait expectantly for the moment when the Queen would say, 'And now you have the rest of the day off from school.' *The Queen!*

Queen Elizabeth coming over our school PA system, right? And we're saying 'Yeah!' We wanted to throw our books up in the air, and out the door we would go because the Queen just gave us the day off. The Union Jack and the Queen's picture were still in our classrooms, although the maple leaf flag was there too. So on the one hand, there was still this very pro-British orientation, but at the same time, we would turn on the radio, and, okay, the Beatles are there – there's a little influence of the British Invasion – but that's where we're getting our Motown, our James Brown, and frankly that seems a lot more real and a lot closer to us. That was the sort of bifurcation that took place. We had one foot in the English Channel and another foot in the Mississippi or maybe the Detroit River or maybe New York Harbor. These American – and specifically these *African*-American – influences were critical, and the phenomenon was reinforced by the arrival of Americans in Halifax. They were draft resisters, people going to art school, and even some civil rights movement traffic. In fact, one way I would characterize the time was that, in the nineteenth century, the most important voyage taken by a black Nova Scotian was by Richard Preston to England to be ordained as a Baptist minister. He came back to Nova Scotia and created the African Baptist Church, the distinctive church of black Nova Scotians. But in the 1960s, the most important trip taken by a black Nova Scotian was probably that of Burnley Rocky Jones, who leaves Truro, Nova Scotia, and goes to Mississippi to work with Dr. Martin Luther King. And *then*, when he comes back to Nova Scotia, he is not ready to be conservative. He is not ready to say, 'Okay, we'll just take it easy and take it slowly.' No. He wants change – and like *that*. Instantly. And so the radical 1960s came to Nova Scotia via Mississippi."

✧ ✧ ✧

OCCURRING AGAINST THE background of the American civil rights movement, the Cuban Missile Crisis of October 1962 was the second of a sequence of geopolitical events that compelled the Canadian psyche into occupying its proper position in the continent of North

America, if only because of the threat of errant missiles overhead. The first novel Richard Wright wrote, *The Weekend Man*, in 1978, confronted the tension of the time directly. It is a pithy, quite wonderful story of a city on the cusp of an unfathomable new age with which Wright's alienated hero, Wes Wakeham, cannot quite come to terms. Wes keeps a "Holocaust bottle" – the whisky he bought on October 24, 1962, the day President John F. Kennedy declared "Defense Condition 2." DEFCON 2 put North America one level of military urgency away from all-out war, and Wes remembers all the mundane details associated with that moment. He struggles for feeling, knows it best when he's at odds with the world – at the publishing house where he works, or in bed. No longer was the war, or what we have come to call the "theatre" of war, far away. Wright grew up in Midland, Ontario, a mill and boat-building port on Georgian Bay that, from the 1920s through the 1960s, was a dry community, the town fathers worried about the ills booze caused. Perhaps for this reason, lovemaking often has a slightly shameful, puritanical air in Wright's novels. Sex, of course, has always enjoyed a leading role in dramas of the apocalypse, and, in the 1960s, the sexual liberation movement was inextricably tied up with America's involvement with the war in Vietnam. It had its seed in scenes of sexual candour and barely containable tension such as Wright wrote in *The Weekend Man*:

> "What makes you happy?"
> "I'm happy enough here."
> "Are you though?"
> "Yes."
> We embrace once more and stroke each other. Helen is suddenly tender again and touches me lightly on the organ.
> "Do you like that?"
> "Yes."
> "How much?"
> "Quite a bit."
> "I want to kiss it."

"Dear God, yes . . ."

"Now . . . I want to kiss it now."

To each his own is what I say and, dear Helen Corbett, with your wild nervous mouth all over me I can only say thanks a million. This is a treat. Molly doesn't like to do this even when her own admirable thighs are crushing my ears. Molly is a selfish person. But then so am I. We suit each other that way. Helen Corbett is a mass of dark hair over my groin. Who would have thought it?

Helen Corbett wants to be happy. Everyone in the land wants to be happy. It's a national goal. The Americans even write it into their constitution – life, liberty and the pursuit of happiness. It's a right bestowed on all; rich man, poor man, beggar man, thief, black man, yellow man, Indian chief. Give me my portion of happiness you son of a bitch or I'll smack you in the mouth. I demand my rights. The only problem is that it's making everyone miserable. Right now – I can only ask that this simple honest muscle in my chest keep working, as dear Helen Corbett transports me to pleasures too rich for the longing, too deep for the telling.

✧ ✧ ✧

"You GREW UP with the idea of all this violence and the prospect of sudden annihilation," said Wright, "and the sense that the whole thing could just go *whoosh*! The Americans were the good guys, the Russians were the bad guys, and the Chinese were coming up fast on the outside, and they were going to have the bomb too. This was really scary stuff. It was as close to hysteria as you would have got back then, though it's nothing like what you're getting today – and then as now, the English had much more sang-froid about it all and were much more laidback. The blitz was only fifteen years behind them, and I remember talking to an old RAF guy who really calmed me down. He said, 'Ah, don't worry. The Russians will back down. Kennedy's got them by the short and curlies, it'll all pass over.' I thought, This guy's been through the mill a few times, so I'm going to pay attention. And, of course, it did, but that was a pivotal moment. All that 1950s stuff, all that *Reader's Digest* stuff, all that House Un-American Activities – the McCarthyism – was still going on, but it was the climax of the whole Cold War for me, and I had to put all that in *The Weekend Man* because it affects the way Wes looks at everything. He's an existentialist. He's thinking, 'What are all these people worried about buying Christmas presents for? We're on a knife-edge.'"

Cold War fear thrust Canadians' attention upon the space in which they were living, but also reinforced that old sense of living at the margins, what with Diefenbaker and his Conservative government having embarked on a non-nuclear path. A feeling of helplessness was a symptom of the times, of course, but the suspicion – the *knowledge* – that one was living on the edge of something bigger has always been a bulwark idea in the national psyche. Now the power that was on people's minds was America's, the new distant authority in politics as it had become in the marketplace. Even the idea of the infinite north as the fount of national identity was formulated, in large part, to countenance anxieties about the sleeping giant to the south – a power that would make up its mind and not be influenced.

One of the best Canadian novels about the early 1960s, Ann-Marie MacDonald's *The Way the Crow Flies*, pays due attention to the country's shifting political allegiances. It captures both the existential fright of the period and its material optimism. The picture it paints of a hopeful society of ice creams and sound futures and white-picket fences is also one of fear and betrayal, the portrait of a country coming to terms with the fierce contradictions of the Cold War and Canada's changing role in it. Madeleine, the child at the core of MacDonald's novel, is molested by the teacher that should protect her. Ricky, the Métis child accused of a young girl's rape and murder, is betrayed by the silence of Madeleine's well-meaning father, Jack, an RCAF officer who might have provided the boy an alibi but who is charged instead with protecting a former Nazi scientist. Jack, in turn, is let down by no one less than

Canada's prime minister, what with Diefenbaker having refused to allow the Americans to arm their missiles in Canada with nuclear warheads in response to the showdown with Russia. Even the corn in the fields around Centralia, where Madeleine's school friend Claire is found raped and murdered, is an emblem of priapic double meaning, the poor child having a cob of corn thrust up her before she is murdered not by Ricky, but by girls. (The book was partly inspired by the alleged wrongful conviction in 1959 of Steven Truscott, then a teenager, for the murder of twelve-year-old Lynne Harper.)

No novel is written in a temporal vacuum. The government's retreat from the nuclear stage, as MacDonald portrays it, can be read as a comment on the current debate about Canada's commitment to its Armed Forces. The mess-hall banter from *The Way the Crow Flies* might have been uttered in Canada any time after 9/11, or in relation to the war in Afghanistan in which Canada is now a player.

From Ann-Marie MacDonald's *The Way the Crow Flies*:

Jack says, "Dief is playing politics with national security 'cause he doesn't want to be seen to be dancing to the American tune."

"I don't get it," says Jack's neighbour, Bryson. "We're all sitting under the same flight path. Part of the same target area."

Jack knows the young officer is thinking of his new baby at home – all the men at this table are fathers. He reaches for his coffee and sees Nolan entering the mess. He lifts a hand, intending to invite him over, but Nolan appears not to notice. He finds a table at the far end and sits with a book.

"Who does he think is going to protect us if we're too gutless to do it ourselves?" says Lawson. "Britain?"

"Fat chance," says Vic.

"Never mind that we saved their bacon in two world wars," says Ted Lawson.

"Dief would rather stand up and sing 'God Save the Queen' while the whole map turns red," says Baxter.

Vic leans forward, his French accent coiling tighter as he speaks. "If we don't be – if we are not prepared to participate in the defence of our own borders, we might as well be the fifty-first state."

"The Americans will defend us whether we like it or not," says Woodley.

"So much for sovereignty," says Jack. "Use it or lose it."

"If you imagine that decade spatially and Canada as a kind of Venn diagram," said MacDonald, "then the Cuban Missile Crisis perfectly illustrated Canada's changing place in the world. It showed how our interests vis-à-vis Britain and the United States had changed, and how our position was seen to shift. Whatever shift had already occurred became apparent in that time."

$$\diamond \quad \diamond \quad \diamond$$

"IMMEDIATELY I THINK of the 1960s as a period of sexual change," said Alice Munro. "That's what hit all the people around my age who didn't think that we should be considered old. We were forty and a lot of the things that were happening were as exciting to us as they were to young people. We liked the music. We adored Trudeau just because he was cool, and there was certainly a shift towards watching the United States and what was happening there. I was born in 1931, and when I was a young child, my father would come in at lunchtime. We had the big meal at noon and we turned on the BBC News. Then I think there was Canadian news after that, but it was the BBC that we would listen to every day, telling us about the Battle of Stalingrad or . . . well, it was terribly important stuff. And the funny thing was that no matter what the news was, if there was something that the Queen had done, then they'd start with that: 'The King and Queen have returned from Sandringham,' and then they would tell you how many planes had been lost. I was aware of everything that was happening in the European war."

The Vietnam War was the third political event of the 1960s that brought rapprochement with the United States at the expense of the country's allegiances to Britain. It transformed Toronto's Yorkville into a countercultural destination, but the famous hippie street was just one expression of the change that was seizing hold of the country from the Atlantic provinces to Victoria – where Alice Munro and her husband, Jim, were working.

"Jim and I had a bookstore – he still does – and it was a centre for everybody who was on drugs and everybody who was against the Vietnam War. Saturday afternoons, you could get high simply from clerking in the store. So, yes, there was this huge awareness of what was happening. The Vietnam War was a huge preoccupation, and there was the FLQ too, which was also very dramatic. But then we were used to this sort of drama. People think the 1950s were a very dull period – my God, they weren't dull at all. You were really scared of atomic war. But it was during the Vietnam War that we started watching the American news – Walter Cronkite, where before that we'd been listening to Earl Cameron tell us about Canada."

✧ ✧ ✧

THE 1960S WERE a high time in Canada, the decade when Lester B. Pearson established the nation's peacekeeping force, the country's cultural identity was realized in its English and French "solitudes," and during which the way was laid for the repatriation of Canada's Constitution. Against a background of simmering Quebec discontent, the watershed moment culminated in the celebrations of Montreal's Expo 67, and the election of Pierre Elliott Trudeau the following year. Out of Pearson's and then Trudeau's efforts to allay the province in the wake of its Quiet Revolution, Canada's multicultural policy was generated. It was the most significant decade for the country since the 1910s and the time of Canada's participation in the Great War, but a regionalism of the mind was another of its consequences and so Canadians have tended to consider the domestic and international events that made it so, in isolation. A reinvigorated quarrel not just with Quebec but all provinces was waiting further down the road, but during the 1960s the Trudeau rose had not yet been tested by the FLQ or blemished by the failure of his National Energy Policy. It was the blossom on a country that had begun to assert itself and to recognize the blessed good fortune of a future that was undecided. Anything seemed possible. A new self-regard saw Canadian borders appear less as the farthest edge of some better place to be, this country vaguely "elsewhere," and more as the threshold of a possibility of creative freedom to be enjoyed by writers and artists, indeed all citizens, knowingly at the start of a special adventure. Canada was at the beginning of its Age of Argument, its stories tantamount to volleys in an enthusiastic national debate. In English Canada of the 1960s, as in Quebec, independent publishers flourished. In the 1970s, they refined themselves.

The novelist Michael Ondaatje was one of those who benefited and contributed. In 1970, a poet and dabbling filmmaker at the time, he published *The Collected Works of Billy the Kid* with House of Anansi and *Coming Through Slaughter*, a pioneering collage of poems and eclectic photographic images, with Coach House Press. I visited him in the Toronto Cabbagetown house he shares with the American novelist Linda Spalding, and Ondaatje spoke of breaking genres and the advantages of *not* being judged – of something that his friend poet b.p. nichol called "border blur."

Ondaatje said, "'Border blur' described that whole questioning of whether or not there existed any meaningful distinction to be made between comic books and poetry, prose, drama, and film, or that linking of the tradition of documentary and poetry that started with Dorothy Livesay. Even being involved, as a writer, with theatre companies such as Théâtre Passe-Muraille was a part of the border blur that existed in the 1960s and 1970s."

I asked, "And did this generation of which you were a part have anything approaching a common creed?"

"There's a line in one of Robert Kroetsch's poems," said Ondaatje, "where he talks about a certain kind of plant that a seed catalogue says, 'flourishes under total neglect.' For a while that was the motto at Coach House."

"The Greeks thought that the best fate for a man was to be unnoticed by the gods," I said.

"It sounds a bit precious," said Ondaatje, "but I think what was very important was that it was a time in which you could try out all kinds of things because you weren't in the public eye. Coach House had a business printing menus and posters, they felt they could survive and publish books that they knew weren't going to do very well. It was a time in which you could try long poems and mongrel forms of literature, and these could be improved and finessed and allowed to develop because there weren't even reviews of the small presses at that time. It's not at all like the way it is now."

Toronto, finally, was acquiring a momentum and identity of its own. It would take another couple of decades to graduate to the full brouhaha of its Age of Argument, but the process started with the country celebrating the diversity it discovered in the mapping that was done in the 1960s and 1970s. A country's Age of Mapping is a giddy, invigorating period of self-discovery, when the work that storytellers do plots not just the history, but the *now* of a society. Katherine Govier, the author of *Fables of Brunswick Avenue*, was one of them, arriving in Toronto from Edmonton in 1971. She had driven across the country with her husband, and settled in Don Mills at first, then leaving Nowhere in Particular for the street in Toronto's Annex that provided her the material and the title of her famous collection. Together we walked the short section of Brunswick Avenue north of Bloor, and Govier explained that the Toronto she then lived in was in the throes of adolescent self-discovery. Eventually, however, the thrill of mapping a place is in danger of turning the pleasures of such revelation into what Govier described as a "moral requirement."

"During the 1970s," Govier said, "during the cultural *naissance* of Canadian literary identity that was flourishing at the time, you had to write about yourself, you had to write a book that was saying something about the future of this country. But by the end of the

1980s, everybody had done that, the immigrant literature was turning heads, and the moral requirement had dissolved. As a writer you looked at your colleagues and thought, 'If they can write about Bombay, why can't I?' Now the borders are all over the map."

◇   ◇   ◇

OR, IN THE CITY, they lose significance. The city, as it develops, becomes bigger and more complex than any of its parts. Consensus falls away and *difference* becomes the lifeblood of a place where a multitude of stories compete for recognition and dispute and build on what has been said before. The City is a "distinct society" because communities live on top and in between one another and no person is any one thing for *all* of the time. Borders do not matter any more because the living is diffuse. The city has its own rules, its own accords. It is a generic place but also multiplicitous. By the late 1990s, Toronto, the Ontario city that was the unremarkable expression of colonized values, had morphed into something else entirely – a place occupied in all its nooks and crannies by a multiplicity of lives and entirely new elites and whole communities jostling for a place at the table. Today, a few of the old rooming houses can still be found in Parkdale, on Roncesvalles, or on Parliament Street and a few blocks west, but across the road are

HOME TO MR AND

MISSISSAUGA

the high towers of St. James Town, where whole families now arrive on airplanes rather than the trains that used to bring new hopefuls to Toronto. The draw of the city is the same, the chance to make good in M.G. Vassanji's new land, but the message of the new dwellings is different. The high apartment buildings and office blocks that have taken the place of the mansions and the rooming houses that once sat comfortably on uncontested terrain are symbols of Toronto's new age, places where entire *populations* can congregate but also disappear from view – here, at Jane and Steeles, or Bathurst and Finch, where the Latvian Jews of David Bezmozgis's collection *Natasha and Other Stories* dominated apartment tenant listings now taken over by Korean and Middle Eastern names. The rooming house that was the architectural emblem of bachelors and their loneliness in the city – and of the *work* that individuals sought – has given way to the apartment block, and its demands for political and cultural freedoms that whole communities now seek.

✧ ✧ ✧

TODAY, NOVELISTS SUCH as Russell Smith and Dionne Brand can explore at their doorstep a city that Barry Callaghan had to work hard to seek and find. Stuff still reigns, but these authors are thrilled by the challenges of a place that is beyond any simple categorizing now.

"I go out a lot at night," said Smith, "and I'm fond of techno music. The performers and the audience at these nightclubs, which gather after midnight, are very multi-ethnic. You cannot be interested in this music and have racism in you because you would not survive at these clubs. I went to a Canada Day concert at a huge complex called The Guvernment, which has about five different rooms, with five different DJ performances going on, and that can hold maybe ten thousand people. We were queuing up at about one o'clock in the morning and being searched by enormous bouncers with headsets, and two tricked-out Honda Civics pulled up right at the head of the line."

"More tailfins, that sort of thing?"

"Yeah, with glowing neon lights underneath them and tinted windows – youthful gangster cars. A group of tiny Asians got out, little guys who were pumped up, but just over five feet tall, with tight T-shirts and their sunglasses up on their head, and three or four tiny women in high-heeled shoes and micro miniskirts. They walked to the front of the line, and they peeled off bills from a wad of cash, which they handed to the bouncer, who opened the velvet

rope and let them go in ahead of us. That was a fantastic example –
particularly on Canada Day – of changing power structures and
classes. Those people were an elite in that place. They belonged
to a really ascendant class. And me, with my private school background and my Queen's education, there I was left standing behind
the rope, waiting to get in."

Calvin becomes Kim and makes good in his motorcar at last.

✧ ✧ ✧

OH, THE CHANGING city. In Toronto, I drove past Mount Pleasant
Cemetery, and on the radio an advertisement promoted the "compassionate, multicultural" services of the necropolis. The city is a
place of contradictions now, and its polyphony is sufficiently a part
of the Canadian fabric that *multiculturalism*, the clunky word that
describes it, now acts as an enticement from birth to the grave.

Anxious commentary in the morning newspapers had tried and
baffled me with their histrionic commentary, after the arrest of
seventeen terrorism suspects in Toronto, as if multiculturalism,
the polyphonic country, was a choice and not a destiny that Canada
had it in her to embrace. It was a *reality*, and not just the hopeful,
binding story that the Age of Mapping's Myths of Disappointment
had worked so hard to promulgate. The truth of it was here already,
the mission of the Age of Mapping achieved but also spent – for
the irony of multiculturalism as an affective national myth is that it
does not even distinguish Canada any more. Force of global circumstance means that it is USAmerica's, Britain's, and Europe's
story too. The business of the Age of Argument is not to celebrate
the players, but the game – to discover *how* to get along. The participation of the multicultures is the key to Canada's new polity.

It was noon, and I made my way to Broadview for a lunch of
duck and pork on rice at the Chinese BBQ eatery I favoured. The
owner was haggling with the young white driver of a butcher's
truck clearly selling him the week's pig for cash illicitly, and the
woman working the floor knew to bring me chili oil and the house
soup and looked at me, as usual, with such an intelligent but weary

expression that I yearned to know more about her life. I'd walked from Cabbagetown through Riverdale Park, watched three ladies in full-length black burkhas remove their platform shoes with their transparent plastic heels so that they might descend the path through the wooded slope more easily. They were laughing gaily and carrying a brass teapot and plastic shopping bags filled with I knew not what. I understood nothing except how strange I must have seemed to them, but the truth was that they had not looked my way at all. Several games were taking place in the park below. Bangladeshis were playing cricket, and Tamils volleyball. A man in a leather jacket, a Serbian probably, was kicking a soccer ball around with his son, bouncing it on his knee a few times and then over to the boy, as his wife looked on. A group of blacks and Hispanics mostly – every colour but not white – had a full match going, red pinnies over one team's shirts. Some whites, young and affluent and wearing T-shirts with their law firm's logo printed on, were warming up for a game of "Ultimate" Frisbee, running around the track and hollering like recruits at boot camp.

Past the Don Valley Parkway, the river that once powered the mills and tanneries that provided work to the mostly Irish slum dwellers of Cabbagetown was now a muddy stream. I crossed the footbridge over the highway and walked up the eastern flank of the old riverbed and along the Danforth where, a couple of years before, I'd strolled among the Greek and Portuguese crowds cheering on their mother countries' soccer teams during the final of the 2004 European Cup. Families crowded the cordoned-off avenue, some born here, as many recently landed and having taken Canada's oath of citizenship in English and French. The swearing in is an oral declaration of loyalty not just to Canada, but to hope and to no racism and the chance of a new beginning. Still, the choice of languages must seem arbitrary to many in the face of Canada's burgeoning forest of voices and patterns of immigration and return that chip away at the resilience of a nation: Italian Canadians electing a member of Parliament to the assembly in Rome; imams teaching their congregations *not* to participate in Canadian politics. If the Canadian multicultural polity is to function, then perhaps it should be supported more pro-actively – so that *not* voting becomes a misdemeanour in this new stage of our country's conversation; aboriginals advocating not land claims, in which First Nations stand apart, but a national network of trails and commons for all Canadians to learn the text of this shared land; a separate army for peacekeeping and another for defence.

"As recently as 1980, the situation was very different," said M.G. Vassanji, the author of several novels that put immigrants at their fore. "It used to be that when people left their country, they knew they would not see their homes again. They felt lucky that they had made it into Canada, and there was no looking back. But now we come from a different world. We come by plane, we hold dual passports, we have email and we have telephones. There are fewer currency controls, economies are interlinked, and when new people come in they bring in the language again and refresh it, so it doesn't happen any more that German disappears or that Gujarati disappears. Families are dispersed in all parts of the world."

Today, refugees of even the worst situations can expect, one day, to be home again – can use the hyphen in "-Canadian" and feel no contradiction. If home is just one thing. One novel that is waiting to be written concerns the immigrant's Canadian-raised son who is sent by the parents from Toronto or Edmonton to fight in an Old-Country war he knows nothing about. It happens.

$$\diamond \quad \diamond \quad \diamond$$

WHETHER IN THE poems of her collection *Thirsty*, or her most recent novel *What We All Long For*, Dionne Brand, a poet and novel-ist of Caribbean descent, has made it the thrilling point of her work to try and capture something of Toronto's bundle of presences. Brand presents the city, as Lisa Moore does St. John's in her novel *Alligator*, in a manner that recalls the Circle of the Myth World. There are no dominating heroes in either of these women's novels, as if a new humility before the contingencies of the world was again being learned – as if people felt helpless before the sheer dimen-sions of modern life, but also in *awe* again. I met Brand, a vibrant and appealing woman, at Dooney's Café on Bloor Street, near Bathurst, in Toronto. She has a wide smile and what Homer used to call "doe-eyes." Workers were pounding the busy street with pneumatic drills, tearing up the pavement for some not immediately fathomable reason. A tied-up Jack Russell yelped. The excitement she conveyed in the midst of it all was derived from her engagement with the city around her.  Noisy, hot, consuming; alternately irritating and satisfying, Toronto was home for her.

"Everyone," said Brand, "when they decide to live in a city, makes a judgment that is profound. It's an agreement about heterogeneity – that we can do this. It's an incredible test of the particular, and of how people see themselves as human in their own cultural space. How do you leap beyond the particular? is the question I was asking. So I drove around a lot, I walked around a lot, I eavesdropped a lot. I'm just fascinated by how people speak to one another, in which languages they speak to one another against the whole background of the politics of the world, whether theirs is the politics of race or gender or class, and how people come to agree to live with one another. And I don't have some kind of naive sense of any of this. I think these things are fought over and constructed through hard experiences. There is a multiplicity of being in the city precisely because we are from various places in the world, but we are also from all kinds of *situations*, benign as well as violent. On any given day, these are the presences we pass."

From Dionne Brand's *What We All Long For*:

Anonymity is the big lie of a city. You aren't anonymous at all. You're common, really, common like so many pebbles, so many specks of dirt, so many atoms of materiality. . . . In this city there are Bulgarian mechanics, there are Eritrean accountants, Colombian café owners, Latvian book publishers, Welsh roofers, Afghani dancers, Iranian mathematicians, Tamil cooks in Thai restaurants, Calabrese boys with Jamaican accents, Fushen deejays, Filipina-Saudi beauticians; Russian doctors changing tires, there are Romanian bill collectors, Cape Croker fishmongers, Japanese grocery clerks, French gas meter readers, German bakers, Haitian and Bengali taxi drivers with Irish dispatchers.

Lives in the city are doubled, tripled, conjugated – women and men all trying to handle their own chain of events, trying to keep the story straight in their own heads. At times they catch themselves in sensational lies, embellishing or avoiding a nasty secret here and there, juggling the lines of causality, and before you know it, it's impossible to tell one thread from another. In this city, like everywhere, people work, they eat, they drink, they have sex, but it's hard not to wake up here without the certainty of misapprehension.

◇　◇　◇

BRAND's "MATERIALITY" IS Michael Turner's "anthology," a multitude of voices in urban practice. An array of populations is what makes our towns and cities fecund. Our "immigrant" literature shows this, though we do not tend to speak of it as such because – unlike in England or Denmark, say – we regard these novels and short stories, even by those who arrived yesterday, less as tales of adjustment to the host country as these communities take the road to true belonging, and more an indication of the diversity of Canadian society and a display of its ethnic riches. In Canada, the lessons of immigrants' literature concern the trials of the *nation* on the road to offering an authentic possibility of belonging for its citizens. The "myth of rescue" that Brand described is a part of it. Readers look to recently landed Canadians for new and unfamiliar stories and for an affirmation of the place we know has the potential to be everyone's best home. Nowhere as an Address with

Virtues. The myth is being contested, however, by several authors feeling their way around the idea of their new home.

Rohinton Mistry, the Mumbai-born Parsi, arrived in Canada at the age of twenty-three and worked for a while as a bank clerk before he turned to writing exemplary short stories and then novels. Mistry's fiction allowed readers to enjoy a literature that was "Canadian" in the broadest sense. No streets, no ancestors, no history that was recognizable. Only the vague conviction that there was something in the country's makeup that helped make these fine and revelatory stories possible. Mistry had lifted the "moral requirement" not just for authors but for readers too. Home is an idea, an aspiration, a sum of relationships. An address is only one small part of it.

"The way that I would like to relate to place," said Mistry, "to a place that is absolutely essential to my being and without which I would pine away – that sort of relationship takes generations to develop."

Mistry has never been keen on talking about writing. He is painfully shy. Conversations about a process he finds difficult and magical really do pain him as writing, for Mistry, is a private matter. And yet he is courteous and in possession of better manners than probably make him comfortable, and because it is hard, if not impossible, for him to behave any other way, then if he says, "Yes, I will discuss my work with you," he does. Mistry, when we met, spoke thoughtfully, economically. The gaps between the words were regular, and long, but each sentence had a remarkable clarity. He spoke, as he wrote, with consideration and grace.

"In the context of the question 'Where is home?'" said Mistry, "a friend of mine once told me, 'I have portable roots, so any place is home where I am able to put my roots down, but can collect these roots up again and transport them with me.' At least the first- and second-generation immigrant, I think, has to accept something like that definition of home, and place."

"So that home, for you," I said, "is an almost archetypal idea depending upon a history of generations –"

"I do remember the reactions to *Tales from Firozsha Baag*, when it first came out, comparing the coldness of Canada to the supposed warmth of the community that I was writing about, and I gently suggested that what many perceived of as 'warmth' would have been intolerable to those living in Bombay, where to try to set yourself apart from your 'friendly' neighbours was often a life's work."

A life's work that may have resulted in a monster home in Mississauga or Richmond Hill. Or the new Hindu palaces of Vaughan or Markham or Brampton.

"Do you consider cities as distinct places?" I asked.

"Cities are certainly similar to one extent, but if you concentrate on them then I am sure that you will find Vancouver or Toronto every bit as interesting as Bombay."

"And yet you have been able to make the break and find home here, in Canada. How would you define your relationship to the immediate place that you find yourself in?"

"I'm very comfortable," said Mistry. "I call it home inasmuch as any place can be home."

"Canada, you mean?"

"Yes, in terms of the ideal. But the ideal, I think, is unachievable."

"The ideal is what, to be perfectly at home anywhere?"

"It's like the idea of perfection. You strive for it, but you never reach it."

"Has Canada entered into your work in any way that you can identify?"

Mistry turned his head and contemplated whatever was the bundle of thoughts prompted by a question that I expect he knew would come. It always did. Yet, such an honest man, Mistry was still visibly thrown, without an immediate answer, considering the question, again, as if it had never been asked of him. Ten seconds passed and I did not interrupt. I worried that I might have sounded like the passenger in the cab who asks the dark-skinned driver, "So where are *you* from" and not "where is your *family* from?"

Seven more full seconds passed and I thought that maybe I

should answer the question for him, or ask another, as Mistry looked so disturbed.

"I think I'd have to say yes," said Mistry finally. "Canada has entered in my work. First, of course, there is the concrete presence of Canada in a couple of the early short stories from *Tales from Firozsha Baag*, and Canada enters in an oblique way in *Family Matters*. But I should say that it is very important to me that the act of writing takes place here. I cannot imagine myself in a room in any other city, in any other country, writing. I'm not quite sure why that is."

Mistry smiled.

"I'll let others try to explain it, but I do feel that way."

"Is your relationship to place defined by work at all?"

"Yes," said Mistry. "There are two places. There is the place where I write and the place that I write about, and I think I have to consider them both as home. If either one was taken away from the equation, then it would collapse for me."

"What notion did you have of Canada when you came?"

Mistry smiled delicately, the face behind the trimmed beard and glasses like that of a student. "I thought it would complete me."

Mistry was silent for a moment, and then he asked, "How do we define Canada these days? As an urban place?"

"Eighty per cent of us live in cities," I said.

"In that case, then it would be urban and it would be multicultural – if multiculturalism is what I think it is. You mentioned America, which made me think of the idea of the melting pot, and that in *Firozsha Baag*, one of my characters says, 'There is not much melting going on.' A lot of the problems in the United States come out of the realization that there is no melting pot there. There have always been the conditions of 'multiculturalism,' but in America you can't call it what it is. You must pretend to be one big happy family. I suppose we need a Third Option now. One has been discredited, and the other is perhaps not satisfactory, but I don't know what third way there is."

"Are writers who know the world through a particular place at an advantage over those whose attachments are less fixed?"

"Perhaps the writer who moves around a lot has more to work with than the writer who realizes there is only the one thing that he has to write about," said Mistry. "But it was V.S. Naipaul, who, after reading books set in London and his mother country, said it took him some time but when he realized Trinidad was 'his place' then he found his voice."

"He also said that he did not know what Englishmen did when they went home at night. Do you ever feel that?"

"Well, who is Canadian? I know what some do."

"It's interesting to me that we don't have the kind of binding mythology that America or even India has," I said. "India so readily describes itself as the 'world's largest democracy,' and America has its Dream. Do you think multiculturalism is a national myth that is comparable?"

"It may not be fully formed yet," said Mistry, "but it may be about a place that is free, and kind, and where you must leave behind the prejudices that belong in the old country – Hindus and Muslims who must leave behind their pasts, for example."

"I hope that we can do that," I said, "but it worries me that often when we describe ourselves as African- or Chinese- or Indo-Canadian, that the epithet matters more than what follows."

"That is the first stage. Canada is the place you come to be free of all those bad things, and the epithet will fall away."

✧ ✧ ✧

IN VANCOUVER, I went over to Strathcona and took a walk there with Madeleine Thien, one of an assortment of young writers from immigrant communities in Canada that render our culture vital. Anosh Irani, a recent immigrant to Canada from Mumbai, India, is another. So is Yann Martel. The list is too long to tabulate. Thien is the Canadian-born child of Malaysian-Chinese parents. In the stories of her collection, *Simple Recipes*, the tension of immigration is felt no more keenly than at home. The drama of arrival takes a couple of generations to play itself out, and in its denouement new stories take root that, in turn, contribute to the maturation of our sense of place and what it means to be a part to the Canadian polyphony.

From Madeleine Thien's "Simple Recipes":

My father pushes at the fish with the edge of his spoon. Underneath, the meat is white and the juice runs down along the side. He lifts a piece and lowers it carefully onto my plate.

Once more, his spoon breaks skin. Gingerly, my father lifts another piece and moves it towards my brother.

"I don't want it," my brother says.

My father's hand wavers. "Try it," he says, smiling. "Take a wok on the wild side."

"No."

My father sighs and places the piece on my mother's plate. We eat in silence, scraping spoons across the dishes. My parents use chopsticks, lifting their bowls and motioning the food into their mouths. The smell of food fills the room.

Savouring each mouthful, my father eats slowly, head tuned to the flavours in his mouth. My mother takes her glasses off, the lenses fogged, and lays them on the table. She eats with her head bowed down, as if in prayer.

Lifting a stem of cauliflower to his lips, my brother sighs deeply. He chews, and then his face changes. I have a sudden picture of him drowning, his hair waving like grass. He coughs, spitting the mouthful back onto his plate. Another cough. He reaches for his throat, choking.

My father slams his chopsticks down on the table. In a single movement, he reaches across, grabbing my brother by the shoulder. "I have tried," he is saying. "I don't know what kind of son you are. To be so ungrateful." His other hand sweeps by me and bruises into my brother's face.

My mother flinches. My brother's face is red and his mouth is open. His eyes are wet.

Still coughing, he grabs a fork, tines aimed at my father, and then in an unthinking moment, he heaves it at him. It strikes my father in the chest and drops.

"I hate you! You're just an asshole, you're just a fucking asshole chink!" My brother holds his plate in his hands. He smashes it down and his food scatters across the table. He is coughing and spitting. "I wish you weren't my father! I wish you were dead."

Thien, a pretty, petite woman, sat on a curbstone at the far end of a yard that had once been the playground of the St. Francis Xavier school, her alma mater. Now it was boarded up, and here she was, a woman in her late twenties living in Amsterdam, home to see the parents who had raised her in Vancouver. Thien spoke gently, nothing in her manner suggesting the lack of ease that her characters struggle with in the new society. Her own family's Canadian adventure was complete. The stories, though set here, are not overtly identified with Canada. They are immigrant stories of a more "universal" nature – the details of place not overly prevalent. I was not altogether convinced this was a good thing. It left me searching, though strangely satisfied. A novel with *only* the universal can be an abstraction – Canada as Nowhere and Off the Map all over again – but I realized that perhaps I was looking for something in the books that I was reading that was no longer germane. Canada in the Age of Argument was a place on the verge of concluding its *own* journey – on the verge of becoming, well, *grown up*.

"When I was writing *Simple Recipes*," said Thien, "I wasn't thinking about ethnicity at all, but about parents who try to do the best for their children and possibly fall short, and about the children who become adults and come to understand their parents in different ways as they grow older."

"And yet that possibility of falling short is emphasized by the fact of their ethnicity," I said. "These are parents who have brought their family to a new country with the hope of a better life. The prospect of failure is very real."

"If I wasn't thinking about ethnicity," said Thien, "certainly I was thinking about immigration and, in particular, about children who try to *catch* their parents. In an immigrant situation there's often no extended family to fall back on. Brothers and sisters and fathers and mothers have been left behind in different countries and so children take on the role of being the immigrant family's support network. They are young but they are also old. They want to save things. They wish to catch their parents as they fall, but of course the parents themselves are in the new country solely to make better lives for their children who carry new hope for them – and this makes for a very different child-parent relationship. To me immigration is both a beautiful and a tragic dynamic. It is about intense connection, but disconnection too."

"I come from a line of Jewish immigrants from Eastern Europe who came to Quebec and New York, and I remember being told by one of my father's generation – like you, the children of those who immigrated – that Canada was the 'destination of second choice.' America was first choice, I suppose."

"Right."

"Was that true for your parents and their friends?"

"No, I don't think so," said Thien. "I believe that my family was always drawn towards Canada and especially towards Vancouver. My mother came from a family of ten sisters and two brothers and most of them met up in New York, but for the four or five that chose Canada I don't think there was ever a doubt. The promise of America is bigger and brighter, but what they were looking for in Canada was stability, I think. They didn't want great things, they just wanted a house, kids, university – *permanence*. They wanted a place where they could settle and wouldn't have to move again. I don't imagine that's what they would have felt when they thought about emigrating to the United States."

✧   ✧   ✧

HOME IS THE place you go and where you know you will be taken in. It is the place where your physical self is at ease, because your very body is so reconciled to the world that it has forgotten its edges. What is "home," after all, but a place to be safe? Does it ever really need to be proclaimed as more than that?

Anosh Irani's first novel, *The Cripple and His Talismans*, is set in the great Indian city the author still calls Bombay, full to bursting with life that is fecund beyond Canadian imagining. India's busy street, its cornucopia of families, its roads filled with trucks and caravans and rickshaws, motorcycle three-seaters and white Ambassador taxicabs; with its gleaming commercial towers, at Nariman Point, that have overshadowed the legacy of Queen Victoria though not the leviathan bustle of the railway station that was named after her; with its cacophonous mix of marriage and funeral processions; its political parties and religions and votes and arguments; its beggars and prostitutes and models and beauty queens; its clerks and students and scholars and monstrously rich; its gay colours and stinking slums; its beaches where families once fished and rivers since reduced to green slime; this was the place of Irani's growing up that, perhaps unsurprisingly, wrote itself in a novel that is best described as a surrealist fable. Yet, as Rohinton Mistry does, Irani will tell you that Canada is home for him.

Irani was in his early thirties when I met him. He had recently taken out Canadian citizenship, having moved to Vancouver in his late twenties in 1998. Before writing his first novel (and during that time), Irani had been a playwright. When I sat with him on Granville Island, on the far side of the Burrard Street Bridge, it was in the empty Arts Club theatre where a play of his was being rehearsed. An empty theatre was as good a place as any for the two of us to have discussed the nature of home, as writers are by nature an alienated bunch and the building was a secular chapel to the work he did. The land that had inspired his work was another matter, for although Irani's cues were Indian, the city he hearkened back to – his first home, and the one that he was writing to – was as false or as true as Saskatchewan had been to Gloria Sawai. The writer's imagination is *affected* by place, but the place is never *real* per se. Irani's second "home," as had been the case for Mistry, was Canada itself, a place that had not yet seeped into his work, though Irani was young and there would be plenty of time for that. Home was the empty theatre, a space in which to work and for him to define as he saw fit. The safety of Canada is the shelter of shared space. A place in which to work and invent. A place where it was possible to think and live freely.

"What is home for you?" I asked.

"Home is two things. It's family, the people you love, and secondly, it's the physical landscape. For me, it is the soil that I stepped on when I was little, the beach that I played on when I was young."

"It's interesting to me that you choose in *The Cripple and His Talismans* and now to refer to the city in which you grew up as Bombay and not Mumbai, which is how it's known on maps these days."

"I grew up in Bombay, so it will always be Bombay for me. It doesn't seem natural to call it Mumbai. Looking back, it's possible to say that it was a conscious choice, but it was also what came naturally to me. When I say Bombay, I'm transported there. When I say Mumbai, I don't know where to go."

"So even if Bombay was your real home, it doesn't exist."

"That's true," said Irani, laughing, "and I don't know if that's a good or bad thing, but it's interesting."

"But you have Vancouver."

"Yes, but right now, the way I live, even if I'm walking down the street in Vancouver, my brain is in Bombay. Because I'm thinking about stories that are set there, my imagination is always in Bombay – and that means that I'm not really observing, one hundred per cent, what is going on around me. But I'm happy here. It's a good place."

"So tell me, if you were walking home from this theatre one night, under the bridge and back into the city, and you saw an Indian white Ambassador taxi careening around the corner choking you on its exhaust as it passed, only for this mysterious apparition to suddenly disappear in some back alley – could you imagine *that* beginning a story?"

Irani was a handsome man – dashing, even. His straight dark hair was parted to one side and flopped across his brow. He wore a crisp white shirt and his cinnamon skin glowed. He held his chin in one hand and stared at the stage. The pose was thoughtful, elegant. Suddenly his face broke out into a debonair smile.

"That's a good idea – you know, to bring Bombay *here*. You would only need one or two elements and then these give you the threads to start a story that is, in a way, 'Canadian.'"

"It's not an obligation," I said.

"None of my writing is set in Canada. At some point it might be, but for now what I like to do is just look back to Bombay because the separation makes the writing easier and gives me more insight into the place. At least, that's what I feel."

"So you think of Canada somewhat along the lines of a hotel, which is the way Yann Martel chose to describe Canada. Not that we check in and leave, indifferent to our surroundings, more that the country is an accommodating place."

"I wouldn't say that it's a hotel for me because I do consider it home now. If it were a hotel, then I would know that I was leaving at some point."

◇ ◇ ◇

"That silly off-the-cuff remark," said Yann Martel impatiently. "Hotels are very diverse places and all kinds of people end up there. All I meant was Canada has the variety of peoples of a hotel. One would hope that people do not come to Canada treating it like a stop on their way to somewhere better. When I said that, I only intended to reflect the diversity of the people that you find here."

Martel had a quality I have known in just a few people, each of them a possible genius, of impeccable courtesy. The civility was a way of keeping others at bay and protecting his artist's utter distraction.

"Where do you write your novels?" I asked.

"I do my research abroad, but I write them in Canada. *Life of Pi* was written mostly in Montreal. I did six months of research in

India, and then most of my more academic research at McGill. *Self* started in Paris, but again, I wrote most of it in Montreal. The stories of *The Facts Behind the Helsinki Roccamatios* were also written in Paris – I was working in the Canadian Embassy though, so technically it was still Canadian territory."

This was amusing, as even I was not about to claim Canada's embassies as exerting a particular influence. Such pressure, there is, and here was I a part of it, for writers to profess love of country when the dogma of nationhood is the last thing most believe in. Writers want most of all to be left alone to work in a quiet place.

"Do you think that the geography of Canada is binding or affecting in any way?" I asked.

"Oh yes, very much so," said Martel, "but I would actually say the *cartography*. There's something about the shape of the country that becomes imprinted on your mind. I really suspect that, were one of the referendums to pass in Quebec, a lot of the pain that would be felt by Canadians would have to do with the change of the shape of our maps – the idea that the Maritimes and the rest of Canada would suddenly become an absurdity, as Pakistan and Bangladesh were when they were meant to be two parts of the same Muslim country. Of course it's ridiculous that Quebec sovereigntists can claim the right to leave Canada, when, no, the First Nations cannot have *their* rights, but I do think that we would also be upset because the shape of our country fascinates us. The cartography has become a part of the consciousness."

"Does Canada's history matter to you?"

"Of course. Our tradition of tolerance doesn't just date from the development of multiculturalism, does it? There's a wonderful letter that a friend showed me from around the time of the Rebellions of 1837, when the governor of Lower Canada decided not to shoot. There was a sense, already, that one does not do that to people who are just protesting something. It was the beginning of this idea that we must tolerate dissent. The very buildup of this country was an act of will. Initially, it was just the English-speaking white men carving out a country, taking in the French because they had no choice, but there was already a tolerance of the francophone element. It was born out of necessity, but eventually we saw the virtue of tolerance for its own sake. And if you think of it, our participation in the two world wars was an act of generosity, of coming to the rescue of what was essentially a foreign country. English Canada wanted to participate out of concern for a country, several thousand miles away, to which they still felt a bond. That bond endured in the second war, and to me, that is remarkable. Yes, Canadian history speaks to me the way it does to most people. Perhaps because I travel so much, I don't feel as strongly about it as I do the history of some countries – I'm something of a chameleon, I travel around, and I'll partake of the local colour for a while – but despite all my travels, I could never, ever imagine not being Canadian. I remember when the Booker short list came out, one of the things that the British papers said was, 'What is Canadian about these writers? None of them was born in Canada –'"

"The English love to say that –"

"Mistry was born in Bombay, Shields was born in the United States, and I was born in Spain. And to one journalist who pointed that out to me, I said, 'Despite the fact that my novel barely takes place in Canada, and there's only a bit of Toronto and the city is not described at all, it's *Canadian* to have novels that don't take place in Canada.' When I'm in Canada, I told him, I see the whole *world* because our country is so multicultural. Conversely, when I travel in the world, often I see Canada because I recognize the peoples that have imported their culture here."

"I've always admired your story 'The Mirror Machine,'" I said, "in which a grandmother speaks her memory into a gramophonelike box, and her words are mixed up with silver paint and create a mirror. Later, the grandson scrutinizes the mirror and discovers that the backing is made up of these minuscule lines that are the memories themselves. Often I wish there was such a mirror here, for Canadians arriving in a country about which they know comparatively little – an ignorance that can be attributed to many of us who live here already. We have a history of being Nowhere, but often we present the place as Nowhere even to ourselves."

"But that is also one of Canada's qualities," Martel said. "Perhaps Canada is a creative void where your East Indian immigrant arrives and is told that to try to speak English or French will definitely help but frankly even that is not a necessity. You're from Montreal. Now you live in Toronto. You will surely know, as I do, immigrants such as the Greek woman who used to be my landlady. The English she spoke was atrocious, even though she had been in Canada for thirty years, but you can get by in the larger urban centres like that. How many Chinese Canadians do not speak English or French? Perhaps Canada is a void that the immigrant can fill bit by bit, in such a way that the country is sustainable to him or her – but in a manner that also sustains our country. In that sense, Canada is a unique experiment. Our federated model has not only political aspects but cultural ones – and it is the way the world will go if it succeeds in muddling through all its problems. And I would suspect that the future of the world is actually the Canadian model – if we manage it. If we cannot, then we shall be another Yugoslavia."

Martel thought for a moment – not for long, the mind was restless, but volatile and quick.

"In 'The Mirror Machine,'" said Martel, "what I wanted to convey was that our past makes us who we are – that acts of remembrance, and of memorializing things, ultimately define us. It was a story about how we imbue objects with spirit, and how valuable objects are never just objects, but objects that have been touched in this way. Can we do that at the scale of a country? Could there ever be a mirror that reflects us as a whole? I'm not sure."

"But isn't that what fiction does?" I asked.

"Yes," said Martel. "But when you create a story, it involves two things – an act of imagination and an act of will. A novel doesn't just come to you without an act of will. You must sit down and devote ten to twenty hours to read that thing. It's an act of will, but it's also a social act in which the imagination of the reader meets that of the writer. And so, in that sense, a novel is like an *agora*, a meeting place, and each of us brings something different to it."

"A theatre of views."

"Yes. And a country is exactly like that. You bring different things to it, and if that contract breaks down then there is failure. Really, there's no inevitability to Canada. The country had to be built and it can be undone. If the act of faith that is Canada becomes too frayed, too tattered, it doesn't seem inconceivable that our sovereignty could disappear. Canada will succeed if we choose."

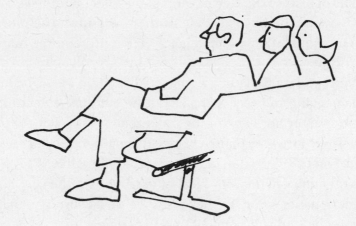

Epilogue

Of course all children sing the world into existence – some joyfully, others not, but nonetheless singing.

Bruce Chatwin, in a postcard to
the author, October 1987

Being Canadian demands a constant effort of the imagination, a working definition of the country that must be conjured out of the ether on consecutive mornings. What exactly *is* this place called Canada? Does it even exist? *How?* What does it mean to be a citizen when patriotism is so problematic?

What does it mean to be a country at all?

Our good fortune is not *because* of us, but it is ours nonetheless. In Canada, the happy accident, we have space – and space, as in the story of Death the Iglulingmiut told – allows for peace. The land has tried us, but it has also taught us how to be sensitive to others and that no one of us has special rights here. We are the "happy accident" because even in these current, anxious days, our lack of an imperial past means that few arrive in this country wanting redress for the ills of history their own colonial masters might have meted out. In Canada, the happy accident, there is still the chance of a fresh start though that will change if we do not enforce our own good fortune.

To contemplate Canada is to have to balance love of country with the nagging and very real possibility that, in the near future, the nation might not exist in the form that we know it today. As Canadians, we love our country, but we do not describe ourselves as "patriots" much. We understand more than the citizens of almost any other country in the world just how tenuous is the very idea of the modern nation-state. We have learned the absurdity of nation-hood from the land and from political experience.

Canada is a nation living in the vivid present. The country has a future that is uncertain and no past that can be agreed upon. It is a happy accident because its peculiar challenges have created the conditions for a nation that is reflective, compassionate, and inventive. The country is an idea, a wish, an argument, and an experiment. To applaud these qualities is not to say they do not exist elsewhere, but here they are attributes of the land, not governments, for the truth about Canada lies beneath any of the superficial borderlines that politicians have made.

We can learn from the novel here.

Canada begins, as novels do, in doubt. And it teaches reason, as novels do. The happy accident will become unhappy if, in the battle of stories that is taking place globally today, we allow epic thinking to gain the upper hand and trumpet an absolute version of society over the malleability and promise of the common humanity that is celebrated here. This task is not easy. It demands that constant effort of the imagination, the rigour and ability to change our minds in the face of the enigma of nationhood. Home, the safe place, the fair shelter, is what we are seeking. Its secular agreements are ones the novel teaches. Argument, but reason. Tolerance, but conviction. Doubt, certainly, but the security that breeds empathy, rather than the chauvinism that teaches confrontation. To think along these lines is not to be weak, or "anti-nationalist," but to *question* nationalism, and in so doing define it afresh and not take the gift for granted. All the ruminations about nationhood that Canadians entertain daily are not, as was the case a generation ago, expressions of some inferiority complex that Canadians were said to have, but a response to the overarching question of what it means to be a citizen of this or any other country.

✧ ✧ ✧

"THE MAP OF CANADA," the geographer Alan Morantz said to me, "is our proper flag."

Canadians consider the map of their country and wonder what shape it should take. In the place of the impact of history, often an ossifying, even stultifying thing, Canadians have looked to *stories* to explain this daunting map, as I have done in this book – and as historians and even our Supreme Court justices do, executors of a brilliant document the authority of which rests not in incontrovertible statutes ("the right of the people to keep and bear Arms shall not be infringed") but in *principles*, stories whose validity must be reasserted as circumstances demand.

All stories must prove themselves; most of all, those posing as absolute. When a historian, writing of the arrival of United Empire Loyalists in Canada in the eighteenth century, says that the country is founded upon flight and not fight, he or she is merely putting forward a *story* that affects our present by virtue of being told. For a story, like water, takes the path that is easiest. The rivulet becomes a stream and then a mighty river. It becomes the course that is taken until some other furrow is dug and the possibility of another channel, another story, exists. Creating this new channel is not always easy. The territory is new, and may fight against it. It may not be the path that the water wants to follow, until you beat back the branches and break up the earth and the path is inviting and obvious. The water runs. The story makes sense. Its possibility was always there.

The stories we tell further our understanding of the country. They help us fathom the disparate facts that Douglas Coupland described as "the news' meaningless little bits." But stories can also incarcerate us, as do the metaphors we choose as shortcuts to meaning. The United Empire Loyalist story has been around for a long time, and is widely told, but it is no more or less true than ones I have put forward about the experience of being colonized or the legacy of the Company Store. In Canada's Age of Invention, the metaphor often used to explain the country was of vast, empty space. In the country's Age of Mapping, the notion of the border became acute. Both filled Canadians with mythic awe and belittled them in the face of the map of the country that is our proper flag. These stories have persisted because the channels these stories have cut are deep, even though the ideas each implies are no longer true. The "empty spaces" that characterized the fears and anxieties of the country's Age of Invention were long ago discovered to be occupied. The sense of limitless territory, but also of Canadians' helpless passivity that was inferred by the idea of a precipitous edge, what with our typically being on the wrong side of it, also has no legitimacy today. The border with the United States is now real – armed in places and soon requiring passports. Even the much vaunted "Idea of North" is an altered one, the open roof towards the Arctic having had a lid put on it by the dispute with Americans over rights of passage, with the Danes over Hans Island, by our impending militarization of it, and the work that scientists are doing to map the Northern seas' beds with a view to the divvying up of mineral resources. Subsequently the modification of Canada's very motto has been proposed – *a mari ad mare* now requiring a third *mare*, our charted Northern sea. The map is finished. Canadian infinity knows bounds.

Now it is incumbent upon us to argue what the map holds with stories. These cannot be legislated, of course, but they can be articulated, spoken into the world to see how each fares. Try this one, then. Canada is not a land of vast, empty spaces, nor even one at some far limit. Canada is a *forest*. Not everywhere, true, though in Canada's Age of Argument – in our third stage of Nowhere as an Address with Virtues – this new metaphor, this change in our thinking, is what's needed. The idea of the forest encourages a change in our imaginative conception of Canada that is true to the spirit of the land and the people who are on it. It is a sensibility that Robert Bringhurst brought to my attention by Heriot Bay, where it struck me that the root of Canadian thinking was grounded in this other metaphor of woods. Cities now have a preponderance in Canadian life, but this does not mean that lessons are not to be drawn from the example of these less humanly populated lands. The forest, remember, was Man's first house. The "multicultural- ism" that we assume defines our age existed in Nature long before we spoke of it as a Canadian virtue. Heterogeneity is a *natural*, not a political state.

"A multitude of voices is the *sine qua non* of our continuing to be," said Bringhurst. "The forest continues to exist *because* it is a multifarious organism. If it is reduced to a monoculture, then it ceases to be self-sustaining. It becomes an artificial plantation that can only keep going by the studious application of more and more fertilizer and more and more human interference, because in a proper ecology the parts feed each other and feed *on* each other. The whole sustains itself by never being committed to one form."

The forest is not daunting – as ideas about vast spaces, rootless nations, or infinite borders are. The forest is about balance, and thinking through co-existence. The forest can be big too, but the quality of it means that wherever you are in it, the world is rich, and full, and close at hand. Even gullies, clearings, and the shore have a place in the forest – they are a part of it. And the forest, like the city, has the promise of surprise. It is a place of wonder, of security – and of danger too, if one does not heed certain basic rules. But what the metaphor of the forest does *not* do is overbear one with the prospect of defeat.

But don't take my word for it.

Canada is a fiction, ours to invent. I have written this book knowing that my entire interpretation of place, all the arguments I have presented in these pages of the iffiness of Canada's borders and the very concept of nationhood, could either be regarded as an effect of the land or, possibly, as a consequence of growing up the way I did. Perhaps it was as a Canadian in England that I learned the virtues of being Nowhere, and to be resentful of class structures too. Perhaps my notion of the Company Store says as much about how I worked my way across the country, in mining, bush, and prospecting jobs, as it does about the legacy of the obstinate land and the Hudson's Bay Company of Adventurers. Perhaps I have always respected stories because they did battle in my house, and my feeling that we all must participate in them came about because I was one in a large brood and each of us needed to speak up to be heard. Perhaps I learned to love the North because my father did, and learned something of the distant authority because his work occupied him so. You be the judge. Certainly, the experience of my family did not put much emphasis on geographical or family roots – not conventionally, at any rate – and that could explain my holding borders in such shallow regard.

I was one of five children of parents who rarely met with their relatives. My father was a poor Jewish child from Montreal's the Main, whose argument with his extended family began when he started writing novels with origins in that community. He did not have a relationship with his family that ours could see, and one of my great surprises, after his death in July 2001, was learning just how regularly he *did* meet with his kin, if out of view. He was keeping in touch with his material, I suppose, though the portrayal, in *St. Urbain's Horseman*, of Jake Hersh's wife, Nancy, and of her tense differences with her Jewish mother-in-law provide some clues to a relationship with in-laws that was not easy and the bendy rules of making things up.

My mother, Florence Ruth Wood, was adopted by an English-speaking family and grew up in Montreal's Point St. Charles, another of the city's poor districts. But for her beloved sister, Muriel, she saw and spoke little of the family that raised her, just as my father told us little of his. My mother had been an actress and a successful model. She left for Europe in the 1950s, in her twenties then and not expecting to return to Canada. In Paris, she modelled for

Christian Dior, Yves St. Laurent, and *Vogue* magazine, but in London she met and fell in love with my father, and he with her. What my parents had was each other. Cousins, aunts, uncles – even countries – did not come into it. We were well off, a middle-class family that lived very comfortably, not ostentatiously, and we moved a couple of times between England and Canada, but really we lived Nowhere and Off the Map. We were neither of one place nor the other. My siblings and I did not possess a distinctive accent or any outstanding idiosyncratic habits. We were not cockneys, or Liverpudlians, or even that Canadian. We were of no particular place, though usually it was more the other place. We lived in between, English or Canadian as suited.

We were not rooted. When I was twelve, the family moved back to Canada, and as a teenager at Collège Stanislas, the French *lycée* in Outremont, in Montreal, I often fought to defend myself as a Jew or as an anglo, my version of the map, learning what it meant politically in fisticuffs. Yet I felt no more at home with the WASPs and rich Jewish children who lived where we did, on the English side of the mountain, in Westmount. I didn't feel that I really belonged anywhere, though I worked hard to make Canada an Address with Virtues.

Even within what might have been our extended family we were insular, spurning roots for the fresh start. The relatives we did occasionally meet seemed oddities to us. They were quasi-fictional characters, strange men and women who intruded from outside of the tight family boundaries, from a historic time before England, before my parents' marriage and the failed unions each of them had also been through. We did not, you might say, relate. Instead, a collection of our parents' closest friends, godparents to one or other of us, took the place of cousins, uncles, aunts. Anyone who claimed to be genuinely a cousin or to have position because they were connected to us by blood was treated with deep-seated suspicion. Because of their fame, even our parents' lives were rendered slightly abstract. We learned about their lives indirectly, through the stories that we read – my father's novels, or articles that were written about them or him – and stories my mother only occasion-ally shared. My fault for not asking, though *neither* parent encour-aged questions about their own upbringing much.

For my mother was secretive, as adopted children often are, and my father was saving his best thoughts for his work. Or he was just not that interested in gabbing with children, and the effect of all those articles – and the books – was that we lived with our parents at the same time as we did the mythology that surrounded them. No matter the truth of them, these myths had their effect. Another point for stories. We floated in the world at large, in our own cocoon of seven – and with occasional shocks. I can remember discover-ing, in *Time* magazine, that my father had previously married. I was eight at the time.

"You never told me about Cathy," I remonstrated.

"You met her," my father said.

"You didn't tell me you were *married*."

"You never asked."

(Interrogate your parents or your children about their lives right now. You won't always have the chance.)

So, is it really any wonder that I find ideas of nationhood so unconvincing? Looking back, I can see that from my early teens I was making a real effort to be a good and true Canadian. And I was making a point vis-à-vis the family's etiolation. I wanted to belong, but had to find a way to do so that did not depend on addresses or the passport that I was holding, and so I took a variety of jobs all over Canada, and learned to know its regions. I worked my way across the prairie, walking from western Manitoba to the Albertan foothills, cut trails in the Rockies, where I stage-managed for a couple of theatre companies too. I worked in the iron mines of Labrador, before the Company Town I was in failed, prospected in the Yukon and British Columbia, and travelled to many other places that had always seemed extraordinary to me. At the same time, I set about proving that I could have been the accomplished Englishman opportunity might have made of me had we stayed in London – studying at Balliol, working at the BBC, though never, for a moment, did I take on the accent. These were my efforts to rebel against our situation of belonging Nowhere in Particular, but I knew, in my heart, where my true home was. So I strove to prove to my mother, who, along with my sisters, had never wanted to leave Britain (there was an interesting patriotic division in my family that ran along gender lines), that we were, if not incontrovertibly Canadian, at least capable of being *happy* in Canada.

And I see now there was something else that I had wanted. Born in Canada but growing up in England, spending my teens in Canada but then attending university and continuing to live a good fifteen years of my adult life there, it is obvious to me now that I had also been attempting to learn about my father, a young Canadian who had been brash and confident enough to forge a living in London in the 1950s and 1960s, writing in the city that was the seat of the novel in the English-speaking world on the strength of no university degree and a lot less support than I had. What my father *did* have was a deep-rooted sense of place, and I am ready to admit that a lot of my feelings about Canadian novelists that I hold in high esteem are derived from admiring their being able to write out of a similarly anchored sense of community. I know now that if I sometimes envy the narrow geographical parameters within which these writers were raised – whether that author be Jacqueline Baker, Michael Crummey, Alistair MacLeod, Lisa Moore, Alice Munro, Guy Vanderhaeghe, Michael Winter, and many others – it has as much to do with knowing they learned an apposite sense of place to the more deracinated one in which I grew up. It is of equal merit to know the world through one place, or many, though the likelihood in our modern age is that we know it through several. As a British friend said to me upon learning of my impending return to Canada, "Wherever you are these days, you need to be someplace else." (He thought he was offering me solace.) And yet I still wonder if novelists who, against the grain, have somehow managed to learn the world out of the one particular place, writers who are steeped in that place, are at an advantage. My belief that a quality of good novels is that they pay attention to place can be attributed, at least in part, to the effect of this intermittent yearning. The "global soul," to borrow Pico Iyer's phrase, understands that his worldliness comes at the expense of a certain authoritative, specific, and slowly learned knowledge of the world, and the irony is that he races *even more* to catch up with what he sometimes thinks he never had.

"Do not look for love, but let it come to you," Jorge Luis Borges said, "otherwise you are just a journalist."

◇ ◇ ◇

I CAME BACK to Canada in October 1998, after fourteen continuous years of being away. I had wanted to live closer to my father, who had gone into hospital for a first bout with cancer in the preceding spring, and to be nearer my brothers, neither of whom I had shared a city with for far too long. I wanted to learn Canada again, and to become reacquainted with much of the territory that I knew and had worked in. And I wanted to contribute to a place where citizens can make a difference, regardless of their class or heritage. This was not true of Britain and consequently I never felt "at home" there, was always in battle with it. Though it took me years to acknowledge, I see now that I had not acquired a British passport deliberately, because I never wished for one. I did not want to be British, not even in my back pocket. And so I left, and returned to the country and the friends and the family that I loved – and to the land that had formed me. I was, in some way that I wanted to embrace, Canadian.

Not a bad decision, really, and here is the book that came out of it.

This is my country, what's yours?

Acknowledgements

I thought this book would take a year to write. It took four. My wife Sarah MacLachlan's help was critical at every step along the way. Without it, there would be nothing in your hands.

A book, wise Sarah has always insisted, is the work of many people. Again she is right. So thanks to Douglas Gibson for buying the book in the first place and, at McClelland & Stewart, to Douglas Pepper for his patience, to Heather Sangster, my editor on a bicycle who went out of her way many times, and to copy editor Jenny Bradshaw, designer Terri Nimmo, and typesetter Sean Tai for deciphering my appalling doctor's handwriting. Thanks also to Sharon Klein of Random House Canada for making sure the book was noticed.

Adrian Mills, then of the CBC, deserves thanks for commissioning the radio aspect of this project, and Jane Chalmers, the CBC's vice-president for English radio, for resuscitating it. Commissioning was the easy part. Very special thanks go to Bernie Lucht, Dave Field, and Richard Handler of CBC Radio One's *Ideas* – the best popular intellectual forum in the country – production team, and to *The Sunday Edition*'s Cate Cochran, who helped with the project in its early stages. This book also owes an indirect debt of gratitude to Richard Bannerman and Louise Greenberg of the BBC, another institution that passionately believes in the merits of cultural inquiry and its importance to a nation, knowing that it cannot always be paid for by market forces.

Ken Alexander, editor-in-chief of *The Walrus*, deserves a grateful mention for providing strong moral support for this book from its beginnings, most of all through the voluble arguments that are so easy to have with him. There comes a time when you realize you are actually putting a book out in the world and that there is no going back, and he was one of a number of readers I was extremely fortunate to have had on this journey. My chapter on Igloolik would not have been possible without the erudite counsel of John MacDonald, before and after, and I would not have felt confident about that chapter or the next without the gifted and meticulous scrutiny of Robert Bringhurst. Shelley Ambrose, Doug Bell (whose loquacious game of squash would stymie even Woody Allen), Nadine Bismuth, Joseph Boyden, Steven Galloway, Rudyard Griffiths, Lisa Moore, Daniel Richler, Emma Richler, Tim Rostron, Timothy Taylor, and Guy Vanderhaeghe were my other readers, giving of their time and intelligence generously. The chapters are greatly improved because of their work, and needlessly said, any errors, lapses of judgment, or advice that I failed to take are my fault entirely.

Thanks also to the Igloolik Oral History Project for the hunting around and the provision of Elders' testimony. Thank you, David Homel for your translations and Michael Winter for the fine illustrations.

John Fraser provided safe haven at Massey College and a library card, and Duncan, Tanya, *et alii* made the House on Parliament my "third place." Margaret Atwood encouraged me to "have a go" early on. John David Gravenor was a tremendous support and helped me source a lot of material, catering to my always at the last moment requests. Alberto Manguel provided inspiring discussion in Turin and an essay, "Seneca in Thunder Bay," that helped with "The Virtues of Being Nowhere." David Stam, the senior scholar at the history department of Syracuse University, and Debra Moore, an archivist at the Hudson's Bay Company Archives in Winnipeg, helped with "Igloolik, 1822" and "The Company Store" respectively.

And, of course, this book would have been impossible without the generosity and goodwill of the writers and storytellers whom I have listed on the following page. Spending time with such thoughtful and remarkably idealistic people was a privilege as well as the source of many good memories.

Thank you, all.

◇ ◇ ◇

These novelists, poets, storytellers, and one filmmaker were interviewed for the book. Not all are represented in the text, but everyone is in the spirit of it.

Robert Arthur Alexie, Nelly Arcan, Margaret Atwood, Jacqueline Baker, Victor-Lévy Beaulieu, John Bemrose, David Bergen, David Bezmozgis, Louis Bird, Nadine Bismuth, Joseph Boyden, Dionne Brand, Robert Bringhurst, Chester Brown, Carol Bruneau, Sharon Butala, Barry Callaghan, David Carpenter, Austin Clarke, George Elliott Clarke, Douglas Coupland, Gil Courtemanche, Michael Crummey, Sheldon Currie, Ramona Dearing, Zsuzsi Gartner, Michelle Genest, Katherine Govier, Lee Gowan, Barbara Gowdy, Rawi Hage, Louise Halfe, Michael Helm, David Helwig, Lee Henderson, Michael Hetherton, Tomson Highway, Lawrence Hill, Jack Hodgins, Anosh Irani, Wayne Johnston, Thomas King, Zacharias Kunuk, Mary Lawson, Nancy Lee, Tim Lilburn, Annabel Lyon, Ann-Marie MacDonald, Alistair MacLeod, Antonine Maillet, Kevin Major, Lee Maracle, Yann Martel, Larry Mathews, Chandra Mayor, Colin McAdam, Ian McGillis, Robin McGrath, Leo McKay Jr., Rohinton Mistry, Mitch Miyagawa, Lisa Moore, Alice Munro, Peter Oliva, Michael Ondaatje, Andrew Pyper, Paul Quarrington, David Adams Richards, Ray Robertson, Eden Robinson, Gloria Sawai, Mauricio Segura, Carol Shields, Alfred Silver, Russell Smith, Karen Solie, Gaétan Soucy, Fred Stenson, Margaret Sweatman, Timothy Taylor, Miriam Toews, Élise Turcotte, Michael Turner, Jane Urquhart, Geoffrey Ursell, Guy Vanderhaeghe, M.G. Vassanji, Guillaume Vigneault, Thomas Wharton, Rudy Wiebe, Claire Wilkshire, David Williams, Michael Winter, Richard Wright, and Alissa York.

The three Inuit Elders whose testimony was acquired from the Igloolik Oral History Project are Hervé Paniaq, George Kappianaq, and Rosie Iqallijuq. Other authors, geographers, painters, philosophers, and everyday thinkers who kindly shared their time and expertise were Gerald Amos, Hugh Brody, Ted Chamberlin, Marlene Creates, Derek Hayes, Jack Hicks, Barbara Le Blanc, Mary Lewis, John MacDonald, Landon MacKenzie, Tara Malinowski, The Two Maxes (Jack Eastwood and Mark Ferguson), Alan Morantz, Leah Otak, George Qulaut, Rupert Sheldrake, Louis Tapardjuk, James Ungalaaq, and Dan Yashinsky.

Notes

Page references refer to the paperback edition unless otherwise noted.

CHAPTER ONE: *THE VIRTUES OF BEING NOWHERE*

1 *No New Land* (McClelland & Stewart, 1991), pp. 28-29.

10 *The Stone Carvers* (McClelland & Stewart, 2001), p. 14.

13 *The Romantic* (HarperFlamingo Canada, 2003), pp. 92-93.

16 *Some Great Thing* (Raincoast, 2004), pp. 329-30. Hardcover edition.

18 *Any Known Blood* (HarperPerennial Canada, 1997), p. 1-2.

21 "W" from *The Broken Record Technique* (Penguin Canada, 2002), pp. 256-57.

25 *A Complicated Kindness* (Knopf Canada, 2004), p. 56.

30 *Family Matters* (McClelland & Stewart, 2002), pp. 234-35.

33 *Hey Nostradamus!* (Vintage Canada, 2004), p. 9.

CHAPTER TWO: *STORIES AND WHAT THEY DO*

39 IN LAING'S MANIC STORY: *Woman of the Aeroplanes* (Picador, 1989), p. 2.

CHAPTER THREE: *IGLOOLIK, 1822*

57 Igloolik Oral History Project (IOHP), interview IE:142.

68 HIS MAJESTY'S SHIPS: *Narrative of a Second Voyage to the Polar Sea* from *Three Voyages for the Discovery of a Northwest Passage from the Atlantic to the Pacific, and Narrative of an Attempt to Reach the North Pole, by Sir W.E. Parry, Capt. R.N., F.R.S.* (Harper & Brothers, Publishers, 1858), pp. 249-50.

68 Parry, *Second Voyage*, p. 249.

75 Parry, *Second Voyage*, p. 298.

77 IOHP interview IE:329.

91 IOHP interview IE:358.

93 IOHP interview IE:445.

94 Parry, *Second Voyage*, p. 262.

98 IOHP interview IE:204.

CHAPTER FOUR: *THE CIRCLE IN THE SQUARE*

110 *Porcupines and China Dolls* (Stoddart, 2002), p. 65. Hardcover edition.

121 *Monkey Beach* (Vintage Canada, 2001), pp. 68-69.

125 *Kiss of the Fur Queen* (Anchor Canada, 2005), pp. 120-21.

139 "Painted Tongue" from *Born With a Tooth* (Cormorant Books, 2005), pp. 75-76.

CHAPTER FIVE: *HOUSE AND GARDEN*

147 "Dead Girls" from *Dead Girls* (McClelland & Stewart, 2003), pp. 104-5.

153 *Stanley Park* (Vintage Canada, 2001), pp. 115-16.

157 GRAHAM MAKES SKETCHES: *Story House* (Knopf Canada, 2006), pp. 130-131. Hardcover edition.

161 "I WAS YOUNG": *Dorothy L'Amour* (HarperCollins Canada, 2000), p. 149.

161 "WE FEAR FOR YOU": Ibid., p. 10.

161 YOUNG DOROTHY: Ibid., p. 54.

161 HIS POEMS WERE: "(viii)" from *Kingsway* (Arsenal Pulp Press, 1995), p. 10.

164 *The Pornographer's Poem* (Vintage Canada, 2000), pp. 171-72.

173 "City of My Dreams" from *All the Anxious Girls on Earth* (Key Porter, 1999), pp. 61-63.

CHAPTER SIX: *THE COMPANY STORE*

181 *The Trade* (Douglas & McIntyre, 2000), pp. 67-68.

184 "The Turkey Season" from *The Moons of Jupiter* (Penguin Canada, 1995), pp. 61-62.

195 "Roots" from *Flesh and Blood* (Anchor Canada, 2003), pp. 54-55.

204 *Like This* (House of Anansi, 1995), p. 25.

210 "Ypres: 1915" from *Alden Nowlan: Selected Poems* (House of Anansi, 1996), pp. 63-65.

211 *River of the Brokenhearted* (Anchor Canada, 2004), pp. 57-58.

223 "The Closing Down of Summer" from *Island* (McClelland & Stewart, 2001), pp. 198-99.

CHAPTER SEVEN: *TRACES*

227 *Make Believe Love* (Vintage Canada, 2002), pp. 12-13.

228 *Homesick* (McClelland & Stewart, 2001), p. 249-50.

232 "East Window, Victoria" from *Short Haul Engine* (Brick Books, 2001), pp. 45-46.

243 "Bloodwood" from *A Hard Witching and Other Stories* (HarperPerennial Canada, 2004), pp. 145-46.

252 *My Present Age* (McClelland & Stewart, 2000), pp. 104-5.

261 *In the Place of Last Things* (McClelland & Stewart, 2005), pp. 78-79.

267 "Gabriel" from *Fever* (HarperPerennial Canada, 1996), pp. 141-2.

CHAPTER EIGHT: *OUR MYTHS OF DISAPPOINTMENT*

287 *Louis Riel: A Comic-Strip Biography* (Drawn & Quarterly, 2003), p. 9.

293 *Broken Ground* (McClelland & Stewart, 1999), pp. 99-100.

297 *Three Day Road* (Penguin Canada, 2006), pp. 205-06.

300 *A Sunday at the Pool in Kigali* (Vintage Canada, 2004), p. 114.

306 *The Colony of Unrequited Dreams* (Vintage Canada, 1999), p. 562.

309 *Pélagie: The Return to Acadie* (Goose Lane, 2004), p. 13.

CHAPTER NINE: *MAKING THINGS UP*

317 *This All Happened* (House of Anansi, 2000), p. 273.

331 Ibid., pp. 141-2.

334 "Nipple of Paradise" from *Degrees of Nakedness* (House of Anansi, 1995), pp. 1-2.

337 *This All Happened*, p. 191.

349 *River Thieves* (Anchor Canada, 2002), pp. 346-47.

CHAPTER TEN: *JE ME SOUVIENS – DE QUOI?*

367 *Scrapbook* (Boréal, 2004), p. 74. Translation by David Homel.
375 *Côte-des-Nègres* (Boréal, 1998), pp. 18-19. Translation by David Homel.
391 *The Body's Place* (Cormorant Books, 2003), pp. 1-2.
400 *Necessary Betrayals* (Douglas & McIntyre, 2002), pp. 187-88.

CHAPTER ELEVEN: *HOME AND AWAY*

418 "The Motor Car" from *Choosing His Coffin: The Best Stories of Austin Clarke* (Thomas Allen, 2003), p. 210.
421 "Crow Jane's Blues" from *The Black Queen Stories* (McArthur & Co., 1994), pp. 8-9.
426 *The Weekend Man* (HarperPerennial Canada, 2001), pp. 146-47.
429 *The Way the Crow Flies* (Vintage Canada, 2004), pp. 227-28.
439 *What We All Long For* (Vintage Canada, 2005), pp. 3-5.
445 "Simple Recipes" from *Simple Recipes* (McClelland & Stewart, 2002), pp. 13-14.

Credits